D1491909

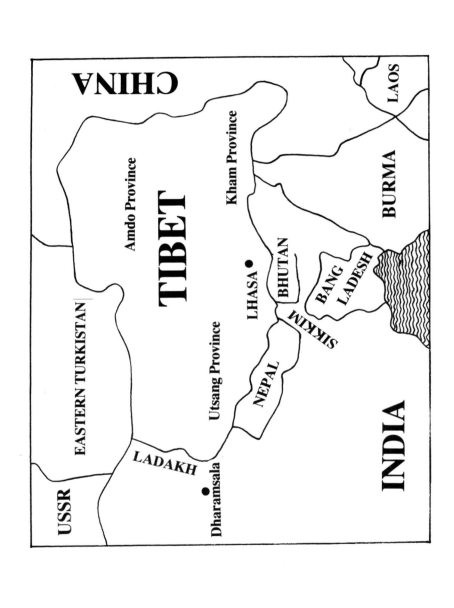

Dogs of Tibet
and the history of the
Tibetan Spaniel

Book World Rugby, Russell Square, Leicester

Printed by de Voyle Litho, Russell Square, Leicester

© 1982 Ann Lindsay Wynyard

All rights reserved. No part of this publication may be reproduced, stored in any retrieval system, or transmitted, in any form or by any means without the prior permission, in writing, of the publisher.

First published 1982 by Book World, Rugby, England

ISBN 0907 948 006

ISBN 0907 948 014

Cover illustration:
'Dogs and a Peony Flower', painted on silk by Shen Ch'uan (1725–1780), A Chinese artist also referred to as Shen Na Ping. (By kind permission of the British Museum.)

To Allister Hamilton

Dogs of Tibet
and the history of the
Tibetan Spaniel

Ann Lindsay Wynyard

I would like to dedicate this book to my husband, Edward Wynyard, and to Miss Helen Forbes. Without their patience, encouragement and support, there would never have been any Braeduke Champions!

Contents

Chronological Table of Major Events in Tibet

1391   The First Dalai Lama was born.
1542   The Third Dalai Lama begins conversion of Mongolia.
1616   The Fifth Dalai Lama born.
1680   The Fifth Dalai Lama dies.
1774–1783   Warren Hastings, Governor General of India, sent British Envoys Bogle and Turner to the Dalai Lama's Court at Tashi Lhun-po.
17th and 18th Centuries saw Christian missionaries in Lhasa.
1876   Thirteenth Dalai Lama born.
1895   The Thirteenth Dalai Lama takes up the full spiritual and secular power.
1904   The British political-military Expedition to Lhasa.
1904   The Dalai Lama flees to Mongolia.
1908   The Dalai Lama is in Peking.
1909   The Dalai Lama returns to Lhasa.
1910   The Dalai Lama flees from the Chinese invasion and arrives in India.
1911   The Chinese Revolution.
1912   The Dalai Lama returns to Tibet and repudiates Chinese overlordship.
1914–1918   First World War.
1923   The Pan-chen Lama flees from Tibet.
1927   Chinese Missions came to Lhasa.
1927   A party from the U.S.S.R. came to Lhasa.
1933   The death of the Thirteenth Dalai Lama.
1935   The birth of the Fourteenth Dalai Lama.
1937   The Pan-chen Lama dies.
1939–1945   Second World War.
1940   The Fourteenth Dalai Lama enthroned.
1950   The Chinese invasion.
1959   The Fourteenth Dalai Lama departed from Tibet into India.

Acknowledgments

The Author would especially like to thank:

Bryan and Marilyn Welsby for making this book possible, themselves devoted Tibetan Spaniel lovers and owners of this breed.

The Lady Freda Valentine for so kindly consenting to write the Preface.

Mrs Sylva Simsova for assisting me in obtaining photostats from early books and magazines.

Mrs Angela Mulliner for some of the original drawings in chapter 13.

Mrs Barbara Burrow of Thomas Fall, Mr Peter Diment, Diane Pearce and Anne Roslin Williams for their help and co-operation over the photographs.

Ugyan Norbu, Secretary of the Tibet Relief Fund for the loan of his Tibetan picture and map of Tibet.

Miss E. Cherry and Mrs A. Keen for their assistance with pedigrees and information.

Dr R. N. Smith Ph.D., D.Sc., F.R.C.V.S. of the School of Veterinary Science, University of Bristol, for permission to use his chart in the Evolution chapter.

The Kennel Club for their permission to use photographs and copy from their *Kennel Encyclopedia* of 1908 and to reprint the three Tibetan Spaniel Breed Standards.

Our Dogs and *Dog World* for permission to quote from their papers.

Mrs Constance Van Den Boom of Holland, Mrs Cosby, Mrs Kohler and Mrs Rosen of the United States of America, Mrs Monica Herjeskog of Sweden, Mrs Sirkka Rautapuro of Finland, Mrs Elaine Vaughan of Canada and Miss M. M. Walsh of Eire for supplying information on the history of the breed in their own countries.

Mrs G. J. Lilley for the loan of her copy of the *Kennel Magazine* of 1911, and for so kindly assisting with the proof correcting.

Mrs G. S. Vines for the loan of *The New Book of the Dog*, 1907.

The British Library and the British Newspaper Library for their permission to use photographs and copy from some of their books and magazines.

The British Museum for so kindly allowing me to use one of their pictures for the jacket cover and for supplying the transparency.

Mrs Elizabeth Davin for so kindly loaning and obtaining for me photographs of Happa Dogs and the Afghan Spaniel, and other references and pictures of early Tibetan Spaniels.

Mr Adrian Stringer for his assistance in obtaining the photographs from his wife's copy of *Toy Dogs and their Ancestors* by the Honourable Mrs Judith A. D. B. Lytton, for the Chinese chapter.

Last, but not least, Mrs Rita Pope for her help in typing and collating and her moral support.

Ann Lindsay Wynyard

Author's Note

Every effort has been made to trace the origin of photographs and quotations and to seek permission for their inclusion in this book. If, however, a photograph or quotation should still remain unacknowledged, the Author would like to apologise for this genuine oversight.

Foreword

I am delighted and honoured to be asked to write the preface to this book, and start by saying that I could not put it down, reading into the small hours of the morning. I am amazed at the amount of research and documentation that has been achieved by the Author – an absolute *tour de force*. Future breeders and judges should be very grateful for all the information in this book with its wonderful illustrations; also for the excellent way in which the story of the trial and errors and triumphs is told.

The Standard of Points for the four Tibetan breeds was thrashed out in our Green Street dining room. The battle raged longest and fiercest over those relating to the Spaniel's ears, some saying, as I did, 'Who has heard of prick-eared Spaniels?' Had the prick-ears happened when the then popular Pomeranian dog in India had been taken north? The matter was settled by the Committee agreeing to the charming lift of the ears next to the head. The lady with the prick-eared dog, Mrs A. R. Greig, who had not spoken during the discussion, was in such a fury that she would not speak to anyone, even the Chairman. At tea-time I insisted that she hand the cream cakes around, so she was forced to talk to everyone in the room, and her daughter, Dr Greig, kindly said: 'These good teas after the meetings do get rid of so much bad blood.'

I hope that breeders and pet owners throughout the world will read this book and so give this charming dog a happy life, and that judges will insist on the following points: the marmoset face, the scowl, the splendid shawl, not forgetting the hare foot, which are keeping this breed alive.

I should like to thank Mrs Wynyard for her foresight in managing to import some new blood, thereby helping to maintain a hardy, healthy breed. May others in the future follow suit!

The Lady Freda Valentine
Patron of the Tibetan Spaniel Association
and its former President

Mrs A. R. Greig of Royden's Stud Dog in 1934. (Photo: T. Fall.)

Author's Introduction

This labour of love commenced nearly three years ago, when I attempted to compile all the information I could find on the Tibetan Spaniel breed, past and present, in order to prevent this and many old and rare photographs – some have never been seen before by anyone in the breed – being lost for future generations of breeders for ever.

The other Tibetan breeds seemed naturally to have historical associations as did the Chinese breeds. If space had permitted, I would have wished to write much more about the Tibetan Mastiff.

I hope that this book will be of interest to both the established breeder and also to the pet owner. I have quite deliberately tried not to force on my readers any of my own conclusions as to whether the Tibetan Spaniel originated as a Chinese dog, or if it was the result of an ancient Chinese breed being crossed with another small indigenous breed of Tibet, or whether it could possibly be one of the oldest pure breeds in the world.

The results of my research may interest owners and breeders of other oriental dogs. The spellings vary with the age of the quotations and sources and I have kept to the original, so these are not printers errors – Lhasa or Lhassa, Thibet or Tibet, Pekinese or Pekingese!

I am still searching for early references and early photographs of Tibetan dogs and will always be happy to hear from anyone who can assist me to add to my store of knowledge and photographic records, which I would like to preserve for posterity.

If anyone, or their dogs, have been omitted, I tender my apologies.

Ann Lindsay Wynyard
1982

1 Tibet, past and present, its religion and its history

Before the reader turns the pages to read about Tibetan dogs, and however much or little is known about these breeds, the Author thinks that it is very important to investigate their background and origins, which, with the history and climate of Tibet, have a great bearing on the composition of the Tibetan breeds we know today.

Amaury de Riencourt, in his book, *Lost World, Tibet Key to Asia*, mentions the birthplace of Lady Wakefield's Tibetan Spaniel, Dolma:

> Phari Dzong is the highest town in the world and it is surely the filthiest. As one traveller wisely remarked, 'it is literally buried in its own filth'. The Pharisians are quite adapted to their surroundings and are the filthiest among the Tibetans, which is a great accomplishment as Tibetans are by far the dirtiest people in the world. The reason for this general uncleanliness is to be found in the extremely cold climate. Glass is almost unknown in Tibet and windows are perpetually open, even in winter, but the extreme altitude destroys most germs.

To criticise the Tibetan people for washing so little is unfair as it must be remembered that winds of almost hurricane force blow throughout the arctic winters of high Tibet. There were no fireplaces in the houses and no glass in the windows. Instead, cotton cloth or paper, sometimes oiled, was tacked or gummed on. The wealthier classes often had windows which ran down the whole length of a fairly large room. The poorer members of the community had small windows with bars arranged either vertically or in the form of a cross, over which some sort of cloth might be hung. All the windows had wooden shutters which were closed at night, but in the poorest houses there were no windows at all, the only openings being the door and the smoke vent in the ceiling.

"A Tibetan village by no means makes a handsome figure", Captain Samuel Turner tells us in his account, *An Embassy to the Court of the Teshoo Lama in Tibet*, published in the year 1800.

> A peasant's house is of mean construction and resembles a brick kiln in shape and size. It is built of rough stones, heaped upon each other without cement. On account of the strong winds that perpetually

1

prevail here it never has more than three or four small apertures to admit light. The roof is a flat terrace, surrounded with a parapet wall two or three feet high; on this are commonly placed piles of loose stones intended to support a small flag or the branch of a tree, or else as a fastening for a long line with scraps of paper, or white rags, strung upon it like the tail of a kite. This is stretched from one house to another acting as a charm against evil genii, as infallible in its efficacy as horse shoes nailed upon a threshold, or as straws thrown across the path of a witch.

Often on one of the walls is a swastika drawn in whitewash. This is an auspicious sign, which gives durability to the house. The swastika is a symbol of good luck. Derived from the Sanskrit words *Su* (well) and *Asti* (is), this sign is very ancient and was also known in India, China, Japan, Iran, Egypt and Greece, as well as among the American Indians.

Above this sign, also outlined in whitewash, are the sun and the moon which draw the household upwards. The roof is of beaten earth, which here and there has holes, to serve the floor below, letting in the light and letting out the smoke.

In the superior dwellings of the wealthy, over the ground floor a larger area of roof projects out on all sides towards the large inner courtyard. Here, partly covered by the floor above, partly under the open sky, the women sit and work. They are the wives and daughters of the tenantry, some weaving carpet rugs, others spinning and carding wool yielded by the *Pa-Lha* sheep which are often grazed as much as twelve miles away, among the mountain ranges. Small children, from babies upwards, sprawl on the flat roof wearing the minimum of clothing. Dogs, too, lie about here and there, mostly asleep.

Sir A. C. Bell in his *Tibetan Notebook* (1934), told us that "there is one breed of dog which is 'very much awake', a well-kept little fellow which runs everywhere. He is the kind known to the Tibetans as the Chinese dog 'Gya Khyi' and to many Europeans as a 'Tibetan Spaniel', and surely one ancestor of the Pekingese, though not quite so puggy in appearance."

W. D. Drury in his book *British Dogs, their Points, Selection and Preparation*, (1903), says: "Occasionally met with is another dog from the same country (ie: Tibet) usually called a Thibetan Spaniel; but as a matter of fact both Mr Jacobs (later Sir Lionel Jacobs) and Mr Clarke are most emphatic in saying that there is no Thibet dog with any of the characteristics of the Spaniel as ordinarily understood."

L.A. Waddell in his record of the Expedition of 1903–4, says about Lhasa, "The Lhasaites are fond of dogs, and especially favour the mongrel breed between the Lhasa Terrier and the Chinese Spaniel. Few of the swarms of ownerless dogs that infest the streets are of this class, most of them being stunted and mangy mastiffs."

To most of us Tibet possibly conjures up the Himalaya Mountains and Mount Everest which is called by the Tibetan people *Chomolungma* or 'Goddess Mother of the World'. Mountains have always been very important to the Hindus who used to go forth on pilgrimages, not to climb the mountains but to die, while poets sang their praises. Buddhist pilgrims from India, Tibet and even China, trekked to the holy ground over high passes to the snows of Mount Kailas. It was thought that hardship and exposure would bring the pilgrims remission from their sins and the favour of the gods.

Mount Everest was discovered by the Great Trigonometrical Survey of India in 1852, long before the sport of mountaineering had been seriously considered. The pioneers of that time discovered that they had to contend not only with the difficulties of rocks, snow and ice, but also with the high altitudes, extreme cold and total lack of any travel amenities. Zoologists and sportsmen had acquired some knowledge of the mountains from observing and hunting such animals as ibex and markhor, but the first real explorers and pioneers of Tibet were Brigadier-General the Hon. C. C. Bruce and Sir Francis Younghusband, who planned to explore and climb Mount Everest.

This mountain, standing on the frontier of Nepal and Tibet, was not easily approached because at that time both Nepal and Tibet still pursued a policy of isolation. In spite of this, Sir Francis Younghusband entered Lhasa at the head of the Political Mission of 1904. Lord Curzon and Lord Minto encouraged the idea of an approach to Mount Everest through Tibet; eventually, after Lord Charles Bell's interviews with the Dalai Lama, whose reluctance was finally overcome, the Reconnaissance Expedition of 1921 was made. Tibetan flora and fauna and the geology of the region were carefully documented. Many beautiful species of flowers have come from Tibet, among them the Blue Gentian, *Incarvilla younghusbandii* and *Meconopsis baileyii*, the latter discovered by Colonel F. M. Bailey on one of his expeditions in Eastern Tibet. There are large white peonies, hollyhocks, marigolds and asters all of which are popular in Tibet, having been grown there from time immemorial. The trees are mostly stunted poplars and willows.

Tibet is the land of the snows, a land of high plateaux and green valleys, of about one-and-a-half million square miles. Geographically it is isolated by the high snow-covered mountain ranges in the south, and by the vast, almost uninhabitable, desert lands in the north where there are less than two inhabitants to each square mile.

In Tibet, the highest land on earth, even the valleys run higher than the summit of any mountain in Europe, Canada, or the United States. There are wide plains, often bare, and it is usually too cold for trees to grow and for hundreds of miles you would see no plant more than six inches high. In the spring flowers bloom – gentians, edelweiss and the famous blue poppies. Grass pushes its way up among the stones, cushion-flowers such as the blue gentians and the beautiful little *Incarvilla younghusbandii*, with its red trumpet-shaped flower, just two inches high, carpet the ground.

A little knowledge of the background and religion of Tibet, and the country of origin of our Tibetan breeds, makes us realise how sturdy and rugged even the smallest of the dogs had to be to survive. Captain Samuel Turner's description, written in 1800, is possibly one of the best we can have. "Tibet strikes a traveller, at first sight, as one of the least favoured countries under heaven, and appears to be in a great measure incapable of culture. It exhibits only low rocky hills, without any visible vegetation, or extensively arid plains, both of the most stern and stubborn aspect."

The winters are very hard in Tibet, with cold and piercing winds in the passes which make winter travelling very difficult. Snow can come early, often in the second half of August, but rarely falls in the valleys where, when shielded from the winds, the climate can be most agreeable. The drawbacks to travel in the months of March and April are cold, wind and dust. In July it is the rivers which impede any progress, with Tibetan bridges few and far between, where in April there had been a shallow easily-crossed stream, by July it would be a strong-running river, swollen by the melting ice of the glaciers, muddy and turbulent, turning over the boulders in the river bed.

The greater part of Tibet is icebound during seven or eight months of the year, and the inhabited areas can be cultivated for only a few months, even if there is not much snow. Snow bridges are formed by layer upon layer of snow, forming bridges over rivers which are strong enough to support a flock of sheep. Other rivers can be crossed by stepping stones strategically placed. The streams are ice-cold, usually with whistling winds whirling around and there are sub-zero temperatures. Narrow paths only about one foot in width zig-zag around the mountains; as one walks slowly on these, shale is dislodged often falling into rivers about five hundred or one thousand feet below. In some places the paths are so steep that it is not possible to attempt them on horseback – the usual form of Tibetan transport.

The rainy months are July and August, with strong cold winds which often reach gale force, sweeping over the land. The winds are especially violent during winter and spring.

The rain clouds come from the south-west, storming over the Indian Ocean and across India, to beat against the gigantic mountains of the Himalayas. This name comes from Sanskrit and means 'The Abode of Snow', and it is this range of mountains which separates India from Tibet. While two hundred inches or more of rain falls each year on the Indian side of the Himalayas, only seven inches falls in Tibet.

There are high altitudes, the average is sixteen thousand feet, and a big danger is dehydration. The Tibetan climate is so dry and cold and so rarified that meat will keep without decomposing for three years and grain for even longer. So clear is the air that distances appear to be an illusion and often the lakes look like mirages. It has been reported that some Tibetan breeds have varying reactions to anaesthetics, which can occasionally be fatal. In the Author's opinion this reaction is most probably caused by their origin, their lungs and respiratory systems obviously being constructed to deal with the rarified atmosphere of Tibet.

The rain and rivers are the two main sources of prosperity for Tibet, which is a nation of farmers and shepherds struggling in a land where water is often difficult to obtain. In some places there may be neither rain nor snow for eight months in a year.

The nomads encamp with their black tents made from spun yak-wool on the high plateaux, where the winds blow long and hard, cold in the winter and hot in the summer, burning their yak-dung fires. The villages are often small, just scattered clusters of houses located near water sources. In higher places the villages consist of no more than a few houses. Here it is possible to ride for days without meeting another human being. The shepherds, stockbreeders and traders farm in the fertile valleys, the crops being mostly grain-crops limited by the climate and soil conditions, some fields being as high up as thirteen thousand feet. In the broad valleys and on the level plains barley, peas, mustard and, to a lesser degree, turnips, radishes, wheat and buckwheat are grown. Rice was a luxury and had to be carried from Bhutan or Nepal, taking between fifteen to twenty-five days to arrive in Tibet, the sacks being carried by donkey, mule, pony, bullock, yak and even by man.

The territory of Tibet historically, culturally and ethnically stretches from the Karakoram on the west to the Holi Shen Range on the east, and the Himalayas and Riwo Jakong in the south, to the Kunlun and the Altyn Tagh on the north. Most of these boundaries

5

were drawn up by treaties and agreements, while others were natural or traditional.

It is very hard to realise that up until the seventh century A.D. there was no such country as Tibet! The people who occupied this region before that time consisted of unknown nomad tribes, steeped in barbarism with no written language, so that there is no recorded history of those times.

The Tibetans are nomads by instinct and inclination. The people of Tibet are accustomed to wander across mountains and valleys and plains for hundreds and thousands of miles. The nomadic spirit is still very strong in them. They belong to the Tartar race, closely resembling the peoples of the steppes and deserts farther to the north, but they are not closely related to the Chinese of the Republic. Before the last Chinese invasion they were still living in a feudal age and their main occupations were farming and herding; one man in three was a monk and one woman in fifteen was a nun. Monasteries were everywhere, some of them huge, and from most families at least one son was sent to become a monk. Although the food and climate produced a hardy race, they were not then a particularly long-lived one, aging rapidly after reaching fifty.

The people of Tibet are racially, culturally, linguistically and historically different from any of their neighbours. Before the Chinese invasion, the population of Tibet was well over six million people. The Tibetan government was in Lhasa, the capital, under the spiritual and temporal leadership of His Holiness the Dalai Lama, who had undisputed and absolute authority in Tibet, over a territory consisting of a staggering 2,333,125 square kilometers. No other power has enjoyed sovereignty over Tibet, especially since His Holiness the Thirteenth Dalai Lama announced Tibet's renewed independence in 1912 after the Manchu occupation had ended. This independence is illustrated by Tibet's neutrality during the Second World War. At this time Tibet had its own legal system, standing national army, postal and telegraph services. Their national currency dates from the year A.D. 1027, which was also the year when astrology was introduced into Tibet. Up until the time of the invasion of Tibet by the Republic of China, they were conducting international trade, a very far cry from the picture of a backward nation imagined by most Europeans.

Tibet has been an independent country since 217 B.C., except for short periods of Chinese imperialist aggression. The Tibetans are a deeply religious and peace-loving nation. The relationship of Tibet with other countries was governed by a policy of peaceful co-existence and the promotion of well-being. Tibet has, in fact, always played an important part in maintaining peace and harmony in Central Asia.

Tibet's history begins in the year A.D. 640, when the region of Central Tibet, with Lhasa as its nucleus, was unified under a King, Songtsang Kampo*, who came from Tzetang in southern Tibet. H. Suyin in his book *Lhasa the Open City* (1977) says:

> Even today, Tibet is far from homogeneous; there are five ethnic groups, the Tsang or Tibetan proper, the Memba, Loba, the Khampa (from the western area of Szechuan, the Hui or Islamic Tibetans, for there is a mosque in Lhasa. In features too, one can see variety; some Tibetans look almost Burmese; others Mongolian; yet others have Persian features, denoting an Afghan or Persian ancestry.
>
> The word Tibet (Tu-Bu) first appears on Chinese maps of the Tang dynasty; the people were also called Tufan, a name which seems to cover a variable area. Later they are mixed up with the Tangut nomads from North Tibet, who are a nomadic Altaic tribe with whom Tibetans in the pastoral regions of northern Tibet seem to have merged. In fact Tibetans are still called Tanguts in Tsinghai province.

Mr Suyin tells us of the reforms made by the young King who was only twenty-three years old in the year A.D. 640, and who was a most energetic, gifted and wise statesman. He unified weights and measures and, with his Prime Minister, created an alphabet for the Tsang (Tibetan) language spoken around Lhasa, deriving its 30 letters from old Sanskrit. A warrior as well, he established a class of armed noblemen, who owed him allegiance, and sought alliances with his powerful neighbour, the Chinese Tang dynasty. He married in A.D. 641 a Chinese Princess, Wen Cheng, the adopted daughter of the Chinese Emperor Tai Tsung who, thirteen centuries later is still revered among Tibetans. She brought with her to Jokka Kang, the holiest Temple in Tibet, a large statue of Buddha and the temple itself was built to commemorate her arrival. Princess Wen Cheng, who was both intelligent and beautiful, brought Buddhism to Tibet; the King was converted and his people followed suit.

King Songtsang Kampo also married a Nepalese Princess and he had a Tibetan wife.

The Dalai Lama, the spiritual and temporal ruler of Tibet, was revered as the highest pontiff of the Buddhist church and had also been the priest or guru of the Mongol kings and the Ming and Manchu emperors of China. This unique priest-patron relationship between the Dalai Lamas and the Chinese emperors was never correctly understood by the rest of the world.

*Also known as Srong-Tsan Gampo in Tibet.

Gotama, the founder of Buddhism, was born during the sixth century before Christ, in Sakya, a small republic in what is now Nepal. The kingdom of Nepal was inhabited by tribes who were mostly Tibetan and not of Indian origin.

Buddhism came to Tibet mainly between the seventh and the eleventh centuries, from India, Nepal and Kashmir. When it came to Tibet it was strongly permeated by the primitive nature worship *Bon* (or *Pön*), that Tibet had known from time immemorial. This was the worship of good spirits and the appeasement of evil demons by the sacrifice of animals.

Buddhism came to an essentially war-like people, who had largely over-run extensive parts of Turkistan, India and China, where they had captured the Chinese capital and exacted tribute for several years. At this time Tibet was one of the chief military powers of Asia and had a very fierce, war-like people. The Tibetans then gave up all their conquests and worldly power, not for economic reasons, nor because they lacked military strength, but solely because of their religion. This great race of soldiers and raiders became pacifist and their priests fought only the evil spirits around them.

After the 11th century the dominant factor in Tibetan history was the progress and spread of Buddhism. The powerful monasteries came to control the economic and military life of the people. The Dalai Lama, the head of the church, was also the people's leader in all things, assisted by a few powerful and wealthy families.

In the middle of the fourteenth century came the birth of the great religious reformer, Tsong-ka-pa, who revived the religion in a purer form, preaching the observance of the laws of discipline, forbidding the consumption of alcohol and insisting upon the celibacy of the priests. His followers became known as the Yellow Hat Sect, the most powerful sect in Tibet, with the Dalai Lama as its head. At this time Tsong-ka-pa founded the great monastery Ganden (the Joyous) about twenty-six miles from Lhasa, the capital. Two of the largest monasteries were Drepung (the Rice Heap) and Tashi Lhunpo (the Mount of Blessing).

The Chinese invaders made the Fifth Dalai Lama the supreme monarch of all Tibet, in order to ensure their complete control. The country was then closed to foreigners, and, with the exception of an occasional visitor, it was virtually unknown to the outside world until 1645. The remoteness of their society, the centuries of Buddhism which did not permit the killing of animals, their political isolation and the inaccessibility of their land, the great distances between the small villages and the loneliness of the nomadic life, earned for the

Tibetan dogs an important place in the lives of the people of Tibet.

Tibetans treat their animals far more kindly than do the Chinese or Indians. The Hindus of India believe in the doctrine of rebirth, but the Tibetans take this doctrine much more seriously, feeling that they themselves may have been animals in some of their previous lives and may be so again in some of their many lives that follow.

Nothing is more important to the Tibetan than his birth in the next life. If his life has been evil, and there is no one to intervene on his behalf, he may even be condemned to one of the hells for five thousand years or more. The Dalai Lama's complete supremacy ensured order throughout Tibet, and unified a large part of the country. As the Dalai is an absolute dictator he can reward or punish both in this life and the next, and only he can help to ensure that you will be reborn as a human in a high position, or better still as a priest in a country where Buddhism flourishes.

The Dalai Lama is looked upon as a god, being regarded by most Tibetans as the fourteenth century reincarnation of Chen-re-zi, the Buddha of Mercy. As Chen-re-zi is held to be the founder of the Tibetan race and is worshipped as its patron deity, this gives the Dalai Lama an overwhelming position in Tibet. Chen-re-zi is said to have achieved Nirvana during his first earthly existence six hundred years ago, and out of compassion for those of us who remain on earth, chose to be continually reborn, so that he may show us the way to Nirvana.

The title Dalai Lama means 'Ocean of Wisdom'. He lived in the vast Potala Palace, which is virtually a self-contained town built on a hill overlooking Lhasa, rising to thirteen storeys and is more than four hundred feet high. It is one of the most wonderful buildings in Asia, and the Dalai Lama lived at the top of it. In the Holy City the Dalai Lama lived in the seclusion of sanctity. Pilgrims turned and faced towards the Dalai Lama's Jewel Park Palace, the Nor-pu-Ling-ka, which was about one-and-a-half miles outside Lhasa and used by the Thirteenth Dalai Lama as his summer residence, the Potala being his home during the winter months. When they passed, the pilgrims would prostrate themselves at full-length on the dusty road before moving on to the Great Temple and other goals of their pilgrimage. When the Dalai passed along the road, all eyes were turned down towards the ground as no one must gaze upon divinity. The only contact that the people had with their Dalai Lama was when they humbly presented their ceremonial scarves of white Chinese silk and other offerings to his attendants – bowing their heads right down to the ground three times, then taking another step or two forward with the head still bowed, to receive his blessing. The Dalai then touched their heads with a tassel attached to a short rod.

The recognised form of Tibetan greeting is by placing a white silk scarf around the neck, or very rarely by placing it over the wrists, an action which disclaims all superiority of rank.

In Lhasa there are three sacred routes for the pilgrims. The first is the Inside Circle which goes around inside the Great Temple. The second is the Intermediate Circle which encloses the Temple. Thirdly there is the Park Circle which surrounds the City of Lhasa and the Potala Palace, and is between four to five miles in length. In his book, *Portrait of the Dalai Lama*, Sir Charles Bell tells us that Lhasa was originally named Ra-sa, (the Place of Goats), as it was built on a lake or marsh which had to be filled up before building began. This was done partly by transporting the earth on the backs of goats. Riding around the marsh on the Lhasa plain, a ten-mile circuit, Sir Charles Bell saw a number of lammergeier under the hills, also ravens, magpies and flocks of sparrows; golden eagles also abounded.

Lhasa was not purely a Tibetan city. There were Mongols from the borders of Siberia and Chinese from the many provinces of China, men from Nepal and Kashmir, also from Chinese Turkistan, as well as Tibetans from the outlying parts of Tibet.

The rosary is in general use throughout Tibet. Each rosary contains one hundred and eight beads which is a sacred number. The prayer wheel and the rosary are carried everywhere, the wheel in the hand and the rosary wound around the left wrist. A pilgrim tells the beads of his rosary with one hand, with the other he turns the prayer wheel. Prayers are written on strings of paper, hundreds of prayers and sacred sentences being packed tightly inside the little cylinder.

The Pan-chen Lama was as great a spiritual force as the Dalai Lama, though not nearly so important on the secular side. In the time of the Thirteenth Dalai Lama the Pan-chen resided in the great monastery at Ta-Shi Lhün-po and was considered to be the incarnation of the Buddha of Boundless Light. The Dalai Lama is the Lord of Mercy and the worldly rule over Tibet belongs to the Dalai. The Pan-chen held a subordinate position as the line of the Dalais started before that of the Pan-chens, although both are identified in the same way.

Asia is considered to be the cradle of the old religions and in Tibet there are many strange survivals of a by-gone age. You would find oracles, as in ancient Greece, which foretold public events, forecast the yield of the crops and predicted whether the year would be peaceful or not. They also were used to help with the finding of the re-born Dalai Lama.

10

Since the Chinese invasion of Tibet, with the disbanding of the monasteries and suppression of the Buddhist religion, there has been a deplorably low standard of education with unqualified teachers; the curriculum obviously concentrates on Marxism, the Chinese language and arithmetic, and the Tibetan language is neglected.

The task of the Tibetan people now in exile in India, Nepal and Bhutan, is to preserve the unique culture of Tibet. Sadly, those left behind inside Tibet have been subjected to a Chinese campaign which is intended to turn Tibet into a modern society. The hard facts are that thousands of Tibetan people have died of starvation, many have been forced to eat cats, dogs, shoe leather and pig food; they are treated as servants by the Communist Chinese, who look down on them as an inferior race.

There is absolutely no freedom; Tibet is, we are told, a barren land with starving people, some of whom have sold their own blood in order to buy food and clothing. Because of the extent of Chinese destruction, the Tibetan people in exile have an extremely important role to play, while delegations are struggling to obtain full freedom, including religious freedom, full human rights and the total well-being of six million Tibetans left inside Tibet.

The Author was very honoured to be invited to a meeting of the Tibet Society and Relief Fund at the Deanery, Westminster Abbey on July 1st 1981, where His Holiness the Dalai Lama of Tibet graciously agreed to receive members of this Society. She was over-whelmed to be introduced to His Holiness and took the opportunity of presenting him with three books about Tibetan Dogs – her own *Dog Directory Guide to Owning a Tibetan Spaniel*, Mrs Mulliner's *Tibetan Terrier* and a book on Lhasa Apsos. His Holiness talked to members present for over half an hour and said that the food situation was now a little easier inside Tibet, but there was still suppression of religious freedom. He stressed the necessity for teaching Tibetan culture, and let us hope it will be possible also to preserve in their pure state the four breeds of Tibetan dogs – five, if one is to include Shih Tzus.

The tragedy is that those of us whose interest in Tibet stems from our ownership and concern with breeding or exhibiting Tibetan dogs, will probably never have the opportunity to visit and find fresh blood. Even if this were to become possible in the future, sadly after the Chinese occupation, things will not be the same again.

Going on to 1964, in S. and R. Gelder's book *The Timely Rain* they describe the festival at Drepung:

Many children carried pet puppies in the folds of their gowns and scores of family dogs had come to the festival with their masters and mistresses. These charming, sleek and well-fed creatures resembled Pekingese, but had more pronounced noses and longer, straighter legs. Others were Shih-Tzus, like small miniatures of Old English Sheepdogs . . . As we passed a little girl*, a puppy popped his saucy head from her gown and licked our hands. His small owner, overcome with confusion, put her hand over her pet's nose. The Lama smiled, but because it was forbidden to bring animals into the chanting house, turned his head and pretended not to see. A grey-haired woman with a fluffy Shih-Tzu in her arms saw the Lama before he saw her and with a smile which asked us to ignore her, bent quickly down and put the dog under her wide skirt.

There are still hundreds of charming pet dogs in the city*. We came upon a delightful scene by the ford at the back of the Potala where there is an ancient chorten (a memorial containing holy relics). A grey-haired old lady was walking round it clockwise – the prescribed ritual – twirling her beautiful, small silver prayer wheel and murmuring prayers as she went. A tiny, fluffy, white puppy trotted close at her heels. When he was tired he sat down, faced the other way and waited for his mistress to come round again. When he got his breath back, he joined in her devotions once more.

The Gelders in their book describe modern Lhasa, saying:

From the roof-tops or from distant mountain peaks the setting of Lhasa is incomparable. But, apart from views of the majestic Potala, at ground level it is a comfortless collection of mean streets flanked by flat grey stone and brown mud buildings completely bereft of charm. Their monotony is relieved only by gay flowers planted in any empty old can the inhabitants can find . . . The overwhelming impression is still of dirt and squalor. There is no domestic drainage system and no arrangement for the disposal of sewage.

Some years before, seven thousand people in the capital had died of smallpox, one of the most dreaded illnesses in Tibet. Eleven years before the Gelders visited Lhasa, the streets were only cleaned once a year, choked with heaps of putrid rubbish in which dead animals as well as household refuse were left to rot. Citizens squatted, wherever they happened to be, to perform their natural functions, or used the yards of their houses.

The city was infested with fierce wild dogs which killed and consumed one another when they were unable to scavenge enough food. Some,

*Lhasa (*Author*).   *In the temple at Drepung (*Author*).

12

driven mad by hunger, attacked humans if they caught them alone. Because theoretically Tibetans as Buddhists must not take life, none of these wretched creatures, however diseased or injured, could be destroyed. There was not one to be seen in the City when we went there. We inquired what had happened to them. It was explained that the new medical authorities couldn't tolerate such a menace to health but neither could they offend religious sentiment by killing animals. So they were rounded up and placed in compounds where they were left to starve and eat one another. The last survivor died of hunger. The Tibetans, relieved of the sin of causing death, were content with this macabre solution.

In early May 1981, Mrs Joan Beard from New South Wales, Australia, went to Tibet. In Lhasa she saw lots of Tibetan Spaniel type dogs everywhere with very thick coats but only a few moth-eaten Lhasa Apsos. In her guest house, the Chinese Guide had a Tibetan Terrier – but didn't apparently know what it was! The Gelders in the early 1960s found that, instead of more than seven thousand monks living at Drepung before the rebellion, only about seven hundred remained. Mrs Beard found in Lhasa in 1981, that instead of ten thousand Lamas there were now only about two hundred and fifty; she also met Tenzing Norgay of Everest fame.

2 Dogs, and their Part in Tibetan Religion and Folklore

For those of us who are intent upon preserving the different breeds of Tibetan dogs, there is little chance of our being able to find and import any from their country of origin. To try and understand just what Tibetan dogs meant to the Tibetan people, we must delve back in time.

The history and attributes of the Tibetan, Chinese and indeed also some of the small Japanese breeds, are all very closely interwoven with those of the various sects of the Buddhist religion.

Bon (or *Pön*) is the nature worship or shamanism that preceded Buddhism throughout Tibet, Mongolia and their borderlands. Buddhism reached China directly from India and, indirectly, as Lamaism from Tibet.

We must understand that Buddhism permits to the dog a closer relationship with man than does Christianity, which in the matter of salvation gives to the canine race not even the proverbial 'dog's chance'. The Buddhist recognises no essential difference on spiritual grounds between man and dog. They credit dogs with having some sort of soul.

In the Buddhist cycle the spirit of man commonly passes into the form of a dog. The Buddhists placed numerous representations of the dog in clay and pottery in early Chinese tombs, in order to retain their services in the life to come. The Lamas of Tibet suggest that the miserable pariah dogs of their country may be the reincarnation of priests who have been faithless to their vows.

The same idea may underly the inclusion of a dog, white for ill luck and mourning, in the scapegoat party, which is recorded by Nain Singh as being annually expelled from Lhasa: "On the 29th day of the first month a man is selected, who is called the *Logon gyalpo*, meaning the 'carrier of one year's ill luck', who becomes a sort of scapegoat for the sins of the people."

For a week the *Logon gyalpo* perambulates Lhasa as a sort of clown with half his face painted white and the other half black. He is also permitted to shake a yak's black tail over the heads of the people, and by so doing he transfers from them to himself the full measure of their ill luck. In payment he receives certain presents from the government, a white horse, a white dog, a white bird and other small gifts and provisions and offerings from the people. Finally, he is driven out of the town by a yelling mob, towards the Samye monastery, where he may be accommodated in the *Khakang* or dead house.

The lion was associated with Buddhism from a very early date, possibly as early as 260 B.C., but the Buddhist religion was not firmly established among the Chinese until A.D. 67. Both the Chinese and Tibetan people undoubtedly bred a race of small dogs to resemble as closely as possible their respective ideas of a Buddhist spirit-lion. The best representatives of the original Buddhist lions are those in stone and bronze which stood originally in the southern doorways of the imperial palaces and the Lama temple in Peking.

The relationship of the spirit-lion and the lion-dog is defined in the Tibetan sacred writings, where they mention that there was a Buddha named Manjusri, who was always accompanied by a small 'Ha-pa' dog (meaning here a pet dog). This Ha-pa dog was transformed into a mighty lion with Buddha riding upon his back, according to the Tibetans. The Chinese refer to the Tibetan Buddha as 'Wenshu'.

It is not known when the Tibetan Lamas began to send the small Tibetan 'shock' or lion-dogs to the Manchus, but it may have commenced as early as A.D. 1583. Laufer, in his book *Annals of Shatung Province* remarks about the dogs which were there in the sixteenth century, "there is a kind from the Western Foreign Country, low, small, clean and cunning, with which you can play. It is called a Ha-pa dog."

Perhaps the association of the Manjusri Buddha with a small pet dog, which on occasions could be changed into a lion, suggested to the devotees of Lamaism that the idea of breeding 'miniature lions' was to be construed as a pious duty and, by so doing, they would acquire heavenly merit.

The Tibetan people, like the Chinese, were willing to call any shaggy-coated dog a 'lion-dog', so it is more than possible that the Tibetan people sent their small dogs as curiosities and presents to the Manchu emperors, intending them to be a flattering reminder of the Lamaist association of the dynastic name with Manjusri, the God of Learning, who was always accompanied by a small pet dog capable of being transformed into a mighty lion, who could then be Buddha's steed.

Sadly we now know that the Red Chinese are systemically destroying the Tibetan dogs in Tibet, when they can find them, mainly because they are consumers of precious food, but also because of what they mean to the Tibetan people. This is another tragic instance of a genocidal reaction towards anything Tibetan.

Another reason why Tibetans consider dogs to be sacred is that when they make their pilgrimages round the town of Lhasa, to visit all the sacred and holy places en route – and there is, apparently, a regular route which circles the town and touches on the main temples – they always take their dogs with them and treat them with great respect, for the dogs are thought to be a receptacle for any evil spirits that might not be pleased with their masters.

M. Harrer, who travelled for seven years in Tibet, confirms that some of these dogs accompanied their owners daily around the five mile pilgrim ring-road, circling Lhasa. After the owner died often the dog could still be seen walking the ring alone until it too died.

The Hon. Mrs F. M. Bailey says that "on the Ling-Kor or sacred road, on which pilgrims circumambulate Lhasa, are a number of dogs of all descriptions, which are fed by the pilgrims as an act of piety. This has nothing to do with the dogs being sacred. All talk of sacred dogs being bred in the monasteries is nonsense, but the Buddhist theory of reincarnation encourages kindness to animals, especially in a holy place like Lhasa."

As early as 1885 Sarat Chandra Das wrote in his book *Narrative of a journey to Lhasa* that the dog was prized as a most useful animal by all classes in Tibet. "Very definitely," he said, "the dogs' lives were very closely interwoven with those of their Tibetan masters, who used their bodies for warmth, their coat for spinning, and their barking as a warning of intruders." Perhaps they even participated with the vultures in the gruesome rites surrounding the disposal of the dead? This is confirmed by Mrs G. Hayes when she wrote in *Our Dogs* (June 3rd, 1932): ". . . the many breeds of mysterious Tibet, dogs of rare intelligence and long lineage, but one breed eats the dead . . . Then there are the Corpse Dogs, which are degenerate descendants of the Mastiffs. These dogs roam wild, and exist on what they can find, like jackals. They eat the dead, who are laid out on little mounds outside the villages so that the dogs can devour them. If the dogs eat the body quickly it is considered a sign of the soul's swift flight to heaven."

In the book *Mongolian Horde* the author mentions the wild dogs, which "hunt in packs, and have nearly exterminated all the small game of the country. They would even attack sambur (the Indian Elk), and often succeeded in pulling it down. Beside the occasional corpses and general scavenging, the packs found a number of dead sheep by haunting the passes going down to India. A great many sheep died of rhododendron poisoning as they were driven down."

The dogs were only about the size of Irish Terriers.

In the *Kennel Gazette* (1934), the Hon. Mrs Bailey wrote: "The late (i.e. Thirteenth) Dalai Lama kept a number of dogs of many breeds up in a garden. Pekingese (of a sort) were kept in a cage."

Mrs Bailey was given some Tibetan Spaniels by the Thirteenth Dalai Lama, but she preferred to keep and bring home her Lhasa Apsos. In 1968 a Mr Ramsay told me that he had visited Tibet before the war and had met the Thirteenth Dalai Lama, who had a pair of Tibetan Spaniels at that time. One was a red sable and the other a very pale gold with a black face and a white tail and trousers. Both had fairly long broad muzzles and very thick coats. Mr Ramsay noticed that in Tibet the longer muzzled dogs had thick coats and the shorter muzzled dogs had a finer coat. His theory was based on the surmise that the shorter-faced Tibetan Spaniels came from the monasteries on the borders of China and Tibet.

In *Portrait of the Dalai Lama* (1946), Sir Charles Bell tells us that the Dalai Lama was very fond of the large Tibetan dogs used for herding yaks and for guarding houses and tents. To be able to give the Dalai Lama a gift of such a dog, the people would pay a great sum of money, the earnings of several months. One of these dogs in the enclosure was a particularly fine specimen; it came, as the Dalai informed Sir Charles Bell, from his own district of Tak-Po. The Dalai was very proud of that dog, but then he was fond of all animals, especially birds. He liked very large or very small dogs; their novelty and strange ways amused him. He played with them after his morning devotions, and after dinner with some of the dogs or other household pets, but especially with the dogs, who were brought in for an interlude. Had he been a Westerner, people would have said that 'He had a way with animals', but Tibetans of course put it much higher than that. In their estimation his spiritual influence moves the animal world; for animals are also 'mind possessors' and are, or should be, on the Path to Buddhahood.

In Sir Charles Bell's book there is a photograph of the Pan-chen Lama taken in 1930, with two small dogs seated on either side of his chair. They look very similar to particolour Pekingeses, possibly black-and-white in colour.

Sir Henry Hayden and Monsieur Cesar Cosson in their book *Sport and Travel in the Highlands of Tibet*, (1927), said that the four most characteristic features of Tibet were the monks, beggars, ruins and dogs. This book gives the distinct impression that one of the most conspicuous features of Lhasa was the hordes of apparently ownerless dogs, which filled all streets, lanes and open spaces. These dogs and a

18

certain number of pigs were, in fact, the scavengers of Lhasa, and the sole representatives of an unofficial Tibetan Municipal Board of Health! The number of dogs seen by these two travellers of the early 1920s must have literally run into thousands, for the most part owner-less. These dogs entered no houses, but roamed about the streets day and night. It is not therefore very difficult to imagine the state of pandemonium that arose nightly throughout the town, whether because of a canine quarrel over a bone, or from some other unexplained night fear.

At every cross-roads they found groups of beggars, blind, lame and diseased, attended by a number of mangy dogs. In Lhasa, and in most of the other Tibetan towns, the bodies of all the dead, except for those of the monks which were burned, were taken away to a convenient rock where they were cut up and thrown to the dogs and vultures. The bones were then pounded and dealt with in much the same way.

This practice is confirmed by Mrs J. Murray Aynsley in *The Kennel Gazette* of September 1890: "The ownerless wandering dogs devour the poorer classes, while the rich are eaten by more distinguished animals."

In the doorway of the underground chamber in the Temple of Reincarnation at Samye, Sir Henry Hayden found hanging from the roof, skins of dogs stuffed with straw. He was told that these dogs, had given good and faithful service to the monks during their lifetime, and that their skins were hung there in the hope that the Distributor-of-Souls would reward them by reincarnation into a higher sphere.

E. R. Huc and Gabet in their book *Travels in Tartary, Thibet and China 1884–1846*, wrote:

Cases of hydrophobia are not unfrequent among the Thibetans; and one is only surprised that this horrible malady does not commit greater ravages, when one bears in mind the terrible multitudes of gaunt, famishing dogs that are always prowling about the streets of Lha-ssa. These animals, in fact, are so numerous in that city that the Chinese comtemptuously say that the three great products of the capital of Thibet are Lamas, women and dogs.

From the book *Die Nomaden von Tibet* (1949), we learn that, in addition to the horse, the dog is also indispensable to the Amdo-pa, who inhabit the province of Amdo, in Eastern Tibet. The dog is, first and foremost, the guardian of the tent. Several keen dogs are to be found near each tent. During the night, while the flocks are resting near the tents, the dogs keep the wolves at bay. There are also particular dogs which accompany the shepherds and protect their flocks by day. Because of these valuable services, the nomads greatly value their dogs and are especially attached and devoted to them. Among the first animals mentioned in Tibetan mythology is the 'white bitch', in Tibetan *Khyi-mo kar-mo*. To throw a stone at a dog, or to strike it, is considered a personal insult by the nomad. When a stranger comes near to a tent, he calls out to the people inside, so that they may come and call off the dogs. Then, and only then, may a stranger approach.

A Tibetan proverb says 'you must never strike a dog you may have called to yourself', which is in Tibetan *Khyi boz na ma rdung*. This does actually have a double meaning and can also be interpreted as 'one must never offend an invited guest, even when he is a bad man'. One also should never suggest to a nomad that he should sell you a grown dog. This would be considered by him as an offence and an insult. He will gladly make a present of a young dog to his friends, but he will never give up a grown dog. Even when his dogs have grown quite old and are barely able to navigate, the Amdo-pa will never put them down, even out of mercy. The dog that has served him faithfully all its life, according to the nomad's ethics, must be allowed to die a natural death. By the same token a nomad will not eat dog, nor in any way use its fur or skin.

However, although the dog is the true friend and companion of man in the great solitude which is the lot of the nomad, the nomads do not endow the dog with any sort of religious adoration. Myths concerning a mystical origin are also unknown to the Amdo-pa.

In his book, *Chinese Creeds and Customs*, which Colonel V. Burkhardt wrote in 1953–58, he mentions Rabies and the belief that the colour of the animal, and the time of infliction of the wound, were of material importance:

In Tibet, where the animals feed on carrion, a regular scale was laid down for the danger to be apprehended; for the poison of a white rabid dog with a red, flushed nose, was mortal at all times. That of a red dog, increased in potency at midday, midnight or sunrise. A parti-coloured brute was most dangerous from 8 a.m. till an hour after noon, whilst spotted dogs were to be avoided at twilight or 9 p.m. The bite of a yellow cur was certain to produce fatal results if inflicted at dusk or 9 a.m. The disease would pronounce itself in man, seven days after the bite of a white dog, but a month must elapse for the diagnosis of hydrophobia if the animal were black. Sixteen days was the period of incubation for a parti-coloured, twenty-six for an ash-grey, and from one month to seven and a half if the beast were red. A blackish-yellow infects man three to seven months after the bite, but it needs a year and fifteen days for a spotted dog to pass on the virus. A bluish-black or tiger-coloured dog has the longest period, namely a year and eight months, but it is difficult to cure if the poison were injected at 7 p.m. or dusk, or in the case of a black dog, at dawn. On the other hand, if a blue dog bites at mid-day, a red one at midnight, a spotted one at dawn, or a white early in the morning, a cure is easily effected.

In so much of Asia, where dogs are usually treated with contempt, all too often neglected and mistreated, the Tibetan people with their attitude towards man's best friend are a pleasure to know. The fidelity and devotion of the Tibetan breeds and the affection of the Tibetan owners for their dogs is well-illustrated in Kaupback's book *Tibetan Trek* from which an extract is given by Mrs Geoffrey Hayes in *Our Dogs* (February 1st, 1935). Mrs Hayes chose this story to illustrate the hardiness and devotion of Tibetan dogs and the Author is sure that readers will undoubtedly jump to the same conclusion, that it must have been a Tibetan Spaniel!

> One of my coolies had a small dog to which he was extraordinarily kind and which was devoted to him, though inclined to be surly to anyone else. When we came to the rope bridge, the fellow decided it was better not to drag the dog across and left it on the bank to go back. Hardly had we reached the other side when we saw it plunge bravely into the water, which was coming down like greased lightning and as cold as ice. It was instantly switched out of sight by the current. We all gave it up for lost and its master broke into despairing sobs; but to our astonishment it came running up ten minutes later, none the worse for its adventure, and as relieved as the owner that they had found each other again. I could never have believed that anything short of an otter could have swum across the river in that state of flood and reached the other side alive.

The fascination with which the Tibetans regarded their animals finds its expression in the pantheon of the ancient Tibetan religion before the advent of Buddhism. The temple banners and frescoes depicted their war-gods with flocks of sheep, herds of yak and hosts of dogs. Behind this lies the human psychological need to find a peaceful inter-relationship between man and his gods and animals.

Even in the Buddhist pantheon, each guardian deity is associated with a particular animal which is depicted as a messenger emanating from its divine master. The functional implication for the devotee was that he should not harm the animal without transgressing doubly the precept of non-injury and the pledge to love it.

Paradoxically concerning the Tibetan Mastiffs, it is a curious fact that the Tibetans, on the whole, are a peaceful, kind people and dog-lovers. They do not appear to consider that the more-or-less permanent chaining of their watchdogs to walls is cruel. They would appear to look upon a chained dog as a piece of household furniture and do not think of the cruel side of it, we are told by Ronald Cardew Duncan who lived in India for about forty years, where he kept many dogs of various breeds and where his small book *Tomu from Tibet and other Dog Stories* was published in 1950.

Mr A. J. Sellar writing about his Tibetan hunting dog in *The Tibetan Terrier Association's 1980 Year Book* mentions the poor condition and nervousness of the dogs in the nomad encampment, which he attributed to the barbarous practice at festival times of having fireworks attached to their tails and then let loose. There were ten or twelve religious festivals held each year in Lhasa.

"Next to his horse, perhaps, the Tibetan favours his dog", says M. H. Duncan in his book *Customs & Superstitions of Tibetans*, published in 1904, obviously referring to the Mastiff . . . "whose almost ceaseless throaty bark, like the sonorous 'rah-rah' of college boys, speeds into a continuous roar when strangers approach his protectorate".

3 The Evolution and Origins of the Tibetan Breeds

Many years ago, Mrs Muriel B. Wood gave me an article on the origin of the Tibetan dog breeds. She also wrote a very interesting article for *Dog World Weekly* (June 2nd, 1967) – 'The Evolution of the Tibetan Breeds', in which she outlined Professor Ludvic von Schulmuth's theories. To understand the Tibetan breeds of dogs, one must go back to the origin of 'Dog and Man'. Mrs Wood said that dogs and men originated at about the same time, quite possibly in one of three places: firstly, in the south-west of the central part of the Gobi Desert; secondly, in what we now call Turkistan south of the Caspian Sea, or between this and the Aral Sea; thirdly, in Central Africa around Lake Victoria and other lakes in this area. All the dogs found near early man were of the 'Spitz' type, or wolf-like, but slowly they altered for a variety of reasons, among them the climate and the amount of food they found. Later, man took to selecting certain dogs for certain work and so the first selective breeding must have taken place.

The peoples from the Gobi Desert area moved north, east, south and west, but the movement to the south-west was slower because of the mountains. Professor von Schulmuth considered that the early people went north-east first, then east, later south and lastly westwards.

Finds relating to these palaeolithic people are sited at Chou-K'ou-tien, thirty miles south-west of Peking; at Ta-Tien-Lu in Western Szechwan; and there have also been finds in Mongolia and Manchuria, as well as in Mongolia at Shabarakh-Usu in the Gobi Desert. The people of this time were hunters and very primitive farmers. Bones of oxen, sheep and horses, also dogs and wild animals, deer and bear, have been found.

There are two sites at Ching-te (Lin-hai) and Ulan Hata (Ch'ih feng), where the neolithic culture was that of sedentary farmers and husbandmen. Here the dogs were heavier in the head. People further north in Northern Manchuria depended on fishing and hunting.

The people who spread further north with their dogs were most likely hunters, and their dogs remained the 'Spitz' type. Those who spread out into and over the great central plains of Asia, became longer in the leg, heavier in the head, and thicker and longer in coat. It is from the dogs of the Gobi Desert people that the small 'Kitchen Midden Dog' and several other breeds descend. Of course it took many thousands of years to produce the dogs we now know, with their different characteristics.

The Professor compared several skulls of the larger type with the skull of the Owcharke and the Tibetan Mastiff and found that they were of similar type, whereas the skulls of the small dogs did not compare with any of the hound types as we know them today, but appeared to be a primitive type of Tibetan Spaniel, Pekingese, Papillon and Japanese Spaniel. Upon comparing the skulls of the Tibetan Spaniel and the Lhasa Apso with the Tibetan Terrier, he found several differences. The Tibetan Spaniel's skull is wider for the length than the other two Tibetan breeds. But the skull of the Shih Tzu and the Pug are halfway between the Tibetan Spaniel and the Tibetan Apso.

It appears that up to late in the 16th century there was a hunting dog in Szechwan and Tsinghai, that was rather long in body. The muzzle was fairly short and rather blunt, the ears which hung down were well-feathered, as were the back of the fore-legs, buttocks and tail. The height would appear to have been about 18–20 inches as these dogs are shown in one or two paintings hunting small deer, and Professor Schulmuth has judged the size of the dogs from the men and deer in the paintings. The tail was carried gaily, the colours were red, fawn and cream and they were not of the Saluki type at all as the skull is far too wide. These dogs also appear to have been known in other parts of China and the Professor believed that the short-legged hound type had been very closely related to the Tibetan Spaniel in the past. Possibly, when the Hound arrived in Tibet with early man, the need for a smallish hunting dog did not exist and the larger type of dog did all the hunting, the smaller then reverting to its former place as a house-pet and vermin killer.

The Professor's theories also concluded that the Afghan Spaniel must have been a close relation of the Tibetan Spaniel. In looks this dog was rather like our Cavalier King Charles Spaniel. About 150 years ago there was a long, or wire-haired, dog of the Pug type found in China, usually in the east, this was called a Loong Chua in some parts, and the Professor considered that this was another descendant of the Tibetan Spaniel, crossed with some other breed.

In *Dog World* (December 13th, 1968), Mr Don H. Rigden wrote asking if any readers could assist him in a research he had undertaken into the history of the Afghan Spaniel, two of which were exhibited at Crufts in 1929. These were described as small, red-and-white, drop-

24

eared, long coated Spaniels. Kennel Club records for March 2nd, 1929, showed one of these as being an import and the other being bred by Mrs Gibbon named Bulbul and Chum. These were black-and-white and both owned by the Hon. Mrs McLaren Morrison. As Mr Rigden correctly says "All sorts of dogs and breed names were accepted by the Kennel Club in the early days, therefore it is quite natural to suspect errors with, possibly, Tibetan breeds". He goes on to quote the change of name and breeds for Lhasa Terriers, as an example.

Mrs M. Weller replied to this reference to Afghan Spaniels in *Dog World* (March 14th, 1969), quoting Mr Jungeling, the Dutch International judge, who recalled having seen dogs of the type described as Afghan Spaniels in the late 1920s and saying that those seen in 1929 will certainly have come from Afghanistan, as Bulbul is a typical Afghan name, not existing in Tibet.

It is a pity that we do not know more about this now little known breed, and of their relationship to the dogs now featured on the modern postage stamps from Bhutan.

Another of the Professor's theories was that the Pug is a smooth-haired offshoot of the Tibetan Spaniel, bred over many centuries and that its short nose was evolved in the same way as that of the Pekingese, by selective breeding and the nose being forced back into the face. It appears that this type of dog was very popular with princes, not of the Imperial House, and with the rich merchants in southern China, where the warmer climate may have accounted for the original short coat, which became even shorter as a result of the breeding that took place in Europe during the past two hundred years.

The Professor's theories concerning the Tibetan Spaniel and Pekingese breeds are borne out in the chapter on early Chinese dogs. He considered that the Pekingese was definitely descended from the Tibetan Spaniel. It was not until the end of the Ming dynasty (1368–1644) that the first paintings of the flat-nosed dogs appeared. The paintings of the Ming dynasty show several dogs of Pekingese type, but all have marked muzzles like the Tibetan Spaniels of today and they are also longer in back than the Pekingese.

To continue with Professor von Schulmuth's theories: during the Ch'ing dynasty (1644–1912) the Chinese Imperial House did much to breed the small Pekingese with no muzzle, even forcing the nose back when they were puppies, binding it close to the face, in the same way that they bound the high-class women's feet. In time, the dogs' noses became flat on the face, but in the early days of the breed in England, right up to 1910, dogs with fairly marked muzzles appeared in the Peke breed in this country, and the Professor was convinced that all the early, so-called Pekes, before about the 1600s were Tibetan Spaniels.

There is another type of dog in China called *Happa*, which means 'a dog with hair over its eyes', descended from the dogs that came to China from the Gobi Desert area, in the early days. It is in part related to the Funlun Mountain Dog. The Professor considered that the Shih Tzu belonged to this group. The name 'lion dog' in Cantonese Chinese is Shih Tzu, the Northern Chinese people called Pekingese type dogs Shih Tzu Gau or lion-dog. He did not think that the Chow Chow was a Chinese dog, but that it originated in Tibet, and there was rather a smooth-coated dog. It was not eaten in Tibet but used as a sledge dog and for hunting, but it did develop its longer coat in China.

One can but ponder whether the Fu Lin dogs mentioned in the Chinese dog chapter could be descended from the Funlun Mountain dogs, just as there existed in the early 1900s the Owtchar or Russian Sheepdog, considered at that time to resemble our Old English Sheepdog. About 31 inches high and very strong in proportion, he was expected to be capable of defending his flock against predatory wolves. These dogs often used to be brought to England in the Baltic trading ships and were frequently called Russian Terriers, although there was nothing of the Terrier about them. They were true sheep and cattle dogs and excellent workers, usually slatey-grey and dirty-white, or sometimes nearly black or rusty-brown.

After careful study, Professor Ludvic von Schulmuth came to the conclusion that the Tibetan Apsos and the Tibetan Terriers were descended from the Owcharke of Russia, via several different breeds:

Owcharke: coat very thick and fairly long, rather inclined to mat, texture rather hard and rough, colour white, light silver-grey, very light red, the first two colours being the most desired, and wolf grey not desirable. Height 24–30 inches, the average height being 28 inches.

The Mongolian Dog: coat rather long and shaggy and sometimes inclined to mat, short under-coat, colour light grey, cream, yellowish-red, fawns, dull brownish-red (undesirable), always with white on the muzzle, chest, feet and often also the tip of tail. Height 22–24 inches.

From the Mongolian Dog descended the Funlun Dog. Also from the Owcharke descended the Inner Mongolian Dog.

The Funlun Mountain Dog: the coat is rather silky and fairly long, the colours cream, reddish, sandy, dark or light grey, sometimes almost black, white on muzzle, chest, feet and tip of tail, height 15–18 inches.

The Inner Mongolian Dog: rather long coat, shaggy and thick, colour grey and white, sandy yellow, always with white on muzzle, chest, feet and tip of tail, height 20–22 inches in the north, but 18 inches in the south.

From the Professor's genealogical chart (p. 32) one can see why he considers the Tibetan Apsos and Tibetan Terriers are closely related.

To get anywhere near to the origin of the Tibetan Spaniel we have to look at the types which descend from the Gobi Desert Kitchen Midden Dog. These types seem to have remained in the East to a great extent.

The various sites where the early hunter-farmers lived, have given up bones of two kinds of dogs: one of these had a heavy head, large bones and long legs, the skull both wide and long, the back fairly long; the other was a lightly boned dog, smaller and lighter, making the dog about 18–20 inches while the larger dog must have been 25–30 inches.

The smaller dog had a shortish muzzle, this was only slightly pointed, the skull was broad and not very long, on some being as wide as it was long, the back was fairly long compared with the length of the legs. The bones were dated by the Professor as being from about 150–950 B.C.

The Professor concluded, according to Mrs Wood, that these short-legged dogs had descended from the Kitchen Midden Dogs, and that the larger, heavier type of dog had descended from another type of the original dogs, and was used to hunt large animals as well as being used to guard. The smaller dogs were probably used to hunt smaller game.

The relationship between man and dog is very ancient and there is evidence that this relationship existed some 10,000 years ago. There have, of course, been various theories of origin, some favouring the wolf, others the jackal, either for the dog in general or for specific breeds or groups of breeds.

There does now appear to be a concensus of scientific opinion that the wolf was the originator of the domestic dog. Konrad Lorenz, who was the original proponent of the theory that the 'Spitz' type of dog was descended from the wolf and the rest were descended from the jackal, has now withdrawn this theory and accepts the wolf hypothesis.

It is interesting to know from those who have worked with them that wolves are organised on the basis of group formations, which may account for their tameability. Most of the work done on wolves is in fact on the zoo behaviour of the North-American wolf. This wolf seems to be much more reluctant to attack humans than the European wolf, which has always had a bad reputation.

Early explorers of the American continent found that the wolves would apparently cooperate with them on buffalo hunts. The American Indians and the wolf appear to have had a working arrangement. Litters were raised within the camps and the whelps played with the children.

The behaviour of the wolf is very similar to that of the dog, except that the wolf communicates more with its tail. It used to be said that dogs bark and wolves howl, but it is now known that wolves do also bark. I can also vouch for the fact that Tibetan Spaniels can howl! It appears that part of the ease with which the dog fits into human society springs from its pack or group loyalty.

Jackals are, however, found only in pairs and have no such complex social organisation. Lorenz's change of mind on the origin of the dog is partly due to the wider range of vocalisation possessed by the jackal. A dog's vocalisation is much closer to that of the wolf.

The wolf shows specialised ability at selective tracking, and does not change from one track to another, thus enabling him to wear down one quarry. The wolf takes food back to the lair and perhaps this accounts for the ease with which dogs may be trained to retrieve. The wolf uses the bark when danger approaches the lair, the howl is a hunting sound, just as the dog's bark is also used as a warning.

Dr R. N. Smith has given me permission to use his chart showing the relationship of wild species to domestic dogs.

RELATIONSHIPS OF WILD SPECIES TO DOMESTIC DOGS

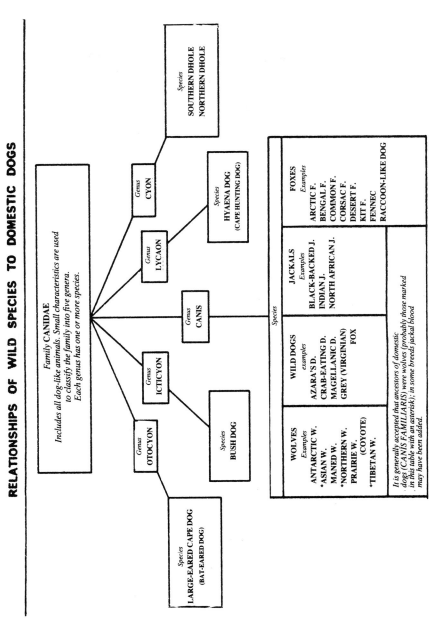

Dr R. N. Smith, Ph.D., D.Sc., F.R.C.V.S. of the School of Veterinary Science, University of Bristol, in his booklet *An Anatomy of the Dog* (published 1972 by Quartilles International Limited) clearly explains with this chart the relationship of the wild species to domestic dogs.

In relation to Dr Smith's chart, I find it interesting to read in the book *Living Animals of the World* published during the very early 1900s, that "Wolves will interbreed with dogs readily, which the red fox will not. The progeny do not bark but howl. The Eskimo cross their dogs with wolves to give them strength".

In the *Book of the Dog*, edited by Brian Vesey Fitzgerald, and published in 1948, we are told that *Canis familiaris* has a background stretching far away through history and, in order for us to understand the evolution of the dog family, it is necessary to delve back to a small flesh-eating mammal called *Miacis* of about forty million years ago. The *Miacis* was an arboreal (living in trees) animal about the size of a polecat with short legs and a tail as long as its body. *Miacis* was the root stock of the family tree from which modern dogs (*Canidae*) and also bears (*Ursidae*) have evolved.

The family *Canidae* is composed of wolves and jackals (*Genus Canis*). Until comparatively recently zoologists regarded the fox as belonging to the genus *Canis* and it was generally supposed that certain of our domestic dogs were descended from the fox; but there are no scientifically attested instances of the dog and fox ever having been interbred.

Detailed anatomy of the structure of the skull and teeth has dis-proved the theory that, because breeds of dogs may superficially resemble a fox or jackal, or some other wild species of the *Canidae*, they are descended from it. There seems little doubt, from the avail-able evidence, that all domestic dogs originate from the common wolf of the northern hemisphere (*Canis lupus*).

G. M. Vevers, F.R.C.S., once the superintendent of the Zoological Gardens, London, in the chapter on phylogeny in Brian Vesey Fitzgerald's book, is quoted as saying that the Soviet geneticist, Iljiin, made the most important scientific contribution towards proving, by genetical methods, the descent of the domestic dog from the wolf, in experiments carried out between the wolf and the dog between 1930 and 1933.

As early as the fourth century B.C., Aristotle recorded wolf–dog crosses, in the first century A.D., Pliny described how inhabitants of Gaul tied up their bitches to trees, when in season, in order to have them served by wild wolf dogs. Even today, Eskimos cross their sledge dogs with wolves to improve the stamina of the breed.

Iljiin's data proved the close similarity in genetic constitution between the wolf and the dog, and the modern dog inherits many habits from the ancestral wolf, for instance, the scratching up of earth with the front feet and pushing it back with the hind feet in order to cover over its tracks after urination and defaecation. Even the smallest lap dog will scratch at the floor as if forming a nest in which to sleep.

Achondroplasia is a congenital disease of the growing bones, in which the cartillage does not develop, resulting in the shortening and deformity of the bones such as the achondroplastic head and legs of the Pekingese, which Stockard has shown to be an inherited dominant factor, was seized upon hundreds of years ago by the Chinese. Unbelievable as it may sound, such breeds as the Pekingese, St Bernard, Great Dane and Belgian Griffon are mutations or 'sports' descending from the wolf alone.

It is considered that the dog was the first of all the animals to be domesticated by man, and throughout the millions of years of physical evolution other subtle changes were taking place in the brain of the *Canidae*, which put the dog on a high plane of intelligence and therefore man selected him above all others as the first subject of domestication.

As Professor von Schulmuth's studies have shown it is likely that the first steps towards domestication commenced as long ago as palaeolithic times, about ten to twelve thousand years ago. Most probably it was the scavenging habits of young wolf cubs which led to their capture and eventual domestication, so in a few generations they came to rely more and more upon man for food and shelter.

Skeletons of dogs have been found in neolithic deposits and the kitchen middens of Denmark. We have evidence to prove that dogs were in Britain in the neolithic period, such a discovery being made by Mr A. Keiller in 1928 at Windmill Hill, near Avebury.

The earliest humans were food gatherers and hunters, with no agriculture or domestic animals of any kind. Living a semi-nomadic life in search of food, they would occupy a site until the local food supply was dangerously diminished, whereupon they would move to another area where food was more abundant. At each of the camps or settlements they would throw the remains of their meals into heaps, whose size would depend upon the length of the stay and the number of people within the group. The odour from these middens must have been quite overpowering. As time went on, it was discovered that the dog was a willing consumer of the left-overs from the 'kitchen' and would thus effectively serve to eliminate the intolerable odours which blew in from the refuse heaps.

Professor Ludvic von Schulmuth's
Genealogical Tree of the Tibetan Dogs

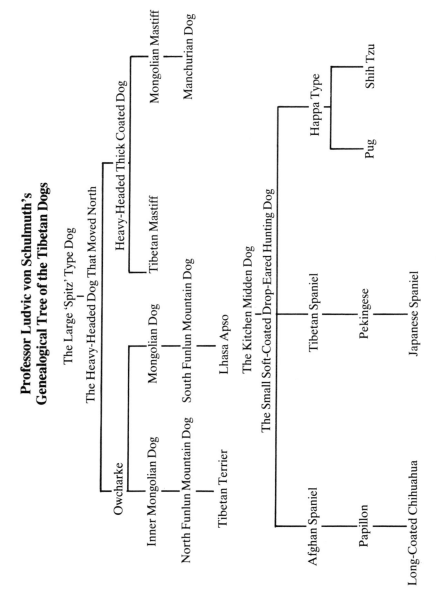

By kind permission of the Editor of *Dog World* from the edition printed 2.6.67.

4 Dogs of Tibet

Food was hard to come by in Tibet, for both humans and for dogs, the canine diet would not be considered well-balanced or adequate for Tibetan dogs in our modern civilisation. For instance, the Tibetan people, even today, advise that no meat should be given to a dog until it is over twelve months old. They like their dogs small, with the exception of the Mastiffs, and they criticise the European dogs saying that, because they are over-fed and given meat at an early age, they always grow big.

The Tibetan people start by giving their puppies *tsampa* mixed with milk. This is a finely ground millet-like grain and is fed to the puppies as soon as they can walk. The Tibetans will sell or give away their puppies at three weeks of age. In spite of this, we do know, from imports into various countries all around the world, that stock bred by the Tibetan people grows into what we consider to be normal-sized healthy animals with good coats.

Tibetan traders are particularly noted for their sparse diet of hard cheese made from dried milk, a bag of *tsampa*, a dried goat or sheep's leg, a small bag of pickled greens, as well as hard bricks of tea which they mix with salt, yak butter and hot water. This is about all they carry on their long, cold journeys.

The herders use grain to make their *chapatti*, a pancake like bread. These people live for months on this bread and goat's milk and are slim, healthy and tenacious.

Mrs G. Hayes wrote in *Our Dogs* (June 3rd, 1932), in her article 'The many breeds of mysterious Tibet':

Dogs of rare intelligence and long lineage but one breed eats the dead [the latter has been referred to in Chapter 2] . . . All Tibetan dogs have certain characteristics in common; very thick coats, great hardiness, and a really remarkable intelligence. For instance a dog used only to the Tibetan language and bought by an European will, in only a week, understand what is wanted of him.

Like the Tibetans themselves, none of the breeds is very prolific, and three puppies are a very large litter. The bitches come into season only once a year, whilst in Tibet. Most of these breeds stand the heat fairly well on being imported into India, provided, of course, that it isn't at the height of the hot season. Their great hardiness is probably due to their being examples of the survival of the fittest, as four out of five dogs die from hardship on the journey from Lhassa.

All the smaller breeds respond at once to European kindness and cleanliness. The only real trouble with them is to avoid over-feeding. After the scanty and poor Tibetan food a little ordinary biscuit and meat has an extraordinary effect, and the diet must always be kept on the meagre side. The dogs kept in the rich families, where they need have no chances of scavenging, are generally free from worms and need little dosing.

When buying a dog in Lhassa it is essential to buy only from a few well-to-do men who breed the dogs. Any dog bought haphazard from a caravan that has come down from India, has quite probably been picked up en route, and may not be pure bred. There are a lot of these half-caste dogs in Bhutan and Balistan, and if the intending purchaser is not personally acquainted with a Tibetan of repute, great care should be exercised.

It is a curious and interesting fact that a primitive and uncultured people such as the Tibetans should be so devoted to their dogs and should actually breed and keep fairly true to type five or six different breeds. There is no Asiatic country of which the same can be said. . . . Year by year English dog owners are becoming more and more interested in the possibilities of Tibetan breeds.

Mentioning A. Croxton-Smith's book, *About Our Dogs* (1931), Mrs Hayes wrote:

Everything I heard is in complete agreement with and substantiates Mr Croxton-Smith's classification and description of these breeds in his book . . . Breeders can be confident of a fixed standard for the different breeds today, though naturally many dogs are not perfect in type, though undoubtedly the breeds will be so after a few generations of scientific breeding. The blood is pure, but the Tibetans' ideas of breeding do not go beyond like to like, and the greater the outcross the better.

So, survival came to only the fittest, any deformities of birth, or sickness, or an undercoat inadequate to enable them to survive the extremes of weather, would doom any Tibetan dog to a short life. The Tibetan dogs were not of course 'bred' in our sense of the word, but the blood-lines were kept 'pure' with the inevitable inbreeding in the isolated areas, and it is more than probable that like was not always mated to like.

As there were no veterinary surgeons in Tibet, the bitches were doomed to whelp in unsterile conditions most probably without human aid. Buddhism ensures that the lives of the dogs, as well as those of the people, were in the hands of the Gods and beyond the control of man.

So centuries of genetically strong and healthy dogs lived and reproduced strong and healthy descendants, who, in turn, survived the rigours of one of the coldest countries in the world, and were, of course, the ancestors of the dogs we own and breed today.

Remember that the unhealthy, the weaklings, the runts and the deformed were culled and discarded by Mother Nature herself. The manner in which the early Tibetan dogs were bred, does, of course, account for why, in some breeds, even today, a changeling or throwback does still appear in pure-bred litters; though I do feel that it is very significant that the Tibetan Spaniel has always bred 'true to type'.

In 1924 W. M. McGovern wrote in his book *To Lhasa in Disguise*:

Tibet abounds with dogs. The natives have no conception of breeding or racial purity as regards their animals, so that the dogs are weird mongrels of a hundred known and unknown breeds. Apart from a few pet dogs kept by the aristocratic families in Shigatse and Lhasa, all Tibetan dogs fall under two main categories, scavengers and watchdogs, both of which are found in great numbers in every village.

The scavengers are all hopelessly hungry-looking animals, usually of a light brown colour. They are left free to prowl about at will, but seem to have been divested of every form of moral or physical courage, and with furtive eye and dropping tail slink around the family courtyard. They are really despicable curs. The only thing one can find to say in their favour is that as scavengers they are really effective, as there is nothing, no matter how filthy, which they refused to eat.

The watchdogs are of an entirely different build, larger and stronger, with a much longer coat, generally black. They are always chained up in front of the great gateway which leads into the courtyard, and thus lead a life of perpetual captivity. They bark vigorously at the approach of any stranger, and generally make a bloodcurdling attempt to bite as well. These dogs are purposely underfed in order to keep them in savage mood.

The largest of the known Tibetan breeds is the Tibetan Mastiff, which is probably one of the rarest pure breeds left in the world today. There are still a few to be found with dedicated breeders, mostly in America and Canada, originating in Tibet and Nepal. Sickan Beckman's American-bred Ausables Mathilda lives in Nyköping, Sweden, is now winning CACIBs, but it took her owner eighteen months to have her registration accepted by the Sweden Kennel Club.

In Switzerland Herr Armin Ritz owns a Tibetan Mastiff imported from Nepal. There are other owners in West Germany, Austria and now also in Holland. The first litter was whelped in America in 1975 and since then thirteen litters have been registered, as in common with the other Tibetan breeds, there is a big demand for female puppies but there seem to be fewer females born in the litters than males. The idea of an American Tibetan Mastiff club, devoted to the preservation of this endangered breed was developed in Nepal in the late 1960s by several people who had the opportunity to observe these dogs at first-hand in their native land. The American Tibetan Mastiff Club (ATMA) was incorporated in the State of Kentucky in 1974 with the form registration and stud book established in 1975. The first National Speciality show was held in California in October 1979 in conjunction with the California Rare Breeds Dog Association. On October 25th, 1980, the American Tibetan Mastiff Club put on their first Club Speciality Match for their members.

Two Tibetan Mastiffs were sent to the United States in 1958, but their fate is not known. In 1969 Jumla's Kalu of Jumla was the first documented Tibetan Mastiff imported into the United States from Nepal, and he became the foundation stud dog on the West Coast.

On the East Coast is the Tibetan Spaniel Club of America (TSCA). Both Clubs have their own quarterly news letter. The first post-war Tibetan Mastiffs to be exported to England were a pair from the Langtang kennel of Miss Ann Rohrer in 1976, but the owners were discouraged from obtaining Kennel Club registration because of all the red tape which is involved when importing from America where no official American Kennel Club Export Pedigree could be issued, and as far as I know they were never bred from. Mrs Pauline Brigden imported another pair in early 1981 for the purpose of showing and breeding, but sadly both were dead from Canine Parvo Virus six weeks after arrival; these came from the Ausable kennels of Mr and Mrs S. Nash of New York, and were accepted for registration by the English Kennel Club.

As the paperback book *Tibetan Mastiff*, (1981), written by Ann Rohrer and Linda Larsen states:

> In his native land the Tibetan Mastiff has three main functions. He is the guardian of the home, the herds and the caravans of the Nomads and the traders. He is a mountain peasant. He expresses his feelings for the things he loves as well as the things he hates. He plays rough and it is hard to avoid being bruised by his teeth and paws as he greets or plays with you. He is a playful, fun-loving dog, and exuberant in showing his affection.

At the present time the Tibetan Mastiff is not eligible for registration with the Canadian Kennel Club nor the American Kennel Club, and the only times that he can be exhibited in Canada are at non-sanctioned matches which are few and far between. In America they do have rare breed shows which allows Tibetan Mastiffs to be seen by the general public. Mr Oscar F. Scholz who lives in Thunder Bay, Ontario, owns two male and three female Tibetan Mastiffs and has bred two litters. Mr Scholz believes that the Kuvasz is a direct descendant of the Tibetan Mastiff. He has found that they are different from his English Setters and Kuvaszok because the bitches only come into season once a year, usually in the fall, and, while he finds the adults very responsive, the puppies and young dogs are extremely independent. He has found the breed to be totally sound both physically and mentally.

As shown in the chapter on evolution, all dogs descend from wolves. In his book *Die Nomaden von Tibet* (1949), Herr M. Hermanns states that the wolf in Tibet was also called 'wild dog' or *Khyi rgod* in Tibetan, and that the original Tibetan Dog* was descended from the black wolf.

Through many dog books, especially those of the 1800s, we can learn a little more about the folklore of this breed. While we know that they were definitely bred centuries before the Christian era, we sadly know little of their origins. Several centuries before Christ the terrible Mastiffs with floppy ears, probably imported from Tibet, and which Alexander the Great introduced into Greece, were depicted in religious sculptures in India. The Buddhist sanctuary of Sanchi-Tope has these dogs sculpted over the arch of a doorway dating from the period of King Asoka (280 B.C.).

In the section on foreign and non-sporting and utility breeds (*New Book of the Dog*, 1907), there is a surprisingly large section devoted to the Tibetan Mastiff, more so than on any other Tibetan breed, confirming the antiquity of the Tibetan Mastiff:

> There can be no doubt that the great dogs depicted in the sculptures from the Palace of Nimrod (640 B.C.) are of this and no other breed. In these carven representations of the gigantic dogs accompanying the sport-loving Assyrian Kings, or pursuing the desert lion or the wild horse, we have the wrinkled head with pendant ears, the massive neck, the sturdy forelegs and occasionally also the heavy tail curled over the level back, all characteristic of the Asiatic Mastiff.

*Considered to be the Tibetan Mastiff (*Author*).

Experts ransacking the age-old evidence concerning early breeds of dogs have discovered an ancient testimony to the antiquity of the Dog of Thibet, contained in Chinese writings in a record of 1121 B.C., where it was stated that the people of Liu, a country situated west of China, sent to the Emperor Wou-wang, a great dog of the Thibetan kind. This fact is also recorded in the *Chou King* (Chapter 'Liu Ngo'), in which the animal is referred to as being four feet high and trained to attack men of a strange race.

Aristotle, the Greek Philosopher (384–322 B.C.) never saw one, but considered the breed a hybrid owing its existence to the crossing of the Tiger and the dog, calling it *Canis Indicus* and *Leontomyx*.

In his *Carmen Venaticum* Gratius Faliscus wrote: *"Sunt qui seras alunt, genus intractabilis irae?"* This untamable wrath has remained a legendary attribute of the Tibetan Mastiff and has followed his reputation down the centuries.

Max Siber in his book *The Dog of Tibet* wrote that the first reliable note about Mastiffs was given by Megasthenes in A.D. 327, who called them Indian Dogs, describing them correctly as possessing drop ears, colossal bone, enormous muscles, large heads and broad muzzles.

The Tibetan Mastiff probably originated in the central tablelands of Asia, but it has also been found in Arabia and Syria and probably arrived in these regions by following the invaders. Big Mastiffs became famous in the arenas and circuses of decadent Rome, and were probably presented to Alexander the Great by Asiatic kings. There is a definite reference to Alexander having received presents of dogs of gigantic stature, dogs of the ancient Indi and Seri (the Seri being the people of Afghanistan).

Marco Polo, the famous medieval traveller and explorer wrote: "The people of Thibet possess a large number of powerful and excellent dogs, which render great service at the capture of musk deer . . . The people of Thibet represent a badly conditioned race; they keep dogs as big as donkeys, which are excellent for hunting wild animals, especially boars".

In Oliver Goldsmith's *History of the earth and animated nature* (1879), mention is made of the Black Dog of Nepaul, or Mastiff of Thibet as being the progenitor in type of all the Mastiff breeds. This theory is confirmed in the *World of Books*, which suggests that the Tibet Mastiff blood features in other breeds such as the St Bernard, the English Sheepdog, the Hungarian Sheepdog and the Newfoundland. Thus, it can be said that the Mastiff breeds are the founders of the canine race. The photograph in *The New Book of the*

Dog of a Thibet Mastiff with a shorn coat, imported from India by H.R.H. the Prince of Wales in 1906, shows this to be more than possible.

The dogs of Tibet travelled all over the world not only along the trade routes, but also as a result of war and invasion. When Julius Caesar landed in Britain he found Mastiffs here, brought, in all probability, by the Phoenicians on their trading expeditions. In America the Conquistadores brought their fierce Mastiffs to terrorise the Quichuas people of the Aztec nation.

The book, *The Living Animals of the World* (1903), mentions very few Tibetan breeds. Among the oriental Spaniels mentioned is the Peking Spaniel to which the Author refers later on. Of the early big dogs are two distinct types:

> From the very early times special breeds of dogs have been trained to guard sheep against the attack of wolves. Some of these were intended to defend the flock on the spot, others to run down the wolves in the open. The former are naturally bred to be very large and heavy; the latter, though they must be strong, are light and speedy. Of the dogs which guard the flocks, several races still survive. Among the most celebrated are those of Albania and the mountainous parts of Turkey, and the wolf-dogs of Tibet, generally called Tibetan Bloodhounds.

Herr M. Hermann, author of the modern German book *Die Nomaden von Tibet*, described a shepherd dog of great stature, with a flat skull, an extended medium-long muzzle with a slight stop, long, drooping ears and a smooth drooping tail. Its hair was long and wispy. These dogs were generally black with tan markings on the face, chest and legs. In the southern region of Amdo, he encountered a bull-type with a massive skull and short muzzle. This dog wore a peculiar ruffle around its neck. In the tent of the chieftain of the Wang-thag tribe, to the west of the lake Koukou Nor, Herr Hermann once met a mighty grey-white Mastiff with black spots, whose fur was short and smooth. He suspected that this dog had been brought there from another region, but he was wrong, as he was told that it was indeed a true native of this region. The dog was strikingly tame and trusting, quite contrary to the other breeds, so much so that he went into Herr Hermann's tent and let his head be stroked.

He went on to describe a particularly prized breed which had never been seen in Koukou Nor, the Hunting Dog. Described as a longbodied, snipey-nosed, wiry-haired little dog, half-whippet and half-pointer*. A good one could fetch the same price as a good riding horse.

Another breed mentioned by Herr Hermann is the actual shepherd dog which accompanied the shepherds with their flocks by day. They are described by him as a distinct type unto themselves. These dogs are smaller, the skull elongated, the muzzle moderately short, the hair is not too long and is curly and always of a light colour.

In other regions of Tibet Herr Hermann came across still more breeds of dogs. Among the various Tibetan breeds several distinct types were discernible. One particularly big and heavy Mastiff type had a massive skull, short broad muzzle, long drooping ears, a long drooping tail and long wispy hair. The most common colour of this type was jet black and it was the one most frequently observed in the company of the Amdo nomads. Still more breeds were seen in other regions but there did seem to have been a lot of mixed breeding between them. In the province of Kham, south of Amdo, there were long-haired dogs measuring up to 50 cm. (i.e. twenty inches), somewhat between a Collie and a German Shepherd in size. These were kept chained-up in the courtyards. With their lovely yellow and black muzzles and black gums, they were a singularly attractive sight!

Herr Hermann's book, published in 1949, gave me the most modern references to Tibetan dogs, with the exception of those mentioned by Peter Matthiessen in his American award winning book *The Snow Leopard* (1979), but those were brief references to sheep dogs and Mastiffs. Hugh Ruttledge in his book *Everest 1933* mentions "Police-ie", the one-eyed Tibetan Mastiff bitch who accompanied the Smythe-Shipton assault, shown on the English television BBC2 programme 'Travellers in Time' on February 25th, 1981.

During her researches for her book, *The History of the Tibetan Breeds*, Mrs Sylva Simsova came across a reference in *Foreign Dog Fancies of Our Dogs*, to the Tibetan Hunting Dog. She was able to locate the owner, Mr A. J. Sellar, who now lives near Chippenham, and who undertook to write an article for the *Tibetan Terrier Association's 1980 Year Book* on 'Kattuk the Tibetan Hunting Dog'.

Mr Sellar acquired Kattuk, a Tibetan Hunting Dog, in Tibet over forty years ago. He found her in a nomad encampment on the road to Gyantse. He was immediately struck by her air of good breeding. She was a lighter colour than the other dogs and more alert. The Tibetan owners, who were not allowed by their religion to kill anything,

*This reference to a Pointer must be compared to a German breed and not the English Pointer (*Author*).

pointed out to him that Kattuk was their best and only hunting dog, which they could not afford to part with. After Kattuk had been bartered in exchange for some stores, she covered the 270 miles back to Sikkim with her new owner in ten days, and from there on to Calcutta. Mr Sellar says that she adjusted well to the hot humid conditions of Bengal and to quarantine in England except that she shed a quantity of hair from her usually thick furry coat, as well as from her tail. She never grew it as thick again. From the photograph in the Year Book she is not unlike an Anatolian Sheepdog (Karabash). She was mated in England to a yellow Labrador, one of her sons eventually went to the Edinburgh Zoo.

Mr Sellar says that Kattuk must not be confused with a Tibetan Mastiff, which is a much larger and more solid animal. Unfortunately he cannot add any more information either about her origin or breeding.

In 1932 Mr Will Hally wrote about

a breed that is completely new to me, 'The Northern Tibetan Hunting Dog', about the size of the St Bernard, with a magnificent body, beautiful legs and great bone, and with the most intelligent expression. The head contains a hint of the Labrador, also of the Golden Retriever and also of the Mastiff, but at the same time it is quite distinctive, with nothing of the cross breed or mongrel about it. Indeed, the whole animal looks the veritable picture of pure breeding. The coat is fluffy from muzzle to tail, the tail is profusely coated, it is not a long or even a feathered coat. The colour is sandy but gets darker in the summer months.

Major W. V. Soman's book *The Indian Dog* published in India in 1963, mentions many of the Tibetan breeds giving a brief description of some of them. The Bhotia, or Himalayan Sheepdog, is found all along the Himalayan border from eastern Nepal to Ladakh in Kashmir. It is a smaller dog than the Tibetan of Bangara Mastiffs with a much smaller head and a pointed muzzle. It stands between 20–25 inches in height and weighs approximately 50–60 lbs. The coat is harsh and thick, black-and-tan of black with some white markings on the toes, chest and collar. There is also a sub-variety of this breed which is a rich golden brown or black and is only found in Kumaon hills. The ears are small and dropped, the tail is heavily plumed and turned over the back. This breed is used by the hill people for herding their sheep as well as for guarding their flocks and houses. The Bhotia dogs of Chamba are like black Labradors in build, though slightly bigger and thicker in body, they have a longer coat than the Labrador but a shorter coat than the Tibetan Mastiff or any of the other Bhotia dogs. This breed was taken up in the late 1950s by the Maharaja of Dumraon. Major Soman said that he bred them true to type and had some lovely dogs in his kennel. In temperament this book says that while it is less suspicious and ferocious than the Tibetan Mastiff, it will never spare an intruder at night, or even during the day; when it attacks it quietly bites the calf or ankle. It is ferocious and savage by nature, but may be transformed by fanciers into a civlised companion. The Bhotia dog does not like to follow its master in his walks, for this purpose it has to be taken on a lead, at night it takes the round of the camp, or of the herd of sheep, or the house, barking all the time! It is also said to be unreliable with visitors. This book warns that breeders of the Bhotia and Himalayan sheepdogs will have to control their nomadic and roaming propensities, when not properly controlled they will go about scavenging. This book makes the droll comment than in Tibet the dogs do a lot of scavenging.

Of the Nepal dog this book says that this is a native of Tibet and about the same size as the Newfoundland. Covered with thick long hair, the coat is harsh and thick, black-and-tan or black with some white markings on toes, chest and collar. Quoting as his source the *Encyclopedia of India*, Volume 1, Major Soman said that it is likely to be a hybrid of the Tibetan dog, standing between 20–24 inches high it too has a pointed muzzle, the weight is given as between 40–50 lbs.

Of the Bisben in the Himalayas, the book notes that it is noted for its size and hardiness, a fine-bred dog which bears a resemblance to a Mastiff. The coat is long and thick, the tail long and bushy, curling up; the colour is usually black-and-white with a little red here and there. The head is somewhat long, pointed like a shepherd's dog, they are covered with long, shaggy hair under the legs, very fine and soft like shawl wool, but the coat changes according to the season. They are very fierce and attain considerable size, but seldom quite as big as a Tibetan Mastiff. They are used as sheepdogs and for hunting all sorts of game, they somewhat appear to be related to the Turkish dog.

The Tibetan Hound is a very swift, short-haired unusual type of dog, usually kept by nomad tribes known as Khampas. They are classified as 'unusual' because they have less hair than any other Tibetan dog, lean, swift as the wind and rather ugly. They cannot be easily described and have not yet been identified or recognised by any of the associations or Kennel Clubs.

We know from Sir Charles Bell that the Tibetan Mastiff was the thirteenth Dalai Lama's favourite dog, used for herding yak and guarding houses and tents. These large dogs have long hair, collars of long-hanging wool dyed in dull red; almost constantly chained up they incessantly tug at their chains to try and spring at strangers, barking with a deep low note which Tibetans say should be like the sound of a well made copper gong. The dogs imported into India are, Major Soman said, of the correct standard; the real true Tibetan Mastiff is both expensive and rare, and are believed to have been bred in Tibet in certain districts only. Major Soman says of this breed that it is the largest of all the Mastiff group, and probably the ancestor of all the Mastiff breeds. Weighing about 130–150 lbs. and standing about 28 inches high at the shoulders, coat is medium in length with a heavy undercoat of wool. The tail is plumed and carried over the back, colours are usually black and tan, it has tan-coloured supraorbital stripes, but can also be of cream, white or brown colour. This breed has a pendulous upper lip and medium size dropped ears on a large round head. The eyes are dark, with a savage look and the face is ferocious. There is no feathering on the legs and the large bushy tail is held up gaily. Used extensively as a guard, the Tibetan Mastiff breed has maintained its purity because it is the most ferocious, costly and exclusive dog. In Tibet it is only the aristocracy and the abbots of monasteries who can keep them.

Of the Sha-Kyi, we have a description from the Hon. Mrs F. M. Bailey who attempted to keep these dogs, but found they were tiresome as they would attack strangers. The young ones were also difficult to rear as they were so delicate. The Sha-Kyi was about the size of an Airedale, creamy-grey in colour with a thick coat. The tail could be carried curled over the back, or down. The head was long and a smokey-black shading into the creamy-grey of the body. The ears hung forward. This dog was used for killing game such as Bharal (wild sheep), musk deer, serow, and it was very keen sighted.

J. Hedley in his book *Tramps in dark Mongolia* (1910), refers to the hunting dogs, who behaved with absolute indifference while the village dogs snapped and snarled at their heels, sticking close to the hooves of the horses which were led about to cool off. These dogs were big and bony, and, save that they had long hair, somewhat resembled our greyhounds.

J. B. Fraser in his 1920 Journal told of a tour through part of the snowy range of the Himalaya mountains, where he noticed that the natives used the dogs as sheep dogs, in the same way as the sheep dogs were in other countries, but they were also used for hunting all sorts of game; the dogs even chased birds on the wing until they fell from the air, exhausted. Some of these dogs were valued at very high prices.

In 1934 Mrs Bailey wrote about the method of hunting in Tibet, where the dog was taken on leash to within sight of the game, and then slipped. When the quarry was pursued it adopted its natural defence against a wolf or dog, where it turns at bay and attempts to butt the aggressor over the precipice. This is where it is wrong, for the dog does not go in and attempt to kill, as a wolf would presumably do, but keeps on barking in complete safety, at a distance, and so distracts the attention of the quarry, while the hunter comes up and shoots the animal at close quarters with his primitive matchlock.

The Kongbo or Kong-Kyi dog is from the district of Kong-po, a province in south-eastern Tibet, but it is not known to have ever been exported from its native land. Mrs Bailey said that when living in Tibet, she kept a Finnish Spitz. The Tibetan people, on seeing this dog, would always point with great surprise and say "Kong-kyi" (i.e. Kongbo dog). The Kong-kyis seen by Mrs Bailey were much heavier in build than the Finnish Spitz, with coarse hair like a Schnauzer and the ears were shorter.

There are other puzzling references to Tibetan breeds. In the *Kennel Gazette* (April 1895) there is a registration for Mr H. P. Paul's Thibet Jack, a Thibet sheepdog.

In *Our Dogs* (January 14th, 1916), Mr E. Lyon of Bull Terrier fame, who was a resident in India for many years, is mentioned by Will Hally as having imported a pair of Mongolian sheepdogs. Mr Hally said that the breed dated back to the times of Kubla Khan, standing twenty-six inches to the shoulder and very strong. He said of them that unlike the Tibetan Mastiffs they were exceedingly good-tempered and affectionate, with a loud and rather terrifying bark.

J. L. Kipling wrote in 1891: "The sheep dogs kept by the Himalay Shepherds are warmly spoken of by their owners, who say that when the mountain paths are hidden in mists, they are infallible guides."

Another breed is mentioned by Ronald Cardew in his 1950 book *Tomu of Tibet*, calling this breed Tibetan Bhutia dogs: ". . . big, savage brutes which have undoubtedly a large strain of the Mastiff in them. These animals are mostly owned by the Tibetan nomads who wander with their flocks and herds for a great part of the year over an immense desolate region known as Chon Ton." One can but wonder how often it was a Tibetan Bhutia and not the true Tibetan Mastiff which has been blamed throughout Tibetan canine history as being the fiercest dog in the world?

Little is known about the Tibetan Bhutia sheepdog, but it is found all along the Himalayas, chiefly with the *gadis* or sheep owners. It is an exceedingly powerful animal, and one or two of them are said to be more than a match for a panther. The real home for this dog is

Bhutan, but, like the Bhutia pony, it is found everywhere along the hills. It is not, as a rule, a pleasant animal to meet on the hillside, for it will often attack Europeans without provocation, in which case sticks are useless – stones are the only things which will keep it off.

The Bangara Mastiff was developed in the district of Tehri Garhwalhas, especially in Bangar. This Mastiff or Bhotia is generally used for herding the yak or sheep when in pastures, and to guard the flocks from carnivorous predators. This breed is powerful and daring with a herding instinct, as a guard it is supreme and would even risk its life. The height is 23–25 inches in males, and 20–23 inches in females. The general colours are black-and-tan or apricot. The coat is coarse but the thick undercoat provides raw material, the muzzle is heavy like the Tibetan Mastiff, the body compact, the tail is set high, heavily plumed and curled to one side. The correct name is Bangara Mastiff.

The Komondor and the Kuvasz are the two largest European breeds of ancient times. Tibet is given as the real ancestral home of the Komondor, while others believe that the Tibetan Mastiffs were used to strengthen many of the other European breeds, both because of their size and their working ability.

One theory in Major Soman's book says that the Kuvasz was imported from Tibet, the cradle of so many large dogs. This theory is subscribed to by Dr Erna Mohr of Germany who also believes that there is a definite relationship between the Hungarian Puli and the Tibetan Terrier. Another theory is that the Komondor and the Kuvasz are descendants of the Mongolian Sheepdog who are also uniformly white. There is no doubt that the Highlands of Tibet were the cradle of these large dogs, and, according to the writers of ancient times the Assyrians and Persians 'took them over' and in many old books the ancient writers persist in writing about 'Indian' dogs which is wrong, for they were alluding to Tibetan dogs, pure and simple. It is quite possible that, in olden times, the Tibetan dogs were considered to be of Indian origin. In the 1930s the countries at the foot of the Himalayas, in Nepal and Bhutan, were found descendants of Tibetan dogs which had been crossed with Pariah dogs. Such cross-breeds were also to be found in Yunan and on the western slopes of the Himalayas, right up to Lahore.

In May 1980 Mrs Hedy Nouc of West Germany saw 42 Tibetan Mastiffs of varying ages at a special show organised by the Indian Animal Protection Authorities. During her whole entire stay in India Frau Nouc saw only one really good Lhasa Apso and that was in the Dalai Lama's residence in Dharamsala. Mrs Nouc in the news letter of the Tibetan Mastiff Club of America describes the gathering of the sheep herds, the shepherds and their Tibetan Mastiffs (which she refers to as the Himalayan Mastiff) as a sight that she will never forget. The sheep herds were mixed with Indian and Tibetan goats, the shepherds had colourful head gear and with each herd was from one to three Mastiffs. Most were black, or black-and-tan, several were golden in colour, not one was mismarked.

Many of these Mastiffs were the embodiment of the Bara Benghalli type (so called), the overwhelming part of the black-and-tans were of the Bharmouri type, and the golden the Lahuali type. The 42 dogs were tied at the appropriate distance to short posts with hand made lines. The idea of holding the show came from a German living in India, who had owned a Tibetan Mastiff bitch; the show was advertised on placards written in Hindustani, in newspapers and by radios and the Indian Animal Protection Authorities provided the owner of the best Mastiff male and also of the best Mastiff bitch with a live Merino lamb, a valuable gift for any shepherd who could improve the quality of his flock. These shepherds did not use their Mastiffs for the same purpose as our shepherd dogs, they are more like protective and fighting dogs against bears and leopards.

These Mastiffs were fed on chappatti's, a pancake like bread, also cornmeal and goat and sheep's milk. None looked weak, none had skin problems, most of them had powerful jaws with a level or overshot bite, none were undershot. Obviously with 42 specimens they were not all going to be of the same preferred type, but all had an elastic gait, strong straight backs because if any dog has a poor topline, hips or hindquarters it is a candidate for death. One of the greatest breeding problems is that almost all of the best males at this show were castrated, the ratio was high with ten out of the thirteen best males neutered, in order to keep them with the herd.

Since then Mrs Nouc has imported a pair of Tibetan Mastiffs brought out over the Tibetan borders.

In *Stonehenge on the Dog* with an engraving by Youatt of 'The Thibet Dog', the author writes about this breed in the section which he calls 'Watchdogs and House-dogs', saying about this group that:

> The peculiarity of this division is, that the dogs composing it are solely useful as the companions or guards of their owners, not being capable of being employed with advantage for hunting, in consequence of their defective noses and their sizes being either too large and unwieldy or too small for that purpose. For that same reason they are not servicable as pastoral dogs or for draught work, their legs and feet, as well as their powers of maintaining long-continued exertion, being comparatively deficient.

In the *Kennel Encyclopedia* (1908), a rare book published in a limited edition of only 1,500 copies, and in four volumes, the Reverend H. W. Bush wrote of the common dog of Tibet, which appeared to be a sort of Collie:

> sometimes black-and-tan, sometimes of a browny colour; it is a lightly made animal, and it is probably a degenerate descendent of the Mastiff. In height it stands about 20 inches at the shoulder, has a long coat, bushy tail, ears almost erect. This dog is the common dog of the people, and is not prized either by the monasteries nor yet by the higher grade Tibetans. Dogs of this breed were commonly known to the Expedition as the Tibetan Collie.
>
> Another large dog constantly found in Tibet was a big black Chow, generally with a white spot on the chest and white forepaws. One of these was brought down to Rawulpindi, but there it died of distemper. From the fact that it has the black tongue and mouth of the Chow, the breed is probably pure Chow though, from the colder climate and higher altitude, they have grown much larger than ordinary Chows. They are described as being very fierce, but when obtained as pups they become very docile and affectionate.

On the larger Tibetan breeds the Hon. Mrs McLaren Morrison wrote in *Our Dogs* (July 13th, 1895):

> Some of the larger breeds of Asiatic dogs are well known to the fancier, as the Siberian Sheepdog, the Persian Greyhound (though indeed I have never seen this splendid creature on our show bench) and the before-mentioned Chou Chou. In one of the fanciers' papers I see there is a pure bred Yak-Hound dog puppy for sale, mother imported from the Thibet frontier. I have never seen this breed, and would be tempted to inquire further about this specimen, but as 'applicants are to be prepared to give a high price', the advertisement is rather forbidding.
>
> The finest big dog I have ever seen, not only in Asia, but also at home, is Shipoo, the glorious dog from the Shipoo monastery in Thibet, which is situated at an altitude of 16,000 feet. This dog has just been taken as a present to the Emperor of Germany and I saw him here before he was embarked. He belonged, no doubt, to the breed known as the 'Thibet Mastiff'. He was immensely powerful, though gentle, also a splendid watch-dog. I could see myself, however, no resemblence to a Mastiff.

There is no picture or photograph of this aforementioned Mastiff in the *Our Dogs* article, so we only have Mrs McLaren Morrison's written description of him to compare with the next big dog of Thibet that she mentioned. Shipoo, the German Emperor's dog, was described as being

> more like that of a Newfoundland; his head, however, with drooping ears, as also his colour, a decided smoke, slate-black at the top and quite light inside the coat, reminded me of a Chou. The texture of the coat is very woolly in fact absolute wool. The coat is very long, very thick and shaggy. The legs are brindled, and tail bushy, and carried over the back like a Chou's tail.
>
> The last photograph in this collection represents another kind of Thibet dog of a brown and brindled colour. I have not seen this dog myself, but he belonged to an acquaintance of mine in Thibet. He seems to me to have a look of the St Bernard as well as of the Collie.

Before closing this article Mrs Morrison mentions one more specimen of large Asian dogs, as described to her by Lord Dunmore, who during his wonderful travels came across it in the Pamirs. He said he had often seen a quantity of these dogs run along the mountain sides, absolutely wild, but was never able to secure a specimen. The size was about that of a Newfoundland, the colour was brindled, the tail carried over the back, the coat was shaggy, the head and ears were pointed. But what impresseed her the most was the description of the 'mane', which was large and shaggy. Mrs Morrison was of the opinion that such a dog would create a sensation on the show bench.

Besides these breeds there was another, a huge kind of dog (a specimen of which was exhibited under the name of the 'largest dog in the world' at Crufts show in 1892), a breed which guards the women in the Himalayan mountains and was known to be indeed a formidable defender.

Later in this chapter, Mr Graham Newell's interview with some of the Tibetan people in exile, has produced references to six distinct Tibetan breeds. We must not assume that these four dogs described by Mrs Morrison were indeed one and the same. With her profound knowledge of the Tibetan dogs they were obviously four distinctly separate breeds.

Travellers to Nepal and India are quick to say that the exiled Tibetan people always treat their dogs with a great deal of tenderness and kindness. They will always keep them with them – on the beds, with them in their homes, beside them in the rug factories where so many of them now work, and the smaller dogs are put into their baskets when they are out on the trail.

Mrs Simsova in her book, *Tibetan and Related Dogs*, considers that the following breeds have a connection with dogs of Tibetan origin or ancestry, the Bangara Mastiff, Bhotia or Bhutan dog, Bhutanese Terrier, Himalayan Sheepdog, Hungarian Puli, Hungarian Komondor, Indian Hound, Kashmir Terrier and the Mongolian Sheepdog.

In *Dog World* (March 22nd, 1940), T. Gray wrote: "War or no war, these breeds must not be allowed to disappear." Referring to Tibetan dogs of various breeds, the article continued: "Through historical contact with other countries Tibetan dogs are related to some other breeds. From China I have included the Shih Tzu and the Happa dog, from Hungary the Puli and Komondor. I have not included the Maltese."

Other related breeds are mentioned in Mrs Simsova's book, among them the Bischur, Buansu, Tibetan Bulldog, Tibetan Death Dragon Dog, Dogue du Thibet, Do-Kyi, Drok-Kyi, Gryphon, Gya-Kyi (Gyaki, Gya Khyi), Happa dog, Tibetan Hound, Tibetan Lion dog, Tibetan Lion Hound, Molossus Thibetanus, Shantung Terrier, Shi-Tsu Pa Erh (Shih Tzu), Yak Hound, in addition to those others already in this chapter. Sad that, out of such a selection, we have only the few recognised Tibetan breeds in the Western world today.

We do know that the Bhuteer Terrier (or Lhassa Terrier) mentioned in Bylandt's book published in Brussels in 1904, was often called Thibet Terrier, Bhutanese Terrier or Kashmir Terrier, as illustrated by dogs owned by Mrs A. Francis of Cadnam named Premier Putima, Navaini and Hurie Sing, Buxa, Absent-minded Beggar, Bootles, Chinna Tumby, and by Mrs McLaren Morrison's Bhutan and Buxa.

In the *Twentieth Century Dog* edited by Herbert Compton and published in 1904, appears the following statement by Mr Lionel Jacob, M.I.C.E., a government official in the Punjab and the organiser of the Northern India Kennel Club, which had originally been published in the *Dog Owner's Annual* for 1901:

The Thibetan, Bhutan, or Lhassa Terrier is now usually allowed to be a distinct breed, and perhaps of all the others it merits the distinction. But even in this case there is a tendancy for the strain to merge into the one Thibet type (which in its ramifications and graduations probably includes all the different Central Asian dogs, from the Thibetan Mastiff to the Chow of China).

There are Thibetan Terriers as large as Russian Poodles, and others almost as small as Maltese. A few would appear to have Terrier instincts but many have the habits of the larger dog of Thibet. The

Lhassa Terrier now* found a foot hold in India, and is bred there, though not in considerable numbers. At one time it was only to be obtained in its purity at Lhassa, and the breed was once, it is said, jealously guarded by the Buddhist priests. But Traders, finding a demand among the dog-loving public of India, contrived to convey specimens westward to Leh and Kashmir, and to Darjeeling, eastward.

Of these little creatures there are apt to be two contrary types – the terrier and the spaniel. At the Murree (an Indian Hill Station bordering on Kashmir) dog show of September 1900, there was for the first time a separate class granted for this breed, and both types were conspicuously represented. The terrier type – though all Thibetan dogs have the tail curling strongly over the back – strongly resembles the Skye Terrier; the other type, puggy and short in face, and undershot, has more affinity to the Japanese Spaniel. There was a so called Thibet Terrier at the Murree show which was a Japanese in all but the name.

Lhasa Apsos

On April 11th, 1970, the first Tibetan Apso show ever organised with Tibetan judges, was held at Tibet House, in New Delhi, India. On this occasion, the panel of five judges, all of whom had owned and bred dogs in Tibet, together with Mr Lobsang Lhalungpa and the members of the Apso Show Committee, sat down together and, for the first time, discussed and recorded their definitions and comments on the various breeds of Tibetan dogs and the standards by which Tibetans judge these breeds.

Among those present were Mr Lobsang Gyaltsen, Mr Thupten Ninjee, Soko Rimpoche, Mr T. Sakchok, Mr P. T. Takla. The organisers of this show were Mr T. D. Gelek, Mrs Khando Chazotsang and Miss Marilyn Silverstone. As a result of this very important, and one can say historic meeting, the following paper was delivered by Mr Lhalungpa at the show.

Perhaps the best known of the Tibetan dogs is the Lhasa Apso, previously named the Tibetan Apso and in the 1930s as the Lhassa Terrier. The Tibetan judges at the New Delhi show in 1970 say that 'abroad these seem to be known as Lhasa Apsos, although we never call them that in Tibet. Probably this is because the first foreigners to acquire Apsos got them from Lhasa.'

The leaflet goes on to say . . .

*i.e. 1900.

although nothing is formally written about Tibetan Standards for these dogs, they are so well known to many of us, the lovers of dogs.

Apsos made their appearance in Mongolia probably at the time of Genghis Khan, and in China during the reign of Kublai Khan and the Manchu Emperors, as the result of contact between them and Tibet.

Apsos were introduced in England in 1904 by Colonel Young-husband after his return home, having led the military expedition to Tibet. Apsos brought to England by the Hon. Mrs. Bailey in 1928 aroused an interest which has since been steadily growing.

These dogs were introduced to the United States much later. Mr C. Suydam Cutting, who was a naturalist and a friend of Theodore Roosevelt, received a pair of Apsos from the 13th Dalai Lama, who had collected the best breed of dogs, both pets and Mastiffs.

The leaflet says that the data we are dealing with is mainly based on oral tradition and gives the following standard for Lhasa Apsos.

Size: Variable, the smaller ones are considered better by us.

Colour: White is considered the best, especially if the hair is silky. Next preferred is the parti-coloured, followed by all black. The other colours are golden, sandy, honey, dark grey, grizzle and brown. It would be wrong to say that Tibetans prefer golden colours above others.

Hair: The longer the better. Silky hair is considered the best. After length, density comes next in importance. Hair should be soft, but not so soft that it gets matted. It should be straight.

Body Shape: The body build and height should be proportional with well-developed fore and hind legs and broad chest.

Head: Big with hair over eyes, forehead roundish but broad, not flat.

Mouth: Short muzzle with roundish mouth, not pointed. Lower jaw should not protrude neither should nose be flat.

Eyes: Big.

Ears: Heavily feathered, with big flaps. Some people prefer matted hair on the ears.

Legs: Short, strong and well-feathered.

Tail: Well-curled over back.

Character: Lively, playful, alert and affectionate.

This leaflet on Apsos goes on to say that the most prized Apsos are those which have small bodies with long soft coats, broad faces, short muzzles, and legs full of hair, carrying a heavy tail well-curled over the back.

A breed, it says, that does not carry its tail over the back in a curl, is regarded as a bad dog, whereas one that has a tightly curled tail is believed to be faithful to its master. There is even a practice of cutting the tip of the tail in order to make the curl stronger.

Any dog with a white nape and a white tipped tail is considered bad, as the traditional saying goes, 'a white-naped one is a bad and strange dog, and the one with the white-tipped tail will lose its master'. The names given to pet Apsos are such as Senge (the Lion), Sentruck (the Lion Cub). Lion here is the 'Snow Lion' which, according to the ancient mythology, as depicted on thangkas, have white fur and a blue mane. Besides these names, others like Dolma (the Goddess Liberator) and Pema (the Lotus), are given to females. Norbu (the Jewel) and Tashi (the Blessed One) are names used for both sexes.

The New Delhi Committee says that there are three distinct types of Tibetan dogs. Type one is listed as pet dogs, of which there are five distinct pet-dog classes in Tibet. The first is the Apso, fluffy breed. The second is the Jemtse Apso, this is the dog known to the outside world as the 'Tibetan Spaniel', the word Jemtse means 'scissored' denoting the shorter coat. This breed has short fur with hairy ears and tails.

Thirdly is the Ursu Apso, which has a thickish hair which is short and rough and a very hairy mouth and beard.

Fourthly is the Goh-Khi, this is so small that it can sit in a Chinese porcelain bowl. Its body is sleek and it comes from Amdo land. This is the dog known as a 'sleeve' dog. The word *goh* means eagle, and some people still believe that these tiny dogs are found in eagles' nests!

Fifth is the Gyakhi (pronounced Gye-Khi) and this is what the Tibetans call the Pekingese in modern times. There is no such thing as a 'prayer dog', despite the popular notion about it abroad. However the Tibetans do teach their pet dogs to stand on their hind legs and salute with their front paws.

The Delhi Committee say that the breed known to us as the Shih Tzu is actually of Apso class. They are descendants of those Apsos that were presented to Yuan and Manchu Emperors of China, by the ruling elite of Tibet. The name itself is, they say, a clear indication of the origin of the breed. *Shih* in Chinese is identical with the Chinese name for 'Tibetan', whereas *tzu* means 'Class'.

Type two is Mastiffs. The Mastiff breed is of three kinds. First the Dhoki – the sleek type, secondly the Dhoki Apso – the fluffy Mastiff, thirdly the Jemtse Apso Dhoki which has shorter fur like the smaller Tibetan Spaniel.

Mastiff breeds are generally called *Dhoki* – meaning 'outdoor dog'. It is interesting to learn that the Delhi Committee considered the name Dhoki Apso described the breed known to us as the Tibetan

Terrier. There is some disagreement about this from some present day Tibetan Terrier breeders, who consider that it refers to the Giant Apso, or the 'tired dog' as mentioned later on in this chapter.

Both the Tibetan Terrier Association and Mr Graham Newell have given me permission to reprint from the *No. 4 Year Book for 1976* the most interesting excerpts from 'The Journey of a Lifetime', in which Mr Newell describes how he explored Nepal and Sikkim and visited Tibetan communities in Nepal, Sikkim and India, to learn all that he could about the breeds from the old Tibetans before it was too late, as, alas, the likelihood of being able to freely travel in Tibet itself now seems very remote.

Kathmandu revealed some passable Lhasa Apsos, but mainly dogs of part Tibetan breeding which Mr Newell refers to as 'perhapsos'! He saw the Tibetan Mastiffs kept by Mr Prabhu Rana and many people spoke most highly of Mrs Pamela Cross Stern who had been there to judge the dogs the year before. The Nepalese are obviously very fond of their dogs and want to do everything to improve their stock. Unfortunately, their Kennel Club is not recognised by our English Kennel Club as yet, which prevents any serious breeders purchasing stock from that country.

Pathan had many Tibetan type dogs but nothing of real quality, mostly a mixture of Spaniel and Apso, in the afternoon Mr Newell visited the Tibetan Refugee centre and saw more dogs of mixed Tibetan origin and only one Tibetan Spaniel. Both Mrs Ammemare Spahr, a Swiss lady who is the Secretary of the Kathmandu Kennel Club and Mrs Amar Rana, President of the Club, expressed the opinion that if they wanted to get first class stock of Tibetan dogs in Nepal they would have to import them from England.

From Nepal Mr Newell went to Darjeeling and, visiting the Tibetan Self Help Centre, found that they were breeding both Spaniels and Apsos commercially. The Spaniels appeared rather coarse but the Apsos were of good quality. The Tibetans were very surprised to be told by Mr Newell that a good quality Apso, which was chocolate and white in colour with a liver nose, would be banned as a show dog in England, as it affected the pigment. The thought had obviously never crossed their minds.

Mr Newell noticed the very natural love of the Tibetans for their dogs which was very evident everywhere he went. He took with him the Frances Sefton book on Lhasa Apsos and the author's book on Tibetan Spaniels and left these with the Tibetan people in Darjeeling. The books were greeted with great delight and some tears. Mr Newell asked them all if the dogs in these two books were typical of the ones they had seen in Tibet and was told that they were. An old Tibetan man was brought to meet Mr Newell, and the translator told him that the old man wished to say 'Thank you to all the people in other countries who are looking after our dogs so well for us, as, unfortunately, we cannot give them all the food and attention that we would like, because we are so poor now.' Mr Newell said he was most moved by the quiet dignity of this dear old man, with a face that had gone through so much sorrow. It was obvious, from the respect shown to him by the other Tibetans there that he was a nobleman. This Tibetan owned a 14-year-old Tibetan Terrier which had come from Western Tibet, and which closely resembled one of Mr Newell's own Champion Tibetan Terriers.

In Gantok, the capital of Sikkim, they saw some Apsos in the big Tibetan monastery there, including a shaved Apso dam tied up in a courtyard. Visiting Kalimpong they saw three Tibetan Terriers. In the Tibetan village of Mussoorie a meeting was arranged for Mr Newell with all the old Tibetans who knew the dogs in Tibet. There was a great deal of discussion on the types of families that kept the dogs in Tibet, and Mr Newell was told that it was mainly the people who had the Apsos, the nobility owned the Spaniels and the Tibetan Terriers lived with the monks. Mr Newell was asked "what is this Standard that you refer to so much?" Through his interpreter he tried to explain and they all looked very serious while listening to him. There was then a long silence, after which a very elderly lady spoke. 'Which of the great Tibetan families that has kept these breeds for thousands of years was consulted?' she asked. Mr Newell says that he felt very small when he tried to explain that not a single Tibetan person had had a hand in any of the Standards. They all obviously thought that this was quite incredible! He felt sure that they were much too polite to ask: "What do English ladies and gentlemen, and Indians, know about the breeds of our country?"

Mr Newell was then asked why he only had books on three (including the *Tibetan Terrier Association's Year Book*) out of the six Tibetan breeds. He professes to being dumbfounded and said that while he knew of the Tibetan Mastiff, he had no idea there were two more! He was enlightened by Thupten Dhundup who, with his wife Tashi Yangzom, had come out of Tibet with some first rate Apsos and Spaniels, which were sitting at their feet at that moment.

He was told that the dog we in England (and people in the rest of the world) call the Tibetan Spaniel is known in Tibet as a Gyaki, and that Apso means 'hairy dog'. They call the Lhasa Apso the 'small Apso', the Tibetan Terrier is known as the 'large Apso'. The Mastiff, known as the Tangki, was becoming rare in Tibet at the time of the Chinese invasion. There was also the Shakhi, which is known as the bad man's dog. As they are Buddhists hunting is forbidden, but the robbers had dogs which they used to hunt small animals. The dog described sounded, to Mr Newell, rather like a cross between a German Shepherd and a Dobermann, and he was assured by all those present that they did breed true to type. The sixth breed was considered by the Tibetan people to be their most interesting; called Dhokey, it is known as the 'tired dog', a big woolly dog rather like a Komondor was described, but with one big difference, the height which everyone agreed upon was between 45 and 50 inches. It had no real function and was quite rare in Tibet. This dog was also known as the Giant Apso.

While in Mussoorie, Mr Newell met Dsela Dorje, an aristocratic Tibetan lady and the widow of the late Prime Minister of Bhutan. From her he learned that the Tibetan aristocracy did occasionally have Apsos, but only the very smallest ones. This was considered a quality to strive for when breeding. When Mr Newell was asked over and over again if he was going to take one of their dogs back to England, he explained that he could not do so because the Kennel Club in England refused to accept Tibetan dogs as they were not registered with a Kennel Club. He said that it was most distressing to witness the look of hurt and bewilderment on the faces of these people who have bred dogs for generations, and were still striving to do so against such enormous odds, and that it was almost more than he could bear. Mr Newell concludes by saying that he came away from that wonderful Tibetan community feeling very humble, and sure that we have only skimmed the surface of our knowledge of the Tibetan breeds.

The leaflet compiled by the Tibetan judges in Delhi, mentions that the average life span of an Apso is 14 to 16 years; a puppy attains its full maturity in a year's time. The diet determines its growth and affects its size. To keep the Apso to the minimum size Tibetans feed a puppy with small quantities of meat, vegetables, *tsampa*, milk and meat soup. Mastiffs are given whey, to deepen their voices, along with *tsampa*, butter, cheese, meat and bones. The Mastiffs also drink milk and *chang* (beer). Shakhis are given meat and not too much liquid, to keep them slim and fast. Apsos should not be fed salty food. This leaflet, compiled by Tibetans, ends by saying that a well-cared-for dog is considered even more fortunate than many human beings. There is a saying that though the life of a dog is the result of bad *karma* in its previous incarnation, the good time that it enjoys keeps it from committing sins in this one.

Tibetan Apsos have found their way into Russia either direct from Tibet or through Mongolia. Just before the second world war began, a German Expedition to Tibet took away specimens of fauna, flora as well as biological specimens, including many dogs – Apsos, Mastiffs, Shakhi and even stray dogs!

According to the leaflet compiled by the Tibetan judges, the word Apso means 'Hairy One'. Apsos of the large and small type originated in Central Tibet where the altitudes range from twelve to sixteen thousand feet. They were generally scattered all over Tibet. The south-eastern areas – Congpo and Dakpo – were known for the Apso-Mastiffs, and a third type, the Shakhi, a hunting dog. However, the judges explained that the word 'Apso' is also considered to be a corruption of the word *rapso* (which means goat-like), as it was originally considered that the long hair gave this breed the appearance of a small Tibetan goat. The Tibetan people looked upon the Apso as a bringer of luck, hence an honour to anyone who received an Apso as a gift. It was not considered to be a sacred dog, and was not kept exclusive to the monasteries. For reasons of honour and good luck these dogs were periodically presented by the Dalai Lamas to the old Emperors of China, and it was still possible in the 1920s to find good specimens in Pekin.

Other interpretations of the meaning of 'Apso' have also been given as the Tibetan name for any long-haired dog, or a corruption of 'Abso' (barking sentinel). Mr Brian Vesey Fitzgerald considers that it could also mean 'Temple Dog', all of which differ from the Tibetan judges' remarks set down at the New Delhi show in 1970.

There were classes for Large and Small Apsos (i.e. what we now know as Tibetan Terriers and Lhasa Apsos) being exhibited prior to the 1914–18 war. After that war, the Lhasa Terrier (Lhasa Apso) almost died out and championship status was withdrawn by the English Kennel Club. Some English dog fanciers brought in Apsos from China in 1924 and said that the breed was known out there as the Lion-dog, but this name was never used in Tibet for the Lhasa Apso, which is, I feel, significant when later in the chapter we refer to the Shih Tzu. The fact that they were known as Lion-dogs (or Seng Kyi) must have caused confusion with the Shih Tzu in the early days of both breeds, which was not helped by the use of the name Lhassa (or Lhasa) Terrier in the 1920s.

In the 1920s and '30s, the breed varied a great deal in both type and size, some owners and breeders considered that only the golden Apsos were the true type, as bred by the Lamas. There was also at one time a dispute as to whether the first parti-coloured Apsos were of pure blood.

A. Croxton-Smith wrote briefly about the Apso in his book *About Our Dogs* (1931):

> Besides Tibetan Mastiffs, Mrs Bailey also introduced to us some small dogs from the same country, which are called Apsos, and they are known in China as Tibetan Lion Dogs. Good specimens are to be found only among the better classes. They do not seem to be unlike Lhasa Terriers of a golden colour. In pre-revolution days the Dalai Lamas of Tibet used to send Apsos as presents to the Emperors of China. They are kept as pets in Tibet, and are intelligent and faithful.

In 1939 H. L. Moulton wrote:

> Once upon a time (any time between 1583 and 1908, from the start of the Manchu Dynasty to the last visit of a Dalai Lama to the Dowager Empress), the present of an Apso was taken to China for the Imperial family. They liked it and asked for more. They got more, but, as such gifts were, in Tibet, considered one of the most esteemed and valuable of all tributes the Chinese Empress didn't get very many. Well, to perpetuate this lovely, exotic dog, a canine talisman, the Chinese crossed their Apsos . . . with their own equally esteemed Palace Dogs or Pekingese.

The Author can only give her readers the facts, leaving them to decide for themselves just what names were given to which Tibetan breeds in the pre-World War Two era. I can only apologise if the facts are contradictory or confusing, but it might just go to show the problems that beset some of the Tibetan breeds in the 1920s and '30s especially.

The Times, Monday, December 1st, 1930, also appears confused about the Tibetan Spaniel, Lhasa Terrier and Apso! The Kennel Correspondent writes:

> On hearing of the Apsos, I began at once to wonder if they could be either Lhasa Terriers or Tibetan Spaniels, but I understand that they are neither. Obviously they have nothing to do with Spaniels, though so far as one can judge from photographs, they do not seem to be dissimilar from what is known in India as the smaller Lhasa Terrier. The standard of the Lhasa Terrier current in India, however, gives the colours as white, cream, grey or smoke, black and parti-colour, whereas the most prized in an Apso is golden.
>
> Good specimens may, I am told, sometimes be found in Peking, where they are known as Tibetan Lion Dogs. One has heard before of

these dogs without being assured that they were not confused with Pekingese. Before the revolution the Dalai Lamas used to make presents of Apsos to the Emperors of China, and a few of their descendents have survived. In Tibet proper they are called Sengtru which means little lion or lion cub.

One can understand that the Tibetans are not too careful in the breeding of their dogs, except among the higher classes, and that those taken into India as merchandise are not always typical.

W. D. Drury in 1903 wrote:

Until Mr Lionel Jacobs enlightened the fanciers of this country by means of his very practical contributions to the Kennel press on the dogs of India, but very little was known here, and much confusion reigned, especially when, as in the case of the Lhassa, two distinct types obtain. Though desirable acquisitions, the true Lhassas are by no means abundant even in that capital, and are correspondingly expensive.

As stated above, two distinct types of Lhassa exist – one (the true) approaching the Skye Terrier in character, but with the tail carried over the back, as is usual with Thibetan dogs, the other more closely approximating to the Japanese Spaniel. In India, as here, separate classes for the breed are provided; but the dogs there do not appear to grow as much hair upon the face, head and ears as do the specimens met with here. This, as Mr R. T. Clarke points out in a letter sent to Mr Lionel Jacobs and by that gentleman contributed to the *Field*, is probably the result of greater attention to the dog's toilet. Mr Clarke describes the Lhassa as 'very affectionate and attached, and do not thrive unless petted and taken a good deal of notice of. They are very jealous, and desperate fighters when their blood is up. When fighting they are determined to kill as any Fox or Irish Terriers, and always attack a vulnerable spot.'

Mr, later Sir, Lionel Jacobs, when dealing with the breed in the *Kennel Gazette* (1901), speaks in terms of the highest praise of the bitch *Marni*, owned by Colonel Walsh, and compares her in type and general appearance to Mrs McLaren Morrison's *Kepvich Tuko*, that had just won in the Bhuteer Class at the Crystal Palace. *Marni* was exhibited very successfully, and, up to the time of her death, she had an unbeaten record. Mr Lionel Jacobs gives the measurements of Marni as follows: length of head 6¼ inches; height at shoulders 10 inches; length of back 19 inches; length of ear 2¼ inches. The same gentleman thus describes the breed in the organ of the Kennel Club referred to above:

Head: Distinctly Terrier-like; Skull narrow, falling away behind the eyes in a marked degree, not quite flat, but not domed or apple shaped. Fore face of fair length, strong in front of the eyes, the nose large, prominent, and pointed, not depressed; a square muzzle is objectionable. The stop, size for size, about that of the Skye Terrier. Mouth quite level, but of the two a slightly overshot mouth is preferable to an undershot one. The teeth are somewhat smaller than would be expected in a Terrier of the size. In this respect the breed seems to suffer to an extraordinary degree from cankered teeth. I have never yet seen an imported specimen with a sound mouth.

Eyes: Neither very large and full, nor very small and sunk, dark brown in colour.

Ears: Set on low, and carried close to the cheeks, similar to the ears of the Drop-eared Skye.

Legs and Feet: The fore legs should be straight. In all short-legged breeds there is a tendency to crookedness, but the straighter the legs the better. There should be good bone. Owing to the heavy coat the legs look, and should look, very heavy in bone, but in reality the bone is not heavy. It should be round and of good strength right down to the toes, the less ankle the better. The hocks should be particularly well let down. Feet should be round and cat-like, with good pads.

Body: There is a tendency in England to look for a level top and short back. All the best specimens have a slight arch at the loin, and the back should not be too short; it should be considerably longer than the height at the withers (note the measurements given of the bitch Marni). The dog should be well ribbed-up with a strong loin, and well-developed quarters and thighs.

Stern: Should be carried well over the back after the manner of the tail of the Chow. All Thibetan dogs carry their tails in this way, and a low carriage of stern is a sign of impure blood.

Coat: Should be heavy, of good length and very dense. There should be a strong growth on the skull, falling on both sides. The legs should be well-clothed right down to the toes. On the body the hair should not reach to the ground, as in the show Yorkshire; there should be a certain amount of daylight. In general appearance the hair should convey the idea of being much harder to the eye than it is to the touch. It should look hard, straight and strong, when to the touch it is soft but not silky. The hair should be straight, with no tendency to curl.

Colour: Black, dark-grizzle, slate, sandy, or an admixture of these colours with white.

Size: About 10 inches or 11 inches height at the shoulder for dogs, and 9 inches or 10 inches for bitches.

In her notes on Tibetan Dogs written by the Hon. Mrs F. M. Bailey in *The Kennel Gazette* of April 1934, she said:

"The word for 'Apso' is the Tibetan name for any longer haired dog. It is a corruption of 'Rapso' which means 'goat-like'.

These dogs are in general appearance not unlike the smaller long-haired goats of the country, though, of course, the dogs are smaller. Apso dogs of many kinds are found in Tibet, but after considerable experience with nobles of Tibet I was able to find out the kind generally preferred. This, as it is purely a pet for the house, is a small dog. Then it must, as the name implies, have long hair, the longer the better within reason. Then as regards colour, the commonest is black or iron grey, but the Tibetans prefer a golden or honey-coloured dog. The long legged dogs in this country would not be admired in Tibet.

As far as I know, the name 'Apso' first appeared in English in connection with these dogs in the Daily Mail of August 19th, 1929.

In 1920–21 Col. R. S. Kennedy was in Lhasa for about a year as Medical Officer with Sir Charles Bell, who at that time was Political Officer for Tibet. In gratitude for his treatment of his wife, the Commander-in-Chief (Tsarong Shape) wished to give Colonel Kennedy some valuable present. This Colonel Kennedy refused but eventually accepted a pair of dogs. The male was named Sengtru and the female Apso. These dogs he took to India, but in 1922 he retired from Government Service and presented the two dogs to me. My husband was then Political Officer for Tibet, having succeeded Sir Charles Bell in 1921, and we lived in Sikkim on the Tibetan frontier for seven years. We visited Tibet each year, taking these two dogs with us. We tried very hard to get more dogs of the same kind. Similar dogs are easy to find, but we were particular to get only the same type in all particulars, including especially colour. This we found impossible. In 1924 my husband spent a month in Lhasa, seeing the Dalai Lama frequently, and through His Holiness himself and other high officers he tried to get more dogs of the correct type. There are, of course, no shows in Tibet, and consequently breeding is not as carefully done as it is with us, and he found it very difficult to get dogs which comprised all the points Tibetans like: size, shape, length and texture of coat, colour, etc. However he found one bitch, the property of a young Tibetan Officer, named Demon. The owner, however, would not part with her, but allowed my husband to take away to breed from. This was essential, as, up to that time, we had only bred from the original pair, and there was danger to the strain from in-breeding. This bitch we named Demon, as the owner called her Apso, the same name as one we had.

A litter was born from her, sired by our Sengtru, and in due course the bitch was sent back to Tibet. She was, however, lost on the road and never seen again.

My husband gave up his appointment in 1928, by which time we had still failed to get any more of the dogs which fulfilled all our requirements. As we did not expect to return to Tibet it was essential to get another dog to bring in fresh blood and so we obtained a male dog, Lhasa, which was what we were looking for in all respects except colour. Lhasa is a white and grey dog and not a uniform colour. We took him as he was the nearest we could find. I am glad to say that his progeny have so far been of an excellent colour.

Lhasa was the property of the late Mr Martin, of the British Trade Agency at Gyantse in Tibet, who had had him for eight years before he presented him to me. He is now the property of Mr Dudley, of the Kennels, Brambledown, Sheerness.

In 1928 we brought to England this dog Lhasa, and also five of the descendents of Sengtru, Apso and Demon. These were Taktru, Droma, Tsitru, Pema and Litsi.

In the book *The Indian Dog* by Major W. V. Soman, published in India in 1963, he says of the Lhasa Apso . . .

In the mysterious land of Tibet, beyond the northern boundary of India, the Lhasa Apso has been in existence for many years. Travel has ever been rare in that wild and mountainous country and visitors to these lands had no opportunity to see these dogs as they were kept within the sanctity of the homes of the mighty, in the villages around the sacred City of Apso. Hence they were never mentioned by early travellers.

The Lhasa Apso is purely Tibetan, known in his homeland as 'Abso Seng Kye' which means 'Bark Sentinel Lion dog'. When it first made its appearance in England, it was known as the Talisman Dog and Sheng Trou, and then, for a time, a few were called Lhasa Terriers; others were called Apsos.

Major Soman quotes from an article by Barrister Mukundilal giving us the information that this breed has been a pet in Tibet since 800 B.C. and he doubts very much if any other breed has been bred to type for centuries together, and that the name is of Mongolian origin. In the Points for the Standard for the Apso as suggested by Barrister Mukundilal are:

Head: Round fully covered with long straight hair, front hair falls on eyes screening them.

Nose: Dark, shining.

Eyes: Dark bright, medium size, not prominent nor sunken.

Ears: Small drooping ears, heart shaped, covered with straight feathers.

Muzzle: Short, square 2 to 3 inches long, covered with hair or whiskers.

Fore legs: Straight covered with straight hair up to or even between toes.

Hind quarters: Straight covered with uniform hair, not feathery nor fluffy.

Feet: Small fully covered with hair closely knit.

Coat: Rough dense, covered with straight hair of uniform length 3 to 6 inches, neither wiry nor curly, fur undercoat, matted hair permissible.

Tail: Curled, carried well up on loins over the back, straight feathers on tail, when frightened down.

Body: Cobby type almost square, erect, straight, upstanding.

Size: Length 14 to 18 inches excluding tail, front 9 to 14 inches, stern 8 to 13 inches; height average 10 to 14 inches; depth from stomach to ground 8 to 10 inches.

Weight: 10 to 16 lbs.

Major Soman also writes of the Apso . . .

The dog itself, in its behaviour and carriage, is an aristocratic dog. It is kept as a guard and pet inside their houses by the Tibetan aristocrats, the high officials and the abbots (Head Lamas) of the monasteries. It is the most exclusive and aristocratic dog of Tibet. It is extremely difficult to get a really good specimen of Apso out of Tibet. What has come out of Tibet is through Sikkim and Bhutan, where the people are really of the same race. They inter-marry with Tibetans and have regular trade with them . . . The true Apso is actually not seen beyond the monasteries, though some traders bring them out of India as Apso, but they are not true to type . . . The Apso adapts itself to any climate, cold or hot, though it is bred in very high lands. It is a hardy dog. It thrives well in India . . . the Apso is a clean dog. It is loving and affectionate. It responds to and appreciates friendly treatment and petting. It is very intelligent, quick of hearing , and ever ready to respond to its owner. It differentiates between strangers and friends quickly. It is obedient. It does not like to walk on wet ground or wet grass. It does not roam about. It is reluctant to go out for walks even with its master. It prefers to remain indoors on the premises. It is really a house or indoor pet. It is a one man's dog. The purity and continuity of this extraordinary breed is due to its indoor, exclusive behaviour and for being confined to the homes of the aristocrats and monasteries. It has been suggested that the Lhasa Apso has a place in the religion in Tibet but the evidence for this belief has never been brought forth from the mysterious land.

Just as there was much confusion between the names Tibetan Poodle, Shih Tzu Kou, Lhasa Terrier, Apso, Ha-pa Dog and the Lion Dog, it was equally confusing to correctly relate the names Bhutia Dog, the Bhuta, Bhutan, Bhutanese dog, or Bhutanese Terrier to the breeds we now know of as the Lhasa Apso or Tibetan Terrier.

In her article on Asiatic Dogs in *Our Dogs* (July 13th, 1895), the Hon. Mrs McLaren Morrison mentions the

little Bhutia dog attracts our next consideration. I have lately seen a specimen that is so perfect that I wish I had its photograph to include in this article. It was black with a little grey front and resembled a splendid animated muff, with just a touch of the Skye, and a vague resemblance in its funny little face to a Japanese Spaniel. As I said before, this is an exceptionally beautiful specimen, that even in its own country fetched a very long price. It is cobby, and short on the legs, the coat is thick, glossy and silky; its size is that of a Yorkshire Terrier – I do not mean a toy specimen of the breed; the face is small, very sweet and short. The resemblance to the Skye is in the coat, particularly where·it grows into the face. I have never seen one of these dogs at home, yet they ought to do well as they come from a cold country.

She goes on to say, about what she considers to be another breed: "the little dog whose portrait is next given, is an inhabitant of Thibet, and resembles also our Skye Terriers. The colour is fawn, and the dog is extremely handsome and makes a charming pet."

In *Our Dogs* (June 3rd, 1932), Mrs G. Hayes wrote about two distinct breeds – the Lhassa Terrier and the Apso Terrier. Of the first she wrote:

Next in size to the Tibetan Spaniel comes the Lhassa Terrier. This is registered by the Indian Kennel Club as a Toydog, though the height at the shoulder is given in the Standard of points as 11 inches, and the usual weight seems to be about 20 lbs. This breed would seem to take its place better among the terriers, the more so as its nature and characteristics are essentially terrier-like.

The Lhassas are hardy little dogs, with a shaggy four-inch coat, a plumed tail, and a bright alert expression. They are of all colours, particolour being the most frequently seen. In the all-blacks, a black tongue is sometimes seen, suggesting a distinct spot of Chow bloods.

Of the Apso Terrier:

. . . is scarcer than the Lhassa, being only bred in the wealthier families, as the Spaniels are. They are a size larger than the Lhassas, and are very decidedly Terriers. About the height and weight of a Scottie, they have beautiful honey-coloured coats, with a few dark hairs on the muzzle and ears. The top hair is long – about four inches – looking more wiry than it feels, and underneath is a thick coat of pure wool, which keeps the dog warm and dry in all weathers. After coming in out of the rain an Apso gives himself a shake and is dry in a few minutes.

These dogs have a distinct mane of long hair around the neck, which gives them a lion-like appearance. The Tibetans call them the Golden Lion Dogs, and it is significant that their pet names in their Tibetan homes is either Singhi (Lion) or Singtuk (Lion-cub).

Besides being pets, they are valued as luck bringers. It is considered very lucky to have an Apso in the house. Years ago Apsos were sent every year as presents to the Emperor of China, which proves that they have long been an ancient and treasured breed, and that they are not allied with any Pekingese blood. They are faithful little dogs, intensely attached to their owners, and extremely intelligent. They are excellent guards, having amazingly keen hearing and wonderful noses.

The New Book of the Dog (1907), says of the Lhassa Terrier, that it is

an interesting native of the tableland of Central Asia, of which few [at that time] have as yet been bred in Europe. In appearance this terrier, with his ample and shaggy coat reminds one of an ill-kept Maltese dog, or perhaps even more of the Dog of Havana. In the best specimens the coat is long and straight and very profuse, with a considerable amount of hair over the eyes and about the long, pendant ears. The colours are white and black, light grey, iron grey, brown or buff and white. In size they vary, but the smaller are considered the more valuable. The Hon. Mrs McLaren Morrison's 'India', imported from Thibet, was perhaps the best of the breed hitherto seen in England. This typical bitch has left many descendants who are well-known on the show bench. Most of the Asiatic breeds of dogs have the reputation of being taciturn, and probably the character is true of them in their native land, but the English-bred Lhasa Terrier is an alert and confiding little companion, extraordinarily wise and devoted.

For dogs associated with the western Mediterranean area also to be associated with dogs of China and Tibet is not in fact as far fetched as it may at first seem! The countries of China, Tibet, the Philippines and Cuba were connected with early trade routes.

I have found the reference to the Maltese and Havana dogs most interesting especially with reference to the next chapter on Chinese dogs and their descendants. The *New Book of the Dog*, in the 'Foreign Pet' section, produced these references to the Havana and Manilla Spaniels:

> These two little toy Spaniels are no doubt varieties of the ancient Maltese dog, from which they differ only in minor points, although owners in both Cuba and the Philippines claim them as native breeds. The Manilla is somewhat larger than the Maltese and may attain a weight of 16 lbs. Usually it is white and the coat instead of falling straight lies in wavy strands.
>
> The Havanese dog has a softer coat, and in colour it may as often be brown as white. A very good bitch was shown by Mme Malenfer at the Tuileries Gardens in 1907, Poulka de Dieghem, bred by M. Max de Conninck, who has kept many of the breed in France. Poulka is a chestnut brown, or café au lait colour, with an excellent consistency of coat, and a good head with large expressive eyes. In general appearance she reminds one of a Lhasa Terrier.

The Havanese is now rarely seen and when searching for a more modern reference to this breed I could only find conflicting references. In Clifford Hubbard's *Observer's Book of Dogs* (1951), where he says of this breed that sometimes it is described as a Spaniel, a member of the Bichon group rather like a Maltese; it is essentially a Toy dog, long coated, white and spirited. Another reference book says that it weighs 2–4 lbs. and is pure white, and attributes the fact that it was also called a Lion-dog to its fighting habits.

The *World Encyclopedia of Dogs*, edited by Ferelith Hamilton, (1971), considers that it is a Cuban breed and one of the Bichon family, of which the Maltese is the best known. The colours for the Havanese given in this book vary from white, which is rare, through light and dark beige to a tobacco brown. They may also be grey or white, marked widely with beige or tobacco brown; here it also says that they may not weigh more than 13 lbs. The coat is described as rather flat, fairly soft and wispy with light curls at the end.

Clifford Hubbard says that some breeders call the larger specimens of the Melita Maltese either Havana or Manilla dogs.

The theme of 'Skye Terrier' has run through the various references, to both the Lhasa or Lhassa Terrier, but also to the Bhutanese, Bhutia or Bhuteer dog. In 1899 W. R. H. Temple referred in the *Kennel Gazette* to Bhuta, a Bhutanese dog, saying that he never saw two Bhutanese dogs of the same type.

In 1902 a copy of *Our Dogs* said: "On the application of the Rev. H. W. Bush, what has been hitherto designated as a 'Bhuteer Terrier' will in future be known as a 'Lhassa Terrier'." We can only assume this was at least one step in the right direction towards differentiating between the breeds now known as the Lhasa Apso and the Tibetan Terrier.

I do not think that I am the only person who has found it very hard to separate the references to the Lhasa or Lhassa Terriers in relation to the Lhasa Apso and Tibetan Terrier breeds of today. Mrs Barbara Burrows of the famous photographic firm of Thomas Fall has told me that all this controversy was, in her early days at Fall's, a positive nightmare until they altered the names in 1934.

The first written reference to the Tibetan Terrier that I could trace was in *Our Dogs* (July 13th, 1895), written by the Hon. Mrs McLaren Morrison: "A rough Terrier (not at all unlike our own rough Terrier), who is also mentioned in Lord Dunsmore's book, and belongs to the Himalayas, though I cannot recall the name of its home. I have seen such a specimen. It is grey, its legs light tan; as said before one might almost at a first glance take it to be neither more nor less than a rough terrier."

In the *Twentieth Century Dog* edited by Herbert Compton and published in 1904, is a photograph of a Lhassa terrier.

> India is illustrated as a fine example. The property of Mrs McLaren Morrison and is a son of Bhutan. Black and white in colour, its eyes are rather dark and very expressive, its coat long, straight and soft; feet well feathered; tail curled over back, ears drooping and silky, and face hidden by the profuse hair on its head. This breed should weigh from 8 lbs. to 15 lbs.

Major W. V. Soman's book *The Indian Dog*, published in India in 1963, mentions the Tibetan Terrier, ". . . which, in appearance and size, is just like the old English Sheepdog, is a cross between a third class Tibetan Mastiff and an Apso. It is not a separate breed in itself, unless just to differentiate it; it may be classified as Apso Tibetan Terrier." Major Soman's book puts forward another theory about the

Tibetan Terrier quoting Dr Erna Mohr of Germany, saying that he does not accept it as an independent breed at all, but calls it a piebald phase of the Puli. The book paradoxically comments that, "it is one of the two small Tibetan breeds that can claim to be pure for centuries, the other being the Tibetan Spaniel".

Hutchinson's *Dog Encyclopedia* of the 1930s said of the true Tibetan Terrier:

> The Tibetan Terrier is one of the two smaller breeds of Tibet that can claim to be of pure descent for centuries – the other being the Tibetan Spaniel.
>
> The Tibetan Terriers are bred in the monasteries in the interior of Tibet and are given to the Gipsy or Nomad tribes as mascots or Luck Bringers. Therefore they are highly prized by the Tibetans and it is very difficult to get the pure-bred specimen out of Tibet unless obtained direct from a monastery.
>
> They are extremely intelligent, can be taught almost anything, and are absolutely one-man dogs. An adult usually will not be bribed by any stranger, hence their value as watch-dogs. The Tibetans use them in a variety of ways, as follows: first and foremost they are mascots and are firmly believed to bring good luck. No Tibetan, other than a lama from a monastery, will sell a pure-bred Tibetan Terrier in case it takes some of its luck with it. The lamas breed them to add to the income of the monastery.
>
> They are also watch-dogs and guards. When the whole of the able-bodied members of the tribe, including the elder children, have left camp to gather fuel or tend the herds, these dogs have to guard their master's possessions from thieves (two- or four-legged), and prevent the young children from falling over the Khud side.
>
> When any possession falls over the khud and lands in a place accessible to man or dog, they are sent to retrieve it. It often falls out of sight among the rocks. The dog then has to use its nose to find it, hence they have good noses and tender mouths. When the master goes on a hunt, the dog is used for pointing out the quarry and for retrieving it if necessary.
>
> During the winter the dogs grow very long thick coats. When the hot weather comes they are clipped, like sheep, and the hair is mixed with Yak's hair and woven into soft warm cloth that is impervious to fine rain or thick, wet mists.

In Mrs A. Greig's advertisement in *Our Dogs Annual* (1927), was written:

> Last year when Mrs Greig's daughter, Dr Greig, returned from India,

she brought her mother these Lhassa Terriers as mascots for good fortune . . . they are the most cherished possession of the Tibetan owners; and in time of famine they will part with every other treasure but still keep their dogs. And it is only as gifts, and for great services rendered, that the Tibetans part with them.

Quoting a letter from Dr Greig in 1930, Mr W. Hally said:

There are two distinct breeds now being classified under the heading of Lhassa Terrier; my mother [i.e. Mrs A. R. Greig] having the one and rarer, and the Hon. Mrs McLaren Morrison the other. I am hoping that the English Kennel Club and the Indian Kennel Club will ultimately separate the two, calling ours, which are the bigger or sporting dogs, Tibetan Terriers, and the other, the smaller or toydog, the Lhassa Terrier.

Not long afterwards, Mr Hally wrote in his *Our Dogs* column that ". . . my long-time friend Mrs Greig, has, by permission of the (Kennel Club) Committee, re-registered her Tibetan Terriers as such. They were previously registered as Lhassa Terriers."

In *Our Dogs* Foreign Dog Fancies column, Mr Will Hally pointed out on October 3rd, 1930, that the name 'Terrier' is very misleading, as the Tibetan Terrier breed is not in fact a 'Terrier breed' in the real sense of the word as we know it today. When this breed was discovered in Tibet it was long before pure-bred dogs were divided into definite breeds or groups. So called 'pedigree' or pure-bred dogs were at that time either big and therefore automatically called 'Guard dogs', or if medium in size they were 'Hunting dogs', if small then they were automatically named 'Terriers'.

In one of Dr Greig's many letters sent from India to Mr Hally in Scotland, she said . . .

The Tibetan Terrier belongs to and is bred by the wandering tribes of the interior of Tibet, and is only seen in India when members of these tribes come down to various hill stations on trading expeditions. The Tibetan Terrier is long in the leg and short-backed; a sturdy, compact dog, powerful for its size and well fitted in every way for its work as guardian of its owner's tents in the wild country, above all it is not a toy.

In *Lhasa* a book written by Percival Landon and published in 1905, is a description of the country and peoples of Central Tibet, it says of Tibetan dogs . . . "the typical Tibetan Terrier, a long coated little fellow with a sharp nose, prick ears, and as a rule, black from muzzle to tail, we found but seldom in a pure state." Mr Landon's theory was that in China the Tibetan Terrier was sometimes crossed with a Pekingese, with a view to introducing more length of coat into that breed. Mr Landon also says of the Tibetan Terrier that he is a "Little fellow", strong in bone, short legged and large-eyed. As prick ears have only been seen in the Tibetan Spaniel the mystery deepens!

There can be little doubt that the mention of the Tibetan Terrier by E. K. Robinson in 1895, in the *Ladies Kennel Journal*, does refer to the breed as we know it today, in spite of the fact that Mr Robinson refers to the dog as the Bhutan dog, as well as calling it a Tibetan Terrier . . .

> At the Punjab end of the Himalayas, the same dogs are procured, with great difficulty, from Tibet through Kashmir and Leh, and they are known as 'Tibetan Terriers'. The first one I ever saw was a waif in the streets of Lahore, mangy and full of parasites. I was living in the Club quarters, and in the dusk of evening saw a longbodied, short-legged animal sneaking in the direction of the servants' quarters and the cook house. It was so utterly unalike anything that one is accustomed to call a 'dog' in India . . . I slung a stone at it, and the waif at once displayed a trait which I have subsequently found to be common to all Tibetan Terriers I became acquainted with. It stopped dead, with its nose and tail to the ground, and awaited in abject humility until I came to examine it, when it crawled fawning at my feet. I was unutterably astonished to see looking up at me through the matted hair ar the near end of the strange beast, those clear, brown, trustful eyes under shaggy eyebrows that one always associates with Scotch dogs, and my heart went out to the poor little wretch . . . a bath brought some of the real beauty of the breed . . . an unusually good specimen of the Tibetan Terrier, a pet household dog among the well-to-do of Central Asia.

Mrs McLaren Morrison confirmed that it was not easy to acquire Tibetan Terriers in the late 1800s, . . . "at the Punjab end of the Himalays, the same dogs are procured, with great difficulty, from Tibet through Kashmir and Leh, and they are known as Tibetan Terriers".

Dr Greig's first Tibetan Terrier was a bitch given to her by a Tibetan trader as a thanks offering for having successfully operated on his wife. This breed, which formed the foundation of the Greig famous Lamleh strain, undoubtedly came from the natives of Tibet where they were used for herding and guarding. This bitch, Bunti, was gold and white and her first litter sired by Rajah was born in 1924; the English Kennel Club registered her in 1926 as Bunty of Ladkok. With Bunty came a son and two daughters, all registered in England as Lhasa Terriers.

Dr Greig's Tibetan Terriers were exhibited in India, and her mother's famous kennels at Royden was the only one in the 1920s and 1930s to breed and exhibit Tibetan Terriers, Lhasa Apsos and Tibetan Spaniels.

Once the Tibetan Breeds Association was formed in 1934 it did much to help separate the breeds and to prevent further confusion between the names for Tibetan Terriers, Lhasa Apsos and Shih Tzus. This was a big step forward for the Tibetan breeds and resulted in the first Breed Standards being published by the English Kennel Club in November 1934.

His Holiness the fourteenth Dalai Lama now in exile in India, owns a Tibetan Terrier, Senge. From the original Lamleh and Ladkok dogs their descendants have gone all around the world becoming the foundation stock for many now world famous Tibetan Terrier breeders and exhibitors.

Mr Hally appears to have conducted a battle with the Kennel Club over sorting out the Tibetan breed standards, over a period of about four years in his *Our Dogs* column. Responding to the Kennel Club's suggestion that Tibetan Lion dogs should be registered as Tibetan Spaniels, Mr Hally firmly said that it would be a calamity if canines other than the true Tibetan Spaniels were permitted to be registered under that name. Mr Hally claimed that these Lion dogs were in fact Lhassa Terriers and that the idea was a real threat to the Tibetan Spaniel breed's purity. That comment brought forth one of the very interesting letters which he received periodically from Dr A. R. H. Greig, of the Lady Dufferin Hospital in Karachi, one of the brilliant daughters of Mrs A. R. Greig of the Ladkok kennels at Royden. In *Our Dogs* of October 3rd, 1930, this letter is quoted . . .

Dr Greig agrees with me that anything which would affect the purity of the rare Eastern breeds would be a calamity, but she adds that such a calamity has already occurred in the cases of the Tibetan Terrier and the Lhassa Terrier, although as far as the dog fancy in the East is concerned, the decision of the Indian Kennel Club to place the Tibetan Terrier and the Lhassa Terrier in their correct categories as distinct and separate breeds will do much to undo what harm has already been done. In recent years in this country there has been very obvious dubiety in judicial circles as to what really is the ideal of a Lhassa Terrier (under which both Tibetan and Lhassa Terriers have been shown here), and while each judge may claim that he or she is right, the fact that awards differ so radically at times is proof in itself that there is at least an absence of unanimity. When Dr Greig says, 'The Tibetan Terrier is the original breed and breeds true to type', she is merely emphasising the difference between the two breeds, and at the same time figuratively italicising her own plea that our Kennel Club emulates the action of the Indian body and differentiates between the two Terriers, Tibetan and Lhassa.

Dr Greig went on to say in her letter that the Tibetan Terrier belongs to, and is bred by the wandering tribes in the interior of Tibet, and is only seen in India when members of these tribes come down to the various hill stations on trading expeditions. "The Tibetan Terrier is long in the leg and short-backed; a sturdy, compact dog, powerful for its size and well fitted in every way for its work as guardian of its owner's tent in the wild country – above all it is NOT A TOY".

Writing of the Lhassa Terrier, Dr Greig added, "it was not originally a pure breed, but has been evolved by crossing two pure-breeds, the Tibetan Terrier and the Tibetan Spaniel; the now pure breed which has resulted from that cross is a Toy dog – low to ground, namely short-legged and long-backed, somewhat after the style of the Skye Terrier." Mr Hally then continues in *Our Dogs*:

The Tibetan Spaniel is only found in Darjeeling, in the villages in the Darjeeling district, and in a small part of Tibet that is adjacent. The Lhassa Terrier – I am now writing of the dog which the Indian Kennel Club now differentiates from the Tibetan Terrier – is likewise found in those same districts, whereas the Tibetan Terrier belongs to central Tibet. It can occasionally be got at the hill stations, but that depends by which route the Tibetan trader comes. I think that everyone will agree that Dr Greig has made out a very strong case for her own plea, that our Kennel Club separates the Tibetan from the Lhassa Terrier.

Dr Greig concludes her letter to Mr Hally thus . . .

I have bred Tibetan Terriers for nine years, and so far all have bred true to type; but Lhassa Terrier breeders out here [i.e. India] will tell you that two Lhassas mated together will sometimes produce a throwback to the Tibetan Spaniel. That tendency is not difficult to breed out, but it proves the necessity of differentiating very clearly between all three breeds – the Tibetan Terrier, the Lhassa Terrier [i.e. the Lhasa Apsos] and the Tibetan Spaniel.

In *Our Dogs* of June 3rd, 1932, on the many breeds of mysterious Tibet, Mrs G. Hayes definitely refers to the Tibetan Terrier breed after her references on firstly the Tibetan Spaniel, the Lhassa Terrier and then the Apso Terrier. As the paragraph on Tibetan Mastiffs follows on after the Tibetan Terrier, one can only assume that they have been taken in graduation of size . . .

The Tibetan Terrier has been registered as a distinct breed by the Indian Kennel Club. It is impossible to discover anything definite about this variety from Tibetans, and it is quite likely that they are only found in parts of Western Tibet and Balistan. They are not bred in the capital itself. They are similar to the Lhassas, but shorter backed and higher on the leg. The ones recently imported into England are attractive little dogs and seem to breed true to type.

Mr Hally returns to the battle criticising the Kennel Club on January 23rd, 1931, . . .

I mentioned a suggestion which had been made to me that Apso Lhassas should be allowed to compete in Lhassa Terrier classes, and I pointed out then that the only section for the Apsos is the mixed Foreign division known as 'Any other variety not otherwise scheduled'. Since my last week's notes were published I have read a report of the Kennel Club General Committee meeting held on January 6th, and from which I learn that a letter was read asking if Apsos could be exhibited in Lhassa Terrier classes. I should have thought that the logical reply to that query would be an unqualified negative; but this committee decided that if the owner of the dogs wished to exhibit them in Lhassa Terrier classes, application should be made for the cancellation of the registration as Apsos and re-registration of the dogs as Lhassa Terriers.

Mr Hally continues . . .

If I had not become accustomed to the Kennel Club's frequent bewildering legislation in recent times concerning Foreign dogs, I would have been astounded at that reply; but whatever one's feelings regarding it may be, there is no doubt that it creates a very dangerous precedent. It has happened from time to time, and in more than one breed, that a registration has been cancelled and re-registration has been permitted.

Now here again, in the case of the Tibetan Spaniels, we have a very old established breed and one long familiar to the British Fancy, so, whatever the Lion dogs were, there should have been no difficulty in knowing at a first glance whether or not they were Tibetan Spaniels. But apparently there is no first glance where the Foreign Dogs are concerned; there is apparently, and practically, a blind registering of such breeds. Had those Lion Dogs been seen by anyone who knows a Tibetan Spaniel, the suggestion to register them as Tibetan Spaniels would never have been made; it would never have been made for the good and sufficient reason that those Lion Dogs were not Tibetan

Spaniels – they were Lhassa Terriers. I do not think that those Lion Dogs have been registered under any name yet; but supposing that the owner had accepted the General Committee's suggestion, and had registered them as Tibetan Spaniels, and supposing that a fancier of real Tibetan Spaniels (seeking for the always desired new blood in that breed) had, on the strength of that registration, sent a Tibetan Spaniel bitch to be mated to that supposed Tibetan Spaniel dog (which was really a Lhassa Terrier), he would, I fear, have had to do some thinking when the resultant progeny arrived.

Mr Hally's justifiable criticism of the English Kennel Club in 1931 continues constructively . . .

if the Apsos are Lhassa Terriers under another name, then they should have been registered originally as Lhassa Terriers, and they should have been prohibited from winning as Apso Lhassas . . . it is quite evident . . . that the Kennel Club Committee are not correcting an original error. The owner who made the request that Apsos be allowed to compete in Lhassa Terrier classes has not said that Apsos are Lhassa Terriers – the request is merely for permission for the Apsos to compete in Lhassa Terrier classes. The Lhassa Terrier is an old established breed, one which has been familiar in this country for about thirty years, and I am not aware that it has ever previously been suggested that any other breed is eligible to compete in Lhassa Terrier sections. Yet, there is only one meaning which can be taken from the Kennel Club General Committee's reply to the referred request, and it is that if one cares to register a dog as a Lhassa Terrier, it can have open sesame to the Lhassa Terrier classes, even though it has been previously registered as a totally different breed . . . If this Apso incident were a solitary example of this sort of Foreign Dog legislation, it might, and I think certainly would, be accepted as a slip on the part of our kennel governors. But it is not a solitary example; not only have Apsos been registered as Apsos, and won as Apsos in a section which was quite as distinct and separate from Lhassa Terriers, but last year there was an application made to the General Committee for the registration of what the owner called Tibetan Lion Dogs. I had never previously heard of Tibetan Lion Dogs, and apparently the Kennel Club General Committee were equally in the dark about them, as the Committee met the request by 'suggesting' that the owner registered the Lion dogs as Tibetan Spaniels.

From the Tibetan Lion Dogs and the Apso Lhassa instances I have quoted it is all too apparent that the Tibetan Spaniel and Lhassa Terrier sections can become, under the Kennel Club General

Committee's present policy, the free dumping-ground of any and every kind of Foreign dog. I do not blame the owner of the so-called Tibetan Lion Dogs, or the owner of the Apsos for making the requests they have done; the requests were made in quite good faith! In the case of the Apsos, indeed, the whole thing has been so obvious that its good faith is glaring for everyone to see. But I cannot find any excuse for our governing body, who in the case of the Lion dogs suggested they be registered as Tibetan Spaniels when they were really Lhassa Terriers, and in the case of the Apsos are ready to re-register them (already exhibited as another breed!), as Lhassa Terriers merely because the owner asks if he may exhibit the Apsos in Lhassa Terrier classes!

If a hitherto unknown Foreign breed (unknown to this country, I mean) comes to us with reasonable credentials as to its being the breed it claims to be, then there can be no objection to its being registered as that breed; if a mistake were made, it could be corrected later, and in the light of fuller information. But surely, in common fairness to our familiar Foreign Breeds, there should be some check by the authorities on the registration of imported dogs, or of dogs of unknown pedigrees, before such dogs are permitted registration at all . . . and unless some such system of checking is inaugurated, our rapidly growing Foreign Dog community is in grave danger of ending up in absolute chaos.

Mr Hally concluded by writing . . .

I would respectfully ask the Kennel Club General Committee to treat this question of Foreign Dog registration with the seriousness which it deserves and with the promptness which it calls for.

As we now know many decades later the Tibetan (or Lhasa) Lion Dog was later known as the Shih Tzu, and so in the early 1930s before the first Standard of Points was drawn up for the Tibetan breeds, did actually introduce yet another 'Tibetan' breed; but in those days it obviously added to the confusion when it came to trying to sort out the different Tibetan breeds for the purpose of Kennel Club registration and exhibition. One can but wonder just how much of this confusion also applied to the breeding side as well?

Shih Tzu
There are many conflicting opinions about the origin of the Shih Tzu; Mr A. de C. Sowerby, Editor of the *Chinese Chronicle*, wrote in 1930: "It is our opinion that the Tibetan Lion Dog is the result of a cross between the Lhasa Terrier and the Pekingese." Mr Suydam Cutting's book *The Fire Ox and Other Years* mentions that Chinese dogs were occasionally brought into Tibet, where they were greatly appreciated,

the menagerie of the Dalai Lama consisting of a 'pair of beautiful Chinese Dogs'.

The chapter on Chinese dogs shows that there has always been, throughout the centuries, through marriages and war, communication between the Chinese Emperors and the early Tibetan kings, then later, with the Dalai Lamas.

In 1930 Mr A. de C. Sowerby, who was also a judge of dogs, told us that all the Tibetan breeds were grouped together, causing confusion in separating the breeds. When judging Mr Sowerby had the Lhasa Terrier or the Tibetan Poodle entered under him at the China Kennel Club Show in Shanghai, and experienced great difficulty in adjudicating as there was no guidance laid down concerning the breed. The matter was not helped by the fact that at that time the Tibetan dogs were called a variety of names, from the Tibetan Poodle, Shih Tzu Kou, Lhasa Terrier, Apso, Ha-pa to the Lion Dog! In 1934 the Peking Kennel Club was formed and the first dog show held with a very large entry of Lhasa Lion-dogs, showing far too great a lack of conformity in size and type. About this show, Mr Sowerby wrote in the *China Journal*: "Is it the same breed that has been given the name 'Apso' in England, and is often called a Lhasa Terrier, Tibetan Poodle, or some such name?"

Much earlier, in 1842, B. H. Hodgson wrote in his manuscript which is now in the British Museum, *Notice on the Mammals of Tibet*: "The ladies dogs are Poodles or Terriers, many of which are pretty and have long hair." A little later L. A. Wadell wrote of Lhasa and its mysteries, in a record of the 1903–4 Expedition: "They are fond of dogs, and especially favour the mongrel breed between the Lhassa Terrier and the Chinese Spaniel."

In the reprint of the original translation of *A Treatise on the Lhassa Lion Dog* by Madame Lu Zee Yuen Nee, translated by M. Chow Sze King, we are told that this breed (the Shih Tzu) had many designations in the past, among them the Tibetan Poodle, Poodle Terrier and the Lhassa Lion Dog.

Mr A. de C. Sowerby wrote in the *China Journal of Shanghai* (February 1933):

It is our opinion that the Tibetan Lion Dog is the result of a cross between the Lhasa Terrier and the Pekingese, which has arisen out of the mixing of the two breeds both in Tibet and China, since the dogs of each country have been taken to the other from time to time by tribute envoys and officials. The cross in Tibet, that has been taken out of that country by way of India, has been called the Apso, while the cross in

Peking has been called the Tibetan Poodle, or Lion Dog. Doubtless the Tibetan cross has more of the Lhasa Terrier in it, while the Chinese cross has more of the Pekingese.

Dr C. Walter Young in his monograph *Some Canine Breeds of Asia* wrote that there is a great deal of evidence to ". . . support the claim that the shock-headed variety of small dogs so commonly seen in Peiping are Tibetan in origin."

There is also some evidence to show that the Shih Tzu has been bred down from a larger-sized breed.

The Manchus were always dog fanciers and dog lovers, and it is considered that the original stock of this breed was introduced into China by the Manchu generals, returning from a successful invasion of Tibet. Manchu court records show that invariably, after successful campaigns, live animals were laid at the feet of the Chinese Emperors by their military lieutenants.

The Shih Tzu is also thought to be a descendant of the Maltese Terrier, which arrived in China in the T'ang dynasty (A.D. 618–906) from the Byzantine Empire.

The Comtess D'Anjou wrote an article for the newspaper *La Vie Canine* of Paris, in which she stated: "Regarding the assertion of rumours circulated that the Tibetan Shih Tzu are a Peke cross, this is utterly false. They are a pure breed originating from Tibet and were presented to the emperors of China two or three hundred years ago."

In 1955 Mrs S. Bode wrote that for many centuries the Shih Tzu had been bred in the Imperial Palace in Peking, along with the Pekingese and the Pug, and that it is more flat-faced than its Tibetan kinsman the Lhasa Apso, which is no reason for supposing that the Shih Tzu is a cross-breed between the Apso and the Peke, especially as the early Tibetan Holy Dog is said to have had, and is depicted as having, a very flat nose.

A. Ferris, who became the Tibetan Breeds correspondent for *Dog World*, commenced writing on February 8th, 1952 and, in one of his articles, he quoted Brian Vesey Fitzgerald as saying:

I have always understood that it was about 1650 that three temple dogs, holy dogs, were sent to China and that from these three came the Shih Tzus. About 100 years later, so I have always understood, the then Dalai Lama (and up until this time the temple dog had always been his special property) gave some away to distinguished visitors, who were Russians. These dogs were stolen before they had reached the border and about the same time, during a civil upheaval, a good many more disappeared from the Dalai Lama's monastery and reappeared in various parts of the country. From that time onwards all sorts of small dogs bearing some resemblance, however vague, to the Apso of old, became an Apso. It was the end of the temple dog, but it was the start of the monastery dog and also of the caravan dog.

The Shih Tzu, or, as it was then known, the Tibetan Lion-dog, was registered as such in 1934, but, prior to this, in the first instance in 1930, these dogs were registered under the then approved name of Apso. Hutchinson's *Popular and Illustrated Dog Encyclopedia* of the early '30s did not help the confusion between the breeds which we now know of as the Shih Tzu and the Lhasa Apso, by giving to the photograph of Madame Aline the caption: "This dog is said to be a Chinese Lion Dog. There is no doubt that there exists considerable confusion concerning this breed. Readers are invited to make their own comparisons with the Pekingese shown on page 1153 [of the Encyclopedia] and the various Apsos on other pages. Surely the resemblance to the latter is overpowering evidence that the Apso, of which the above is an example, does not resemble a lion." In my humble opinion Madame Aline can only be a good early example of what we now know of as a Shih Tzu! Little wonder that Lady Brownrigg deliberately avoided the gold colours, in order to discriminate her breed from that of the Lhasa Apso!

Just as there was at one time confusion between the Lhassa Terrier and the Tibetan Terrier, Norman and Carolyn Herbel in their book *The Complete Lhasa Apso*, mention that in America there were, in the mid 1950s, Shih Tzus exported from England to the States and registered there as Lhasa Apsos.

This revelation is probably no more shocking than that of Dr Greig writing in 1930 to her friend Mr Will Hally saying: "It was not originally a pure breed," of the Lhassa Terrier (i.e. Lhasa Apso), "but has been evolved by crossing two pure breeds, the Tibetan Terrier and the Tibetan Spaniel; the now pure breed which has resulted from that cross is a Toy-dog – low to the ground, namely short-legged and long-backed, somewhat after the style of the Skye Terrier."

The four Tibetan Breeds' Standards published in *Our Dogs* (November 9th, 1934) then left no shadow of doubt as to the ideals issued by the Tibetan Breeds Association.

There is little doubt that Tibet has made a very wonderful contribution to the canine world. Let us hope that there will always be responsible and dedicated breeders concerned for the welfare and future of all the Tibetan breeds of dogs.

5 Chinese Dogs and their Descendants

The fact that the chapter on Tibetan dogs has come before this one is not deliberate policy, but it did seem to be in the natural order of things. We must now go further back into history if we are to find out more about the Tibetan Spaniel and its possible relationship to other breeds including the Pekin Spaniel and the Pekingese.

It is thought that eastern Asia had domesticated dogs originating in China before Christianity, but as there are no records we have nothing concrete. Pauthier, who translated the sacred book of Chou-King, said that the Chinese imported all their dogs. However about 3468 B.C. Fo Hi was already encouraging the breeding of 'sleeve dogs' and later, 2188–2160 B.C., Tai Kang who was a great dog lover too, was also said to be doing so.

The Foo (or Fo) dog, or Buddhist Lion Dog, is not a dog but an imaginary animal. In countless porcelain and wooden figures it is an animal with the mane of a lion, a shaggy tail and the head of a Pekingese. Usually, a ball is held under the foot, as the Foo dog was the Keeper of the Jewel of the Law.

From China, has come the terracotta dog (*circa* 3rd century B.C., during the Han dynasty) with its massive body, its Bulldog head and its amusing expression. There are also the famous Korean dogs of Fo which guarded the temple doors up to about 550 B.C., in appearance similar to heavy-jowled dragons and reminiscent of the modern Pekingese, and the squat Mastiffs placed at intervals on the steps of the Buddhist temple at Kathmandu in Nepal.

Silk was introduced into Rome and Greece by a northern overland route as early as 225–206 B.C. during the time of the Ch'in dynasty, and also to Egypt about the time of Ptolemy (247–222 B.C.). Mrs Neville Lytton in her book *Toy Dogs and their Ancestors* (1911), traces the origins of the long-nosed Spaniel-type dogs from China to Italy via the Silk Route, and then to England. Illustrations in this book show the close affinity between the English Toy Spaniel and the Tibetan Spaniel, who could possibly have shared the same ancestor – or is it more probable that the Tibetan Spaniel is the ancestor of the European Toy Spaniel types? Greuze (1725–1805) painted a black-and-tan dwarf Spaniel in his portarit of the Marquise de Chauvelin.

Fragonard (1732–1806) painted Papillon Spaniels into nearly all his work.

Buffon's family tree of the dog *Table de l'ordre des Chiens* (18th century), shows the *Bichon*, the *Chien Lion*, the *Gredin* and the *Pyrame* as being related and the forerunners of many of today's small breeds of toy Spaniel types. The little 'Spaniel' depicted in 'The Lady with the Unicorn' from a detail of a fifteenth century French tapestry, could well be one of our Tibetan Spaniels.

The northern overland caravan route became established in the Han dynasty (206 B.C.–A.D. 220) hundreds of years before the Christian era. In Laufer's book *Chinese Pottery of the Han Dynasty*, first published in Leiden in 1909, the author states: "The representations of dogs on the reliefs of Han pottery and the Han bas-reliefs of Shantung, naturally give rise to the question – what race of dogs were they intended to portray and what breeds of dogs then existed in China?"

Lady Gloria Cottesloe in her article in the *Field* (October 22nd, 1970), tells of a "gilt-bronze reclining model of a dog, only an inch and a half long, now in the Seattle Art Museum and made by a Chinese craftsman between A.D. 220 and A.D. 589, shows what could easily be a tiny Tibetan Spaniel, its elegant forelegs crossed in a familiar attitude, with well-defined eyebrows, slanting eyes, well-set ears and the characteristic mane and tail. It is a far cry from the short-nosed Pekingese that appeared in China in the 19th century when the Chinese inclined towards dogs with broad skulls and short-nosed faces."

Wealthy Romans wore silk which came from the looms of Han, in exchange for goods from the West. It is probable that pet dogs, for which the Roman Empire and Greece were then famous, went to China. At the time, it was customary to include these small pet dogs as gifts and objects of exchange. This theory is supported by the Emperor Kao Wei of the northern Ch'i dynasty, who reigned in A.D. 550–577, who owned a small Persian dog which rode on a mat placed in front of his saddle. The wars of the Huns and Tartars severed the trade routes until the 5th century.

In A.D. 609 (the Sui dynasty) the Emperor of the Turkoman country visited the Honan emperor; later, he went on an expedition to Korea and married a Chinese princess upon his return home. His successor sent an envoy to the Emperor Kou Tzu with two small dogs, one male and one female, of about 7½ inches high and 12 inches long, which were born in the Fu Lin country. These two little dogs were trained to lead horses by the reins and each was taught to light its master's path at night by carrying a torch in its mouth. It is considered that it is more than possible that these little dogs were the ancestors of the Maltese.

Before the Maltese dogs arrived in China in the T'ang dynasty, this small, white silky *Canis melitaeus* was alluded to by Aristotle more than three hundred years before the Christian era. Strabo writing in A.D. 25 said: "There is a town in Sicily called Melita whence are exported many beautiful dogs called *Canis melitei*". The *New Book of the Dog* (1907), is of the opinion that the Maltese dog is the most ancient of all the lapdogs of the western world, and that this breed came originally from the Adriatic Island of Melita rather than from the Mediterranean Island of Malta. Confusingly there were three islands called by this name, the third being adjacent to Sicily. Indeed, the breed did exist in a number of islands and obviously had become separately established; Publius, the Roman governor of Malta, owned a Maltese bitch named Issa.

The Maltese breed was subsequently called 'shock dog'; Johnson, writing in 1755, describes the Maltese as being "either short-haired, or long-haired, or maned", but prior to this they were first mentioned by Dr Johannes Caius, physician to Queen Elizabeth I who wrote of them in 1570 as '*Meliteï*' from the Island of Melita. Dr Caius was of the opinion that these dogs were the ancestors of the Maltese and Pomeranian breeds.

The *Observer's Book of Dogs* (1972 edition) edited by S. M. Lampson, confirms that the Shock dog was first mentioned in Europe in the 16th century, but it did not become popular until the 18th century when it was more fashionable to be seen in society with one or more of these little dogs. The height was about 12 inches and the weight about 14 lbs., the colour white, or with black or red markings, the coat was soft and curly, with a top knot and it was probably akin to the Maltese.

In 1841, a Mr Lukey found a pair of Maltese dogs in Manila and it is thought that this pair could be the forerunners of the breed in Great Britain and the United States of America.

Throughout history there has always been a strong link between China and Tibet, through marriages and war. Lhasa, the capital of Tibet, was founded by Srong-Tsan-Gampo, who married one of the Imperial daughters of China. In A.D. 633 the Chinese sacked Lhasa and burned the royal palace. Another Tibetan King, Khri-srong-Ide-Tsan, born in A.D. 730, had a mother who was the daughter of one of the Chinese emperors.

In the T'ang dynasty (A.D. 618–906) Islam interfered with the trading missions to China; even though Islam considered dogs to be 'unclean' the Turks were not averse to accepting gifts of rare canines.

In the Sung dynasty (A.D. 960–1279) about 1041, the Emperor Ren Tsung sent officials to search Ssuchuan for a place named Lo-chiang, famous for its dogs. He specified that he must have a dog with a red coat, because these were very quick of ear and that they should be bred in the palace so as to give early warning of trouble outside.

In the twentieth century, no special breed of dog was found to exist in Lo-chiang, but it was discovered that the name for a pet dog in the district of Ssuchuan was said to be 'Peking' dog. As all Ssuchuan place names had the suffix 'sze' this may well account for how the name Lo-chiang could have been altered to Lo-sze, later this was the name given in Peking to the short-haired Pug breed. The Chinese Lo-sze (or Pug) dog was known to exist right up to 1914.

The origin of the Chinese Pug, as well as that of the European Pug, is wrapped in obscurity. The first recorded use of this name appeared in 1731. In Butler's *Hudibras* there is a reference to a Stygian Pug kept by Agrippa. It is thought that the Pug came to England early in William III's reign (1688–1702) and that it was then called the Dutch Pug. There appear to be very few references to European short-mouthed dogs, with the exception of Bulldogs, before the nineteenth century. The first mention of abnormally short noses is by Youatt in 1845, who wrote of the new short-nosed type of dog as an innovation. This ties in with the theory that there was no Pekingese before the seventeenth century.

If the Pug was brought to England from Holland, at that time, it should be remembered that the Dutch East India Company was in constant communication with the Far East. Others declare that Muscovy was the Pug's original home; James Watson's *Dog Book* says that the best English Pugs were of Dutch origin and that the Willoughby strain came from St Petersburg. The theory in this book is that the best English Pugs of prominence from 1800 to 1900 can be traced back to Click, a dog of pure Chinese descent. It is more than possible that the Portuguese may also have introduced the Chinese Pug into Europe.

In J. Hedley's book *Tramps in Dark Mongolia* (1910), he mentions a fine little Peking Pug found in K'u Lu Kou. K. A. Carl in her book *With the Empress Dowager* (1905), comments about Her Majesty . . . "She has some magnificent specimens of Pekingese pugs and a sort of Skye Terrier. The pugs are bred with great care and perfection, their spots being perfectly symmetrical and their hair beautifully long and silky, and they are of wonderful intelligence. The King Charles

82

spaniels are said to have been bred out of the first of these dogs ever carried to Europe."

The Hon. Mrs McLaren Morrison wrote in *Our Dogs* (July 13th, 1895): "I have to mention the short-haired, black Thibet Spaniel; and the knowledge that such a dog exists brings us a step nearer on our way to the discovery of the origin of the black Pug."

The Chinese name for Pug is 'Lo-sze' and the same Chinese writing characters are used to designate the old name for Russia, which supports one theory that the Pug breed originated in Russia and from there doubtless went to China. It is possible that this Chinese name for the Pug breed is connected with the city of Lokiang or Lochiang, in the province of Ssuchuan, which was famous for its dogs in the eighth and eleventh centuries. Yet, strangely, in the early 1900s the name for the breed had been forgotten in its birthplace in China, and at that time the common name for a short-nosed dog in Ssuchuan was Ching-Kou or Pekingese!

Chinese records do in fact prove the existence of short muzzled dogs in the time of Confucius in 1700 B.C. There was also another distinct race, the Loong chua Lo-sze, or the Dragon Claw Pug, which became extinct in the late 1800s. This was a short-coated dog except for the ears, toes and behind the legs, with a chrysanthemum flower tail, all of which were feathered.

One can but wonder just how short was 'short', considering the cold climates of both China and Tibet. Even today, the Tibetan and Chinese peoples combat the cold by increasing the amount of clothing worn, and not by increasing the heat in their living rooms, so the production of a shaggy-coated or long-coated dog was natural to their climate.

In the last part of the twelfth century, two breeds were known to the Chinese, the Chinese Lion Dog and the Lo-chiang. The Lo-chiang was definitely referred to as early as A.D. 990 when the Emperor T'ai Tsung of the Sung dynasty (A.D. 960–1279) was given a Lo-chiang dog which had been found in Ho-chow, about fifty miles north of Chungking. It was small, extremely intelligent, and, when the Emperor held his official audiences, the dog preceeded the Emperor to his throne room, announcing his impending arrival by barking. On its royal master's death it refused to precede the new Emperor and was pining away. The poor little dog was eventually put into an iron cage, with white cushions as a sign of mourning, and carried in the Imperial Chair to its master's tomb, where it expired.

Tibet was conquered by Genghis Khan in about A.D. 1206, in the Chin (Nü-chen Tartars) period. In 1253, his grandson Kublai Khan conquered the whole of Tibet. In 1653 the Dalai Lama paid a visit to the Emperor of China in Peking, doubtless taking among the gifts of tribute some of the small dogs of Tibet to delight the ladies of the Imperial court. Later, in 1720, the Chinese army again invaded Tibet.

Dogs have always been used as political gifts, all over the world. The Tudors and Stuarts used to give dogs to many European monarchs as well as to the rulers of the countries of the Far and Near East. So, at this time, there was a very definite interchange of canines between many European and Asian countries.

Some of the Tibetan and Chinese breeds must have travelled to Europe through the silk routes, as well as through the travels of the Jesuit priests between Peking and Rome. When the Manchus captured Peking in A.D. 1644, at the end of the Ming dynasty, they permitted the Jesuit fathers to reside at the Court of Peking and even encouraged trading with foreigners.

The Manchus, being of Mongolian origin, encouraged the Lamaist form of Buddhism. An early Chinese scholar has suggested that the sending of lion-like dogs to the emperors of China as part of the annual tribute, symbolised the presentation of lions to the Wen Shu Buddha.

It is also possible that the 'golden-coated, nimble dogs which are commonly bred by the people in their homes' mentioned by an ancient Chinese historian as existing in Peking in Kublai Khan's time, were introduced into Europe because, during the last part of the Yüan dynasty (A.D. 1260–1368) Chinese princes were received at the Papal court of Rome.

The Lags K'yi (or Hand Dogs) of Tibet were called Chinese Lion-dogs or *Shih-tzu-kou*, chiefly because of the long shaggy coat, but then the Chinese applied this name to any long-coated dog, whether native or foreign, large or small. They were referred to in China as early as A.D. 1662–1722 in the reign of K'ang Hsi.

The Emperor Ch'ien Lung (A.D. 1736–1795) was supposed to have kept Lhassas. He was very eager to expand and explore the western part of his empire. It was only in the days of the decadent Manchu dynasty that the so-called 'Poodles' became a palace fashion, which probably encouraged the regular breeding of the strain established by the Peking Kennel Club as the Lhassa Lion-dog, which has also been called the Chinese Lion-dog, the Tibetan Lion-dog or, today, the Shih Tzu.

In 1667 Kircher wrote about a monarch of the Tartar empire, possibly K'ang Hsi, having a short-coated dog of Spaniel-size with a long nose and straight legs. In those days, the word 'Spaniel' described a toy-dog or a lap-dog, just as the French word *Epagneul* did, but looking at a picture in Holland painted by Simon de Vos (1603–1676) entitled 'A Tibetan Spaniel', leads to the conjecture that the dog may have belonged to a famous nobleman of that time, who was anxious to have his very rare dog painted. This dog has the hare feet and the 'ape-like look' which makes him recognisable as the ancestor of our breed today.

The first Chinese mention of a 'Lion-dog' was in 1371 and possibly referred to the long-coated variety mentioned before as the Shih-tzu. There are references to this dog as being a fair size, and a Chinese legend about the breed says that, in about A.D. 1131 one followed and attacked the murderer of its master.

Many breeds have been called Lion-dogs, but, with the exception of the Rhodesian Ridgeback, they have all been small dogs. The Ridgeback's original name was the Rhodesian Ridgeback Lion-dog, so it can be discounted as having any Buddhist connections, but, ironically, it can be considered to be the only breed with any real right to the title as these dogs were used in packs for hunting lions.

Other breeds known to use this name have been the Pekingese, Lhasa Apso and various members of the Bichon family. The latter includes the Maltese (which used to be clipped in lion fashion), the Havanese and the Manila. Another is the Löwchen ('Little Lion') and this breed appears to be closely related to the Bichon family.

In the Foreign Pet section of the *New Book of the Dog* (1907), the 'Little Lion' breed is mentioned as coming from Russia; the breed description says that it weighs 5 lbs. and has a long wavy coat.

Collier's book published in 1921 only briefly mentions the Chinese Crested and the Lion-dog; in Rees' *Encyclopedia* of 1820 there are pictures of dogs closely resembling the Löwchen.

Overland communication between China and the Byzantine Empire 'existed up until the time of Hung Wu in A.D. 1371. Constantinople was taken by the Turks in 1543; therefore, the exchange of dogs may have taken place up to this period between the Turks and the Chinese, but there are no records since the T'ang dynasty (A.D. 618–906). Literature of this period continued to call the race of small imperial dogs 'Fu-Lin', or 'Folin', right up until the seventeenth century.

During the seventeenth and eighteenth centuries Christian missionaries, mostly Jesuits and Capuchins, lived in Lhasa and the last were driven out of Tibet in 1745. Perhaps they returned to Italy with some of the Tibetan dogs.

Collier's book expresses the opinion that the Chinese imperial breed (i.e. the Pekingese) had ancestors which came from Byzantium, and that it was more than likely that they were connected with the Maltese of this period.

During the Ch'ing or Manchu dynasty (A.D. 1644–1912) the first flat-faced dogs appeared in paintings. It is interesting to note that there is no reference to the Pekingese breed in China until the seventeenth century. No Pekingese breed of dog is recorded or mentioned by Lord MacCartney's embassy to Peking in 1792. There were no paintings on porcelain or china models of this breed known to exist before the nineteenth century.

K. A. Carl's book *With the Empress Dowager* (1905), confirmed that the peak of breeding Pekingese was reached in the nineteenth century and that colour and distribution were considered of more importance than make or shape. To the Chinese, every colour had its value, laid down by the immutable laws of geomancy which permeated their lives. After the fall of the Manchus, and before the expulsion of the last emperor from the Palace, the small dogs were exclusively the province of the eunuchs. The Emperor himself abhorred them, on account of the mess that they made, and Colonel V. Burkhardt's book *Chinese Creeds and Customs* (1953–1958), commented that it is significant that the Mings, the only true Chinese dynasty since the Hans, banished the dogs, and lavished their affection on cats, to the great discontent of the eunuchs, who made a handsome profit out of supplying pets to rich officials.

Dr Rennie remarked in 1861 that the breed of Peking dogs was a very peculiar one, something between the then King Charles (English Toy Spaniel) and the Pug. Dr J. E. Gray in 1867 saw these dogs, which were then called the Chinese Pug-nosed Spaniel.

Just as the Tibetan lamas modelled the dogs they bred in the monasteries on the image of the Lion of Buddha, the eunuchs of the Imperial Palace in Peking used pictures from the good dogs displayed on scrolls and depicted in the Imperial Dog Book with the same object.

The Dowager Empress of China objected to the artificial dwarfing of dogs, but she encouraged the comparison of her Lion-dogs to the Spirit Lion of Buddha. Tzu-Hsi, the last Empress of Imperial China, had a great fondness for the Pekingese breed and a great interest in breeding dogs. She, with the Eastern Empress, had nearly 100 dogs in the late 1800s.

The Dowager Empress Tzu-Hsi did not approve of distorted or grotesque dogs, but the eunuchs of the Palace used many methods, some of them very cruel, to reduce the overall size of the dogs and also

86

to shorten their noses. Some were enclosed in small cages, others had their food and water severely restricted, silver masks were bound over their muzzles and others even had the cartilages of their noses broken.

The docking of tails was carried out among the Palace dogs during the Hsien Feng (A.D. 1851–1861) period, the wife of Tao Kuang (A.D. 1821–1850) had a passion for breeding dogs. During this time it was said that over eight distinct varieties of Palace dogs were evolved, their differences in some cases appear to have been largely a matter of colour and length of coat.

Collier mentions that the hard times and the overthrow of the Manchus did much to extinguish Chinese interest in breeding dogs. The Chinese might have eventually succeeded in perpetuating several varieties of Pekingese, each with characteristic markings, instead of the one race produced in the Empress' lifetime which started the breed in Europe and America.

When the Communists came to power in China all the dogs, the few exceptions being those owned by high-up officials and party members, were destroyed as being consumers of food, possibly also because they were considered a legacy from the decadent Manchus.

The difficulty of obtaining dogs from the Imperial Palace prior to the Boxer Rebellion, together with the long sea voyage from China to Europe, probably accounts for why so few of the Palace Dogs were imported to Europe prior to the death of the 'Old Buddha', the nick-name for the late Empress Dowager. The finding of the small Pekingese dog, known to everyone as 'Looty', by Captain (later General) Dunne, at the destruction of the Yuen Ming Yuan Palace in 1860, is now a matter of canine history.

In *The New Book of the Dog* (1907), Robert Leighton, assisted by eminent authorities on the various breeds, gives an interesting account of the 'Pekinese' in the section 'Pet and Toy Dogs' written by Lady Algernon Gordon-Lennox, about the breed Browning described as "a crush-nosed, human-hearted dog".

Lady Gordon-Lennox said that of their early history little was known beyond the fact that, at the looting of the Summer Palace of Pekin in 1860, bronze effigies of these dogs known to be more than two thousand years old, were found within the sacred precincts. She explained that Pekin Spaniels could be imported without difficulty, as they abounded in various towns of China, but in the case of the Palace Dog it was an altogether different matter, and the two (i.e. breeds) should on no account be confounded.

Admiral Lord John Hay, who was on Active Service, gave a graphic account of the finding of five of these little dogs in a part of the garden frequented by an aunt of the Emperor, who had committed suicide on the approach of the Allied Forces. Lord John and another naval officer, a cousin of the then late Duchess of Richmond, each secured two dogs. The fifth was taken by General Dunne who presented it to Queen Victoria. It is from the pair that lived to a respectable old age at Goodwood, that so many of the breed now in England can trace their descent. Before this the Palace Dogs were jealously guarded under the supervision of the Chief Eunuch of the Court, and few ever found their way to the outside world.

Some years later Mr Alfred de Rothchild tried, through his agents in China, to secure a specimen of the Palace Dogs for Lady Gordon-Lennox, without success, even after two years of correspondence. They did learn that the Palace Dogs were rigidly guarded and that their theft was punishable by death. In the late 1800s Mrs Douglas Murray, whose husband had extensive interests in China, had after many years managed to secure a true Palace Dog, which had been smuggled out of the Imperial Palace. This dog, Ah Cum, was mated to two Goodwood bitches.

Lady Gordon-Lennox with Lady Samuelson and Mrs Douglas Murray drew up the original standard of points and fixed the maximum weight at 10 lbs. But, later on, in order to secure a larger Club membership, the maximum weight was raised to 18 lbs.

Apparently, there was then some confusion as to the true type and some felt that there should be two distinct classes at shows, one for the Palace Dog and the other for the Pekin Spaniel.

As a Tibetan Spaniel breeder the Author is extremely interested in Lord John Hay's letter to Lady Gordon-Lennox, of which the following is an extract:

> Now there is another breed which is confounded with the Palace Dog; they present the same characteristics; appearance very similar, and disposition equally charming, but they are *much larger* [i.e. than the then desired 10 lbs.]; they are also called Pekin Spaniels, but they are as different breeds originally, I feel sure, as a Pegu pony is from an English Hunter; they are seldom so well provided with hair on the feet, and the trousers do not go down far enough, also the hair on the stomach and sides does not grow long enough.

Lady Gordon-Lennox was quite in accord with Lord John in his appreciation of the 'larger type', for they were just as attractive and, in many ways, as handsome as the Palace Dogs; but Lord John Hay, Lady Gordon-Lennox, Lady Samuelson and Mrs Douglas Murray felt that they should not both be judged in the same classes.

The book *Toy Dogs and Their Ancestors* (1911) by the Hon. Mrs Judith A. D. B. Lytton shows paintings of a black-and-white Chinese dog, about 1700, which is probably the ancestor of the Japanese Chin and also of the King Charles Spaniel. There is also a photograph of a picture of a Chinese Spaniel of the best type, painted in 1700 of a red-and-white dog which belonged to one of the Chinese Emperors. Another picture of the same date is of a Chinese Spaniel (Coarse type) and it is noticeable that this is the only one of the dogs portrayed to have the very bowed front legs which we now associate with the Pekingese breed. In the Standard of Points given in this book it states Legs – Short, and front legs not bowed. Mrs Lytton stresses the point that she does not believe the present type of Pekingese to be correct and that the true Pekingese should not have bent fore legs, and that the present breed is absurdly too large. Mrs Lytton says that these statements have been borne out by her own researches. The big Pekingese seems to have been a separate variety from the Toy Pekingese kept by the Emperors of China, which was a very delicately made little dog with short but straight legs. The toes sometimes turned out, but the legs were not twisted. The crooked legs do not appear to have been introduced until the 18th century and belong to the coarse, common variety. The deformity was very likely caused by the bigger and coarser puppies growing too heavy for their legs and thus bending the bone like a fat child that walks too soon. Commenting that the small dogs never had these bowed fronts, Mrs Lytton quotes Mrs Ashton Cross as saying: "Many puppies of great promise are spoiled in the bringing up, e.g. exercise is necessary but it may straighten the legs". Mrs Lytton says, "Comment is needless."

Mrs Lytton writes:

Great stress is always laid on the fact that our best Pekingese originated from five dogs taken, in 1860, from the Summer Palace at Peking, when the Court fled to the interior. It has, however, been ascertained that the Court took with them to Jehal a number of dogs, and it is quite unlikely that they should have left first-class specimens behind. I think we in England have yet to learn what good Chinese Palace Dogs are like. If the Court took the trouble to remove any of their dogs, it is highly improbable that they would have left others unless they did not consider them worth taking. If the theft of one such dog is, as Lady A. G. Lennox says, punishable by death, five perfect dogs would not have been abandoned by the Chinese to be looted.

In 1908 the thirteenth Dalai Lama visited the Empress Dowager of China and presented her with several dogs, but the Empress found great difficulty in rearing Tibetan dogs, which were somewhat delicate, being very susceptible to pneumonia and they required more care than the breed now known as Pekingese. Thankfully no Tibetan Spaniel owner will agree with that statement over 70 years later!

We know, from Collier's book *Dogs of China and Japan in Nature and Art*, that the Dowager Empress of China bred Tibetan Spaniels, also from other sources at the time of the Boxer Rebellion that only "Spaniels, Pugs and Poodles" were found remaining in the Imperial Palace when it was occupied by the Allied Forces, the true Palace Dogs having fled with the court to Si-gnanfu. As to what the 'Poodles' were, we must use our imagination and the previous information in the Tibetan chapter, but they were not of course the French Poodle we know today.

The Japanese Chin was almost certainly introduced from China, the breed name in Japanese is 'Chin' and the Japanese writing characters for this name are composed of roots denoting 'China' and 'Dog'.

In *Our Dogs* (July 13th, 1895), Mrs McLaren Morrison wrote about this breed:

> The next dog I propose to mention is the Japanese Spaniel, now well known to the fancy in all its beauty and diminutiveness. It was only yesterday that an old traveller in Japan assured me how almost impossible it is to get a really good, tiny specimen now in Japan. There seemed to me to be so many varieties of the Japanese Spaniel, in size and texture of coat, that this was always a most puzzling matter to my mind. But at last I think that I have cast some light on the matter – namely that the Japanese and the Nepalese Spaniels are two different kinds of Spaniels, though closely resembling each other in colouring, both being generally black and white. But the Nepalese Spaniel is always a fair size, never smaller than our King Charles, whereas the really beautiful Japanese ought to be very diminutive, and according to size and shortness of nose is prized in his own country. I think that this will throw light on the so-called Japanese Spaniels that, though large, have every right to be called handsome, as they are Nepalese.

Mrs Morrison's own opinion was that the Japanese Chins were related to the short-nosed Spaniels of Thibet and the variety was an offshoot from the Spaniels of Pekin and she was fairly certain that they were indigenous to the Far East.

James Watson's *The Dog Book* (New York, 1909), contains Mrs McLaren Morrison's theory upon the origins of the Japanese Chin:

90

The presumption is that the Japanese came either from the Pekinese dog or both came from a common origin. Mrs McLaren Morrison is of the opinion that they came from the Thibet Spaniel and that the English dogs had a similar origin. To that we can hardly subscribe, for the short-faced Toy Spaniel of England is a London product, the result of selection, starting about 1835 with very ordinary-faced Spaniels. We have not the slightest idea that the Asiatic Spaniels had anything to do with the European Toys, and when it comes to Asiatic dogs it cannot be gainsaid that the Pekinese is by far the most impressive dog in the way of character. Either the Tibet dog (i.e. Tibetan Spaniel) was wonderfully improved at Pekin or not having the same ideal to breed to, the Tibetese took no pains to keep up what they had got from Pekin. The Japanese must have come from the mainland and that means China, so that we must conclude that the Pekinese and the Japanese are of one origin, bred along divergent lines and thus assuming difference of type and character which have become established. At the show of 1882 at New York there were 9 entries of Japanese but by far the best of breed was entered as a Pekinese (China) Spaniel by Mrs W. H. Appleton in the miscellaneous class.

During the period of Tien Wu Ti (A.D. 673–686) and of Ch'ih T'ung Hi (A.D. 690–696) both Korea and China were constantly presenting pet dogs to Japan. In the *Our Dogs* article, Mrs McLaren Morrison mentioned that some years before she had exhibited a 'Corean Spaniel',

and though I won a medal with her, also a first prize at the Crystal Palace, I was not a little astonished to hear her called 'half-bred'. I was very much taken aback at this information. The Captain who bred her had been in the Coreas, and few people have done that. The Kennel Club, however, did not share the view expressed for when at one time an objection was lodged against her, it gave it in favour of the little Corean stranger.

In this same article Mrs McLaren Morrison mentioned the 'Chinese Spaniel', describing it:

they much resemble the Japanese or Nepalese, except in colour, as they are of a deep orange or brindled. They are never so small as the Japanese 'small' specimens, though I have heard it said that some are seen in Pekin small enough to be put in a pocket, but cannot venture an opinion on this point. They are very handsome, their coats being rather thick and flowing, and their faces rather short. I think they are also called 'Lion Dogs' and they certainly bear a resemblence to the King of Animals.

Other breeds once found in China were the Chinese Royal Coated Greyhound and the Kansu Greyhound, but the Author could not trace any relationship to any of the other Asian breeds. The Chinese Crested, as with most of the hairless dogs, have come from tropical countries and probably have Turkish origins, though hairless dogs are usually found to have their origins in Mexico and Africa. The Chinese Crested were referred to in books on China about four hundred years ago. The Chinese Greyhound found in Kansu and Shensi districts were possibly a mixture of English Greyhounds with a small Indian Greyhound – which had probably been sent to China as gifts. The Chinese Coolie dog was alleged to have been introduced into England in the 1920s and it appears to have been a product looking like something between the Akita and the Chow Chow, of a definite Spitz-type, but it was not recognised by the China Kennel Union.

Clifford Hubbard refers to the Lo-Chiang dog as a short-faced breed of Pug-type, well known in the Ssuchuan province of China in the 8th century, probably the ancestor of the modern Pug. The same source says of the Loong Chua, that it is a now extinct variety of Pug, which was always rare. Infrequently, long-coated Pugs are met with in France, but they are not Loong Chuas.

The Shantung Greyhound Mr Clifford Hubbard tells us is a little known Chinese variety, similar to the now extinct Long-haired Whippet.

In spite of the belief of the Reverend H. W. Bush that the Chow Chow has Tibetan origins, the breed name appears to originate from 'pidgin English', a trade language mainly composed of a mixture of the most easily intelligible words used chiefly in trade intercourse in southern China, in this was also a large element of Portuguese. The name 'Chow' was applied to the breed of dog most commonly found in Canton, and simply means 'Chinese' dog, and does not refer to its having been used for food. Shan Dog was another name for a smooth coated Chow Chow.

In Colonel V. Burkhardt's book *Chinese Creeds and Customs* (1953–58), he says: "The Chinese attitude to dogs is entirely different to that of Europeans. The Chinese regards the dog purely as a burglar alarm, and it is no more a member of the family than the wretched cur chained to a kennel in the yard. Even the rich, who purchase pedigree foreign dogs hardly ever take them for a walk, but entrust their exercise to a coolie."

The public marketing of dog's flesh was prohibited by the Chinese Republique in 1915, but undoubtedly this practice has not been discontinued. While many Chinese are revolted by this eating of dog flesh Colonel Burkhardt says that "proof of the wideness of the practice is furnished by the Calendar, which lays down the days on which it should not be consumed . . . *The Book of Rites*, according to a Chinese commentator, classified the canine race as hunting-dogs, watch-dogs and those commonly known as the edible variety, which were bred for the pot . . . The Chinese attribute all sorts of consequences to partaking of a particular diet, and a dish of dog meat was credited with the power of reducing fatigue due to lack of sleep."

Mrs Beard and her party travelling in Tibet and China in May 1981 confirms that the Chinese do still eat Chow-type dogs and also cats. Therefore it is interesting to learn from Colonel Burkhardt that the dog plays an important part in Chinese mythology, "for the T'ien Kou or Heavenly Hound, outshines his master Erh Lang, as the sun does the moon."

The Chow, or a close relation, was noted for his powers of scenting and was used in Chinese fowling before the European bird-dog was invented. The breed appears to have extended north to Tibet, which would account for the Rev. Bush's remarks referred to in the previous chapter. In 1905, Percival Landon described some of the dogs which swarmed over Tibet as: "Every breed of dog known to the fancier seem to have been mixed with this sandy-coated pack. It is curious, however, that in spite of the out-of-door life which is led by them, the type to which they have reverted is not that of the wolf or Collie, but rather of the Esquimaux sledge-dog."

At one time, the most popular dog in Tibet was the Gya-Kyi, which could also be spelled Gya-Khi or Gyaki, meaning 'Chinese Dog'. This was more like a smooth-haired Pekingese; specimens were exhibited in this country in the 1920s and early 1930s. The Hon. Mrs F. M. Bailey believes that this breed is the Chinese Pug, probably the same as, or else akin to, the Chinese Ha-pa dog that she was once given by the thirteenth Dalai Lama.

Mrs Parsons of Ottershaw, Surrey, imported a pair of Gyakis in 1950. The dogs were golden-brown and black with white, smaller in size than Lhasa Apsos, flat-chested, with bushy tails. As the male had a bad heart she did not breed from them.

The Chinese Hound or Ma-chu-gou, is thought to be descended from the Buansu, a long-coated wild dog (*Cyon primaevis*), or Buansuah, found in Kashmir, Nepal, Assam and Eastern Tibet. It has an excellent nose and hunts in packs and is probably the breed referred to earlier, in the book *The Mongolian Horde*.

The Chinese Shar-Pei, or fighting dog, is listed in the Guiness Book of Records as the world's rarest dog; the name refers to either the colour or the gritty, stiff textured coat, and actually means 'sandy coat'.

The Chinese agree that the Shar-Pei breed has existed for centuries. Over two thousand years ago it was the all purpose, general utility dog kept by peasant farmers of the southern provinces, bordering on the South China Sea. They were used for hunting mongoose or wild boar, or to protect their masters' livestock from predators, but mostly they were guardians of the home. In appearance the dog stands firm on the ground with the stature of a warrior. It was probably because of their strength and appearance that these dogs were introduced to combat at a later time in history. The Shar-Pei were trained for dog fights and with their association with the combat ring could be considered an oriental version of our Bulldog. We know that the Shar-Pei were sometimes trained for dog fights, now those days are behind the ease with which this breed has slipped into the role of companion, pet and protector, leads one to consider that they must have been either drugged or tormented before engaging in dog fights. The Shar-Pei's temperament now enables them to meet all situations in a calm and unruffled manner.

The first Shar-Pei to come to England left quarantine in October 1981, imported by Miss H. Ligget from Hong Kong; there are also specimens in Denmark, Switzerland and Holland and their popularity is spreading far and wide in America. Not only is the Shar Pei an intriguing animal but also something of a clown, but it does present a very startling and unusual appearance. The weight is forty to fifty pounds, the males being heavier, the height is about eighteen inches. In size it is about equal to a strongly built Bull Terrier. Viewed from the front the head reminds one of a Hippopotamus, while the wrinkles and folds on the head and body are one of the outstanding features, only the correct amount is needed. Like the Chow, the tongue is bluish-black.

In the *New Book of the Dog*, mentioned before, the Hapa Dog, (Happa Dog, Chinese Pug or Peking Pug) is described as "a variety of the Pekinese Spaniel, to which it is similar in general shape, the great difference being that the Hapa is a smooth-coated dog, and is therefore destitute of one of the chief attractions of the Pekinese." It was very like a short-coated and short-backed Pekingese, with the faults of both and the attributes of neither.

Few specimens have been seen in England. Mrs Jardine Gresson of Pershore, Worcestershire, advertised her 'Happa Dogs' in the *Illustrated Kennel News* (December 12th, 1913), her prefix was E-Wo, from the supplement to *Our Dogs* of December 12th, 1913, came the description:

> E-Wo Lung as Golden Fawn with dark mask and shadings and E-Wo Ah as Biscuit Fawn, both being Mrs Jardine Gresson's 'Happa' dogs at Birlingham House, Pershore, Worcestershire. An interesting breed of foreign dog recently brought to this country from China by Mrs Jardine Gresson and at present the only ones of their kind in England, is the Happa dog. Mrs Gresson has for some years past been trying to get specimens of this breed without success until last Spring, when she was fortunate enough to secure the two dogs and the bitch whose photographs appear on this page. As will be seen from the photographs they are quaint looking. E-Wo Ah, the right hand of the two dogs particularly, having the appearance of a stone image.
>
> The bitch E-Wo Feng-Huang, is black with white breast and feet. Of the dogs E-Wo Lung is golden fawn, dark mask and shadings and E-Wo Ah biscuit fawn. Mrs Gresson hopes before long to put some puppies on the market.

One named Ta Jen was imported by the Hon. Mrs Lancelot Carnegie, and exhibited at the first show of the Pekinese Club in July 1907. It was led into the ring by a Chinese nurse in native costume. In appearance, Ta Jen was not unlike a tiny Miniature Bulldog, with a quaint, fierce face and large eyes set far apart, and with ears 'like the sails of a war junk'. His tail was short, but not docked. His weight might be 5 or 6 lbs., and in colour he was black-and-tan. A dog of the same variety, but fawn-and-white, was owned by Lord Howe. Both were imported by Mrs Carnegie from Peking, where they were said to have been purloined from the Imperial Palace.

We are told in *The Observer's Book of Dogs* that the Happa Dog, or Chinese Pug or Peking Pug is "like a short-coated, short-backed Pekingese, with the faults of the Peke and the Pug and the attributes of neither. It is extremely doubtful whether the dogs seen in Europe were ever pure bred. The origins and history remain rather mysterious. Height about 9 inches, weight about 5–10 lbs. Colour: black and tan, black and red, red, fawn and cream. Coat short and smooth. Head comparatively large. Tail docked short."

Before completing her article on Asiatic Toy Dogs, Mrs Morrison said:

> Before closing on Toys, I wanted to mention one dog, the existence of which I have always doubted, but since I have been promised a specimen needs must doubt it no more – this is the genuine 'sleeve' dog. It is said to be found in China, but the one I have been promised is

to come from Tibet. It is to be extremely tiny, and all white, like a ball of wool. Should I safely receive it, I shall be able to give further information about it. How many Asiatic Toy Dogs are yet perfectly unknown to the fancier it would be impossible to guess, for some parts of Asia are even now so inaccessible to Europeans that their customs, peoples, and dogs are alike a sealed book to us.

As the Author could not trace any further reference to this dog she can only assume that Mrs McLaren Morrison never received her sleeve dog. Could it have been the Pen-Lo, even smaller than the popular sleeve or miniature Pekingese? Clifford Hubbard tells us that the Pen-Lo was only bred in China. From the Tao Kuang period (A.D. 1821–1850) onwards, the smallest of this breed were carried in the sleeve but, with the disappearance of this custom, about the year 1900, they ceased to be Sleeve Pekingese proper and then took the name Pen-Lo. The variety is still the smallest of all Pekingese and was becoming quite rare even in China; the height was 3½ to 5 inches, length 8 inches and weight about 2½ lbs.

On page 32 of Mrs A. Mulliner's Tibetan Terrier book is a photo-graph of some of Dr Greig's dogs taken at the Karachi dog show in 1931. Two of the dogs might well be mistaken for Tibetan Spaniels, sitting on the benches next door to the obvious Tibetan Terriers, but Mrs Mulliner assures me that they are Champion Pekingese! Perhaps totally out of coat because of the heat.

Many of the Tibetan Spaniels sighted in the East up until the second world war were reported to be all black or a combination of black-and-white; so, combining all the information on other oriental breeds, the Author is going to leave her readers to decide for them-selves as to whether the Tibetan Spaniel originated as a Chinese dog, or has resulted from the mating of an ancient Chinese breed crossed with another small indigenous breed of Tibet, or even, perhaps, is one of the oldest pure-bred breeds of dogs in the world and the ancestor of many more small toy dogs and toy Spaniels.

6 Tibetan Spaniels from 1895–1937

It is almost impossible to pin-point just when the first Tibetan Spaniel came to the British Isles, but the Miss Russell-Allens of Dalhabboch owned a dog called Ching, purchased by their father in 1895 from a sailor who had been in the Far East. Ching was bright red with good but not excessive coat, he had a definite shawl, was small and well-balanced, with a well-carried tail. His nose was short with a lot of cushioning on his muzzle, giving him a very ape-like appearance.

The earliest record that the Author has been able to trace of a Tibetan Spaniel being exhibited was in 1898, when the Hon. Mrs A. McLaren Morrison entered two at a show for breeds under 10 lbs. in weight. As the history is traced in this chapter, one thing will become very obvious, the immense interest of this lady in our breed. She was known as a keen and enthusiastic fancier and lover of animals; her kennels were situated at Kepwick Park, far from a railway station, in the neighbourhood of the Yorkshire Moors. Mrs McLaren Morrison was a daughter of Lord Pirbright, who had a distinguished political career and was formerly known as Baron Henry de Worms. She made frequent visits to India with her husband, who held an appointment out there, but this did not stop her dogs from being exhibited at most of the major dog shows all over England. Mrs McLaren Morrison owned, bred and exhibited Chows from China, Samoyeds from the Arctic regions, Bhuteer Terriers from India, Spaniels from Thibet, Spaniels from Japan and she was probably best-known for her King Charles (English Toy) Spaniels. Mrs Morrison did not confine her attentions to dogs alone, for a considerable number of years she kept both long and short haired cats, which won numerous prizes at the Crystal Palace and at other shows.

In the book *Dog Shows and Doggy People* (1902), by C. H. Lane, there is a photograph of Mrs McLaren Morrison's Thibet Spaniel, Everest, "one of the rarest varieties shown, is most typical and interesting."

In the *New Book of the Dog* (1907), there is a small piece on the Thibet Spaniel, illustrated by a picture of Mrs Morrison's kennel man with a group of 'Thibet' Spaniels: the second dog in this group we are told is Yezo (imported) and next to him his son, Grand Lhama:

Until comparatively recently the engaging little Thibet Spaniel was not known in England, but it is now frequently to be seen at shows where foreign dogs are admitted; thanks mainly to the efforts of the Hon. Mrs McLaren Morrison, who has probably done more than any other dog owner of the present time to introduce and acclimatise unfamiliar breeds.

Mrs Morrison is no doubt right in her belief that the Thibet Spaniel is the true ancestor of all Pekinese, Japanese and even English Toy Spaniels. The similarity in appearance and type between her imported dog Yezo and the Spaniels from Pekin is too close to admit of any questions as to their relationship. The examples of this breed first imported from the monasteries of Thibet were black-and-white, and also black-and-tan; but Mrs Morrison has succeeded in breeding specimens of a beautiful self-coloured sable, and some of a rich tan and ruby, as well as brown, are now to be seen. They are fascinating little dogs, of a most loving and devoted disposition; and their sagacity is remarkable. They are hardy and by no means difficult to rear in our climate, and there is every probability that they will soon achieve the popularity which they deserve.

It is important to know that there are two types of Thibetan Spaniel, each of which has its particular votaries among English breeders. Mrs Frank Wormald, for instance, who has imported several from the original source, is strongly in favour of maintaining the long-nosed variety, in contradistinction to those who hold that the Thibetan should resemble in regard to nose its relative the Pekinese. Mrs Wormald considers that the long nose is characteristic of the true type. It is not a very uncommon breed in Northern India, as these dogs are frequently brought over the frontier.

For some years there was in the South Kensington Museum a stuffed black-and-white Tibetan Spaniel, rather coarse in type, brought into England about 1897. When our eldest daughter was quite small her favourite occupation was to visit the museum to gaze at this dog – and others, but the verdict was always the same: "It is not in the least bit like any of yours, Mummy!"

Before the early 20th century little was to appear in print about the Tibetan Spaniel, in the *Illustrated Kennel News* (January 5th, 1906), on the 'Ladies Page' written by Lady Betty, the nom de plume of Miss Lilian Smythe, appeared the first real article on our breed:

There is interesting news this week, Mrs Barnett is taking up a new breed and in addition to her Pekingese and Pomeranians is going in for Thibet Spaniels. It was at the Kennel Club show that Mrs Barnett fell in love with what she considers the most fascinating, quaint rare dogs, and now she has purchased two.

The article continues:

Monica, a beautiful, black, sixteen-months-old bitch, and Tan-Tan, a seven-months-old black-and-tan, a rare variety, from Mrs Walker of Woodheys Park. Mrs Walker and the Hon. Mrs McLaren Morrison are practically the only owners of the breed at present in England, and Mrs Morrison has imported several from their land of origin. One of the greatest attractions of the Thibet Spaniel is their extreme hardiness, which is a valuable point in all Oriental dogs, and I hear that they are also very sweet tempered, and possess that saving grace in a pet, they recognise but one master or mistress to whom they owe allegiance. Their attendants may feed them and look after them, but 'cupboard love' has no part in their dispositions, and they give their devotion to one mistress only.

As they are easy breeders, and need little attention Mrs Barnett should do well with her new pets. She tells me that there will be classes for the breed at Crufts and Westminster, so there is every prospect that the public may learn to appreciate the breed.

In Herbert Compton's book *The Twentieth Century Dog* (1904), the Tibetan Spaniel is listed under Foreign Spaniels; others in this category are the Pekinese Spaniel, the Japanese Spaniel, the Lhasa Spaniel or Terrier. Mr Compton quotes the Hon. Mrs McLaren Morrison on the photograph of Yatsu* as saying: "This is the rarest and latest recruit to 'Foreign Spaniels'." Mrs Morrison continued:

As far as the Thibetan Spaniel is concerned the breed has been very much in the background. I have seen some splendid specimens in the East and I am of the opinion it would be much appreciated in England, and take its place by the side of the Pekinese and Japanese Spaniels. The Thibet Spaniel is intelligent, very affectionate, very smart, a good follower and companion and not delicate, like so many other toy varieties are. They are, moreover, very devoted to each other, and my dog, Lhama, takes his share of the care of the infants.

The natives of the frontiers of Tibet know well the value of these dogs and they are recognised as a breed as, say, the King Charles is with us. I have seen them all black, black with white markings, and black-and-tan. The colours seem to somewhat coincide with those of our varieties of King Charles Spaniels†, though I myself have never

*The name Yatsu has also been spelt Jatsu in books of that era (*Author*).
†i.e. Ruby, Blenheim, Black-and-Tan and Tricolour (*Author*).

seen an all-tan Thibet Spaniel to correspond with our ruby variety, but I know that they exist.

It is a great pity that the Thibet Spaniel is not more fancied. A more settled understanding as to type would perhaps encourage the judges to place it. There are several in England besides my own, by my Karpo, very rare on account of his black and white colouring. He is one of the best specimens. Miss Fairman has a most typical dog in her Yatsu. The Thibet Spaniel should, as a breed, be incorporated with the Pekinese and Japanese varieties; it might then come to the enjoyment its merits deserve, and ultimately obtain a separate registration*.

About Yatsu, Herbert Compton tells us, quoting Mr H. C. Brooke:

Yatsu is an imported Thibet Spaniel, and the property of Miss Fairman, the well known animal artist. It weighs 11 lbs., the coat is glossy black with white points; the tail is carried more erect than in a Pekinese and Japanese Spaniels; the legs are short, thick and slightly bowed; the ears cocked in a striking way. Miss Fairman adds . . . 'He never forgets a friend but asserts his rights, and is a delightful companion. I have heard that the Pekinese Spaniels originally came from Thibet; there is certainly a strong resemblence between them.' Yatsu has won many prizes in variety classes, but there is no special classification for the breed. Mr H. C. Brooke, another high authority on foreign dogs, considers that the Thibet Spaniel is quite a distinct breed, and thinks the specimens exhibited show marked type of their own.

In his *20th Century Dog Non Sporting book* of 1904, Herbert Compton says:

I am glad to be able to present my readers with an illustration of Yatsu, the specimen Mrs McLaren Morrison considers so typical. Although somewhat favouring the Pekinese dog, it has an individuality of its own, and the shape of the head and ears, the comparatively narrow skull, and the tail not carried over the back, distinguish it from the Toy Spaniels of the Farthest East.

James Watson's Dog Book (1909), gives us additional information of interest.

It has been the good fortune of the Author [i.e. Mrs McLaren Morrison] to see the authentic photographs of the dogs of Tibet taken by the Grand Lhama himself . . . The Tibet Spaniel is now also well known in England and already between 50 and 60 specimens are in

*Refers to the Lhassa Terrier and Tibet Spaniel (*Author*).

100

Great Britain. The Thibet Spaniel is the true ancestor of the Pekinese, Japanese and English Toy Spaniel, of that there really can be no doubt and as such they are doubly interesting. The monasteries of Tibet enclose many beautiful specimens of this fascinating breed, and the monks know their value well. The black and white and the black and tan variety are now fairly familiar to show visitors, who however, have yet to learn that self-coloured sable specimens as well as those of rich tan and ruby as well as brown etc, should also soon be found at our shows. In conclusion let me assure the reader that these various little Asiatics are of a most loving and devoted disposition, showing great sagacity and by no means difficult to rear in our climate where they are therefore able to be our constant companions. To know them is to love them! One can but trust that soon they will have the position in England and also in America which they so truly deserve.

In 1915 in his 'Foreign Fancies' column in *Our Dogs*, Mr Will Hally bemoans that: "Lhassa Terriers and Tibetan Spaniels are doing little more than holding their own." A far cry from the fifty to sixty Tibetan Spaniels in Great Britain around 1909.

In 1925 Mr Hally wrote:

I cast regretful eyes at the apparent extinction of the Tibetan Spaniel, but find some consolation in the determined presence of the Lhassa Terrier, which, with a little more 'go' applied to their cult, would go a long way.

To go forward in time, it is very interesting to read Mr Hally's remarks in *Our Dogs* (June 24th, 1932), when he wrote:

In all that has been written about the Tibetan breeds, it will have been noticed that the Tibetan Spaniel is exemplified as one of the most ancient origin. And yet, Mrs McLaren Morrison has just remarked to me that the Tibetan Spaniels which she sees today are different from those which she and other importers owned a quarter of a century ago and more. Some of the early importations were sent to this country by the then Governor of Bengal (I cannot remember his name at the moment) while some others of the same period came from Sikkim, sent home by the then British Resident there.

Old exhibitors will remember Mrs McLaren Morrison's Kina (if I remember rightly that exhibit was undefeated in this country) and another notability was Miss Fairman's Jatsu. I do not remember at this late day the history of all those early exhibits, but I do remember that they all came from absolutely authentic sources and were only secured by influence; I think that Kina was born in a Tibetan monastery, but the interesting feature of those long-ago Tibetan Spaniels was that they were mostly, though not invariably, black with white shirt fronts, and at that time that colouring was considered the most prized by the native breeders.

Those early Spaniels were generally more massive (of course I am speaking comparatively), than the present Spaniels, while their legs were straight and their faces were not short. Here again, we have to allow for evolution, and, anyhow, the little differences between the original Tibetan Spaniel importations and those of today, are not serious, while the important point is that the later importations, no matter from what source they have been secured, are all of the one type. That applies to those just out of quarantine and still in quarantine which have been imported by Mrs McLaren Morrison herself. I mention this because I do not want to give the impression that Mrs McLaren Morrison, while recognising the difference between the earliest and the latest importeds, is in any way questioning the latter. Another matter which I would like to make clear, is that modern importeds all represent what is now the generally accepted standard of the breed.

This chapter shows that, between the two world wars, there was just as much variation in type as is still considered to exist over fifty years later – which should be heartening to those of today's breeders who worry about it!

The mention by various sources of a shorter-coated, smoother-haired Tibetan Spaniel must pose the question as to whether the Gya-kyi was ever inadvertently bred with a Tibetan Spaniel, or one of the other smaller Tibetan breeds. In his book *Tibetan Notebook* (1934) which is referred to in the first chapter, Sir A. C. Bell mentions his visit to a Tibetan village where ". . . dogs too, are lying about, here and there, mostly asleep. But one of them is very much awake, a well-kept little fellow which runs about everywhere. He is the kind known to Tibetans as 'Chinese Dog' (Gya-khyi) and to many Europeans as a 'Tibetan Spaniel', and surely one ancestor of the Pekingese, although not so puggy in appearance".

In Sir Edward Wakefield's book *Past Imperative*, the Gya-kyi is again mentioned, meaning a Tibetan Spaniel.

So it can be seen that Tibetan Spaniels obviously varied in type. In the early part of the century the Reverend Bush wrote about the distinction in heads, and in 1895 Mrs McLaren Morrison wrote about the short-haired black Thibet Spaniel as being one of the original ancestors of the black Pug.

Going back in time, the Reverend H. W. Bush's article, 'Dogs of

India and Tibet', appeared in J. Sidney Turner's *The Kennel Encyclopedia* (1908), a very rare book indeed, with only 1,500 copies printed. As a result this work is very scarce today and I would like to thank Lt.-Cdr. John Williams, the late Secretary of the Kennel Club, for permitting me to obtain copies of the Tibetan Spaniel photographs, and to Miss Prudence Cuming for her co-operation in this matter.

In the chapter 'The Dogs of Tibet', the Rev. Bush wrote:

Since the return of the Tibet Expeditionary Force in India a couple of years ago, much that was previously known about the breeds of dogs in that land has been confirmed, and the existence of others, not so well known, has been revealed. Up to the time of the Expedition, Tibet was a closed land, and all information to be obtained about the dogs was what the Tibetans visiting India either could or would give. The existence of the larger dog of Tibet, the so-called Mastiff, has been known to the 'outer' world for a number of years, but from time to time, specimens both good and bad, have found their way into India whence some have been taken to Europe and England. It is a well established fact that the Tibetans have not, as a rule, parted with their best, and small blame to them for that. Of the smaller breeds, the Lhasa Terrier and Tibetan Spaniel are the best known, they have been easier to get, and thrive both in India and England very well indeed. The same cannot be said of the Mastiff, he cannot stand the plains of India even in winter for any length of time, while diseases, especially distemper, prove very fatal.

Tibet is rich in small breeds. The Lhasa Terrier and the Tibetan Spaniel of the broad-nosed kind, like the type originally shown by the Hon. Mrs McLaren Morrison, are recognised by the Kennel Club. There is, however, another small breed, called by some the Tibetan Spaniel, in which the nose is pointed; it is not so long in the back, its legs are not so feathered, the coat is dense and only fairly long; legs straight and of moderate bone, tail curled up over the back. The usual colour is black, generally with a white mark on the chest, white paws both fore and hind, and under the belly two small white patches exactly corresponding. This dog has been called the 'Spitz-like Tibet Dog' – a name without meaning. Sometimes the colour is sandy-red, and even parti-colour, it is a small dog, but varies a bit in size. We have seen them of 10 lbs. weight, while others would scale 15 lbs. It appears to be quite a distinct breed and breeds true to type.

The other illustration of a Spaniel that comes into Northern India from Tibet via Leh, is a perfectly different class of dog. To begin with it is very much bigger, coat much longer, feathered much more, head much broader and nose much blunter. And here appears the difficulty; how are these breeds to be distinguished? They cannot all be called by the name 'Spaniel', which at best is a misnomer. They represent three distinct breeds, and might be designated by three distinct names, but what those names ought to be we do not venture to suggest.

There now comes the question as to how far Tibet has derived her smaller breeds from China. It is difficult to answer, and we are inclined to think also, one that can never really be satisfactorily solved. As we all know, China has constant communication with Tibet, and it practically has always been so. It may be that China's small dog, the Pekingese, found its way by caravan to Tibet, and there would be nothing strange in that, and has in time degenerated to the present type of 'Tibetan Spaniel'. Many of those who were in Tibet spoke of 'the Chinese small dogs in Tibet', and yet it has been asserted that China owes her small dogs to Tibet. Anyway, there is a very distinct resemblence between the breeds. This was emphasised by the arrival of some Tibetan 'Spaniels', golden tan and white in colour, which were exactly like some Pekingese dogs in size, colour and type – that came from Peking after the late China War. It would be very interesting if we could find out the exact case; at present it is impossible to get reliable information from the Tibetans, for they will tell the inquirer whatever they think would please him, so much that has been culled from them is hardly worth having without severe sifting. However let us live in hopes. Summing it up, it may be said of the known breeds of Tibet, probably two only are actually indigenous, namely the Mastiff and the Lhasa Terrier, the other large dogs being merely inferior varieties of the aforesaid Mastiff, while the origin of the 'Spaniel' and the 'Spitz-like' breeds is most likely traceable to Chinese importations, unless it can ever be authentically proved that it is the other way around.

The Reverend Bush certainly gives us plenty of food for thought! In the same edition of *The Kennel Encyclopedia*, in the chapter 'Dogs of India and Tibet', the Hon Mrs A. McLaren Morrison says,

The Tibetan Spaniel gains in daintiness what it loses in quaintness over the Lhasa Terrier; he is my lady's lap-dog, the 'King Charles' of the East. His small-featured feet seem made to rest on silken cushions, not like the soft, big, shaggy paws of the little Lhasa made for duty in the snow!

The Tibetan Spaniel is far more numerous in England than is the Lhasa Terrier, but he is still waiting for Championship Show rights which the latter has already obtained. A short time ago we found in all descriptions of Tibetan Spaniels the colour described as black with some white, or white with black markings. In recent years tan with black, cream and other colours have been imported; and brown, bright orange, and brindle specimens, have been bred in this country. A lovely white-and-tan dog has been imported, which was brought back by the recent expedition after having, with the charming little female, his kennel companion, walked nearly the whole way from Tibet to India. They are a pair of Tibet Spaniels similar to those already in England, who undoubtedly came straight from Tibet – the genuine article. Their appearance at a leading show should give an impetus to the breed.

It is stated with some authority that the Tibet Spaniel, known for hundreds of years in the monasteries of Tibet, is the original ancestor of the Pekingese, Japanese and English Toy Spaniel. The writer firmly believes this to be the case. The monks of the Far East know both their value and their good points, and it is very difficult to obtain a good one from them to take out of the country. The Tibet Spaniel is rather long in body and low to the ground, but withal a small dog, quite a toy; bigger ones are often excellent specimens, but the smaller ones should be most valued and encouraged by exhibitors. The legs are straighter than those of the Pekingese, and the mane is not so prominent, though a good frill adorns the throat of the dog when in full coat. The tail should be carried plumed over the back. The most important feature in the Tibet Spaniel is the head, which should never at all approach to that of the snub-face of the Pekingese. The female has the longer face as a rule, but in good specimens there is a somewhat square-looking muzzle, which is still more marked in the best males. The eye is large, but not so prominent as in the Japanese, yet most expressive. The Tibet Spaniel is very intelligent and engaging, whilst his pretty ways and charming appearance make him presentable amongst the daintiest sofa cushions of his mistress. Even if the larger specimens be kept in the 'kennel', the smaller ones should grace the drawing room and have the run of the house, as is the custom in Anglo-Indian homes where this charming little oriental is constantly to be found. It is to be hoped that the Tibetan Spaniel will take his proper place on the show benches before very long.

It was of course a good many more years, from the late 1800s to the mid 1900s, before this wish of Mrs McLaren Morrison's came true!

The editor of *The Kennel Encyclopedia*, Mr J. Sidney Turner, doubted whether either the Japanese Chin, the King Charles Spaniel or the Pekingese originally came from Tibet. Mr Turner's theory was that it was quite probable that when the Chinese overran Tibet in the 13th century, when Tibet was still quite a barbarous country, that they introduced their native breeds of dogs into Tibet at that time. We must remember that, even in the 13th century, China had already been civilised for very many hundreds of years.

Our Dogs (July 13th, 1895), includes with Mrs McLaren Morrison's article on Asiatic Breeds, a photograph of a black dog, Zezo (who has also been referred to as Komo Zezo or Yezo). Mrs McLaren Morrison says of him:

> I now come to another kind of Spaniel, and one indeed that is very little known. Again, when I exhibited a specimen a year ago, the all knowing critic (who probably had also been in Thibet, though that country is as good as unexplored by Europeans), whispered 'No true breed'. This time, however, I am able to give him facts. This portrait of Zezo, my Thibet Spaniel, to my belief is the first specimen ever exhibited in England. These dogs are brought from Central Thibet, and are very difficult to get. I have seen two specimens besides Zezo, both black like he is, and I am now in possession of a 'grey' female, who I hope may live to show herself to English judges. The coat of this breed is thick, the legs not very high, the body rather long, and the tail is carried over the back in a graceful curl. The face is shorter in some specimens than others, its shortness being prized. . . . Secondly, I have to mention the short-haired, black Thibet Spaniel; and the knowledge that such a dog exists brings us a step nearer on our way to the discovery of the origins of the Black Pug.

Mrs McLaren Morrison was obviously greatly interested in the colours of the Tibetan Spaniel. In the *Kennel* (July 1911), she writes:

> The coloured Tibet Spaniel was until quite recently a very rara avis among dogs. Quite lately I have known several outside my own kennels, and curiously though from two quite different specimens, one resident in the Emerald Isle.
>
> The first coloured Tibetan Spaniel I owned was bred when I lived in India, and both parents were black, though the mother's black could be called the deepest brown-black, or black-brown. Hence, no doubt, the colour of her puppies. Next I imported two perfect coloured females, a cream and a fine red-brindle. The family of the former and a black sire was truly extraordinary – one cream, one black, one deep chocolate brown and one orange! The brindle had two males; one was my noted first prize winner Karpo, curiously enough the cream daughter of the cream mother had two black puppies, thus throwing back to her black sire. The sire of the puppies was also black. The orange female gave me two males, a biscuit colour and a light brown.

A pure black female and a pure black sire produced a brown and white puppy; in this case I cannot trace any colour in the mother's pedigree, which I know far back, but the sire being imported probably accounts for it. It is rare to have Tibets with very much white, but the black sire (whose dam is deep black-brown, the female spoken of above) gave me a white female with a little tan, her mother being dark. The light shade of biscuit is one I particularly admire in Tibets, and curiously enough two of my now living Lhasa Terriers are of this beautiful shade. I think that the colours here are so beautiful and manifold that to all colour-breeders the breed should offer particular interests. The shades are really lovely. The little dogs themselves, apart from the colour question, are hardy, most fascinating, intelligent and attractive, and whether coloured, or black with white, or all black, are, apart from the immense antiquity of the breed, (cultivated and preserved in the monasteries of Tibet from times unknown), delightful companions, who need only to be once known to establish a firm hold in this country.

There are already a great many in England of various strains, if only all Tibet Spaniel lovers would come forward the classes would soon be filled. I earnestly hope such will shortly prove the case, as the interest in the breed is growing far more general, and enquiries for specimens as well as interchange of strains more frequent.

Mrs Geoffrey Hayes gives an interesting insight about the breed in her article 'The Many Breeds of Mysterious Tibet', in *Our Dogs* (June 3rd, 1932). The Tibetan Spaniel heads the list and of it she writes: "First of all for ancient lineage, comes the Tibetan Spaniel. This charming little toydog is greatly prized and is only owned by the wealthy [i.e. in Tibet]. It is bred by the present Dalai Lama, among others. It should be very small, of a light fawny colour preferably, with fluffy, silky coat."
Her article continues:

They are very active, but not used to walking exercise, as they practically never leave the house in which they were born, unless they are carried. Owing to the constant society of human beings, these little dogs develop extraordinary intelligence and learn all kinds of little tricks. They hold the position of court jester in a country of few amusements. Like all Tibetan dogs, the Spaniels are inclined to become very stout, and should be kept on a short and scanty diet; though this is difficult as they are terribly greedy and will do anything to get extra titbits.

All Tibetan dogs have certain characteristics in common; very thick coats, great hardiness and really remarkable intelligence. For instance, a dog used only to the Tibetan language, and bought by a European will, in only a week, understand what is wanted of him.

Like the Tibetans themselves, none of the breeds is very prolific and three puppies are a very large litter. The bitches come into season only once a year, whilst in Tibet. Most of the breeds stand the heat fairly well upon being imported to India, provided, of course, that it isn't at the height of the hot season. Their great hardiness is probably due to their being examples of the survival of the fittest, as four out of five dogs die from hardship on the journey down from Lhasa.

In 1915 Mr Will Hally, who wrote the Foreign Dog Fancies column regularly in *Our Dogs*, bemoaned that "Lhassa Terriers and Tibetan Spaniels are doing little more than holding their own." In 1921 Mr Hally wrote:

The War period seems to have put an end to the publicity which the Tibetan Spaniel, and likewise the Lhassa Terrier, at one time enjoyed. If Tibetan progress was never very noteworthy, it was undoubted for a time, and ten or eleven years ago the breed's promise was so encouraging that the Hon. Mrs McLaren Morrison, to whom these dogs owed practically all of their British appreciation, suggested the formation of a specialist club. Kennel Club recognition and the coveted championships were even on the horizon; but that is furthest the Tibetans ever got, and it does not look as if they would ever get as far again.

In 1929 Mr Hally wrote: "No Tibetan canine is ever very easily secured, but not only in overcoming difficulties in that way, but in reviving what threatened to be a completely 'lost' breed in this country, I do congratulate Mrs Greig on her enterprise."

In 1932 Mr Hally in his column said: "Mrs Brownlees feels that if the romantic history of the Tibetan Spaniels was more emphasised there would be a much bigger fancy for this breed, especially as the Tibetans are so highly intelligent. Tibetan Spaniels are the prayer dogs of the Tibetan Temples and great care must be taken in keeping the breed pure."

In the *Kennel Magazine*, number 11 (February 1911), edited by A. Croxton Smith, in the chapter 'Our Portrait Gallery', there is an article describing the Hon. Mrs McLaren Morrison's Tibetan Spaniels kept at Kepwick Park, near Northallerton in Yorkshire:

As a nucleus of the breed in England, this kennel is important as it contains no less than seven distinct strains of Tibet blood, so that there

108

is no danger of too close inbreeding, as often befalls when a rare breed becomes popularised. There is little doubt but that as soon as Tibetan Spaniels are better known they will become popular, for they are not only very hardy dogs, healthy and long-lived, but charming companions. Kina, whose portrait appears on our front cover this month is the constant companion of Mrs McLaren Morrison, in hotels and trains, etc., his manners are perfect, and he is very affectionate and intelligent, bright and very game.

Among other dogs of this breed in the kennel should be mentioned the two imported pioneers of the coloured variety of Tibetans, whose descendents are now flourishing, one of them is the cream-coloured Tibet Spaniel. Kamba, a 1st prize winner, is no more but Tuna, also a prize winner, is still living. And as the coloured dogs may be as popular as the blacks, it is interesting to hear of its recent addition to the kennel of a beautiful puppy from golden coloured parents, which will probably prove the same lovely hue. Mrs Morrison has a pair of gold-coloured Tibetans of her own breeding in the kennel. The dog, Naringe (an 'orange' in Hindustani), and is the sire of puppies of the same colour ex an orange bitch. Another Tibetan dog, of the best type, now at Kepwick Park, greatly resembles his great-great-great-grandfather, Grand Lhama, who is still living at 15 years. But Chumbi is, alas, now dead from an accident, a sad loss to the breed. It should be born in mind that a different standard of points obtains in Tibetans than in the better known oriental dogs. The short flat face of the Pekingese is quite taboo among Tibet Spaniel breeders, but a square short muzzle is accepted, rather longer in the bitch than the dog, and Tibetans are not and should not be short-faced.

So that these Eastern breeds could be protected and their interests promoted in England, a new Club was formed at this time with the title of 'Tibetan Spaniel, Lhasa Terrier, and other Foreign Dogs Club'. Sir John Bourdillon was the President, and the Hon. Secretary was the Hon. Mrs McLaren Morrison.

Percival Landon's book *Lhasa* (1905), clearly shows the confusion over breed names for Tibetan dogs, mentioning "The typical Tibetan terrier*, a long-coated little fellow with a sharp nose, prick ears, and, as a rule, black from muzzle to tail, we found but seldom in a pure state". The reader could well be forgiven for not recognising this description of a Tibetan Spaniel as we know the breed today, because

*The photograph of Gantak Sebu shows her to be a Tibetan Spaniel leaving us in no shadow of doubt as to the breed referred to, but incorrectly named, by Mr Landon. Little wonder that there was confusion prior to the 1930s over the names given to the Tibetan breeds by the Kennel Club.

Mr Landon mentions further on with a definite reference to this 'Tibetan terrier', "The finest specimens of this breed* are owned by Mrs Claude White – 'Tippoo', 'Jugri' and scantily-coated 'Nari' came up with us to Lhasa with their master. But 'Sebu' a sable freak in the same family, and beyond question the most beautiful of them all, remained at Gantok."

In this same edition of the *Kennel Magazine* (1911), Mr John C. White, C.I.E., tells us in the chapter, 'Some Interesting Breeds of Dogs':

Among dogs that are only beginning to be known in England, are the breeds designated Tibetan Spaniels and Lhasa Terriers, most interesting in themselves, and also on account of the fact that countries of Tibet, Nepal and Bhutan, where these dogs are indigenous, are practically closed to European travellers, and good specimens rare even in these places, are consequently almost impossible to obtain.

I have had a kennel of Tibet Spaniels for very many years, and claim for them to be the best of their kind. I began with a black and white dog from the Royal Palace at Khatmandu, and at his death he was replaced by an almost similar dog, only entirely black, with a little white on his chest, who was got from a travelling Tibetan as quite a pup on the Tibetan frontier during the Sikhim Expedition of 1888, and from him, Tibet, and his mate Tabitha, descended my present family.

My contention is that the Nepalese Palace Dogs differ from those now known as the Tibet Spaniel only in colouring, in which the former resemble the Japanese breed, and my readers have only to compare the accompanying photographs to see how alike the points are in both. But as my experience of Nepal is quite 25 years ago, the dogs then known as Palace Dogs no longer exist, though at that time they were known and spoken of as Palace Dogs.

These little Spaniels are unusually intelligent and quick, very affectionate and adaptable, excellent watch dogs, as they hear and bark at every sound. They are used by travelling Tibetans as watch dogs to guard their packs of merchandise when halting, and the men are very kind to and fond of their little dogs. Really good specimens are very rare, and the owners are unwilling to part with them. I saw only one good specimen in Lhasa, a very old dog, the property of a beggar, and all the time I was in India (apart from those I bred myself) I do not think I met with a dozen good dogs, although I kept a sharp look out for them.

In colour they are generally black with a little white, but occasionally coloured brown with black points to the hairs, occasionally grey, and I have one puppy as yet only six months old, a bright yellow. They are very slow in development, and do not attain their best under two years, and often a dog that at a year seemed ungainly and not worth much, at two years becomes a strikingly handsome animal. Their most distinctive characteristics are a small head with large expressive eyes, set fairly wide apart; a rather long and somewhat pointed nose; dropping ears and a profuse mane, forming a ruff around the neck. The coat is long and silky, with a soft thick undercoat, and the legs well-feathered, with long tufts of hair on the toes. The tail has long thick hair, and is usually carried curled over the back, except when running, when they use it as a rudder, holding it straight out behind. They have extraordinary powers of jinking, and it is a pretty sight to see three or four of them racing over the ground, making the most wonderful twists and turns to avoid each other. They generally weigh from 10 lbs. to 14 lbs. I am afraid no attention is paid to careful breeding, although Natives will always point out a dog they consider good.

A. Croxton Smith in his book *About Our Dogs* published in 1931 confirms Mr White's remarks about the eye size. Nowhere in any of the early books can I find any reference to the small or almond shaped eyes, and I do wonder if it is this alteration to the eye shape in our breed standard which has produced the watering eyes? Even a human-shaped eye (which the present day standard requires) waters in dusty or smokey atmospheres and this is also very noticeable in today's Tibetan Spaniels as well!

In a chapter headed 'Lesser known Foreign Breeds', Mr Croxton Smith says:

The other breed of which mention should be made is the Tibetan Spaniel, with which we are also familiar through the instrumentality of Mrs McLaren Morrison, who thinks that it is the ancestor of the Pekingese. Others, however, say that it owes its origin to the Chinese dogs, which were taken into Tibet and crossed with Lhasa Terriers. He is a small toy standing on short legs and having a rather long body. The legs are straighter than those of the Pekingese and the jaws are of a natural shape. The eyes are large but not prominent. The coat is long and flat. Colours are various, such as black with some white, white with black markings, black and tan, and various shades of brown and brindle.

The Hon. Mrs F. M. Bailey wrote in the *Kennel Gazette* (August 1934):

The dog known in this country as the Tibetan Spaniel, has as far as I know, no special name in Tibet. There seem to be more of them in the

Chumbi valley than in any other part of Tibet. Mr Claude White, who was the Political Officer in Sikkim, had a fine kennel of these dogs many years ago. My husband got a very nice dog of this breed when in Lhasa with Sir Francis Younghusband's Expedition of 1904. This dog accompanied him on a journey of over thousands of miles through Tibet to Simla, and a photograph was taken on that expedition while crossing a high snowy pass. This dog was called Lhasa and later on he was given to Mrs Frank Wormald, who brought him to this country in 1905. He was shown and won prizes and died at the age of 18. I myself parted with them and confined my attention to Apsos.

It is interesting that the late Mrs Veronica Wormald of the famous Knaith Labrador kennel in Scotland, criticised the Tibetan Spaniels of the early 1960s, saying that they were quite different from her sister-in-law's dog Lhasa, who was a much more substantial animal and more like a scaled-down working Spaniel.

The Hon. Mrs F. M. Bailey has kindly written to me about the Tibetan Spaniels given to her by the 13th Dalai Lama. One was a lovely cream colour, and she does not recall ever having seen one of this colour in this country. Mrs Bailey tells me that the Spaniel was always known in Tibet as the 'Chinese Dog', referred to as Gya-Kyi (Gya = Chinese) (Kyi = Dog). It was also called the Chumbi Dog, as they were only found in Yatung, a small town in the Chumbi Valley of Tibet, where there had always been a Chinese Customs Officer until the Sun Yat Sen revolution in China in 1912, when all the Chinese were kicked out of Tibet by the Tibetans.

With such very dedicated and enthusiastic people as Mrs McLaren Morrison and Mr White, it is very hard to understand why the breed appeared to die out during the first decade of the 1900s, and then again during the war years. The Distemper virus possibly played a great part in the reduction of the breed and, in 1926, Mr Theo Marples in his book *Show Dogs* wrote: "The average man who did not know what breed they really were, would at once put them down as mongrels." Harsh words, but looking at the photographs of some of the Greig imports, so kindly given to me by Mrs Janet Beasley, with the one exception of Doma of Ladkok, one can but feel that Mr Marples was only voicing the general opinion of the breed among dog fanciers of that time.

Dr Agnes R. H. Greig (Nancy to her friends) worked in the Women's Medical Services in India at the Lady Dufferin Hospital in Karachi. One of the daughters of Mrs A. Renton Greig of the Ladkok Kennels at Roydon in Hertfordshire, she saw Tibetan Spaniels when up in the foothills near to the borders of Tibet. Dr Greig was able, through her contacts and patients, to obtain some Tibetan Spaniels, Lhasa Apsos and Tibetan Terriers, as well as Pekingese which were exhibited in India. These were sent to England and exhibited under the mother and daughter's prefix-affixes of Lamleh and Ladkok.

Going on now to some of the first championship shows where the breed was exhibited, without championship status or CCs, at Crufts Dog Show of February 6th and 7th in 1935, the Tibetan Spaniel breed had five classes, Open Dog, Open Bitch, Special Breeders (mixed sexes), Brace and Team classes with three cups to be won. Colonel G. Hayes, D.S.O., was the judge and there were eleven Tibetan Spaniels making sixteen entries. At this same show there were twelve Lhasa Apsos making nineteen entries, nine Tibetan Terriers making fifteen entries and two Tibetan Mastiffs making three entries.

In his show report in *Our Dogs* Colonel Hayes, says in his Tibetan Spaniel critique:

> Kinsae, an imported dog, more typical in head and expression and stern than those below him. Dukkoo of Ladkok, nice little dog, moved nicely. Rajah – similar in type to the second, not quite so compact. Chand Bibi an imported bitch, good expression and type of face, typical stern, lacked bloom and did not move too well, but stood out for type. Dullee Doma of Larwich, imported, typical, unfortunately not very fit at present. Tina of Ladkok in better bloom than those above her, but not quite such a typical head. Dizaree of Ladkok very similar to third. Brace – McLaren Morrison, Team – Mrs A. R. Greig.

It is a great pity that Colonel Hayes' critique did not tell us the colours and a little more about the dogs. Judges, please remember that you are writing show critiques for posterity!

The Ladies Kennel Association Show of 1935 had two Tibetan Spaniel classes guaranteed by the Hon. Mrs McLaren Morrison. There were nine exhibits from four kennels, and the winning dog was Mrs A. R. Greig's Seu of Ladkok who was also Best of Breed, with Mrs McLaren Morrison's imported Chand Bibi the best bitch.

At the Richmond Show in 1935, judged by Mr A. C. Dudley, were exhibits owned by Mrs McLaren Morrison, Mrs A. R. Greig and Mrs Abbott, as well as from Mr Lapwood's kennels. The cutting also states that, after the show, Shan of Ladkok was sold to a lady in Monte Carlo.

Mr Crufts' Golden Jubilee Show of 1936 records that Lhasa Apsos had eleven dogs entered making twenty entries, Tibetan Terriers had eleven dogs making seventeen entries, Tibetan Spaniels eight dogs making eleven entries. The only Tibetan Mastiff entered was absent.

113

One amusing aside is Mr Hally's notes in *Our Dogs*, in which he tells us about the judge Mr W. H. Lapwood: "He obviously made his awards according to the Standards, everybody seemed to be in the most contented and optimistic frame of mind." So, who says that a judge cannot please everyone, or were the early exhibitors more friendly and less critical?

Lady Wakefield has given the Author some interesting information about the many people who served in India, whose tours of duty took them to the high hills near Simla, Almora and the surrounding districts. They often acquired an enchanting and probably 'lousy' Tibetan Spaniel puppy. She remembers that an aunt of hers had a brownish bitch, Peri, brought home to England at the beginning of this century. There must have been others who did likewise. Lady Wakefield has explained that there was the indoor, rather pampered, dainty, smaller type, which was owned and bred by the higher class Tibetans of noble background, or by an abbot of a Tibetan monastery. Then there were the 'Hill Dogs', much bigger and coarser and more common in type. Lady Wakefield's Dolma was much esteemed by the Hill People who admired both her size and type.

Dr Greig considered that the Tibetan Spaniel was only found in Darjeeling, or in the villages in the Darjeeling district and in a small part of Tibet that is adjacent to it. The Lhassa Terrier (i.e. the Lhasa Apso) was likewise found in those same districts, whereas the Tibetan Terrier belonged to Central Tibet. Dr Greig, in her letters to Mr Will Hally, states: "I have bred Tibetan Terriers for nine years, and so far all have bred true to type; but Lhassa Terrier breeders out here will tell you that two Lhassa Terriers mated together will sometimes produce a throw-back to the Tibetan Spaniel."

Dr Greig and her mother were supposed to have imported about six of the really fine monastery-bred Tibetan Spaniels, but in the Author's opinion of those shown in this book only Doma could be considered typical by today's standards. Yet some of these probably figure in the pedigrees of Tina of Ladkok and Skyid! The Hon. Mrs F. M. Bailey has told me that she does not recall thinking that Dr Greig's Tibetan Spaniels were very good specimens of the breed. Readers may have guessed from reading the preface to this book by the Lady Freda Valentine that there was considerable controversy among the pre-war breeders about ear-carriage. G. Harowitz in the supplement to *Our Dogs* (December 5th, 1930), wrote in the review of Mrs A. R. Greig's kennel, "The little Tibetan Spaniels are known as the 'Prayer Dogs' of the monasteries of Tibet. They are sweet little things and can have either drop or prick ears." They were not at all like the present day Tibetan Spaniels in England, nor at all similar to the ones given to Mrs Bailey by the late Dalai Lama, as can be easily seen from the photograph of Miss Daisy Greig with a trio of her mother's and sister's dogs, the exception being Doma in the centre of the picture.

Hutchinson's Encyclopedia in the 1930s, referring to our breed, gives us some interesting information:

> The Tibetan Spaniel is a dainty little toy dog, which can boast of being of pure descent for centuries. They have many fascinating ways and should appeal to anyone who wishes to get away from the ordinary Toy Dog. They have been bred in certain monasteries and villages in Tibet. The Tibetan Spaniel and the Pekingese have a common ancestor, but, whereas the Peke has been selectively bred to produce the grotesque dog of today, the Tibetan Spaniel has been left to develop as nature willed, hence the great difference between them.

Apart from the Greigs, the only other breeder in the 1920s and '30s about whom we have any knowledge, is Mrs Stutely Abbott, who commenced in the late 1920s with Cairn Terriers. Meeting Dr Greig who had imported two Tibetan Spaniels a year or two earlier, Mrs Abbott obtained from her a bitch, Pitti Sing of Ladkok, on breeding terms. Eventually, six puppies arrived sired by the imported dog Zemu of Ladkok. Mrs Abbott particularly fancied one of them, a red and white dog puppy, and was terrified that Dr Greig would choose to take him as one of her choice of two puppies! Mr J. L. S. Abbott can still remember his mother's sigh of relief when this puppy was not chosen. She grabbed the one that she had wanted to keep all along – he became known as Fanthorpe Nanki Poo. Mr Abbott says that, from that moment on, the Tibetans (including a Terrier) ruled the home, but Nanki always remained Mrs Abbott's favourite.

Another charming Fanthorpe anecdote, told me by Mr Abbott, concerns the late Lord Lytton, recently returned to England having been Viceroy of India. He telephoned Mrs Abbott, asked if he might see her Tibetan Spaniels, and was invited to tea. He arrived with about half a dozen scarlet morocco-covered photograph albums tooled in gold. After tea, the Tibetan Spaniels trooped into the drawing room for his inspection. His Lordship, solemnly looked at them then, turning to Mrs Abbott, said: Beautiful little dogs, but they are not Tibetan Spaniels." Apparently you could have heard a pin drop! This, after they had won at nearly every championship show in the southern half of England!

Lord Lytton then opened the photograph albums and showed them page after page of what we now know are Lhasa Apsos. Mr Abbott remembers clearly that it was a very difficult moment, but somehow they all remained very cool and terribly 'British'.

A little light relief eventually came when Lord Lytton's chauffeur, who was having tea in the kitchen, returned to his car – of which the driver's door had been left open – to find young Mr Abbott's old Bulldog bitch sitting there and daring him to get in. When Mr Abbott was called upon to remove her from the car, Lord Lytton asked if he could try. "I've never been beaten by any dog yet," he said. He was this time! When he departed, the Abbott family felt that honours were even.

Miss Peggy Abbott recalls that her stables were always full of crates of tinned salmon – for the dog! It was sold in those days for ninepence (old money) a large tin! Miss Abbott says that Fanthorpe Nanki Poo was not a small dog, but an extremely attractive, well marked red and white particolour. Unfortunately Rajah, purchased from Mr Lapwood, went blind while still quite young and, because of this, was killed by a car while sitting in the drive.

It is tragic to think of all the imported blood-lines that were once in England and are lost to us now. The only pre-war blood-line to be found, when Sir Edward and Lady Wakefield started their new dynasty after the Second World War, was through Fanthorpe Nanki Poo's son, Skyid, who also carried the Greig imported blood-lines. The breed never did gain the popularity that it should have done, perhaps because of the controversy mentioned by Mr Will Hally in *Our Dogs* (June 22nd, 1934): "The Tibetan Terriers and Tibetan Spaniels are being affected by the prejudiced judging because of confusion over the Apso–Shih Tzu breeds." Mr Hally explained that the judges were very chary of having anything to do with Tibetan canines while the discussion over this state of affairs continued. Mr Hally's opinion was that this judicial attitude was a very stupid one; he could clearly see that there was no controversy, and never had been, over the Tibetan Terrier and Tibetan Spaniel. To quote him: "These are definitely different breeds and so there is no excuse for anyone not being aware what the respective standards are . . . both Tibetan Terriers and Tibetan Spaniels are quite non-controversial as the public are realising, even if the judges are failing to do so."

It is a fitting conclusion to this chapter to acknowledge the great debt that the Tibetan breeds owe to Mr Will Hally for his careful writing which gives us most of the documentation on all the Tibetan breeds between the two world wars. Mr Hally's articles, in *Our Dogs*, breathed sanity into some rather fraught situations concerning judicial and Kennel Club confusion, especially in the 1920s and '30s.

116

He firmly supported Dr Greig's opinion that different parts of Tibet had their own breed of dog. In his Foreign Dog Fancies column, he constantly hammered this point home and, as a result, eventually achieved acceptance of the idea that the various Tibetan breeds with which we were dealing were not, as it then seemed to some people, simply variations of type within one single breed, but were a number of totally different breeds.

Mongolian Princess Telema
with a particolour Tibetan Spaniel.

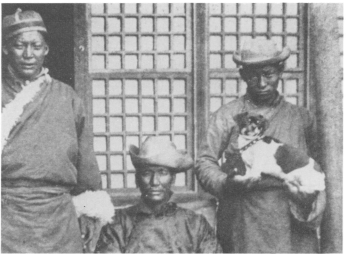

The Dzongpon and his two Clerks, of Shen-Tsa, which lies in the middle of a plain about five miles wide, in an altitude too great for any cultivation. Shen-Tsa consisted in the late 1920s of 40–50 small houses built of sun dried bricks or of sods, standing in the middle of what was then a windswept, desolate waste, surrounded by swamps. The Dzongpon was a charming and courteous old gentleman, a martyr to rheumatism. Like most Tibetan officials he had discarded the head dress of the country; he wore a lady's straw hat, broad brimmed and high in the crown and innocent of all trimming, a European hat of which he appeared to be inordinately proud and which he wore when Sir Henry Hayden and M. Cossin photographed him as they passed through Shen-Tsa. Undoubtedly another prized possession was his particolour Tibetan Spaniel. From *Sport and Travel in the Highlands of Tibet*, by Sir Henry Hayden and Cáesar Cosson published in 1927.

A Tibetan woman with a particolour Tibetan Spaniel from the book *Everest the Challenge* by Sir Francis Younghusband, published about 1936.

Man with his Tibetan Snow Lion, from a Tibetan painting (loaned by Mr Ugyan Norbu of the Tibet Society).

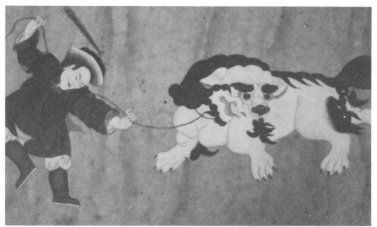

Zazzela, a novel type of dog exhibited at Crufts in 1929, an Afghan Spaniel, the property of the Hon. Mrs McLaren Morrison. (Photo: T.P.A.)

Drenjong Dakpa, A Tibetan Mastiff owned and imported by the Hon. Mrs F. M. Bailey in 1934. (Photo: T. Fall.)

The dogs Malenki and Malchik from Sven Hedin's book *Adventure in Tibet*, published in 1904, showing the rare spotted Mastiffs of the friendly dispositions, mentioned decades later by Herr M. Herrman in his book *Die Nomaden Von Tibet*, published in 1949.

Ch Jana of Lamleh, Tibetan Terrier owned by Dr Greig in 1939. (Photo: T. Fall.)

Zara of Ladkok, a Lhasa Apso
owned by Dr Greig in 1938.
(Photo: T. Fall.)

Ch Ta Chi of Taisan, Shih Tzu
owned by Lady Brownrigg in
1949. (Photo: T. Fall.)

Poulka de Dieghem, a
Havanese dog, the property of
Mme Malenfer of Paris in the
early 1900s.

Mrs McLaren Morrison's
Lhasa Terrier, India, in winter
coat.

Tomb figure of dog in glazed
earthenware, a good example from a
Chinese grave from the 1st–2nd
century A.D. (*c*.167–191). (By kind
permission of the Victoria and Albert
Museum.)

A gilt-bronze reclining model of a dog,
only an inch and a half long, now in the
Thomas D. Stimson Memorial
Collection at the Seattle Art Museum,
made by a Chinese craftsman of the Six
Dynasties, A.D. 220–589 (By kind
permission of the Seattle Art Museum,
U.S.A.) 57.128)

Recumbent dog in jade, Sung dynasty (10–13th century) from the Eumorfopoulos collection. (By kind permission of the Victoria and Albert Museum.)

'Puppy carrying Pheasant Feather', by Yi Om (a Korean artist born 1499), a 16th century hanging scroll, watercolour on silk. (By kind permission of the Philadelphia Museum of Art, U.S.A.)

'Chinese Puppies' by Marsuyama Okio, 1733–95, Shijo School.

Ch Braeduke Jhanki of Wimaro, a 1968
Tibetan Spaniel Champion. (Photo: Sally
Anne Thompson.)

A Tibetan Spaniel by Simon de Vos (Antwerp
1603–76), this is a very unusual subject for
Simon de Vos to have undertaken and leads
to the conjecture that the dog may have
belonged to a famous nobleman who was
anxious to have it painted.

'Dog in the Bamboo Grove', A.D. 1426–35, painted in the Emperor
Hsuan-Teh dynasty.

Chinese Spaniel (Coarse Type) 1700, Painter Shen Li.

Chinese Spaniel of the Best Type, this dog belonged to one of the Chinese Emperors, and was red and white. Painter Shen Cheng of P'ing-Chiang, 1700. (From Frau Olga Wegener's collection.)

Black and White Chinese Dog, about 1700. Painter Shen Chen-Lin (Feng-ch'ih).

Chinese Bowl, Taokwang period 1820.

Lady Decies' Ch Pekin Poppy, Pekingese of the early 1900s.

E-Wo Lung and E-Wo Ah from the supplement to *Our Dogs* of December 12th, 1913.

E-Wo Feng-Huang, Happa dog, also known as Chinese Pug or Peking Pug.

Dandelion, a Chinese Shar-Pei or Fighting dog, listed in the Guiness Book of Records as the world's rarest dog. He is owned by Miss Heather Ligget, imported from Hong Kong in 1981, at the time of publication he is still awaiting English Kennel Club registration. The first of this breed to come to England.

Mr L. Carnegie's Chinese Happa Dog, from the book *Toy Dogs and Their Ancestors* by Judith A. D. B. Lytton published in 1911.

A Chinese Pug or Ha Pa.

Zezo, Thibet Spaniel owned by the Hon. Mrs McLaren Morrison in 1895, and the first specimen ever to be exhibited in England, he has also been called Yezo and Komo Zezo.

A group of the Hon. Mrs McLaren Morrison's Thibet Spaniels. The second dog in the group is Yezo (imported) and next to him is his son, Grand Lhama.

Thibet Spaniel – Yatsu, an imported Thibet Spaniel.

Everest, a Thibet Spaniel owned by the Hon Mrs McLaren Morrison, one of the rarest varieties shown, considered to be most typical and interesting.

Thibet Spaniel Karpo, Property of the Hon. Mrs McLaren Morrison, London.

Lhasa, Thibet Spaniel, 1904.

Thibet Spaniel from the *Illustrated Sporting and Dramatic News* periodical of May 4th, 1912. (Photo: The British Library.)

Tibetan Spaniel in the early 1900s. (Photo: Prudence Cuming Associates.)

Tibetan Spaniel that comes from Tibet via Leh. (Photo: Prudence Cuming Associates.)

Tibetan Spaniels, the property
of J. C. White, Esq., C.I.E.
(Photo: Prudence Cuming
Associates.)

Kina, the property of
the Hon. Mrs McLaren
Morrison, Kepwick
Park, Northallerton.
(Photo: The British
Library.)

Sintu 1. A black dog purchased from
Tibet. (Photo: The British Library.)

Boojum, a black and white Palace dog
from Khatmandu, Nepal, in the
possession of Mr J. C. White from
1884–89. (Photo: The British Library.)

Gantak Rags, a black Tibetan Spaniel.
(Photo: The British Library.)

Gantak Tippu, a black dog bred by Mr J. C. White. (Photo: The British Library.)

Gantak Sebu, a sable-coloured bitch. (Photo: The British Library.)

Doma of Ladkok (imported) "Tibetian Foreign Dog, owned by Mrs A. R. Greig, winner at the Ladies Kennel Association Members show at the Crystal Palace on December 4th, 1930". (Photo: Sport & General.)

A trio of Tibetan Spaniel puppies, owned and bred by Mrs A. R. Greig in the early 1930s, showing the variation of type even then.

Miss Daisy Greig with a collection of Tibetan Spaniels, Doma of Ladkok is in the centre.

Miss Daisy Greig with a group of her mother's Tibetan Spaniels, Doma of Ladkok in front.

Kim of Ladkok. (Photo: T. Fall.)

Seu of Ladkok. (Photo: T. Fall.)

Fanthorpes Nanki Poo
(from the left) with
Fanthorpe Nanki Tu and
Rajah. (Photo: T. Fall.)

Mughiwuli, Sir Edward and Lady Wakefield's first Tibetan Spaniel, dam of Garpon and Potala.

Miss Diana Hawkins with Garpon (on the left) and Potala, born in 1941.

Mrs (later Lady) E. B. Wakefield of Breadsall, Derby, with her three Tibetan Spaniels seen at Crufts on February 11th, 1950. From the left: Chuni La with her sire Lama (believed to be the only picture of him in existence), and her dam Dolma. (Photo: Northcliffe Newspapers Group Ltd.)

'The Duchess' – Dolma, with a Tibetan teapot.

Dolma's first litter sired by Lama. From the left, Shipki La, who was to become Mrs Bagot's stud dog, Sing Trub La who died young, Bogo La who later won a Best of Breed at Crufts show, Shemo La who was a brood bitch and show winner. (Photo: Westmoreland Gazette.)

From the left: Kye Ho S'Gokyi, Toomai of Furzyhurst and Kye Ho Tumi.

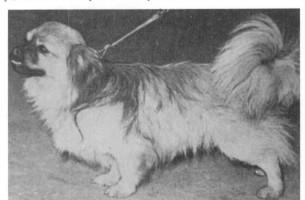

Kyipup, winner of two
Challenge Certificates, a
son of Garpon and
Potala.

Miss H. Elam with (left) Shim Rde La of Padua, a
son of Seng Ge La out of Shemo La; and one of her
two foundation brood bitches, Furzyhurst Pyari
Larki of Padua.

Mrs D. M. Battson's foundation brood bitch Szufung Lotus of Furzyhurst born in 1957; aged 8 months old.

From the left: Mrs F. Dudman with Ch Ramblersholt Ram-A-Din, the judge Miss H. Elam, and Mrs F. Davies with Ch Kando of Furzyhurst, at the Ladies Kennel Association Championship show in 1963. (Photo: C. M. Cooke & Son.)

Momo of Szufung, half-sister of Ch Tomu of Szufung, born in 1962, CC winner in 1965, bred and owned by Mrs D. M. Battson. (Photo: C. M. Cooke & Son.)

Miss S. Selby's Ama of Szufung winner of two Challenge Certificates. (Photo: A. Roslin-Williams.)

Pontac Keun Chang, owned by Mrs S. Rank and bred by Mr and Mrs Gill, winner of one Challenge Certificate, sire of Ch Sivas Wimaro Ti Mu and of Sivas Karamba. (Photo: C. M. Cooke & Son.)

Sivas Lotus, a black and white bitch bred by Mrs Bagot, sired by Pubu Levens out of Gser Pho La, Miss S. Selby's foundation brood bitch and dam of Ch Braeduke Sivas Padmini. (Photo: A. Roslin-Williams.)

Ch Braeduke Lotus Bud of Szufung, bred by Mrs D. M. Battson, sired by Ch Khan Dee of Curwenna out of Ch Yaso of Szufung, Best of Breed at Crufts show 1968. (Photo: Sally Anne Thompson.)

Sivas Gombu, black-and-tan male owned and bred by Miss S. Selby, sire of Miss P. M. Mayhew's Mingshang Sivas Tamarisk. (Photo: A. Roslin-Williams.)

Ch Ma-Ni of Amcross a 1971 Champion bitch, owned and bred by Mrs D. Jenkins and Miss M. C. Hourihane. (Photo: Diane Pearce.)

From left to right: Mrs C. Jeary (now Mrs Clapham) with Ch Braeduke Channa, the judge The Lady Freda Valentine and Mrs R Bichener with Ch Tze-Tze of Curwenna, at the Three Counties Championship show in 1969. (Photo: C. M. Cooke & Son.)

Ming-Y of Northanger, Mrs K. Newbury's Challenge Certificate winner, who is in the pedigrees of many of today's winning Tibetan Spaniels. (Photo: Diane Pearce.)

Rutherglen Lho-Ri, owned and bred by Mrs J. M. Smith, winner of one Challenge Certificate, photographed as a puppy. (Photo: Diane Pearce.)

Ch Rowena of Padua, the first ever Tibetan Spaniel Champion in 1961, winner of 12 Challenge Certificates and for many years the holder of the title of the top winning bitch in this breed. Bred and owned by Miss H. Elam and Miss Braye.

Ch Kye Ho Za-Khyi, bred by Mrs L. Jones, who still holds the title of the joint top winning male in this breed with 15 Challenge Certificates. (Photo: Diane Pearce.)

Ch Windameres Braeduke Champa, a 1972 Champion dog, winner of 15 Challenge Certificates, bred by the Author, owned and campaigned by Mrs G. S. Vines. (Photo: Diane Pearce.)

Ch Huntglen Braeduke Ta-Ra-Ni, bred by and campaigned by the Author, dam of four Champions and winner of 13 Challenge Certificates, for many years the breed's top winning bitch up until her death in June 1980, at fourteen and a half years old. (Photo: Sally Anne Thompson.)

Ch Wildhern Genghiz Khan, owned and bred by Mrs J. D. P. Micklethwait, the first Anglo-Indian male to win his title in England in 1975 and the first Wildhern Champion.

Ch Windameres Lho-Zah-Mi, the first Tibetan Spaniel in England to win a Utility Group in 1977 at Birmingham National Championship show, bred and owned by Mrs G. S. Vines. (Photo: Diane Pearce.)

Ch Braeduke Whitewisp Hara Nor, a 1972 Champion, bred by Mr and Mrs G. W. Grounds and owned by the Author, dam of six Champions sired by three different stud dogs; she holds the British brood bitch record. (Photo: Diane Pearce.)

From left to right: A group of Amcross Champions, Ch Part-Li Amcross a particolour male; Ch Amcross Parti Peace a particolour bitch; Ch Amcross Vosta Kushi Kee the winner of 15 Challenge Certificates and joint title holder for this breed's top winning Tibetan Spaniel; Ch Amcross Am-Ban, an Anglo-Chinese descendant and the second ever Tibetan Spaniel to win a Utility Group in England, at the West of England Ladies Kennel Society's Championship show in 1979. (Photo: V. Hourihane.)

Ch Northanger Kenchira Dikki of Wildhern, a 1975 Champion male from the Indian born imported bitch Dikki Dolma, sired by Ming-Y of Northanger. Bred by Mrs H. Joyce and owned by Mrs J. D. P. Micklethwait. (Photo: D. Pearce.)

Ch Braeduke Poo-Khyi, a 1979 Champion, the present title holder of this breed's joint top winning Tibetan Spaniel in England, with 15 Challenge Certificates. Bred by Mrs H. Butler and owned and campaigned by the Author. (Photo: F. Garwood.)

From the left: Kendoman Misty Moonbeam and her litter brother Kendoman Midnight Shadow, sired by Ch Tsingay Master-Ly. Showing how black-and-tans can vary in colour and markings. Owned and bred by Miss J. Chapman.

Ch Tsingay Master-Ly, a son of Ch Ram Chandra of Amcross, won his title in 1977. Owned and bred by Mrs P. Atkins. (Photo: Diane Pearce.)

Ch Sebastian of Deanford, a son of Ch Amcross Tarquin, a 1980 Champion owned by Mrs A. Keen.

Kensing Rhum-Me of Dockenfield, winner of three Reserve Challenge Certificates, a daughter of Ch Braeduke Rhum-Bu of Kensing owned by Mrs A. Hamer, bred by Mrs G. J. Lilley. (Photo: Diane Pearce.)

Dockenfield Cedar, son of Ch Kensing Oscar out of Kensing Rhum-Me of Dockenfield, a Reserve Challenge Certificate winner owned by Major J. E. Tye. (Photo: Sally Anne Thompson.)

Left to right: Ch Kensing Ra, a 1980 Champion, and his litter-sister Ch Kensing Rosetta, owned and bred by Mrs G. J. Lilley, photographed at 8 months old, sired by Tangwell Gu Cham Midas out of Ch Kensing Ri-Tse.

Ch Parkplace Prim Rose, a 1980 Champion bitch, owned and bred by Lady Dalrymple-Hay. (Photo: Diane Pearce.)

Ch Tan Ku from Amscor, a 1978 Champion bitch sired by Ch Windameres Lho-Zah-Mi, owned by Miss V. Hourihane and bred by Mrs G. S. Vines. (Photo: Diane Pearce.)

A Shamau family group: (front, left to right) Silverset Shireen, Shamau Pipitang, Ch Shamau Ba-Ti-Ka, Shamau Dege Taikala, and at the back Ch Shamau Tranka the first English particolour Champion; all owned by Miss M. Sharp who bred them all with the exception of Shireen, her foundation brood bitch.

Ch Rutherglen Tai-Mar of Taimani a 1976 Champion, owned by Mrs A. Wilson and bred by Mrs J. M. Smith, a daughter of Ch Windameres Braeduke Champa out of Rutherglen Lho-Ri. (Photo: Diane Pearce.)

Left to right: Champions Both, Ch Amcross Jimbu and Ch Amcross Jinda, litter-brother and -sister, sired by Ch Part-Li Amcross, bred and owned by Mrs D. Jenkins and Miss M. C. Hourihane. (Photo: T. Fall.)

Ch Simpasture Topaz, a 1980 Champion, bred by Mrs S. W. Beale and owned by Mr and Mrs T. Sowerby, a son of the Anglo-Indian black-and-tan dog Wildhern Magic Dragon of Simpasture out of a Ch Braeduke Nimmi daughter. (Photo: F. Garwood.)

Braeduke Colphil Seng-Kyi, winner of the Dog Challenge Certificate, Best of Breed and Best in Show at the Tibetan Spaniel Association's fourteenth Championship show in 1981, bred by Mrs H. Butler and owned by the Author. (Photo: P. Diment.)

Ch Su-Li of Braeduke, a 1980 Champion bitch, bred by Miss D. Dodson and Miss M. Flint and owned by the Author.

Ch Braeduke Nimmi, sire of seven Champions and litter-brother of three Champions, sired by Ch Ram Chandra of Amcross out of Ch Braeduke Whitewisp Hara Nor, owned and bred by the Author. (Photo: T. Fall.)

Huntglen Rosaree Akasha, bred by Mrs J. Hubbersty, later owned by Mrs A. Young, the first ever English particolour Challenge Certificate winner. Trophy winner for Best Particolour at Crufts show in 1966, 1967, 1969, and 1970. Her daughter won this in 1968. (Photo: Diane Pearce.)

Ch Friarland Bo-Peep of Sharbonne a 1981 Champion, daughter of T.S.C.A. Ch Braeduke Dung-Ka out of Colphil Ku Lu, owned by Miss Y. Border and bred by Mrs V. Armstrong; Bo-Peep won the Bitch Challenge Certificate and Best of Breed Crufts show 1981. (Photo: Diane Pearce.)

Bruesown Dun-Dun, a son of Ch Amcross Tarquin, winner of two Challenge Certificates, bred and owned by Miss B. E. M. Croucher. (Photo: P. Diment.)

English and Irish Champion Braeduke Am-Ra, bred by the Author, son of Rama of Amcross out of the Hawaiian born Import English Ch Braeduke Ama Kuluh. Ch Am-Ra is now owned by Miss M. M. Walsh and Miss M. E. Flynn in Dublin. (Photo: Diane Pearce.)

Swedish Ch Ba-Ba, particolour male born in Hawaii and litter-brother of English Ch Braeduke Ama Kuluh, photographed at 8 years old. Owned by M. and B. Herjeskog. (Photo: Pax.)

International and Nordic Ch
Lässebackens Afrodite, sired
by Swedish and Norwegian Ch
Strömkarlens Bzanba, himself
a son of Swedish Ch Ba-Ba out
of Ch Colphil Chu-Li. Owned
by M. and B. Herjeskog.
(Photo: Wilhelm Dufwa.)

International and
Nordic Ch Braeduke
Amdo Chu, litter-
brother of English Ch
Amcross Am-Ban, bred
by Mrs D. Jenkins and
Miss M. C. Hourihane.

International and
Nordic Ch Fieldlan
Fatima.

English Ch Braeduke Sivas Padmini, a 1966 Champion, dam of International and Nordic Ch Huntglen Rampa and the great-great-great-grandmother of English Ch Braeduke Poo-Khyi. (Photo: A. Roslin-Williams.)

Finnish Ch Habanas Charli, owned and bred by Mrs Riitta Amperla.

Nordic Ch and Winner 1978 Central Point Virginia, owned and bred by Mrs Orvokki Keskinen of Finland, a daughter of International and Nordic Ch Zalatino of Zlazano out of Finnish Ch Zessica of Zlazano.

From left to right: Habanas
Chaana, Zinos of Zlazano
(Santtu) and their daughter
Sandriina, all owned by Mrs
R. Amperla. (Photo:
Kennel Habanas.)

Mrs Salme Vestelin's
Finnish and Norwegian Ch
Sajasan Belinda, the top
winning Tibetan Spaniel in
Finland for 1981, winner of
the Toy Group on 20.7.81 at
the Lappeenranta show. A
great-grand-daughter of
T.S.C.A. Ch Braeduke
Dung-Ka, Wildhern
A-Rabella, Ch Braeduke
Lotus Bud of Szufung and
of Ch Braeduke Sivas
Padmini.

Norwegian and Swedish Ch Eicie-
Ka-Gawa, a daughter of English,
Nordic and International Ch Lho-
Cham of Windameres, owned by
Solveig Berge of Larvik, Norway
and bred by Fru Aina Skarin.

International and Danish Ch Braeduke Mingmar Choden, who became the 52nd Braeduke Champion in October 1981, owned by Fru Bente Jörgensen.

Danish, Luxembourg, German and International Ch U Wong of Jo Gya Kang, sired by Braeduke Chumna the litter-brother of Ch Heyvan Jola, out of a Ch Beaver of Eulyn daughter. Owned by Fru Bente Jörgensen of Denmark and bred by Frau Irmgard Wienekamp of West Germany.

Left to right: International and World Ch Braeduke Pat-Me, with International and Italian Ch Braeduke Norbu Asma, Asma's son Yadruk-Pa Kang Tchup at nine months old with his mother Braeduke Rje-Doma. All owned by Mrs Nina Alexander of Italy.

Braeduke Gser Phur, a first prize winner in Oregon, U.S.A. in a Miscellaneous class, now owned by Mrs D. Lilley in British Colombia, Canada, and the sire of the first ever Canadian Tibetan Spaniel bitch Champion. (Photo: Carl Lindemaier.)

Mr Leo Kearns, the 'father' of the Tibetan Spaniel breed in America, with his English Champion male Yakrose Chiala of Amcross.

'Missie', or Doghouse Dream Baby, aged twelve years old.

Witneylea Kulha, imported December 1969 at five months of age. The first T.S.C.A. Champion in the breed, he is owned by Mrs Joan Child.

English Ch Peterstown Drom of Szufung, sire of Doghouse Dream Baby, he is a son of Ch Tomu of Szufung out of Szufung Lotus of Furzyhurst, owned by Mr C. F. Poole, M.R.C.V.S., and was bred by Mrs D. M. Battson. (Photo: C. M. Cooke & Son.)

A historical photograph of Mrs Peter Neckles on the left, and Mrs Patrick Child in 1971, with some of the foundation stock sent to America from England.

Lower left to right: T.S.C.A.
Ch Braeduke Gantsa with
Ambrier's Bet R Parti Girl.
Rear left to right: Daji Dynasty
Warlord of Bet R, Bet R Suey
Sauce, and Braeduke Litsi. Far
rear (smiling): B.D.A.
Bermuda Ch and T.S.C.A. Ch
Kharekhola Lasya. All owned
by Mr and Mrs Herbert Rosen.

T.S.C.A. Ch Braeduke Dung-
Ka with co-owner Mrs P.
Kohler at the Annapolis
Kennel Club show in 1979.
Winner of the Miscellaneous
class under judge Mr Stine.
(Photo: Wm P. Gilbert.)

T.S.C.A. Ch Bim's Twin Socks
Kamla, sired by T.S.C.A. Ch
Braeduke Dung-Ka out of
Bim's Dusty Tara, owned by
Ms Mallory Cosby and bred by
Mr and Mrs T. Whiting from
their Indian imported blood-
lines.(Photo: Wm P. Gilbert.)

A Californian Match, showing (left to right) Judge Mary Walsh, Mrs R. Wells with Camas Tibs Bhabu, Mr Bill Wells with Camas Tibs Clarion Call of Tudor's, and Mrs M. Jennings with Camas Tibs Moon of Jade of Tudor's, where they won Best of Breed Adult, Best of Breed Puppy and Best Opposite Sex Puppy as well.(Photo: Jayne Langdon.)

Australian Ch Leagay Jholi La, daughter of Aust. Ch Braeduke Lhakpa Chedi out of New Zealand and Aust. Ch Braeduke Regina, owned and bred by Mrs M. Leach. (Photo: K. Barkleigh-Shute.)

Australian Ch Leagay Gelugpa, owned by Mrs M. and Miss L. Dogger. (Photo: K. Barkleigh-Shute.)

New Zealand Ch Braeduke
Mingmo, bred by the
Author and sired by
Braeduke Lu-Ting out of
U.S.A. Import Kalimpong
Ming Dordja of Braeduke,
owned by Mrs D. Cassells.
(Photo: Ann McSweeney.)

Ladakh Djouley, Tibetan Terrier male, found by
his American owner Mr Thomas Leathers
Caldwell at Swayambho in Nepal, in July 1975,
and now resides outside Paris. Because he does
not have a pedigree he is unable to win the title of
International Champion, but he has nine
CACIBs and seventeen CACs to his credit. In
addition he was Champion of Spain in 1981, the
first Champion in the breed born in Asia since
Thoombay of Ladkok, who was born in Tibet in
1927 – and became an English Champion in 1938.
Djouley has also won three times Vice Champion
of France and the Reserve CAC at the Paris show
in 1978, 1979 and 1980.

Jigme Khampa, the sire of Yasodhara and Dikki Dolma. He was born in Tibet and is registered at the Indian Kennel Club.

Yangchelna, the dam of the Indian Imports Yasodhara and Dikki Dolma, she too was born in Tibet and is registered at the Indian Kennel Club.

Honeybun, a particolour bitch born in Hong Kong from unknown parents who came from Tibet. Dam of Swedish Ch Ba-Ba and also of English Ch Braeduke Ama Kuluh, Honeybun now has many Champion descendants all over the world.

English Ch Braeduke
Ama Kuluh, born in
Honolulu, Hawaii and
the founder of the
English Anglo-Chinese
dynasty, bred by Mrs J.
Hacker and owned by
the Author. (Photo: T.
Fall.)

Tashi Dorji, found and
imported into America by
Mrs P. H. Sorum (formerly
Miss Marguerite Cotsworth
Perkins). Found in
Darjeeling, India, this
black-and-white particolour
dog is the sire of the
Author's bitch Kalimpong
Ming Dordja of Braeduke.

Kalimpong Ming Dordja of Braeduke, bred by Mrs P. H. Sorum in America and imported and
owned by the Author. Ming is an English Reserve Challenge Certificate winner and the dam of
three Champions from her first litter. Photographed on the day she came out of quarantine
kennels at just over one year of age. (Photo: P. Diment.)

Clawson Raibrai Yin, bred by Dr B. Holcombe in Finland and imported and owned by Mrs M. Gidman.

Dr B. Holcombe's Yang, born in Russia and the sire of Clawson Raibrai Yin.

Amroth's Own Tigger, a Nepal born male owned by Mrs P. Child in America.

His Majesty The King of Bhutan, Jigme Dorji Wangchuk, with his constant companion, a particolour dog named Khomto (said to mean 'My Little Baby'). (Photo: *The Asia Magazine*, Aug. 1968.)

Chuni La, winner of the first ever Bitch CC awarded in England, at Crufts show 1960, under Mr Leo Wilson.

A historical photograph of Crufts show 1960. Left to right: Mrs Taylor with Lama of Szufung, Lady Gloria Cottesloe with Dolma of Szufung, Lady Wakefield with Seng Ge La, Squadron Leader Dewar with Chemo of Szufung, and Mrs D. M. Battson with Szufung Lotus of Furzyhurst. Seng Ge La was the sire and Lotus the dam of the other three in this photograph. (Photo: F. W. Simms.)

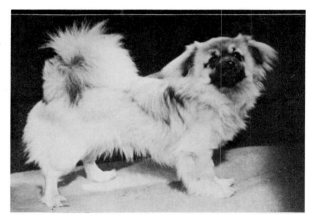

Kye Ho Tumi, the Dog
CC winner at Crufts
show 1960.

Seng Ge La, the
Reserve Dog CC winner
at Crufts show 1960.

Richard Taylor holding Sherpa of Padua bred by
Miss Elam and sired by Ch Kye Ho Za-Khyi, Mr
Shaw Taylor, the well known Television
personality is holding Redgame Artist, a son of
Kensing Ano-Rak of Amcross.

Fanthorpes Nanki Poo owned and bred by Mrs S. Abbott.

Left to right: Yang Gau-U La and Toomai of Furzyhurst.

Ranee of Glenholme.

Chumurti La winner of Best of Breed at Crufts shows before CCs were allocated to the breed. Owned by Mrs R. Bagot.

Left to right: Bogo Poo (looking up) and Ran-Ba, two Kye Ho brood bitches owned by Mrs E. Peach. Bogo Poo was a daughter of Dolma, of the original type fine silky coat and with a small pointed face. Ran-Ba had a thicker, woolly coat with a broader head.

Ch Tomu of Szufung a 1965 Champion dog owned and bred by Mrs D. M. Battson. (Photo: C. M. Cooke & Son.)

Ch Sivas Ten-Sing of Myarlune, winner of nine Challenge Certificates including Crufts show 1965. (Photo: A. Roslin-Williams.)

Braeduke Tamara of Szufung, a daughter of Ch Tomu of Szufung out of Szufung Lotus of Furzyhurst and full sister of Amcross Seto of Szufung, dam of three Champions. Owned by the Author and bred by Mrs D. M. Battson. (Photo: A. Roslin-Williams.)

7 The New Tibetan Spaniel Dynasty from 1938

Centuries before the beginning of the Christian era, at a time when our own woad-painted ancestors were roaming the forests of Britain, Tibetan Spaniels were the treasured pets at cultured oriental courts. Indeed so highly were they prized in ancient times, that they formed part of the tribute which was paid annually to the Emperors of China in Pekin, by successive ruling dynasties at Lhasa, the capital of Tibet.

It was as a result of this practice that the breed, which is considered to have originated in Tibet, became established in China. There is no doubt that it is the Tibetan Spaniel that is portrayed in the most ancient Chinese paintings, tapestries and ceramics; so it is more than possible that they could have become, through being crossed with the Chinese Pug or another of the ancient Chinese breeds, the ancestor of the Pekingese; perhaps also of other toy breeds.

This is the legend that the Author was told when she owned her first Tibetan Spaniel in 1962, and which eventually fired her imagination and caused her to search deeper into the background of the breed. She could well believe that being the proud possessor of a Tibetan Spaniel would make any Lama or Monk set a very high value upon them; they were treasured for their gaiety and animation, for their intelligent companionship and for the practical services they could render. Their fur was used for spinning, they lay on the battlement walls of the Dzongs and Gompas, giving tongue to warn of the advent of strangers to the gates, or of wolves attacking the monastery flocks below.

At one time, it was thought that these little dogs were trained to turn prayer wheels. Sadly, this myth has been exploded. It was a charming thought that these little dogs should have been trained to turn a revolving cylinder containing tightly rolled parchment on which is recorded, over and over again, the mystic Buddhist formula, '*Om Mani Padmi Haum*' (O God in the Jewel of the Flower of the Lotus). It is believed that with each revolution of this cylinder the prayers are given an impetus which takes them directly to Heaven.

Due to the efforts of Lady Freda Valentine, the Tibetan Breeds Association was formed in 1934 for all the Tibetan breeds. This Association remained active until 1957 when the Tibetan Apso people, (as the Lhasa Apso breed was then known), broke away to form their own breed club. There were very few Tibetan Spaniel members in the Association: Lady Wakefield, Mrs R. Bagot, Miss J. Hervey-Cecil, Miss Braye and Miss Elam. Funds were low, most of the cups and trophies were for Apsos and Mastiffs, so the Club started with just two Tibetan Spaniel trophies. A few months later, Mrs E. Peach and Mrs L. Jones joined, then Miss Simmons and Mrs Thornton, so it must have been a bitter blow when Dr Greig told them, in 1958, that she wished to form her own Tibetan Terrier Association.

Miss Theobald who, for a short time, had been the Honorary Secretary of the Tibetan Breeds Association, then retired. Miss Hilda Elam of the Padua kennel took over in her place. The newly-formed Tibetan Spaniel Association held its first Committee Meeting at the Friends Meeting House, Euston Road, London, on August 18th, 1958. The first Annual General Meeting was held at the Holborn Town Hall on January 31st, 1959, where Major John Hubberstey, whose wife had the Rosaree Tibetan Spaniels, was appointed as Honorary Treasurer.

When Miss Elam retired in 1964, her office was taken by Major J. Hubberstey, until 1967. Then Miss P. Burnett, of the Tibskips Tibetan Spaniels, held office until her retirement in 1976. Since then, the Author, then Mrs Joan Smith of Rutherglen, and currently Mrs June Tomlinson of Jaykay, have been Honorary Secretaries of the Tibetan Spaniel Association.

Very few of today's breeders and exhibitors will be able to recall how necessary it was, in the 1950s and 1960s especially, to encourage every puppy buyer to join the Association, just as it was absolutely essential to boost the annual Kennel Club Registrations for our breed in order to obtain Challenge Certificates which had first been granted in 1960. The year 1976 brought forth a new Kennel Club system of registration which no longer clearly gives any precise indication as to how many puppies have been born annually. The old system meant that dedicated breeders, like Miss Selby of Sivas and Miss Hervey-Cecil of Furzyhurst, often registered puppies sired by their stud dogs and born to pet-owners' bitches, even registering puppies which had died after birth.

Slowly and gradually, the breed began to make progress. The Association fought hard to get classes for the breed put on at both Open and Championship shows, and, even where there were no Challenge Certificates, the classes were well supported in those days. This often meant the Association guaranteeing the classification and paying up when entries did not cover the prize money.

The novice and the newcomer to the breed should remember that a small band of dedicated people worked very hard indeed to get the Tibetan Spaniel breed in the strong position that it is today. It was often very difficult to sell the puppies of what was then a rare, little known breed. This was extremely discouraging to the dedicated breeders who had to curtail their breeding programmes and thereby lessen the genetic pool of blood-lines. More often than not the stud dogs were 'difficult' about mating bitches – one of them would only mate a bitch if her head was covered with a piece of black velvet! There were very few keen studs and, of course, these were more widely used than the others.

Interest began to increase after the first milestone in 1960, when the Kennel Club granted to the Tibetan Spaniel breed Championship show status with Challenge Certificates. It was necesssary to try and keep up the annual Kennel Club registrations in order to get classes and CCs at the Championship shows, but with the small numbers of litters born, and the small size of the litters – often one, sometimes two and three puppies was then considered to be a very good-sized litter – indeed, it was difficult to make up Champions and to win Junior Warrant points.

In 1965, Sivas Lakshmi won the first Junior Warrant in our breed, with Braeduke Jhanki of Wimaro in 1967 becoming the first male to do so. In 1969 Braeduke Sivas Supi Yaw Lat was the first black-and-tan to win a Junior Warrant; in 1970 Witneylea Tupence was the first black-and-tan male to win one. In particolours the first Junior Warrant winner was Ch Tomarans Lotti Lu in 1973, followed by the first particolour male to win a Junior Warrant, Ch Part-Li Amcross, in 1976. This will perhaps show how difficult it was to win with the rarer and more unusual colours, all too often judges have been, and some still are, colour biased. It is time that everyone learned that a good Tibetan Spaniel can be any colour and, unlike some of the other Asian breeds, there is no incorrect coat colour in Tibetan Spaniels – even liver is permitted!

Other important milestones in the history of the Tibetan Spaniel breed in this country, have been the Utility Group winners at general Championship shows. The first to do so was Ch Windameres Lho-Zah-Mi at the Southern Counties in 1977; he was then followed by two more in 1979, all three were males; Ch Amcross Am-Ban won the Utility Group at W.E.L.K.S. Show; then Ch Amcross Pundit at the Border Union Show a few months later. It is interesting to note that two of these dogs descend from imported bitches: Ch Lho-Zah-Mi from Dikki Dolma and Ch Amcross Am-Ban from Ch Braeduke Ama Kuluh.

Ch Sivas Mesa and her half-sister Ch Huntglen Braeduke Ta-Ra-Ni were the first ever Tibetan Spaniels to win a Best in Show at an All Breeds Open Show. The ultimate ambition of most Tibetan Spaniel exhibitors has not yet been achieved – for a Tibetan Spaniel to win a Best in Show award at a general Championship show, preferably at Crufts!

English Kennel Club Annual Registrations for Tibetan Spaniels from 1959–1980

1959	1960	1961	1962	1963	1964	1965	1966	1967	1968	1969	1970	1971
58	64	48	113	98	101	154	137	197	284	305	445	511

1972	1973	1974	1975	1976	1977	1978	1979	1980
582	616	669	559	289*	221*	484*	591*	516*

*denotes a change in the English Kennel Club's registration system, these are the totals for those dogs entered into the Active Register and are by no means representative in any way of the dogs being bred in this country.

In 1967 the late Mr Fred Cross drew, what was for those days, a record entry of one hundred and thirty dogs making three hundred class entries, for the first ever Tibetan Spaniel Association's breed club Open show. This was in fact the first ever show confined just to Tibetan Spaniels in the British Isles. Best in Show was won by Miss Selby's Ch Sivas Wimaro Ti-Mu.

Another historical milestone for the Tibetan Spaniel Association was in 1968 when the first breed club Championship show was held. The Tibetan Spaniel Association's first ever Championship show was judged by Mr J. H. Braddon on October 19th in that year. There were one hundred and six dogs making two hundred class entries in twenty-one classes. Best in Show and winner of the Bitch Challenge Certificate was the Author's Ch Braeduke Tam-Cho who is now owned by Miss M. Heaton, and she is still alive at the time of writing this manuscript. The Dog CC winner was Mrs L. R. M-Donaldson's Ch Kye Ho Za-Khyi; at the time he was over ten years old.

In 1968 there were only twelve sets of Challenge Certificates to be won at twelve general Championship shows. To compare and assess the progress of the breed, we have twenty-six sets of CCs in 1981 at general Championship shows, plus three more additional sets for each of the three British breed clubs. A 'set' is two, one for each sex. There has been a tremendous upsurge of interest in the breed, both as pets and also for showing.

The next breed club to be formed was the South Western Tibetan Spaniel Association, inaugurated by Mrs Donaldson of the Eulyn prefix in the spring of 1975. This Club held its first Open Show in August of the same year, and their first Championship show was in March 1978.

The next English breed club was formed by Mr Norman Charlton of the Copdene prefix, in the north of England; the Northern Tibetan Spaniel Club was officially recognised by the Kennel Club in 1977, and they held their first Open show in that year. In November 1980 the Northern Club held their first Championship show.

The increasing interest in Tibetan Spaniels produced a world record entry for Mrs Gwen Broadley to judge in October 1980, with the Tibetan Spaniel Association's Championship show producing one hundred and ninety-seven dogs making over four hundred class entries. Both the Challenge Certificate winners descended from the imports, Best in Show winner Ch Braeduke Poo-Khyi won her thirteenth CC which made her the top winning living bitch in the British Isles. Mr and Mrs T. Sowerby's male Ch Simpasture Topaz won the Dog CC and Best Opposite Sex, he is a double descendant of Dikki Dolma and Ch Poo-Khyi is a granddaughter of Ch Braeduke Ama Kuluh.

There are various differences between *Kennel Gazette* entries and show catalogues and it is virtually impossible to know which is correct. Fanthorpe also appears with an 's'; Ama Dablam of Furzyhurst also appears as Furzyhurst Ama Dablam, Kye Ho as Kyeho, and so on. Senge La has also been written as Seng Ge La or as Seng Gela, and so I have used what I consider to be correct.

To explain to overseas readers how our Kennel Club system works, and what is required to make up a Champion in England, it is necessary to start at the beginning and try to make it as simple as possible.

Up until and including 1966, there was just the overloaded Non-Sporting group with thirty-three breeds. This was sub-divided in 1967 and the Utility Group was formed with nineteen different breeds (excluding some without Challenge Certificate status which are virtually non-existent in this country). All the so-called Asiatic breeds are now in the Utility Group (i.e. Chow Chows, Lhasa Apsos, Shih Tzus, Tibetan Spaniels and Tibetan Terriers). At the present time there are two Tibetan Mastiffs registered at the Kennel Club who died in quarantine before they could be exhibited and in September 1981 the breed has officially been included in the Working Group.

Prior to 1977, the allocation of Challenge Certificates was based upon the total number of dogs registered during the previous three years. Commencing in 1978, the new system is based upon the number of exhibits for each breed entered at the general Championship shows in their own breed classes. In 1980 Tibetan Spaniels had twenty-six sets of Challenge Certificates for general Championship shows in England, Scotland and Wales which indicates the progress of the breed.

CC is an abbreviation for Challenge Certificate: The Kennel Club's award for Best of Sex in the Breed at a Championship show.

RCC or Res. CC: an abbreviation for Reserve Challenge Certificate; this is the Kennel Club's award for the Reserve Best of Sex in breed at a Championship show, the exhibit being of such merit as to be worthy of the CC should the winner be disqualified.

Ch: the title of Champion, again an abbreviation. The title of Champion shall attach to any dog awarded three Challenge Certificates under three different judges, at least one of them to be awarded when the dog is over the age of one year.

J.W. or Junior Warrant: awarded by the Kennel Club to a dog (or bitch) that has obtained, whilst under 18 months of age, the twenty-five points necessary to qualify in accordance with the schedule of points. For each 1st prize in breed classes at Championship shows with CCs for the breed – three points. For each 1st prize in breed classes at a Championship show without CCs for the breed, or at an Open show (no CCs awarded at Open shows) – one point.

Unfortunately, there is not space to list everyone's Junior Warrant winners, nor to mention their names or owners; just as it impossible to name all breeders or owners of Champions or CC winners. The choice of dominant stud dogs and brood bitches is entirely the Author's own, based on observation over the years. They are not written down in alphabetical order because so many are closely linked together genetically. Believing that sensibly *line-bred* pedigree produces better type and quality than a total outcross or inbred pedigree, those considered to be dominant and influential have been picked out.

Injudicious breeding will of course weaken dominant strains and it is sad to think that the modern breeders tend to use the winning stud dog rather than the dog that sires the winners. Doubtless it is due to economic reasons and those of time and distance that we have now reached an era when even the smallest breeders keep their own stud dog, regardless of whether he carries the same faults as their own bitches, or whether his pedigree produces the dominant line-breeding for which they should be aiming. But as we all have to find out – often the hard way – you learn more by your mistakes than your successes!

The pedigrees in the appendix will help when reading this chapter. They should enable most people to work back their pedigrees to the Greig imports of the late 1920s and early 1930s.

The Author apologises to anyone whose name, or those of their dogs or photographs have been omitted, but space was limited. The rest of this chapter is intended to make the point that certain stud dogs and brood bitches have good dominant blood-lines which for many generations continue on down to their descendants.

Sir Edward Wakefield and his wife were responsible for reintroducing the Tibetan Spaniel to England after their almost complete extinction during the Second World War. In Sir Edward's book *Past Imperative* (1966), he refers to the Tibetan Spaniel as the Gyakhi. Writing of Dolma, Sir Edward said:

> The Maharaja of Sikkim wanted to reward me for my services but I could not, of course, accept a present in the usual sense of the word. However I did tell him that, if he could obtain from Tibet a Gyakhi (Tibetan Spaniel) bitch, my wife who wanted to re-introduce the breed to England, would be delighted. Gyakhis are the treasured pets and watchdogs of Tibetan Monasteries, and the monks are no more ready to part with a Gyakhi than a desert Arab to part with his mare. I did not know it at the time but the Maharaja was patron of a monastery at Phari Dzong in the Chumbi valley of south Tibet and had no difficulty in obtaining a young Gyakhi bitch for me. I had forgotten all about my suggestion to the Maharaja when, some months later, his emissary clothed in a long broad-sleeved robe, arrived at my house in New Delhi. He held in both hands a purple silk cushion and on the cushion, fast asleep, lay a golden-haired Gyakhi. Her name was Dolma and she was about four months old. Her children, and grand-children and great-grand-children have won countless awards at Crufts; and she herself ruled our Derbyshire household until in 1962, old age led (she was a Buddhist) to her translation.

Sir Edward in his book told of another Gyakhi:

> Lunching with a Tibetan official of high rank was a novel experience for me, I was entranced by his Gyakhi which was his constant companion and shared his bed and board. It was literally a lap dog for, when he was sitting, it lay across his hands, concealed in the broad

sleeves of his robe. An animated hot water bottle, it kept him warm by day and night. The cold can be intense in Tibet, but it is greatly mitigated for those honoured human beings who have the privilege of a Tibetan Spaniel.

In his Maiden Speech as a Member of the House of Commons, on November 20th, 1950, Sir Edward Wakefield spoke of the Communist invasion of Tibet by the Chinese, and said:

I strongly support what the Honourable Member for Birmingham Northfield (Mr Blackburn) has said about the pacific nature of the Tibetans. They really are the most peace-loving nation on earth, and are incapable of fighting. They have no wish to fight. They have no means wherewith to fight. I have attended a Military display in Gartok, the capital of Western Tibet, and the arms used were bows and arrows. I have at this moment, living in my home in Derbyshire, a family of Tibetans. They are actually Tibetan dogs, but they manifest all the characteristics of the Tibetan people. When a stranger appears they will go and bark at him; but if he advances they themselves retreat to another point of vantage, and then go on barking. If, in due course, the intruder establishes himself, they accept the fact.

Tibetan Spaniels can still occasionally be found in monasteries, but perhaps not always in their pure form. Dr Lotte Kahler from West Germany travelled to Northern India and Nepal in 1970 and found some in the Gelugpa monastery at Bodsnath, Kathmandu, the last little village before Tibet on the China road.

Miss Ann Rohrer, who spent three years in Nepal while with the United States Aid, saw large Tsampa cups strung up to the ceilings of the homes of Tibetan Refugees, high enough to prevent the little dogs sitting in them from falling out, presumably with their heads almost touching the ceilings. The smallest dogs were only taken out for feeding, exercising and fondling. They literally lived and slept strung up in these cups. Miss Rohrer said that they were definitely of a small Tibetan Spaniel type.

The new dynasty, or the Wakefield dynasty – as Lady Wakefield did not have any prefix or affix, except that her registered dogs are distinguished by the suffix 'La' after their names – really started in 1938 when Sir Edward and Lady Wakefield were living in the Punjab and were presented with a Tibetan Spaniel bitch puppy by Dr Khanshi Ram, the Trade Agent at Gartok, in western Tibet. The *Indian Kennel Gazette* (1941) reported that Mughiwuli was born at Lahore, but that both of her parents came from western Tibet. At the time of this publication her father was dead, but her mother came from a monastery at Taklakot and accompanied her master back to Tibet each year.

Mughiwuli raised two litters in India with four puppies in each; and by the sale of five of these eight puppies 1,000 rupees was donated for patriotic purposes to the Viceroy's Spitfire Fund. One of these puppies went to H.H. the Maharani of Sabibeh of Patiala who became devoted to it; when it died as a result of accidental poisoning, there was mourning at the Patiala court.

In 1940, Dr Khanshi Ram was able to borrow the services of a Tibetan Spaniel dog, Tashi, from the monks of the monastery at Tashigong. At this time, Mughiwuli was living with her owners in the Punjab State of Nabba, where she became a great favourite of H.H. the Maharajah Sir Pratep Sing, Malvendra Bahadur. Mughiwuli was sent to Simla in the Maharajah's private Rolls Royce, for her 'marriage' to Tashi. The *Indian Kennel Gazette* gave the information that Tashi's owner was a Mr Lakshaan Sing, who was himself half Tibetan and was the Accountant to the British Trade Agency for Western Tibet.

Mughiwuli was exhibited in India and won prizes, one of her sons was subsequently providentially returned to Lady Wakefield when his owners retired and returned home from India. This dog, Lama, eventually came back to England with the Wakefields when they returned with Dolma in 1946. The only existing photograph of this dog was taken at Crufts Dog Show in 1950, when Lady Wakefield exhibited him with Dolma and their daughter, Chuni La. Lama was sable with a good mane and shawl, his ears had a slight lift to them, but were not so erect as Mughiwuli's. Dolma was small and dainty and a light red in colour. She had a slight lift to her ears when alert or listening and I understand that some of her photographs are rather misleading and exaggerate her ear carriage.

Lt.-Col. and Mrs A. W. Hawkins returned to England from India in 1946, bringing with them Garpon, a bright red male, and his black-and-tan litter-sister Potala. Born in 1941, they were the offspring of Tashi and Mughiwuli and therefore full brother and sister of Lady Wakefield's Lama.

Garpon and Potala were mated together and a bitch from their first litter, Susan of Deddington, was purchased by Mrs O. Sabin to mate to her red dog Skyid. Skyid was the only remaining descendant of the Greig pre-war imports from Tibet, and, when mated to Susan, they produced a rather large dog Ramba of Armadale and his full sister Ta Le.

Lady Wakefield has told me that she did not consider Skyid at all typical. Foxy-red in colour, he was big, coarse and heavy, also very long in muzzle and very undershot. Mrs L. Jones, cousin of Lady Wakefield, has told me that at this time there were definitely two different types; every now and again a big coarse puppy would appear in a litter for no apparent reason, and there would also probably be one which was very high on the leg. The explanation could be that Dolma was the true small type from the Chumbi valley and that Skyid's ancestors had come from another part of Tibet. Looking at the two photographs of Miss Daisy Greig with a collection of her mother's and sister's Tibetan Spaniels, it can clearly be seen that Doma of Ladkok was of similar type to Dolma, and the others were much bigger and coarser and did not have the correct type of head.

Kyipup, the winner of two CCs, was bred by Colonel Hawkins and owned by his wife from their original pair. The photograph of this dog clearly shows a breed fault, with his bottom row of teeth definitely showing when his mouth was closed. Another male from Garpon and Potala was The Prince of Dzun, a bright red dog whose daughter Milady Zetta was owned by Miss Mason.

Ramba of Armadale was to influence the breed through his son Toomai of Furzyhurst and his grandson, Ch Kye Ho Za-Kyi.

When Kyipup was mated to the litter-sister of Ramba, Ta-Le, they produced Ama Dablam of Furzyhurst. When Ama Dablam was mated to Ramba of Armadale, she produced Furzyhurst Virtuous Dragon and his litter-sister Furzyhurst Tiger Lily. Mated together, Virtuous Dragon and Tiger Lily produced the outstanding brood-bitch, Szufung Lotus of Furzyhurst and her sister, Furzyhurst Tamar.

In Dolma's first litter by Lama there was the particolour bitch Shemo La and her two litter-brothers, Bogo La, who won Best of Breed at Crufts before the breed had Championship status, and Mrs Bagot's Shipki La. In a repeat mating of Lama and Dolma, was a particolour male, Mondo La, who was later exported to Germany. In 1950, Lama and Dolma produced Seng Ge La who was rather too long in leg, but he won Best of Breed at Crufts Dog Show in 1959. He, in turn, sired Mrs D. M. Battson's Ch Yaso of Szufung when mated to Szufung Lotus of Furzyhurst.

Nak Lok La, a rather rangy black dog, was born in 1955 sired by Seng Ge La out of his full sister Shemo La, he was the brother to Shim Rde La of Padua owned by Miss Braye and Miss Elam. When Sir Edward and Lady Wakfield went to Malta, Nak Lok La joined Colonel and Mrs Hawkins, and Lady Wakefield's bitches went to Mrs L. Jones in Wales.

Miss J. Hervey-Cecil found it difficult to attend many shows as she lived on the Isle of Wight. She started in 1949 with Chuni La, a red-and-white daughter of Lama and Dolma. Chuni La made history by winning the first Challenge Certificate offered to bitches in our breed in 1960. She also proved herself to be a valuable brood-bitch by producing Toomai of Furzyhurst, as well as the two foundation brood-bitches for Miss Braye and Miss Elam of the Padua prefix. Also descending from Chuni La are the influential Champions, Ch Rowena of Padua, the first ever Champion in our breed, Ch Kando of Furzyhurst and her son Ch Khan Dee of Curwenna, also Ch Tze Tze of Curwenna the litter sister of Khan Dee, and Ch Kye Ho Za-Khyi.

Chuni La's son Toomai of Furzyhurst was owned by Mrs Jones. Sadly, the poor dog seems to have been survived by his unfortunate nick-name of 'Elephant Boy'. Mrs Jones has told me that this red dog was very handsome and a good, well-proportioned specimen of the breed, even if he was then considered to be too big. He also had a bold temperament and was a strong red colour.

Toomai's daughter, Ran-Ba, was the dam of Kye Ho Tumi, but perhaps his most famous offspring was Ch Kye Ho Za-Kyi, the winner of fifteen Challenge Certificates, winning the last one at well over ten years of age. Ku Sburpa, the dam of Ch Kye Ho Za-Kyi, was a daughter of Nyi Khyi, who was himself the result of a full brother and sister mating from Shipki La and Chimurti La. Ch Kye Ho Za-Khyi, bred by Mrs L. Jones, was owned by Mrs E. Peach, so taking on her prefix of Kye Ho. Later he was owned and campaigned by Mrs J. Hubberstey and then passed into the hands of Mrs L. Hitchings (later to become Mrs Donaldson).

Another very successful stud dog at that time was Mrs Peach's home-bred Kye Ho Tumi, winner of two Challenge Certificates. Both Tumi and Rory of Padua are sons of Nak Lok La. Mrs Peach started in the breed with two bitches obtained from her friend Mrs Jones. Bogo Poo, a daughter of Dolma, was of the original type with a fine silky coat, and rather high on the leg. Ran-Ba had a thicker, woolly coat and a broader head. Other descendants from Kye Ho Tumi were Rosaree Peri Lustre and his litter-sister Ch Rosaree Mai Lei.

Mrs L. Westbrook lives on the Isle of Wight, and although she is no longer active in the breed, we have her Armadale and Glenholme blood-lines in the back of most of today's pedigrees.

Mrs F. Dudman started in Tibetan Spaniels with Cham Pu I Chuni, a daughter of Chuni La bred by Miss Hervey-Cecil. Initially, Mrs Dudman became interested in the breed during her visit to northern India in the 1930s, she endeavoured to purchase one from Tibetan traders but without success. It was not until she herself lived on the Isle of Wight and assisted Miss Hervey-Cecil with showing and breeding, that she definitely decided to have this breed. As Dr Greig had no stock at that time, Mrs Dudman booked, on Miss Harvey-Cecil's behalf, a bitch puppy from Lady Wakefield's Dolma. From Dolma's first-born litter came Chuni La, who was to become the grandmother of Mrs Dudman's Ch Ramblersholt Rupon.

Rory of Padua purchased by Mrs Dudman from Miss Braye and Miss Elam, was a son of Nak Lok La out of Ch Rowena of Padua, and was to win a CC. Rory was also to become the sire of perhaps one of our greatest ever stud dogs Ch Ramblersholt Ram-A-Din. The dam of Ram-A-Din was a daughter of the unshown sire Glenholme Skyid out of Furzyhurst Tamar. Another influential son of Rory of Padua was Ch Ramblersholt Rupon, the sire of Curwenna Rupert of Padua. Rupert, when mated to Ch Kando of Furzyhurst sired Ch Khan Dee of Curwenna.

Mrs Dudman of Ramblersholt has held office as Chairman of the Tibetan Spaniel Association.

A point to make here is that two of the most influential and dominant dogs and bitches of the early 1960s were Mrs Battson's foundation brood-bitch Szufung Lotus of Furzyhurst and Mrs Jenkins and Miss M. C. Hourihane's Ch Ramblersholt Ram-A-Din, who both descended from the mating of brother and sister – Furzyhurst Virtuous Dragon and Furzyhurst Tiger Lily (the sire and dam of Furzyhurst Tamar and Szufung Lotus of Furzyhurst).

The Padua kennel of Miss Braye and Miss Hilda Elam commenced in 1930 with Chow Chows and Pugs; the partnership ended with Miss Braye's death in 1961, although Miss Elam did carry on with the dogs. In August 1954, they purchased their first two Tibetan Spaniels from Miss Hervey-Cecil; litter-sisters, the dark-red bitch Furzyhurst Pyari Larki of Padua and the golden sable Furzyhurst Sermo of Padua, daughters of Ramba of Armadale (the son of Skyid and Susan of Deddington) out of Chuni La.

In October 1954 Shim Rde La of Padua, a son of Seng Ge La out of his particolour litter-sister, with the two sisters formed the foundation of the Padua strain. Miss Elam recalled that they did not look much like litter-sisters, Sermo had a much shorter coat, was rather high on the leg similar to Seu of Ladkok in type, she had a lovely head carriage and grew into an attractive bitch. Sermo's teeth had a level bite and Pyari Larki's were slightly undershot which gave her the monkey-like look which was then so desired. Miss Elam commented, in later years, that she was sorry that this look was fast disappearing in today's show dogs and this has also been commented upon by the Lady Freda Valentine in the foreword.

Sermo was to become the dam of this breed's first ever Champion, Rowena of Padua, sired by Shim Rde La of Padua. Other notable winners bred here were the CC winner Rory of Padua, and the Reserve CC winners Hazel of Padua, Rupert of Padua, Remus of Padua and Rosemary of Padua. Rupert sired Ch Khan Dee of Curwenna and his litter-sister Ch Tze Tze of Curwenna, and Ranee of Padua the dam of Mrs F. Davies' Ch Kando of Furzyhurst (the dam of Ch Khan Dee and Ch Tze Tze). Miss Hilda Elam was, for many years, the Honorary Secretary of the Tibetan Spaniel Association.

The Rosaree Tibetan Spaniels were in Mrs Hubberstey's name; her husband, Major John Hubberstey, was the Honorary Secretary of the Tibetan Spaniel Association from 1964, when he took over from Miss Elam, until 1967. Before this he had held office as Honorary Treasurer. They did much to campaign the black-and-tan Tibetan Spaniel, commencing with two daughters of Ch Rowena of Padua and a daughter of Furzyhurst Sermo of Padua. Chloe was purchased first, in 1957, and when she was mated to Nak Lok La, they retained Sheka of Rosaree. Next a dog and a bitch puppy were purchased from Miss Mason: Rosaree Peri Lustre, who was later owned by Mr and Mrs E. Gill, and the bitch Rosaree Mai Lei. Mai Lei made history by becoming this breed's first black-and-tan Champion and her daughter Huntglen Rosaree Akasha, was the first particolour in England to win a Challenge Certificate. Ch Rosaree Anak Agung, a black-and-tan son of Ch Rosaree Mai Lei was exported to Sweden shortly after winning his English title in 1956.

Ch Kye Ho Za-Khyi, who won his title when owned by Mrs Hubberstey, was to have a great influence on the breed. His double grandson, the Author's Huntglen Rosaree Bhabu was the sire of eight Champions, and from Bhabu's offspring yet more have descended. Other dominant lines have come from Ch Kye Ho Za-Khyi through his son Ch Tomu of Szufung, owned and bred by Mrs D. M. Battson. Ch Tomu's son Mingshang Toto of Szufung, owned by the late Miss P. M. Mayhew, and Rama of Amcross a grandson of Ch Tomu, have also been very dominant.

Ch Kye Ho Za-Khyi's female descendants have included a pair of full sisters, bred by Mrs Battson from her dominant brood bitch Szufung Lotus of Furzyhurst. Amcross Seto of Szufung founded a dynasty for Mrs D. Jenkins and Miss M. C. Hourihane. Braeduke Tamara of Szufung founded a dynasty for the Author.

Ch Kye Ho Za-Khyi himself clearly demonstrated the longevity and lasting qualities of this breed by winning his last CCs when over ten years old. He was, at that time, owned by Mrs Donaldson and, with fifteen CCs, he held for many years the title of the top winning Tibetan Spaniel. This was later lost to his descendant Ch Windameres Braeduke Champa, also the winner of fifteen CCs and, to date Mrs Jenkins and Miss Hourihane's Ch Amcross Kushi Kee, bred by Mr and Mrs Foster, is the top-winning, living British Tibetan Spaniel with fifteen CCs, yet another descendant of Ch Za-Khyi.

The first ever Champion in this breed, Ch Rowena of Padua, was, for many years, the title holder of the top winning Bitch with twelve CCs. This was then held by the Author's Ch Huntglen Braeduke Ta-Ra-Ni, a daughter of Ch Sivas Ten Sing of Myarlune out of Braeduke Tamara of Szufung. Ch Ta-Ra-Ni died in June 1980 and, by the end of that year, her great-great-granddaughter Ch Braeduke Poo-Khyi had succeeded to this with a total of thirteen CCs, won at two and a half years of age. Ch Poo-Khyi is sired by the Anglo-Chinese male Irish and English Ch Braeduke Am-Ra and is out of Braeduke Pye-Mi who descends from Sivas Lotus and Braeduke Sivas Kiki. On December 18th, 1981, Ch Poo-Khyi made history by winning her fourteenth CC, beating all previous bitch records.

Not only has Mrs D. M. Battson's small Szufung kennel been very successful in the show ring, but also in its breeding programme, producing the foundation stock for other top winning kennels. There cannot be many Champions anywhere in the world that are unable to trace back their pedigrees to a 'Szufung'.

In 1958, Mrs Battson obtained, from Miss Hervey-Cecil, a bitch named Szufung Lotus of Furzyhurst. Lotus came from a litter-brother and -sister mating of Furzyhurst Virtuous Dragon and Furzyhurst Tiger Lily. Her full sister was Furzyhurst Tamar and from both these bitches have come dominant and influential blood-lines. In 1960, another bitch, Traza Truly Fair, was obtained from Miss J. Thirlwell (later Mrs Whitworth) who had commenced in the late 1950s with a bitch, Rosella of Padua. When mated to Ch Kye Ho Za-Khyi, Truly Fair produced for Mrs Battson, the dog Ch Tomu of Szufung.

Both Ch Tomu and Szufung Lotus of Furzyhurst have proved themselves to be dominant, especially Lotus who, when mated to Ch Kye Ho Za-Khyi, produced Ama of Szufung, later owned by Miss Selby and winner of two CCs, and the winning Momo of Szufung. Both these bitches were to have a profound influence on the Mingshang kennel, through Ama's daughter Mingshang Sivas Tamarisk, and Momo's son Mingshang Toto of Szufung.

Ch Tomu, with Lotus, produced the foundation stock for the

Amcross, Braeduke, Mingshang and Peterstown strains; and, through their descendants have spread their influence all over the world. In the list of progeny under Lotus' name only Ch Yaso of Szufung was not sired by Ch Tomu, her sire being Lady Wakefield's Seng Ge La.

SZUFUNG LOTUS OF FURZYHURST (Bitch)

Sire: Furzyhurst Virtuous Dragon   **Owner:** Mrs D. M. Battson

Dam: Furzyhurst Tiger Lily   **Breeder:** Miss J. Hervey-Cecil

Dam of:
Ch Yaso of Szufung
(dam of Ch Braeduke Lotus Bud of
Szufung)
Ch Mingshang Yang Zom of
Szufung
(dam of two Champions)
Ch Peterstown Drom of Szufung
(whose daughter started an
American dynasty)
Danish Ch Braeduke Ti-Phu of
Szufung
Amcross Seto of Szufung
(dam of three Champions)
Braeduke Tamara of Szufung
(dam of three Champions)
Momo of Szufung
(one CC)
Ama of Szufung
(two CCs)

Others of note owned or bred by Mrs Batson:

Ch Braeduke Lotus Bud of
Szufung
(dam of two Champions)
Mingshang Toto of Szufung
(sire of four Champions and a Res.
CC winner)
Mingshang Tamarisk of Szufung
(one CC)

Dolma of Szufung
(Res. CC)
Ch Tomu of Szufung
(sire of three Champions)

Through purchasing the lovely bitch Chuni of Szufung, Mr C. F. Poole, M.R.C.V.S., who came into the breed in 1963, started his Peterstown strain. His first Champion was Ch Peterstown Drom of Szufung, a son of Ch Tomu of Szufung out of Szufung Lotus of Furzyhurst. This male Champion influenced the Northanger strain through his daughter Pan-Zi of Northanger and through another daughter, founded Mr Leo Kearns' American dynasty. Mr Poole bred Drom's grandson Ch Peterstown Tobo-An. Through Pan-Zi of Northanger also descend some of the Wildhern blood-lines.

Another small kennel of the late 1950s and '60s was that of Mrs F. Davies of Curwenna, who purchased, from Miss Hervey-Cecil, a bitch which became Ch Kando of Furzyhurst. From Miss Elam came the son of Ch Ramblersholt Rupon, the Reserve CC winning Curwenna Rupert of Padua. When mated together, Rupert and Kando produced two Champions, litter-brother and -sister, Ch Khan Dee of Curwenna and Ch Tze-Tze of Curwenna. Ch Tze-Tze had only one litter when in the ownership of Mrs R. Bichener.

From Ch Khan Dee came four influential Champions. He sired Ch Zimbu Vaida, bred and campaigned by Miss C. Adams and later owned by Mr A. Bridge. He also sired Ch Braeduke Lotus Bud of Szufung, bred by Mrs Battson, and owned and campaigned by the Author before going to Mrs C. Clapham. The third, also a bitch, was Ch Braeduke Tam Cho. Ch Lotus Bud's two daughters, both sired by Ch Ramblersholt Ram-A-Din were to influence the breed, Braeduke Li-Ka-Ra being the foundation of the Rutherglen strain, and International and Nordic Ch Huntglen Braeduke Lhotse founding a dynasty of her own for the Zlazano kennel in Finland. From Ch Braeduke Tam Cho came two dominant stud dogs; Ch Windameres Braeduke Champa, owned by Mrs Vines, was the sire of nine Champions, and the winner of fifteen CCs. Her other son, Ch Braeduke Channa is the sire of ten Champions.

The fourth Champion Khan Dee daughter was Ch Kensing Kempton Karma, bred by Mrs D. Ormsby and owned by Mrs Lilley, and she has had considerable influence on the Kensing kennel.

Ch KANDO OF FURZYHURST (Bitch)

Sire: Wonghsi of Furzyhurst

Owner: Mrs F. Davies

Dam: Ranee of Padua

Breeder: Miss J. Hervey-Cecil

Some of Kando's Champion descendants:
Ch Khan Dee of Curwenna
(sire of four Champions)
Ch Tze-Tze of Curwenna
Ch Braeduke Tam Cho
(dam of four Champions)
Ch Braeduke Lotus Bud of
Szufung
(dam of two Champions)
Ch Zimbu Vaida
Ch Kensing Ra
(sire of one Champion)
Ch Kechanta Li-Sa
Ch Kensing Kempton Karma
(dam of one Champion)
Ch Benagh Chelsea
(dam of one Champion)
English and Finnish Ch Benagh
Chensa
Swedish and Norwegian Ch
Kensing Mikki
(sire of one Champion)
International and Nordic Ch
Huntglen Braeduke Lhotse
Ch Ysa of Braeduke
Ch Roma of Copdene
Ch Kensing Oscar
(sire of one Champion)
Ch Braeduke Shipke-La
Ch Windameres Braeduke
Champa
(fifteen CCs, and sire of nine
Champions)
Ch Heyvan Jola
(sire of one Champion)
Ch Braeduke Channa
(sire of ten Champions)

Ch Lho-Cham of Windameres
(sire of twelve Champions)
Ch Windameres Lho-Zah-Mi
(sire of two Champions)
Ch Windameres Lho-Lita
Ch Peterstown Tobo-An
Ch Braeduke Whitewisp Hara
Nor
(dam of six Champions)
Ch Braeduke Nimmi
(sire of seven Champions)
Ch Rutherglen Tai-Mar of
Taimani
(dam of two Champions)
Ch Braeduke Patlin
Ch Braeduke Lhalu
(dam of five Champions)
Ch Shamau Ba-Ti-Ka
Ch Braeduke Poo-Khyi
(fifteen CCs)
Ch Ybroc Eskimo Nell
Ch Su-Li of Braeduke
Ch Taimani Tu-Bo
(sire of three Champions)
Ch Kensing O-So Special
Ch Rutherglen Jamba
Ch Wildhern Genghiz Khan
Ch Amcross Tarquin
(sire of six Champions)
Ch Kensing Rosetta
Ch Kensing Pandora
Ch Braeduke Ama Dablam
Ch Cham Bu of Windameres
Ch Friarland Bo-Peep of
Sharbonne
Ch Taimani Se-Ba of Rutherglen
Ch Velindre Ankas Amne

Miss Sara Selby of Sivas saw her first Tibetan Spaniel in 1949 and purchased a bitch, Sivas Lotus, from Mrs Robin Bagot in 1960. This

136

black-and-white particolour bitch was a daughter of Pubu Levens out of Gser Pho La; Pubu Levens being a son of Shipki La out of Chimurti La, and Gser Pho La was a daughter of Nyi-Khyi out of Shemo La, and so stemmed from Lady Wakefield's original dogs.

Miss Selby can recall that in the early 1950s the only northern breeders of Tibetan Spaniels were Lady Wakefield, Mrs Bagot, Mrs Caldwell and Mrs Crowther. Miss Selby's second bitch was purchased from Mr and Mrs McKay, namely Yang Chenla Sakya Trayerpa. The story goes that there was a mix-up over her Kennel Club registration and, instead of being given her first two names or alternatively the last two, she got the lot!

Miss Selby's third Tibetan Spaniel was a male, a younger full-brother of Lotus, a black-and-white particolour, Sivas Sherpa. He distinguished himself by mating Miss Bailey's Kyungu who produced a litter containing the dominant stud dog Ch Sivas Ten Sing of Myarlune, winner of nine Challenge Certificates and the sire of four Champions. Later, Ch Ten Sing passed into the ownership of Mr N. Charlton of the Copdene kennels.

Without any difficulty I have traced over sixty-five direct Champion descendants from Ch Sivas Ten Sing of Myarlune, most of them descending through his son Ch Braeduke Channa and two daughters Ch Huntglen Braeduke Ta-Ra-Ni and Ch Sivas Mesa. At the time of her death in the summer of 1980, Ch Ta-Ra-Ni had over thirty-seven British Champion descendants.

Ch Ten Sing's dominant influence has promoted the Braeduke, the Whitewisp and Colphil strains among others. Ch Mesa's black-and-tan daughter International and Dutch Ch Braeduke Sivas Supi Yaw Lat was the foundation for Mrs Van Den Boom's Fanfare kennel in Holland.

Sivas Mara (the black-and-tan litter-sister of Ch Mesa) and Sivas Ang Akalu, are two more dominant daughters of Ch Ten Sing, influencing the Wimaro and Northanger strains. Mesa's son Ch Sivas Wimaro Ti-Mu when mated to Ang Akalu produced Ch Braeduke Jhanki of Wimaro, the sire of ten Champions. Jhanki's most dominant influence has been in Sweden, through his progeny.

Braeduke Cilla of Curwenna another black-and-tan was unrelated to the Author's strain, and was purchased out of sympathy at an Open show held in Alexandra Palace; she was then given to Miss Selby. Cilla produced Ch Sivas Zodi, and his litter-brother International and Nordic Ch Daleviz Sivas Zebe who was then owned by Mr A. Bridge before going to Sweden. Miss Selby had the greatest variety of blood-lines of any Tibetan Spaniel breeder of the 1960s.

Ch SIVAS WIMARO Ti Mu (Dog) (owned by Miss S. Selby and later by Mr N. Charlton)

SIVAS KARAMBA (Bitch)

Sire: Pontac Keun Chang   **Owner:** Mrs G. Howard Joyce

Dam: Sivas Mara   **Breeder:** Mrs S. Rank

Some of their Champion and winning descendants:
Ch Northanger Kenchira Dikki
of Wildhern
Northanger Kam Bu Dikki
(sire of two Champions)
Braeduke Northanger Cu Li
Dikki
(dam of five Champions)
Ch Northanger Da-Ra
Ch Northanger A-Su
Ch Lho-Cham of Windameres
(sire of twelve Champions)
Ch Windameres Lho-Zah-Mi
(sire of two Champions, 1977 Utility
Group winner)
Windameres Lho-Lita
Ch Windameres Azah-Mi
(dam of two Champions)
Ch Cham Bu of Windameres
Marles Abba Ann
(one CC)
Ch Wildhern Genghiz Khan
Ch Roma of Copdene
Ch Shamau Tranka
(sire of one Champion)
Ch Braeduke Lhalu
(dam of five Champions)
Ch Sivas Zodi
(sire of one Champion)
International and Nordic Ch
Daleviz Sivas Zebe
Ch Amcross Tarquin
(sire of seven Champions)
Ch Hexwood Timini

Ch Braeduke Whitewisp Hara
Nor
(dam of six Champions)
Ch Braeduke Jhanki of Wimaro
(sire of ten Champions)
Ch Kechanta Li-Sa
Ch Braeduke Rhum Bu of
Kensing
(sire of three Champions)
Ch Braeduke Patlin
Ch Braeduke Poo-Khyi
(fifteen CCs)
Ch Braeduke Re-Ba
(dam of one Champion)
New Zealand and Australian Ch
Braeduke Re-Gi-Na
Ch Su-Li of Braeduke
Weiden Sy-Mon
(one CC)
Ch Braeduke Nimmi
(sire of seven Champions)
English and Finnish Ch Benagh
Chensa
Ming-Y of Northanger
(one CC)
Braeduke Shan Hu of
Northanger
(dam of four Champions)
Braeduke Su-Lin
(one CC)
Braeduke Rab-Shi
(one CC, sire of three Champions)
Ch Chamdoh Shi-Sel of Akbar
Ch Kensing Rosie
Ch Part-Li Amcross
(sire of two Champions)
Windameres Salvador
(sire of three Champions)
Ch Kensing Kempton Karma
(dam of one Champion)
Ch Kensing Oscar
(sire of one Champion)

Ch Lho-Cham of Windameres
(sire of twelve Champions)
Ch Bridgrove Tashi
Rutherglen Lho-Ri
(one CC, dam of one Champion)
Ch Rutherglen Tai-Mar of
Taimani
(dam of two Champions)
Ch Taimani Se-Ba of Rutherglen
Braeduke Lu-Ting
(one CC, sire of four champions and
a dual English CC winner)
Ch Braeduke Ama Dablam
Ch Kensing Pandora

Ch Sivas Kabru of Amcross, a son of Yang Chenla Sakya Trayerpa, was bred by Miss Selby who sold him to the Amcross partnership at a year old. The Zlazano kennel in Finland also purchased their first Tibetan Spaniels from Miss Selby and her blood-lines have been dominant, have influenced many of the top breeders, and lie behind most of the top winning dogs and bitches of today.

Sivas Lakshmi was the first ever Tibetan Spaniel to win a Junior Warrant in 1965, and subsequently won a CC, the male Sivas Eusabio was another CC winner. Miss Selby obtained Ch Sivas Wimaro Ti Mu from Mrs Rank and campaigned him to his title, he later went to Mr Charlton.

Miss Selby sold to the Author Braeduke Sivas Kiki, the winner of two CCs, before her early death after an accident. Her daughter Braeduke Koko Nor, owned by Mr and Mrs Grounds, is the dam of Ch Braeduke Whitewisp Hara Nor who must hold the British record as the dam of six Champions, from three litters by three different sires. The most successful of her litters was sired by Ch Ram Chandra of Amcross, a son of Ch Ramblersholt Ram-A-Din, and produced four Champions.

Ama of Szufung, bred by Mrs Battson, was a litter-sister of Momo of Szufung; when mated to Sivas Gombu she produced the influential bitch Mingshang Sivas Tamarisk, who in turn produced Ch Mingshang Jason. Momo herself also influenced the Mingshangs with her son Mingshang Toto of Szufung.

Mrs Sylvia Rank did not attend many shows, her first major win was with her CC winning male, Pontac Keun Chang, the sire of Sivas Karamba and also of her full brother Ch Sivas Wimaro Ti Mu. Nowadays there is a little confusion about the validity of the birth dates of this pair, bred by the late Mrs Rank; Ch Ti Mu's birth date is given as 2.5.65 and that of Sivas Karamba as 4.10.64, giving rise to the conjecture that could Sivas Mara have conceivably produced both? Ch Ti Mu's son, Ch Braeduke Jhanki of Wimaro, was bred here and sold to the Author at five and a half months old. Mr Charlton's CC winning bitch Wimaro Tu Maraz of Copdene and Mr Poole's CC winning Ti-Ga of Wimaro were also bred here. Mrs Rank owned the black-and-tan bitch Sivas Mara, dam of Karamba and Ti Mu, and I can still recall being very shocked to see how badly undershot she was – more pronounced than Kyipup, showing her teeth when her mouth was closed!

Mrs Howard Joyce of Northanger commenced in the mid 1960s with Silvas Karamba, ostensibly a full sister of Ch Ti-Mu, descending from Rosaree Peri Lustre. In her first litter, sired by Ch Peterstown Drom of Szufung, Karamba produced Pan-Zi of Northanger who when mated to Ch Braeduke Jhanki of Wimaro was to become the dam of Northanger Ti-Bo. Black-and-tan Ti-Bo was the first bitch and the foundation bitch for Mrs C. M. Micklethwait of Wildhern.

Northanger Ti-Bo's litter-brother is Nordic Ch Huntglen Northanger Tai T'sung, a dominant stud force in the Zlazano kennel in Finland. Pan-Zi of Northanger was also to become the great-grandmother of the American-bred Kalimpong Ming Dordja of Braeduke, who was imported by the Author.

Sivas Karamba, in her first litter to Huntglen Rosaree Bhabu, produced Mrs K. Newbury's CC winning male Ming-Y of Northanger and his litter-sister Braeduke Shan Hu of Northanger, owned by the Author, who was the dam of four Champions.

In her second litter to Bhabu, came Mrs Vines' Ch Northanger Da-Ra, in her third litter, also sired by Bhabu, came Mrs Micklethwait's Ch Northanger A-Su.

Through the Author's search for fresh blood-lines, Mrs Howard Joyce purchased and imported Dikki Dolma, who came to England with her litter-sister Yasodhara who was jointly owned by the Author and Miss H. F. J. Forbes. Two of Dikki Dolma's sons and one daughter, all from the same litter sired by Ming-Y of Northanger, have been very influential in the breed. Northanger Kam Bu Dikki was purchased and owned by Mrs Vines, through his daughter Ch Windameres Azah-Mi and his grandson Ch Lho-Za-Mi have come more Champions. Through Mrs Micklethwait's Ch Northanger Kenchira Dikki of Wildhern have come yet more successful strains such as Simpasture, Tsingay, Mobella, Perjena (formerly Lydgrove), and Kharekhola.

Mrs Howard Joyce's Pan-Zi of Northanger was also to influence the Wildhern strain through her daughter Northanger Ti-Bo sired by Ch Braeduke Jhanki of Wimaro, a son of Ch Sivas Wimaro out of a Ch Sivas Ten Sing of Myarlune daughter.

In 1968, Mrs C. M. Micklethwait purchased her foundation brood bitch Northanger Ti-Bo and then the male Ch Northanger Kenchira Dikki of Wildhern, both as puppies; through them, and also by using Ch Windameres Braeduke Champa, she has produced the English Ch Wildhern Genghiz Khan, T.S.C.A. Ch Wildhern Ambassador and T.S.C.A. Ch Wildhern Winni Too. Others descending from her original nucleus are the CC and Reserve CC winners Wildhern Wicked Won, Wildhern Warlock, Wildhern Partli President, Wildhern Warrior, Wildhern Mowgli, Wildhern Wolf and Wildhern Water Lily.

Mrs P. Atkins started in 1973 with the litter-sister of Ch Wildhern Genghiz Khan, Wildhern Taranatha. When mated the first time to Ch Ram Chandra of Amcross, she produced Ch Tsingay Master-Ly who has influenced the small Kendoman kennel of Miss J. Chapman. From a second repeat mating came the bitch Ch Tsingay Taraminta and the dog T.S.C.A. Ch Tsingay Tambolin.

Through an unshown son of Ch Northanger Kenchira Dikki of Wildhern has come the 1981 Champion bitch Sweet Whisper of Carnbech owned by Mr A. Gillett and Mr P. Bell, and bred by Mrs P. Harris of Mobella prefix. Ch Sweet Whisper was sired by Mrs M. Coulthwaite's home-bred Reserve CC winning Kenmo Fernando, a son of Ch Heyvan Jola and therefore descending from both Braeduke Dung-Ka and Ch Braeduke Channa. Ch Sweet Whispers is a double descendant of the Indian-bred import Dikki Dolma.

Mrs S. W. Beale's Simpasture kennel is based on Pan-Zi of Copdene, a daughter of Ch Sivas Wimaro Ti-Mu, and upon a black-and-tan male Wildhern Magic Dragon of Simpasture. Through Magic Dragon being mated to his granddaughter Simpasture Imandra, has come the lovely male Ch Simpasture Topaz owned by Mr and Mrs Sowerby. There are other Simpasture CC and Reserve CC winners descending from Mrs Beale's original pair.

One of the most famous and successful kennels is that of Amcross, the kennel name of the partnership of Mrs Deidre Jenkins and Miss Mary Clare Hourihane. Starting in 1964 with their foundation brood-bitch Amcross Seto of Szufung, bred by Mrs D. M. Battson from Ch Tomu of Szufung and the dominant brood-bitch Szufung Lotus of Furzyhurst, Seto is the younger full sister of the Author's Braeduke Tamara of Szufung. Both these bitches were to have tremendous influence on the breed.

In the Author's opinion the combination of Seto with Ch Ramblersholt Ram-A-Din has been the most successful and from these two have come many Champion descendants. Purchased from his breeder, Mrs F. Dudman, after he had been campaigned to his title, Ram-A-Din's influence has spread far and wide through his children, especially those from Amcross Seto of Szufung and all their descendants.

Of all the stud dogs in the post-war dynasty, the Author considers that Ch Ramblersholt Ram-A-Din, the sire of eight Champions, has been the most dominant and influential; but we must not forget the strong dominant lines which lie behind him, which can be seen in his pedigree in the appendix section of this book.

Many other Champions and CC winners have been owned and bred by Mrs Jenkins and Miss M. C. Hourihane, and another dominant line has come through a Ch Ram-A-Din great-great-great-grandson, Ch Amcross Tarquin, who is out of a Ch Sivas Wimaro Ti-Mu daughter.

Although not bred by Mrs Jenkins and Miss Hourihane, Ch Yakrose Chiala of Amcross was purchased by them and campaigned to his title before being exported to Mr Leo Kearns in America, where this dog founded a dynasty with a daughter of Ch Peterstown Drom of Szufung. Another Ch Chiala son, Ch Rimpoche of Amcross, was the sire of Mrs Lilley's foundation male Kensing Ano-Rak of Amcross.

Another Amcross brood-bitch was Shari of Myarlune who later passed into the ownership of Miss C. Adams of Zimbu.

It would be almost impossible to list all the other successful breeders and kennels of Amcross descendants, but Miss V. Hourihane's Amscor is an offshoot, with the first Amscor litter registered in 1973 which included Mrs Vines' Ku-Li of Windameres who produced the first Amscor Champion in Ch Tan-Ku from Amscor.

Others of note bred or owned by the Amcross Partnership:

Ch Amcross Gu-Pa of Kethmora
(sire of one Champion, later owned
by Mrs Donaldson)
Ch Bu-Po of Amcross
Swedish and English Ch Amcross
Kam-Dar
(sire of two Champions)
Ch Amcross Tarquin
(sire of seven Champions)
Ch Seto of Rowcourt
Ch Ma-Ni of Amcross
Ch Rani of Amcross
Ch Amcross Rak-Ha
Ch Amcross Ni-Ma
Ch Sivas Kabru of Amcross
Ch Rimpoche of Amcross
(sire of one Champion)
Rama of Amcross
(sire of six Champions)
Ch Ram Chandra of Amcross
(sire of six Champions)
Ch Copdene Marpo of Amcross
Ch Amcross Parti-Peace
(dam of three Champions)
Ch Amcross Kai-Tei
Ch Amcross Jinda
Ch Amcross Jimbu
Ch Amcross Justice
Ch Yakrose Chiala of Amcross
(sire of one Champion, exported to
U.S.A.)
Finnish and English Ch Amcross
Pax
(sire of one Champion)
Ch Amcross Pa-Che
Ch Part-Li Amcross
(sire of two Champions)
Ch Amcross Tar-Ka
(sire of two Champions, now owned
by Mr A. Bridge)

Ch Amcross Pundit
(sire of one Champion, 1979 Utility
Group winner)
Ch Amcross Am-Ban
(1979 Utility Group winner)
Ch Sivas Kabru of Amcross
Ch Ramblersholt Ram-A-Din
(sire of eight Champions)
Swedish Ch Braeduke Atisha
Chu
International and Nordic Ch
Braeduke Amdo Chu

AMCROSS SETO OF SZUFUNG (Bitch)

Sire: Ch Tomu of Szufung

Owners: Mrs D. Jenkins and
Miss M. C. Hourihane

Dam: Szufung Lotus of
Furzyhurst

Breeder: Mrs D. M. Battson

Dam of:
Ch Ma-Ni of Amcross
Ch Copdene Marpo of Amcross
Ch Rani of Amcross
Rama of Amcross
(Res. CC, sire of six Champions)
Mu-Tig of Amcross
(one CC)

The Author considers that the Amcross strain is dominant in stud-dog blood-lines, as is shown in the other charts, especially through Ch Ram-A-Din and his two sons Rama of Amcross and Ch Ram Chandra of Amcross. Through Mingshang Toto of Szufung's son Ch Amcross Tar-Ka, who is now owned by Mr A. Bridge, when mated to a double descendant of Szufung Lotus of Furzyhurst produced the dominant sire Ch Amcross Tarquin.

Ch RAMBLERSHOLT RAM-A-DIN (Dog)

Sire: Rory of Padua

Owners: Mrs Jenkins and
Miss M. C. Hourihane

Dam: Ramblersholt La Tru

Breeder: Mrs F. Dudman

Sire of:
(In addition to those listed under Amcross Seto of Szufung's list)
Ch Mingshang Jason
(sire of four Champions)
Ch Ram Chandra of Amcross
(sire of six Champions)
Nordic Ch Ulvus Argon
(Sweden)
International and Nordic Ch
Huntglen Braeduke Lhotse
Ch Tibskips Rinchin
(dam of one Champion)
His other Champion descendants are too numerous to list.

RAMA OF AMCROSS (Dog)

Sire: Ch Ramblersholt Ram-A-Din

Dam: Amcross Seto of Szufung

Owners and breeders:
Mrs Jenkins and
Miss M. C. Hourihane

Sire of:
Ch Bu-Po of Amcross
Ch Amcross Rak-Ha
Ch Roma of Copdene
T.S.C.A. Ch Braeduke Dung-Ka
(sire of twelve Champions)
Ch Amcross Gu-Pa of Kethmora
(sire of one Champion)
Ch Tibskips Dan-Rog
English and Irish Ch Am-Ra
(sire of seven Champions)

Among his other descendants:
Ch Ima Blossom of Amcross
Ch Heyvan Jola
Ch Amcross Tar-Ka
Ch Kechanta Li-Sa
Ch Ybroc Eskimo Nell
Ch Braeduke Poo-Khyi
Alvinas Lil-Li-An
(two CCs)

Ch RAM CHANDRA OF AMCROSS (Dog)

Sire: Ch Ramblersholt Ram-A-Din

Owners: Mrs Jenkins and Miss M. C. Hourihane

Dam: Heronshaw Hansi of Amcross

Breeder: Mrs D. Chapman

Sire of:
Ch Braeduke Nimmi
(sire of seven Champions)
International and Nordic Ch
Braeduke Nalina
(Sweden)
Australian Ch Braeduke Numa
Finnish Ch Braeduke Narpo
Ch Tsingay Master-Ly
Ch Tsingay Taraminta

Ch AMCROSS TARQUIN (Dog)

Sire: Ch Amcross Tar-Ka

Owners and Breeders:
Mrs Jenkins and
Miss M. C. Hourihane

Dam: Ro-Sana of Copdene

Sire of:
Ch Amcross Vosta Kushi Kee
(top winning living male with
fifteen CCs)
Ch Vosta Kala Anka
(sire of three Champions)
Ch Sebastian of Deanford
International and Nordic Ch
Braeduke Amdo Chu
Swedish Ch Braeduke Atisha
Chu
Ch Amcross Am-Ban
(sire of one Champion)
Ch Chanda of Cloudsmere
Cresimen Aphos
(one CC)
Ch Velindre Ankas Amne
Chaylmolen Desdemona
(one CC)

Chaylmolen is the kennel name for Mr and Mrs P. Diment. Mrs A. Diment's home-bred Chaylmolen Desdemona and her litter-sister Emilia both won their Junior Warrants in Spring 1981, with Desdemona winning the Challenge Certificate at W.E.L.K.S. show in the same year, they are both daughters of Ch Amcross Tarquin.

Among successful sons of Ch Amcross Tarquin are the litter brothers Ch Amcross Vosta Kushi Kee and Ch Vosta Kala Anka. Mr and Mrs R. Stanley's Champion bitch Velindre Ankas Amne, a daughter of Ch Kala Anka, was bred by Mr and Mrs Moores.

The late Miss P. M. Mayhew is known to many readers through her two privately published paperback books on Tibetan Spaniels which came out in 1972 and 1974. Her Mingshang Tibetan Spaniel kennel commenced in 1965 with a bitch puppy from Mrs D. M. Battson who became Ch Mingshang Yang Zom of Szufung, sired by Ch Tomu of Szufung out of Szufung Lotus of Furzyhurst. In 1966, Miss Mayhew purchased Mingshang Toto of Szufung; he won a Reserve CC, and Miss Mayhew considered him to be her leading stud dog. Toto was the son of Ch Tomu of Szufung out of the CC winning Momo of Szufung, sister of the dual CC winner Ama of Szufung. This pair of sisters was influential in the Sivas and the Mingshang strains. Toto's progeny and their descendants have also been very dominant as can be seen from his list.

Later two more bitches joined the Mingshang kennel, the first was Chibu of Szufung, a descendant of Kye Ho Tumi and Dolma of Szufung. The second was Sivas Tamarisk, a particolour daughter of Sivas Gombu out of Ama of Szufung. From this nucleus came the Champions and CC winners Mingshang Chintz, Ch Mingshang Jason, Ch Mingshang Zena, Ch Mingshang Zita of Kempton owned by Mrs D. Ormsby, Swedish Ch Mingshang Benjamin, Australian Ch Mingshang Bino, Australian Ch Jayne of Mingshang, International and Dutch Ch Mingshang Zenith and Mrs Battson's CC winning Mingshang Tamarisk of Szufung.

Ch MINGSHANG JASON (Dog)

Sire: Ramblersholt Ram-A-Din   **Owner-Breeder:**
Miss P. M. Mayhew

Dam: Sivas Tamarisk

Some of Ch Jason's Champion and winning descendants:
Ch Mingshang Zena

148

Mingshang Chintz
(one CC)
Windameres Salvador
(sire of three Champions)
Mingshang Chena
(dam of Ch Windameres Azah-Mi)
Australian Ch Mingshang Bino
Australian Ch Jayne of
Mingshang
Ch Windameres Lho-Lita
Ch Mingshang Zita of Kempton
Ch Windameres Lho-Zah-Mi
(sire of two Champions)
Windameres Lho-Mar-Ni
(two CCs)
International and Dutch Ch
Mingshang Zenith
Swedish Ch Mingshang
Benjamin

MINGSHANG TOTO OF SZUFUNG (Dog)

Sire: Ch Tomu of Szufung

Dam: Momo of Szufung (one CC)

Owner: Miss P. M. Mayhew

Breeder: Mrs D. M. Battson

Champion and winning descendants:
Nordic Ch Rutherglen Shu-Sha
(Sweden, dam of one Champion)
Ch Braeduke Su-La
Ch Su-Li of Braeduke
Ch Amcross Tarquin
(sire of seven Champions)
Mingshang Tamarisk of Szufung
(one CC)
Ch Rutherglen Jamba
Ch Braeduke Shipke La
Ch Tar-Ka of Amcross
Braeduke Colphil Seng-Kyi
(one CC)

Mrs G. S. Vines is a very successful exhibitor; she exhibited her first Tibetan Spaniel in 1969, a black-and-tan bitch, An-Ke of Balgay, who was to become the dam of the black-and-tan bitch Ch Windameres Loo-Di-Pa who was sired by the black-and-tan Witneylea Tupence. The first Champion male to be made up by Mrs Vines has greatly influenced the breed, Ch Windameres Braeduke Champa, a son of Ch Clawson Braeduke Rampa out of Ch Braeduke Tam Cho. On both sides he descended from Ch Tomu of Szufung and Szufung Lotus of Furzyhurst and was line-bred to Braeduke Tamara of Szufung. Ch Champa won fifteen CCs before his early death when about five years old; he was the sire of nine Champions and years after his death he is still the joint title-holder of the Top Winning Tibetan Spaniel. His son, Ch Lho-Cham of Windameres, is a very influential stud force in Sweden, and his grandson Ch Windameres Lho-Zah-Mi was the first Tibetan Spaniel in England to win a Utility Group at any general Championship show.

In bitches, Mrs Vines' Mingshang Chena has shown herself to be influential; a daughter of Ch Mingshang Jason she descends on her dam's side from Ch Tomu of Szufung and Szufung Lotus of Furzyhurst.

MINGSHANG CHENA (Bitch)

Sire: Ch Mingshang Jason   **Owner:** Mrs G. S. Vines

Dam: Mingshang Chibu of Szufung   **Breeder:** Miss P. M. Mayhew

Champion and winning descendants:
Ch Windameres Azah-Mi
(dam of two Champions)
Ch Windameres Lho-Zah-Mi
(sire of two Champions)
Ch Windameres Lho-Lita
Windameres Salvador
(Res. CC winner, sire of three
Champions)
Ch Bridgrove Tashi
Ch Cham-Bu of Windameres
Ch Taimani Se-Ba of Rutherglen
Marles Abba Ann
(one CC)
Ch Windameres Lho-Mar-Ni
(two CCs)

Ch WINDAMERES BRAEDUKE CHAMPA (Dog)

Sire: Clawson Braeduke Rampa

Dam: Braeduke Tam Cho

Owner: Mrs G. S. Vines

Breeder: Mrs A. L. Wynyard

Sire of:
Ch Rutherglen Tai-Mar of
Taimani
(dam of two Champions)
Ch Tomarans Lotti Lu
Ch Wildhern Genghiz Khan
English, International and
Nordic Ch Lho Cham of
Windameres
(sire of twelve Champions)
Swedish and Finnish Ch
Braeduke Sinha
International Ch Braeduke
Cham Kusho
(Holland)
International Ch Braeduke
Chamba Sopa
(Holland)
Nordic Ch Braeduke Champa
Namgyal
(Sweden)
Braeduke Su Lin
(one CC)
Tangwell Gu Cham Midas
(sire of three Champions)

Other descendants:
Ch Kensing Ra
(sire of one Champion)
Ch Shamau Ba-Ti-Ka
Windameres Lho-Mar-Ni
(two CCs)
Ch Windameres Lho-Zah-Mi
Ch Kensing Rosetta
Ch Taimani Se-Ba of Rutherglen
Ch Windameres Lho-Lita
Marles Abba Ann
(one CC)

Ch Cham-Bu of Windameres
Ch Kensing Pandora
Tomarans Gwe-N-Daw
(one CC)

Other Champions owned or bred by Mrs G. S. Vines:
Swedish and Norwegian Ch
Windameres Tarquin
Ch Windameres Loo-Di-Pa
Ch Windameres Lho-Tsh-Hi
Ch Tan-Ku from Amscor
Ch Windameres Azah-Mi

Miss M. H. Heaton's Sketchley prefix is linked with the Szufung blood-lines and the Windameres, through owning in her later years Ch Braeduke Tam Cho, who is still alive and over sixteen years of age at the time of writing this book, and being the owner-breeder of her grandson Sketchley Yee-Cho, a son of Ch Windameres Braeduke Champa. Yee-Cho is the sire of Mrs Vines' 1981 Challenge Certificate winning bitch Windameres Lho-Mar-Ni and also of Miss Heaton's home-bred particolur bitch Ch Sketchley Miranda.

Mrs M. Marsden of the Marles prefix commenced in 1974 with the purchase of a Ch Windameres Braeduke Champa daughter, who was to become the dam of Mrs Vines' Ch Cham Bu of Windameres and his CC winning litter-sister Marles Abba Ann.

Unusually, the Kensing strain commenced in 1968 with a male; he was Kensing Ano-Rak of Amcross, a descendant of Ch Ramblersholt Ram-A-Din and of Amcross Seto of Szufung. In 1970 he was joined by two bitch puppies; they were Kensing Kempton Karma, a daughter of Ch Khan Dee of Curwenna out of a Res. CC winning daughter of Ch Braeduke Jhanki of Wimaro and of Ch Yaso of Szufung bred by Mrs D. Ormsby. The other bitch was Kensing Tibskips Re-Sa, a daughter of Ch Clawson Braeduke Rampa and Ch Tibskips Rinchin. Both were campaigned to their Champion titles, and Ch Re-Sa was the leading Brood bitch for 1974. Ch Braeduke Rhum Bu of Kensing joined the Kensings as a puppy, and from him have come three Champions; he is a son of Northanger Kam Bu Dikki out of Ch Huntglen Braeduke Ta-Ra-Ni. The dominant lines of the Kensing strain can be traced back to Ch Sivas Ten Sing of Myarlune and Ch Ramblersholt Ram-A-Din in the male lines, and to Szufung Lotus of Furzyhurst in the bitches.

KENSING ANO-RAK of AMCROSS (Dog)

Sire: Ch Rimpoche of Amcross

Dam: Ch Ma-Ni of Amcross

Owner: Mrs G. J. Lilley

Breeders: Mrs Jenkins and Miss M. C. Hourihane

Sire of:
Ch Kensing Ri-Tse
(dam of three Champions)
Swedish and Norwegian Ch
Kensing Mikki
(sire of one Champion)
Kensing Mini-Bean
(dam of a Champion)
Kensing Roger
(one CC)
Kensing Ru Bear of Parkplace
(Res. CC and sire of one Champion)

All the above are out of Ch Kensing Tibskips Re-Sa except for Mikki who is out of Ch Kensing Kempton Karma.

Champion and winning descendants of Kensing Ano-Rak of Amcross:
Ch Kensing Ra
(sire of one Champion)
Ch Parkplace Prim Rose
Ch Kensing Rosetta
Kechanta Kali-Ko of Kensing
(Res. CC and dam of a Champion)
Ch Kensing O-So Special
(dam of two Champions)
Dockenfield Cedar
(one Res. CC)
Ch Kensing Pandora
Ch Kensing Rosie
Kensing Hugo
(one CC)
Kensing Rhum-Me of
Dockenfield
(three Res. CCs)
Kechanta Zarina of Kensing
(two Res. CCs)
Dockenfield Clover
(Res. CC)

Parkplace Maybelle
(Res. CC)
Ch Kensing Oscar
Ch Hexwood Timini
Kensing Marmaduke
(two Res. CCs)
Alvinas Lil-Li-An
(two CCs)

Ch KENSING TIBSKIPS RE-SA (Bitch)

Sire: Ch Clawson Braeduke Rampa   **Owner:** Mrs G. J. Lilley

Dam: Ch Tibskips Rinchin   **Breeder:** Miss P. Burnett

Dam of:
Ch Kensing Ri-Tse
(dam of three Champions)
Kensing Ru-Bear of Parkplace
(Res. CC and sire of one Champion)
Kensing Hugo
(one CC)
Kensing Roger
(one CC)
Kensing Mini-Bean
(dam of one Champion)
Ch Kensing Oscar
(sire of one Champion)

Other Champion and winning descendants:
Ch Kensing Ra
(sire of one Champion)
Ch Kensing Rosie
Ch Kensing O-So Special
(dam of two Champions)
Dockenfield Cedar
Ch Parkplace Prim-Rose
Kensing Rhum-Me of
Dockenfield
(two Res. CCs)
Ch Hexwood Timini
Kechanta Zarina of Kensing
(two Res. CCs)

Ch Kensing Rosetta
Parkplace Maybelle
(Res. CC)
Ch Kensing Pandora
Kensing Marmaduke
(two Res. CCs)
Dockenfield Clover
(Res. CC)

Combining both the Amcross and the Kensing blood-lines with her foundation brood-bitch, Amcross Kos-Pa, purchased in 1971, and with the male, Kensing Ru-Bear of Parkplace, purchased in 1972, Lady Sylvia Dalrymple-Hay had her first home-bred Champion made up in mid 1980; she was Ch Parkplace Prim Rose, whose half-sister Parkplace Maybelle won a Reserve CC, as did Kos-Pa and Ru-Bear.

Mrs V. White's small Kechanta kennel started in 1971, with the dam of the Author's Ch Kechanta Li-Sa, purchased in 1972 from the Redgame kennels. This bitch, Redgame Luna, is from a Champion son of Rama of Amcross out of a litter-sister of Ch Braeduke Channa. Mrs White also bred the Reserve CC winners Kechanta Kali-Ko of Kensing (the dam of the Author's Ch Kensing O-So Special), and Kechanta Zarina of Kensing.

Mrs W. Wallis' home-bred CC winner Tangwell Gubi Glops is a daughter of Ch Ramblersholt Ram-A-Din out of a Wimaro bitch. When Gubi Glops was mated to Ch Windameres Braeduke Champa Mrs Wallis retained a dog and a bitch. Tangwell Gu Cham Midas is the sire of Mrs Lilley's Ch Kensing Ra and Ch Kensing Rosetta, and Miss Sharp's Ch Shamau Ba-Ti-Ka. His litter-sister, Tangwell Gu Cham Gemini, is the dam of Reserve CC winner Tangwell Galaxy, and another Tangwell bitch, Call Me Carmen, is the dam of Miss M. Heaton's Ch Sketchley Miranda.

Mrs A. Hamer of Dockenfield acquired her first Tibetan Spaniel in 1973 and owns a CC winner, but her main blood-lines stem from her triple Reserve CC winning Kensing Rhum-Me of Dockenfield, a daughter of Ch Braeduke Rhum Bu of Kensing out of Ch Kensing Ri-Tse. Her daughter, Dockenfield Clover, and her litter-brother, who is owned by Major and Mrs J. E. Tye in Dockenfield Cedar have both won Reserve CCs; they were sired by Ch Kensing Oscar.

Mrs A. L. Weller, of the Witneylea prefix, started in the early 1960s. One of her first bitches was a particolour litter-sister of Huntglen Rosaree Akasha, but she did not produce any puppies. Mrs Weller's home-bred black-and-tan male Witneylea Tupence, was the first male of this colour to win his Junior Warrant and the second male to do so. Through being mated to Mrs Vines' black-and-tan bitch An-Ke of Balgay, he sired the second English black-and-tan Champion bitch, and only the third English Champion of this colour, Ch Windameres Loo-Di-Pa. There are many other successful winners from the Witneylea blood-lines which are based on Ramblersholt and Amcross strains, among these are Champions in Scandinavia including the first ever particolour Champion in this breed in the Finnish and Swedish Ch Witneylea Patchi Penny Piece. Mrs J. Child's Amroth kennel in America was influenced by Witneylea Kulha, who became a Tibetan Spaniel Club of America Champion.

Miss P. Burnett's first bitch Gyak of Amcross, obtained in 1965, was sired by Ch Sivas Kabru of Amcross out of a daughter of Ch Sivas Ten Sing of Myarlune and the dual CC winner Ama of Szufung. The first Tibskips Champion bred by Miss Burnett was Ch Tibskips Rinchin, who founded her own dynasty when mated to Ch Clawson Braeduke Rampa, through her daughter Ch Kensing Tibskips Re-Sa who was to become Mrs G. J. Lilley's first Kensing Champion.

Ch Rinchin and her CC winning litter-brother, Tibskips Grothan, were both sired by Ch Ramblersholt Ram-A-Din. Miss Burnett's second foundation bitch was a black-and-tan daughter of Ch Peterstown Drom of Szufung who became the dam of Ch Tibskips Dan-Rog. When Ch Rinchin was mated to Ch Bu-Po of Amcross, they produced Tibskips Kham Dong. With a descendant of Ch Dan-Rog and Sivas Shalimar (a litter-sister of International and World Ch Braeduke Sivas Supi Yaw Lat), Kham Dong produced Mr Arthur Bridge's home-bred CC winning Daleviz Kam-Bu. Mr Bridge also owns Ch Amcross Tar-Ka, sire of the dominant stud dog Ch Amcross Tarquin.

Nothing is more difficult than to write about one's own dogs and bitches, so the Author hopes that this information upon the dominant Braeduke blood-lines will help to show the continuation of the 'pattern' already set, of the dominant past and present stud-dogs and brood-bitches. The Author's first bitch was purchased in mid 1962, Braeduke Pema of Szufung, a daughter of Curwenna Rupert of Padua (the sire of Ch Khan Dee of Curwenna), out of Ch Yaso of Szufung, herself a daughter of Seng Ge La out of Szufung Lotus of Furzyhurst; from Pema have descended many Champions and CC winners, although Pema herself did not produce any Champion progeny.

The second bitch, also purchased from Mrs Battson in 1962, was Braeduke Tamara of Szufung, a daughter of Ch Tomu of Szufung out of Szufung Lotus of Furzyhurst, and the older full sister of Mrs Jenkins and Miss Hourihane's Amcross Seto of Szufung. Tamara's two English Champion daughters have continued the dominant strain from Szufung Lotus of Furzyhurst through their sons and daughters. Later on the Author was lucky enough to be able to purchase a twelve months old Tamara daughter sold to Mrs M. Harper of the Huntglen prefix, which is no longer active in this breed; she was Ch Huntglen Braeduke Ta-Ra-Ni, destined to become this breed's top winning bitch with thirteen Challenge Certificates, a title held after her death at fourteen and a half years old, in June 1980. With Huntglen Braeduke Ta-Ra-Ni came the eleven months old male Huntglen Rosaree Bhabu, both descendants of Ch Kye Ho Za-Khyi. Next was purchased a five months old male from Mrs S. Rank who was to become Ch Braeduke Jhanki of Wimaro, a son of Ch Sivas Wimaro Ti Mu out of a Ch Sivas Ten Sing of Myarlune daughter. He was the sire of ten Champions, but possibly his greatest influence on this breed came via his progeny in Sweden. Jhanki was also the first male in this breed to win his Junior Warrant.

Ch Braeduke Lotus Bud of Szufung was purchased from her breeder Mrs Battson at seven months old, a daughter of Ch Khan Dee of Curwenna she shared the same dam as the first Braeduke foundation brood-bitch Pema, in Ch Yaso of Szufung. Ch Lotus Bud's influence on the breed has come through three of her daughters, from her first litter sired by Ch Ramblersholt Ram-A-Din came International Ch Huntglen Braeduke Lhotse, who was owned as a small puppy for a short time by Mrs M. Harper. Lhotse later founded her own dynasty for Mrs P. Kangassalo's Zlazano kennel in Finland. Braeduke Li-Ka-Ra, litter-sister of Lhotse, became Mrs J. M. Smith's foundation brood-bitch for the Rutherglen strain and subsequently also influenced the Taimani strain of Mrs A. Wilson. Another Lotus Bud daughter Ch Braeduke Lhalu was bred by Mrs C. Clapham, sired by Ch Jhanki she produced Australian Ch Braeduke Lhak-Pa Chedi owned by Mrs M. Leach, whose influence has continued through Mrs J. Cassell's Ten Sing kennel in New Zealand. Another Lhalu son, International Ch Braeduke Lham, has again influenced the Zlazano kennel. In their middle years the Author gave both Ch Jhanki and Ch Lotus Bud to Mrs C. Clapham who was, before she re-married, Mrs Jeary of the Heyvan prefix. The Heyvan kennel is no longer active.

From Ch Ta-Ra-Ni's first litter sired by Bhabu came Mrs M. Gidman's Ch Clawson Braeduke Rampa, two of Rampa's three Champion children were to influence the breed. When mated to the half-sister of his dam Ch Braeduke Tam Cho, they produced Mrs

Vines' Ch Windameres Braeduke Champa who was for many years to hold the title of top winning living Tibetan Spaniel in this breed, with fifteen CCs. Siring nine Champions the Ch Champa blood-line has been dominant in the Windameres, Marles, Rutherglen, Taimani, and Kensing strains in England. Overseas his progeny and their descendants have influenced the Strömkarlens kennel in Sweden and the Fanfare kennel in Holland. Unfortunately Ch Champa died at under five years of age before his full potential could be realised.

Through only five influential children of Ch Ta-Ra-Ni have come more than fifty direct Champion descendants, which is a remarkable record for a brood-bitch of any breed, but especially so in this numerically small breed and from so few progeny. Through Bhabu and Ch Ta-Ra-Ni's sons, Ch Rampa and his black-and-tan litter brother Braeduke Rimche Surkhang, have descended the dominant lines from both Ch Kye Ho Za-Khyi and Szufung Lotus of Furzyhurst. Rimche was exported as a puppy to Mrs S. Hacker and, when mated to the Hong Kong-born bitch Honeybun produced two Champions with a completely fresh unknown blood-line, in the Author's Ch Braeduke Ama Kuluh and Mr and Mrs Herjeskog's Swedish Ch Ba-Ba, litter-sister and -brother. These two founded the Anglo-Chinese dynasty in England and Scandinavia, from whom many Champions have now descended, all around the world.

Perhaps the most dominant of the Ch Braeduke Tam Cho progeny has been the stud dog Ch Braeduke Channa, sire of ten Champions. Bred by the Author and sired by Ch Sivas Ten Sing of Myarlune, he won a CC when exhibited by his first owner Mrs Clapham, before passing to Mr and Mrs G. W. Grounds of Whitewisp Samoyed fame, who campaigned him to complete his title. Channa's influence has come through the Colphil kennel of Mrs H. Butler and also through his daughter Ch Braeduke Whitewisp Hara Nor, owned by the Author. Ch Hara Nor must hold the British breed record as the dam of six Champions sired by three different stud dogs, four of these Champions coming from one litter sired by Ch Ram Chandra of Amcross. The most dominant are probably the Author's stud dog Ch Braeduke Nimmi who is now the sire of seven Champions, and his litter-sister owned by Mrs A. Reis in Sweden, International and Nordic Ch Braeduke Nalina. A litter-brother of these two is Mrs M. Leach's premier stud dog Australian Ch Braeduke Numa.

The first ever Champion to be made up in this breed by the Author was Ch Braeduke Sivas Padmini, purchased as a puppy from Miss S. Selby and a daughter of Sivas Lotus. From Ch Padmini has descended Ch Braeduke Patlin and her granddaughter Ch Braeduke Poo-Khyi, both bred by Mrs H. Butler from bitches obtained from the Author under a breeding terms agreement, which is why they do not carry Mrs Butler's Colphil prefix. Ch Poo-Khyi is now this breed's top winning British bitch with fifteen CCs to her credit, inheriting the title from her great-great-paternal grandmother Ch Ta-Ra-Ni. Through her sire International Ch Braeduke Am-Ra, son of Ch Braeduke Ama Kuluh, Poo-Khyi is actually an Anglo-Chinese descendant.

The pair of litter-sisters imported from Poona, India, arrived in England in early 1968. Found by the Author, who with Miss H. F. J. Forbes co-owned the cream sable Yasodhara, it was to be her litter-sister Dikki Dolma, a bright rich red, purchased by Mrs G. Joyce, who was to have the greatest influence. Both these imported bitches have Champion descendants and founded the Anglo-Indian dynasty.

In Dikki Dolma's first litter sired by Ming-Y of Northanger, a son of Huntglen Rosaree Bhabu out of Mrs Joyce's foundation brood bitch Sivas Karamba, came Mrs Micklethwait's Ch Northanger Kenchira Dikki of Wildhern and Mrs Vines' Northanger Kam-Bu Dikki who were to influence the Wildhern, Simpasture and Windameres kennels. Their litter-sister Braeduke Cu-Li Dikki owned by the Author produced five Champions, three of which came from one litter sired by Ch Windameres Braeduke Champa. Another Dikki Dolma daughter sired by Ch Champa was the dam of Mr and Mrs A. Seymour's first home-bred Champion, Ch Chamdoh Shih-Sel Akbar. His sire, Braeduke Rab-Shi, was out of Ch Ta-Ra-Ni.

When Ch Ta-Ra-Ni was mated to Northanger Kam-Bu Dikki she produced Mrs Lilley's Ch Braeduke Rhum-Bu of Kensing, the sire of three Champions. One of Ch Rhum-Bu's sons is Ch Part-Li Amcross, who in turn sired the Champion litter-brother and -sister in Amcross Jimbu and Amcross Jinda. Through a Rhum-Bu daughter Ch Kechanta Li-Sa, bred by Mrs V. White and owned by the Author, has come the CC winning stud dog Braeduke Lu-Ting, a rare silver sable and white particolour. Lu-ting is sired by Ch Channa and he has so far sired four Champions. Three are from the American import Kalimpong Ming Dordja of Braeduke and the other from the Hawaiian import English Ch Braeduke Ama Kuluh, he also has a daughter with two CCs.

Braeduke Dung-Ka descends on both sides from Szufung Lotus of Furzyhurst as he is sired by Rama of Amcross out of a Dikki Dolma granddaughter, Northanger Do-Lo Dikki, thereby combining the blood-lines of both Amcross Seto of Szufung and Braeduke Tamara of Szufung. Dung-Ka is now the sire of thirteen Champions, two of them American Tibetan Spaniel Club Champions, and it is very difficult to say which have been the most influential. Perhaps his sons English Ch Heyvan Jola, International and Nordic Ch Braeduke Lham and International and Nordic Ch Zalatino of Zlazano.

In the summer of 1978 the Author had stud dog problems arise between Ch Braeduke Am-Ra and Braeduke Dung-Ka, which were resolved by giving Am-Ra to Miss M. M. Walsh and Miss M. E. Flynn of Dublin, Ireland, and giving Dung-Ka to be co-owned by Mrs P. Kohler and Ms Mallory Cosby of Virginia, U.S.A. Dung-Ka is currently the top T.S.C.A. Champion producing sire in America.

The Author also purchased Braeduke Shan Hu of Northanger as a puppy from her breeder Mrs Joyce, she was the litter-sister of Ming-Y of Northanger. Through Shan Hu's daughter, Ch Braeduke Su-La, one of four Champions produced in Shan Hu's three litters, has come Mrs Butler's stud dog Ch Braeduke Shipke La who was actually bred by one of the Author's daughters, Edwina. Braeduke Colphil Seng-Kyi the Dog Challenge Certificate winner and Best of Breed at the 1981 Tibetan Spaniel Association's fourteenth Championship show, is bred by Mrs Butler and sired by Ch Shipke La out of a Braeduke Pema of Szufung descendant, Camleigh Shan Tsung, who was ten years old when Seng-Kyi and his litter mates were born.

Clawson Che-Pa of Braeduke who was line-bred to Ch Kye Ho Za-Khyi and bred by Mrs M. Gidman, came to the Author at a year old, under a breeding terms agreement. Before being exported in whelp to Northanger Kam Bu Dikki, to Mrs M. Baurne in Sweden, Che-Pa had two litters by Braeduke Channa. From the first litter a bitch puppy returned to Mrs Gidman, she was registered as Clawson Me-Tsag and sold to Miss M. Moorhead in Southern Ireland, to become the foundation brood bitch for the Benagh kennel. There was another repeat mating and from those two litters came three overseas Champions. Other notable descendants of Che-Pa are Ch Ybroc Eskimo Nell, Ch Benagh Chelsea and her daughter English and Finnish Ch Benagh Chensa.

Miss D. Dodson's partnership with Miss M. I. Flint shared the Weiden prefix, they commenced with two Balgay black-and-tan bitch puppies.

Subsequently a male puppy was purchased from the Author, Braeduke Su-Sun, and his litter-sister went to them under a breeding term agreement. From this bitch, Braeduke Su-Ra, a daughter of Ch Heyvan Jola out of Ch Braeduke Su-La, came the Author's Ch Su-Li of Braeduke and later, from a repeat mating, Mrs Cochrane's CC winning male Weiden Sy-Mon. These two were sired by Ch Taimani

Tu-Bo who descends from Ch Ramblersholt Ram-A-Din and Ch Braeduke Lotus Bud of Szufung.

The Author purchased three other bitches, from Mrs G. J. Lilley came Ch Kensing O-So Special, a particolour double descendant of Ch Ta-Ra-Ni; from Mrs W. Wallis came Tangwell Galaxy, a double descendant of Ch Ramblersholt Ram-A-Din; from Mrs V. White came Ch Kechanka Li-Sa, all purchased as puppies. Ch O-So Special has produced two Champions in two of her litters. From three of Galaxy's litters all by different stud dogs, have come dogs and bitches who have been influential in Canada and America. In one litter, her first, sired by Ch Amcross Am-Ban, Galaxy produced International and Danish Ch Braeduke Gonpo, Mr and Mrs Honey's English Reserve CC winner Braeduke Gartok, Braeduke Gser Phur in Canada who sired the first ever Canadian bitch Champion in this breed, and in America Mrs L. Hosticka (who is now Ms Tamura)'s Braeduke Garpon. Garpon was handled by Mrs Wells who tells me that he had 'finished' and qualifies for his T.S.C.A. Champion title, but this has never been officially confirmed. In Galaxy's second litter, sired by Ch Windameres Lho-Zah-Mi, came two winning bitches, Mr and Mrs Rosen's T.S.C.A. Champion Braeduke Gantsa and, in Southern Ireland, Mr A. Mulcahy's Reserve Green Star winning Braeduke Galinka. In her third litter by Braeduke Su-Sun came Mr and Mrs Mulford's English Reserve CC winning Braeduke Geruda, also Mme Brouilly in France owns his litter-sister Luxembourg Ch Braeduke Gyara. It is interesting to note that Galaxy's dam, Tangwell Gu Cham Gemini, is the litter-sister of Tangwell Gu Cham Midas who is the sire of three British Champions.

Charts showing the 52 Braeduke Tibetan Spaniel Champions, which are numbered.

(*denotes has imported bloodlines)
(Ch denotes British Champion)

BRAEDUKE TAMARA OF SZUFUNG (Bitch)

Sire: Ch Tomu of Szufung

Owner: Mrs A. L. Wynyard

Dam: Szufung Lotus of Furzyhurst

Breeder: Mrs D. M. Battson

Dam of:
1. Ch Huntglen Braeduke
Ta-Ra-Ni
(winner of thirteen CCs, dam of four
Champions)
2. Ch Braeduke Tam Cho
(dam of four Champions, including
the winner of 15 CCs)
3. Finnish Ch Braeduke
Tin-Ti-Lin

Ch BRAEDUKE TAM CHO (Bitch)

Sire: Ch Khan Dee of Curwenna

Owner: Now Miss
M. H. Heaton

Dam: Braeduke Tamara of Szufung

Breeder: Mrs A. L. Wynyard

Dam of:
4. Ch Windameres Braeduke
Champa
(winner of fifteen CCs, sire of nine
Champions)
5. Ch Braeduke Channa
(sire of ten Champions)
6. International and Dutch Ch
Braeduke Chura
7. Swedish Ch Braeduke
Chu-Cel
(dam of one Champion)

Ch HUNTGLEN BRAEDUKE TA-RA-NI (Bitch)

Sire: Ch Sivas Ten Sing of Myarlune

Dam: Braeduke Tamara of Szufung

Owner and Breeder:
Mrs A. L. Wynyard

Dam of:
8. Ch Clawson Braeduke Rampa
(sire of three Champions)
9. Ch Braeduke Re-Ba
(dam of one Champion)
10. Ch Braeduke Rhum-Bu of
Kensing*
(sire of three Champions)
11. International and Dutch Ch
Braeduke Rincen
Braeduke Rab-Shi
(sire of three Champions)
Braeduke Rimche Surkhang
(sire of two Champions)

Over fifty of her direct Champion descendants, via five of her children:
12. International (English and
Irish) Ch Braeduke Am-Ra*
(sire of seven Champions)
13. Finnish Ch Braeduke Dolpo
Dikki*
(jointly bred with Miss H. F. J.
Forbes)
14. International and Italian Ch
Braeduke Norbu Asma*
15. Australian Ch Braeduke
Lhak-Pa Chedi*
16. New Zealand Ch Braeduke
Mingmo*
17. New Zealand Ch Braeduke
O-Pam-Ra*
18. New Zealand and Australian
Ch Braeduke Re-Gi-Na*
19. International and Nordic Ch
Huntglen Braeduke Lhotse
20. Italian Ch Braeduke
Rgul-Po*

21. Ch Braeduke Ama Dablam*
(who did in fact become the 50th
Braeduke Champion)
22. Australian Ch Braeduke
O-Panka*
23. International and Dutch Ch
Braeduke Phu-Phu
24. South African Ch Braeduke
O-Puku
25. South African Ch Braeduke
Lhuntse*
26. International and Nordic Ch
Braeduke Lham*
27. Nordic Ch Braeduke Sinha
28. International and Dutch Ch
Braeduke Spo-Sel
29. International and Danish Ch
Braeduke Gonpo*
30. Australian Ch Braeduke
Sa-Di*
31. Nordic Ch Braeduke
Champa Namgyal*
32. International and Dutch Ch
Braeduke Cham Kusho*
33. International and Dutch Ch
Braeduke Chamba Sopa*
34. Finnish Ch Braeduke
Nan-Pai
35. Luxembourg Ch Braeduke
Gyara*
36. Finnish Ch Braeduke Oso
Pando*
Ch Kensing O-So Special*
Ch Kensing Tibskips Re-Sa
Ch Kensing Ri-Tsi
Ch Kensing Rosetta
Ch Kensing Ra
Ch Kensing Rosie*
Ch Kensing Pandora
Ch Kensing Oscar
Ch Braeduke Ama Kuluh*
(import)

Ch Braeduke Poo-Khyi*
Ch Su-Li of Braeduke*
International and Nordic Ch
Braeduke Amdo Chu*
Swedish Ch Braeduke Atisha
Chu*
Ch Windameres Braeduke
Champa
Ch Ysa of Braeduke*
Ch Rutherglen Jamba
Nordic Ch Rutherglen Shu-Sha
Ch Rutherglen Tai-Mar of
Taimani
Ch Taimani Tu-Bo
Ch Taimani Se-Ba of
Rutherglen*
International, Nordic, English
Ch Lho Cham of Windameres
Ch Windameres Lho-Za-Mi*
Ch Windameres Lho-Lita*
Ch Cham-Bu of Windameres*
Ch Windameres Lho-Tsh-Hi
Ch Kechanta Li-Sa*
Ch Part-Li Amcross*
Ch Amcross Jimbu*
Ch Amcross Jinda*
Ch Amcross Am-Ban*
Ch Tan-Ku from Amscor*
Ch Nimana Lhamu*
Ch Shamau Ba-Ti-Ka
Ch Wildhern Genghiz Khan*
Irish Ch Balgay Aka-Ru*
Ch Parkplace Prim-Rose
Ch Sweet Whisper of Carnbech*
Ch Hexwood Timini
Ch Chamdoh Shi-Sel Akbar*
Finnish and English Ch Benagh
Chensa
Ch Heyvan Jola*
Ch Tsingay Taraminta*
Ch Tsingay Master-Ly*
Ch Tomarans Lotti-Lu

Ch Sketchley Miranda
Ch Ybroc Eskimo Nell*
Ch Friarland Bo-Peep of
Sharbonne*

Some of the other Champions bred or campaigned by the Author:
37. Ch Braeduke Nimmi
38. International and Nordic Ch
Braeduke Nalina
39. Australian Ch Braeduke
Numa
40. Finnish Ch Braeduke Narpo
41. Finnish Ch Braeduke Sinji
42. Ch Braeduke Su-La
43. Ch Braeduke Shipke La
(bred by Edwina Wynyard)
44. International and Nordic Ch
Braeduke Phola
45. Swedish and Norwegian Ch
Braeduke Chamdo Culi*
46. Nordic Ch Braeduke Chung
Culi*
47. South African Ch Braeduke
Lhak-Pa-Lo
48. Swedish Ch Braeduke Pulak
49. International and World Ch
Braeduke Pat-Me
50. Swedish Ch Braeduke Lhiki
Khola
Ch Braeduke Whitewisp Hara
Nor
Ch Braeduke Sivas Padmini
Ch Braeduke Jhanki of Wimaro
Ch Braeduke Lotus Bud of
Szufung
Ch Benagh Chelsea
Ch Braeduke Patlin
Ch Braeduke Lhalu
51. Finnish Ch Braeduke
Mingbo
52. International and Danish Ch
Braeduke Mingmar Choden

166

Under the rules of the Tibetan Spaniel Club of America these have won their T.S.C.A. Champion titles, also bred by the Author; Braeduke Dung-Ka, jointly bred with Miss H. Forbes, and Braeduke Gantsa.

From the bitches mated by the Author and exported in whelp have come these Champions in addition to those already listed: Nordic and Finnish Ch Zuni of Zlazano, International and Nordic Ch Zodi of Zlazano who are both from Huntglen Braeduke Lhotse. From Braeduke Sivas Supi Yaw Lat has come International and Dutch Ch Fanfare for Jampo. From Wildhern Arabella has come International and Nordic Ch Zalatino of Zlazano; also Swedish and Norwegian Ch Zalamander of Zlazano. From Colphil Chi-Lo there is South African Ch Sonnings Tong Woo, and from Braeduke Chu Cel the first Swedish-bred Nordic Champion in Ulvus Argon.

HUNTGLEN ROSAREE BHABU (Dog)

Sire: Rosaree Khen Chung

Dam: Rosaree Lady Gillian

Owner: Mrs A. L. Wynyard

Breeder: Mrs J. Hubberstey

Sire of:
Ch Clawson Braeduke Rampa
(sire of three Champions)
Ming-Y of Northanger
(one CC)
Braeduke Shan Hu of
Northanger
(dam of four Champions)
Ch Shamau Tranka
(sire of one Champion)
Ch Northanger Da-Ra
Ch Northanger A-Su
Finnish Ch La Buska of Copdene
Nordic Ch Braeduke Chung-Culi
Swedish and Norwegian Ch
Braeduke Chamdo Culi
Swedish Ch Rutherglen Tashi

Ch BRAEDUKE CHANNA (Dog)

Sire: Ch Sivas Ten Sing of Myarlune

Dam: Ch Braeduke Tam Cho

Owners: Mr and Mrs G. W. Grounds

Breeder: Mrs A. L. Wynyard

Sire of:
Ch Braeduke Whitewisp Hara Nor
(dam of six Champions)
International Ch Braeduke Phu-Phu (Holland)
International and Nordic Ch Pho-La
(Finland)
Nordic Ch Braeduke Pulak
South African Ch Colphil Chi-Lo
Swedish Ch Whitewisp Chomolungma
Swedish Ch Colphil Chu-Li
Swedish Ch Colphil Shan-Hu
Ch Braeduke Patlin
Finnish and Swedish Ch Braeduke Oso Pando

T.S.C.A. Ch BRAEDUKE DUNG-KA (Dog)

Sire: Rama of Amcross

Dam: Northanger Do-Lo Dikki

Owners: Mesdames P. Kohler and M. Cosby (U.S.A.)

Breeders: Mrs A. Wynyard and Miss H. Forbes

Sire of:
Australian Ch Braeduke Sa-Di
New Zealand and Australian Ch Braeduke Re-Gi-Na
Swedish and Norwegian Ch Zalamander of Zlazano
International and Nordic Ch Zalatino of Zlazano
International and Nordic Ch

Braeduke Lham
Italian Ch Braeduke Rgul-Po
Ch Nimana Lhamu
Ch Heyvan Jola
(sire of one Champion)
South African Ch Sonnings Tong
Woo
South African Ch Braeduke
Lhuntse
T.S.C.A. Ch Bim's Twin Socks
Kamla
T.S.C.A. Ch Phylmarko
Tong-Ka
Ch Friarland Bo-Peep of
Sharbonne

Ch BRAEDUKE AMA KULUH (Bitch) (Import)

Sire: Braeduke Rimche Surkhang   **Owner:** Mrs A. L. Wynyard

Dam: Honeybun (unregistered)   **Breeder:** Mrs J. Hacker

Some of Ama Kuluh's Champion and winning descendants:
English and Irish Ch Braeduke
Am-Ra
(sire of seven Champions, 1979 Irish
Championship show Utility Group
winner)
Braeduke Norbu Ambu
(two Res. CCs)
Ch Braeduke Poo-Khyi
(winner of fifteen CCs)
Finnish Ch Braeduke Dolpo
Dikki
New Zealand Ch Braeduke
O-Pam-Ra
International and Italian Ch
Braeduke Norbu Asma
Irish Ch Balgay Aka-Ru
Australian Ch Braeduke
Lhak-Pa Chedi
Irish Ch Kilmologue Am-Ra
(1981 Irish Championship show
Utility.Group winner)

Ch Amcross Am-Ban
(sire of one Champion, 1979
W.E.L.K.S. Utility Group winner)
International and Nordic Ch
Braeduke Amdo Chu
Swedish Ch Braeduke Atisha
Chu
Ch Braeduke Ama Dablam
Ch Amcross Justice

Ch BRAEDUKE WHITEWISP HARA NOR (Bitch)

Sire: Ch Braeduke Channa

Dam: Braeduke Koko Nor

Owner: Mrs A. L. Wynyard

Breeders: Mr and Mrs
G. W. Grounds

Dam of:
Ch Braeduke Nimmi
(sire of seven Champions)
International and Nordic Ch
Braeduke Nalina
Finnish Ch Braeduke Narpo
Australian Ch Braeduke Numa
Finnish Ch Braeduke Nan-Pai
International and Italian Ch
Braeduke Norbu Asma
Braeduke Norbu Ambu
(two Res. CCs)

(The first four listed were all sired by Ch Ram Chandra of Amcross and came from the same litter.)

Some of her other Champion and winning descendants are:
Swedish Ch Braeduke Lhiki
Khola
South African Ch Braeduke
Lhak-Pa-Lo
Finnish and Swedish Ch
Braeduke Sinji
Finnish Ch Braeduke
Lho-Tho-Ri
Ch Braeduke Pat-Me
(Italy)
Ch Taimani Tu-Bo
Ch Braeduke Shipke La

170

Tangwell Galaxy
(Res. CC)
Braeduke Star-Skyi of Ybroc
(one CC)
Braeduke Lham-Tang
(Res. CC)
Braeduke Colphil Seng-Kyi
(one CC)
Waesfjord Potala
(one CC)

Mrs J. M. Smith's foundation brood bitch Braeduke Li-Ka-Ra was bred by the Author, and started a strong bitch line for the Rutherglen strain in 1966. Li-Ka-Ra and her litter sister, International and Nordic Ch Huntglen Braeduke Lhotse, were sired by Ch Ramblersholt Ram-A-Din out of Ch Braeduke Lotus Bud of Szufung. When Li-Ka-Ra was mated to Ch Clawson Braeduke Rampa she produced Rutherglen Lendzema, who was to become the dam of Ch Rutherglen Jamba and her litter brother Nordic Ch Rutherglen Shu-Sha. Through their sire Mingshang Toto of Szufung, Jamba and Shu-Sha carried five lines to Ch Kye Ho Za-Khyi. Another Li-Ka-Ra daughter sired by Ming-Y of Northanger was the CC winner Rutherglen Lho-Ri. When Lho-Ri was mated to Ch Windameres Braeduke Champa, she produced Mrs A. Wilson's first ever Champion bitch Ch Rutherglen Tai-Mar of Taimani. When Mrs Wilson combined the blood-lines of Rutherglen Sakura and Rutherglen Lho-Ri she produced Mrs J. M. Smith's young 1981 Champion bitch Taimani Hi-Ra of Rutherglen.

Miss H. Simper and Miss E. Scoates of the Clydum partnership, purchased as an adult the CC winner Rutherglen Ze-To, whose daughter Clydum Matilda won her first CC in September 1981. Other Champions, CC winners or Reserve CC winners bred by Mrs Smith are Swedish Ch Rutherglen Tashi, Rutherglen Lav-en-Del, Rutherglen Li-Ka-Ra and Rutherglen Sari.

In 1974 Mrs A. Wilson purchased from Mrs Smith a bitch puppy to become her foundation brood bitch Ch Rutherglen Tai-Mar of Taimani. Tai-Mar has, in turn, produced two Champion daughters. In 1975 the adult bitch Rutherglen Sakura joined the Taimani kennel, a daughter of Ch Amcross Tar-Kar out of Rutherglen Lendzema. When Sakura was mated to the Author's Ch Braeduke Nimmi she produced the first home-bred Champion for Mrs Wilson, and her first stud dog Ch Taimani Tu-Bo. When he was mated to Miss Dodson and

Miss Flint's Braeduke Su-Ra, Tu Bo produced in the first litter the Author's Ch Su-Li of Braeduke and in the second, the CC winner Weiden Sy-Mon. Another Ch Tu-Bo son won his title in 1981 Ch Taimani Chomo Lhari and a daughter Ch Taimani Hi-Ra of Rutherglen.

Mr and Mrs K. Tomlinson's first Tibetan Spaniel was non-pedigree, or a more apt description would be of pedigree unknown. This was in the days before either of them had seen a Tibetan Spaniel. Suzi-Wong, named because she looked like a Peke gone wrong, was found by them as a stray in Nairobi in 1962. She came to England with her owners and after her death she was replaced in 1964 by the purchase of Braeduke Laya from the Author. Laya was the daughter of International Ch Braeduke Am-Ra out of Braeduke Lho-La, herself a daughter of Ch Clawson Braeduke Rampa out of Ch Braeduke Lotus Bud of Szufung. When mated to Ch Braeduke Nimmi, Laya produced a Reserve CC winning daughter in Jaykay Mar-Ti-Ni, subsequently, when mated to Ch Amcross Tarquin, another daughter Jaykay O-Mei was retained and won the Reserve CC at the fourteenth Tibetan Spaniel Association's Championship show in 1981.

Mrs H. Butler of Colphil prefix obtained two bitches as her foundation stock, Camleigh Shan Tsung bred by Mrs M. Catlin was a descendant of Ch Sivas Wimaro Ti Mu and of Sivas Lotus, Braeduke Kailas Kyaring, bred by Mrs Newbury; the second, a daughter of Ming-Y of Northanger out of Kailas Braeduke Po-So, who descended from Ch Sivas Wimaro Ti Mu and Sivas Lotus. Under a breeding terms agreement with the Author the first ever Champion bred by Mrs Butler was produced from Kyaring when she was mated to Ch Braeduke Channa, this was Ch Braeduke Patlin. From Braeduke Pye-Mi, a Ch Patlin daughter sired by Ch Braeduke Nimmi, came this breed's top winning British bitch Ch Braeduke Poo-Khyi. Poo-Khyi was sired by International Ch Braeduke Am-Ra and as she returned to the Author under another breeding terms agreement she does not, like her grandmother, carry the Colphil name.

Mrs Butler mated both her foundation bitches to Ch Braeduke Channa which gave her a successful start; Swedish Ch Colphil Chu-Li and her litter-sister South African Ch Colphil Chi-Lo have their own successful dynasties. When in England in the ownership of Mrs Clapham, Chi-Lo produced Mrs Quinn's Ch Heyvan Jola, who was sired by T.S.C.A. Ch Braeduke Dung-Ka. Another successful Colphil line has been the Irish Green Star winner Colphil Ki-Ki, dam of Ireland's first ever Irish-bred Champion in Miss Walsh and Miss

Flynn's bitch Waesfjord Little Yellow Peril. Mrs Butler's stud dog is a Ch Nimmi and Ch Su La son, Ch Braeduke Shipke La, who sired bred the Author's youngest stud dog Braeduke Colphil Seng-Kyi, a son of Ch Shipke La out of Camleigh Shan Tsung's last litter

In Scotland both Mrs V. Armstrong's home-bred Champion bitch, Friarland Lu-Lha and her CC winning dog Friarland Mhy Ling, are descendants of Colphil Ku-Lu. From the last of the Ch Channa and Camleigh Shan Tsung matings came Mr and Mrs Herjeskog's Swedish Ch Colphil Shan-Hu. Miss Y. Border in Scotland owns another Ku-Lu descendant, Ch Friarland Bo-Peep of Sharbonne.

In 1968, Miss M. W. Sharp of the Shamau prefix, purchased as a pet the particolour bitch Silverset Shireen, of Sivas and Wimaro blood-lines. In her first litter sired by Huntglen Rosaree Bhabu, Shireen produced the first English particolour Champion, the male Ch Shamau Tranka. Shireen won trophies for the top British Brood bitch both in 1972 and 1973, she was also runner up for this trophy in 1974. Miss Sharp's small select kennel has been fearlessly campaigned, promoting the rare and unusual colour – particolour. Among the CC and Reserve CC winners bred here are Ch Shamau Ba-Ti-Ka, Shamau Tagster, Shamau Pipitang, Shamau Kaspa and Shamau Dri-Bo. Mrs A. Young in Scotland owns the particolour dog Irish Ch Balgay Artali, a son of Ch Tranka.

Miss K. Williamson's small Nimana kennel commenced in 1975 with the purchase of her foundation brood bitch, Braeduke Rinchi-Ta, a daughter of Ch Braeduke Nimmi out of Ch Ta-Ra-Ni's daughter Ch Braeduke Re-Ba. In her first litter sired by T.S.C.A. Ch Braeduke Dung-Ka came Ch Nimana Lhamu, and her litter sister Nimana Khara of Twinley owned by Mrs P. Block. In the second litter bred by Miss Williamson, sired by Ch Amcross Am-Ban out of Ch Lhamu, combining both the Anglo-Indian and Anglo-Chinese blood-lines, came Nimana Kelma who distinguished himself in May 1981 by winning Supreme Best Puppy in Show at the Bath Championship All Breeds show, the first time ever for a Tibetan Spaniel and no mean feat!

The Ybroc kennel of Mrs C. Quinn and her daughter Miss A. Leslie is now not very active; they started with a male puppy bred by Mrs Clapham which they campaigned to his title, in Ch Heyvan Jola. Their first bitch was Braeduke Ba-Byi of Ybroc who won a CC, the mating of Ch Jola to Ba-Byi produced the Author's and Miss H. F. J. Forbes' co-owned red-and-white particolour bitch Ch Ybroc Eskimo Nell. From this same litter came Mrs J. Holsapple's T.S.C.A. Ch Ybroc Terribly Twee. Miss Leslie owns the litter-sister of Ch Su-Li of

Braeduke and the CC winning male Braeduke Star-Skyi of Ybroc.

Mrs A. L. Gulliver of the Alvinas prefix owns two Tibetan Spaniel bitches; from Churlswood Mimosa she bred Mr D. Chapman's dual CC winning bitch Alvinas Lil-Li-An; Mimosa is sired by Ch Amcross Tarquin and is out of a descendant of T.S.C.A. Ch Braeduke Dung-Ka, and was mated to Braeduke Lu-Ting.

Mr Chapman also owns the dual CC winning male Braeduke Lingbu, a son of Ch Braeduke Nimmi out of Braeduke Lin-Ga-La who is the litter-sister of Braeduke Lu-Ting.

It is interesting to trace the progress of the Tibetan Spaniel breed in other parts of the British Isles. In Wales the only current active exhibitors are Mrs Ruth Croucher and her daughter Miss Bridget Croucher with their jointly owned Bruesown prefix-affix. Based on the Amcross blood-lines, their Bruesown A-Ne has two CCs and four Reserve CCs, in males Bruesown Zir-Tan-Ce has one CC and another male, Bruesown Dun-Dun, a son of Ch Amcross Tarquin, now has two CCs. These are all home-bred and they are campaigned all over the British Isles.

Other Welsh owners are not so active, like Mr Halley Jones of the Brynshal prefix, Mrs M. Edwards of the Dolhfryd prefix and Mr and Mrs B. Johnson of the Megburn prefix. To date Mrs and Miss Croucher are the only consistent Welsh exhibitors who attend most of the Championship shows.

In Scotland Mrs A. Young of Balgay prefix-affix, commenced in 1967 with a black-and-tan daughter of Ch Braeduke Jhanki of Wimaro out of Braeduke Tamara of Szufung. Huntglen Rosaree Akasha was purchased as an adult in 1968 and she has had the greatest influence on the Balgay kennel. Akasha was the particolour daughter of Ch Kye Ho Za-Khyi out of Ch Rosaree Mai Lei and the first particolour to win a CC in the British Isles. Her son Balgay A-Li-Ka-Li sired by Ch Sivas Ten Sing of Myarlune, was tragically killed after winning his Irish title and before he could complete his English title, having won two CCs. His litter sister An-Na-Ma-Na of Balgay was the foundation bitch for Mrs M. Wilson's Woldfoot strain. Mrs Young has campaigned the breed all over the British Isles including Southern Ireland, and she can claim to have made up the first ever Irish champion. Other Champions, CC or Reserve CC, or Irish Green Star winners here are Irish Ch Balgay Artali, the sire of Mrs Armstrong's Ch Friarland Lu-Lha, Irish Ch Balgay A-Ti-Wa, Balgay Tsed-Pa and Balgay Ardhui.

Among the small nucleus of Tibetan Spaniel breeders and exhibitors in Scotland, mostly sited in Ayrshire and Perthshire, is Mrs

V. Armstrong of the Friarland prefix who can clain to have made up the first Scottish-bred British Champion in her home-bred bitch Ch Friarland Lu-Lha, a granddaughter of her first bitch Colphil Ku-Lu obtained in 1973. A half brother of Ch Lu-Lha is the CC winning male Friarland Mhy Ling, a son of Braeduke Lu-Ting and out of Friarland Minni.

Miss Y. Border has her small select Sharbonne kennel based on her foundation brood bitch Ch Friarland Bo-Peep of Sharbonne, a daughter of Braeduke Dung-Ka out of Colphil Ku-Lu. Miss Border exhibits her three bitches outside Scotland and appears to specialise in breeding the rare rich auburn red coat colour, which is occasionally referred to as the true 'Indian Red'.

Other Scottish breeders and exhibitors who do not exhibit very much and seldom venture outside Scotland or the North of England, are Mrs L. Clarke of the Tuyat prefix, Mr and Mrs W. G. Dick of the Niord prefix, Mr and Mrs S. Main of the Niam prefix, Mrs N. Stewart who owns and bred the Irish Green Star winner Muirhall Ki-Khan, lastly Mr and Mrs Wedderburn-Ogilvy of the Puchill prefix. More recently new exhibitors are Mr B. Stevenson and Mrs P. M. Scott, who do not yet have their own prefixes.

The Author considers that the biggest lack in Scotland is a variety and choice of stud dog blood-lines, the enormous distances to the southern dogs discourages the Scottish breeders from venturing far afield when mating their bitches. This must undoubtedly inhibit expansion and very few of the Scottish owners and breeders are regular exhibitors outside their own immediate area.

Crossing the sea to Northern Ireland, the only general all breeds Championship show is Belfast. For the first time, in 1980, there were Tibetan Spaniel classes with no CCs and only nine entered. In 1981 there were 10 dogs entered at this show, still without CCs*.

Not many of the Northern Irish Open shows give Tibetan Spaniel breed classes so that there is really very little encouragement and dedicated exhibitors are forced to travel to the South. Mrs P. McAfee of the Carnam kennel was the first person to import in 1968, but Cavaliers are now her main breed. Mr and Mrs R. Mackenzie own a Carnam-bred dog and bitch and a Kilmologue male. Mrs P. Reynolds of the Hollybough prefix does exhibit in the South, her two males Braeduke Lhari of Hollybough and Braeduke Nge-Drup Dorje are both Irish Green Star winners, but they are not at stud, as Mrs Reynolds does not breed. Mrs V. Robinson of Deetree prefix emi-

*The Northern Ireland Belfast Championship show, is subject to English Kennel Club rules, and is not under the jurisdiction of the Irish Kennel Club.

grated with her family and the three Tibetan Spaniel bitches to the Cape Cod area on the East Coast of America in November 1981; but as yet, in the north, only Mrs McAfee has bred any litters.

In the South Miss M. Moorhead was the first breeder in Eire, her foundation brood bitch, Clawson Me-Tsag, was a litter-sister of International and Nordic Ch Braeduke Pho La. From Me-Tsag's first litter sired by Irish Ch Balgay A-Li-Ka-Li came the Green Star winner later to become an English Champion, Benagh Chelsea. It was Chelsea's daughter, Benagh Chensa, sired by Braeduke Rab-Shi, who made history by becoming the first Irish-bred English and Finnish Champion. Benagh Chang of Ybroc, litter-brother of Ch Chensa won a CC and also sired the mother of Ch Ybroc Eskimo Nell. In the last litter bred by Miss Moorhead were the Green Star winning male Benagh Sage owned by Mr M. Hogan, and his litter-sister Benagh Rue who was exported to Canada. Now Mrs Hockin in England has her Aunt's Benagh prefix and another Benagh registered litter was born in 1981, but not from the original blood-lines.

The Irish Kennel Club first recognised the Tibetan Spaniel as a breed in 1968, and since then there have been 209 Tibetan Spaniel registrations.

Other active breeders and exhibitors are Miss M. M. Walsh and Miss M. E. Flynn, who jointly own the Waesfjord prefix-affix; they are the owners of the first ever 1978 Irish-bred Irish Champion in the bitch Waesfjord Little Yellow Peril. She was bred by Mrs J. Wynne Jones and descends through T.S.C.A. Ch Braeduke Dung-Ka from the dominant Ch Ramblersholt Ram-A-Din line.

English Ch Braeduke Am-Ra joined the Waesfjords in mid 1978 as an adult, he was the second Irish Tibetan Spaniel to win a Utility Group at the Dublin Show Society's Championship show in 1979, and the first Irish male to do so. He subsequently won enough points for his Irish Champion title and is the first International Tibetan Spaniel Champion in the British Isles, also he is the sire of seven Champions. A son of Ch Braeduke Nimmi out of Ch Braeduke Patlin, Braeduke Puk-Pa of Waesfjord, winner of an Irish Green Star, sired his first litters in 1981. The Author owns his daughter Waesfjord Potala, out of the Irish Champion bitch, who won her first CC at 11 months old in November 1981.

Mrs M. Tobin now owns Colphil Ki-Ki, dam of Ch Little Yellow Peril, and bred her daughter Irish Ch Tobhog Madame Y. Mrs E. Lynch owns the two Green Star winners, Tomarans Zorba a male and a bitch, Tamar of Tobhog.

Mr P. Murphy owns the second Irish-bred Champion, also a bitch, in Ch Ballymore Thami who was bred by Mrs McKeever. His 1981 Champion bitch the black-and-tan, Ballymore Tarim, made history by being the first ever Tibetan Spaniel to win a Utility Group in 1977. Mr Murphy's home-bred Ch Kilmologue Am-Ra was the top winning Annual Champion for 1980, and was the third Irish Champion to win his title in 1981, he is also a Utility Group winner. Mr Murphy also owns the English-bred particolour Irish Champion male, Avenel Robin, bred by Mrs P. Ffoulkes.

Other exhibitors are Mr A. Mulcahy with his Green Star winning bitch Braeduke Galinka and his Reserve Green Star winning male Kensing Friend, Mr H. Graham of the well known Cocker Spaniel prefix Hardet, Mrs R. Donohue, Mrs E. Lynch of the Curralyn prefix, Mrs M. McGrath, Mrs A. O'Brien, Mr and Mrs Duggan and Mrs C. Kennedy.

There are many more Tibetan Spaniel owners both in the North and South of Ireland, but they appear to have their dogs as pets and do not wish to show them or breed from them. Until the show classification improves in Ireland and more specialised and knowledgeable judges are appointed to adjudicate on the breed, there is not a great deal of encouragement with scanty, often mixed sex, classes offered by the Irish Championship shows. Though, to be fair, 1981 has seen a big improvement in the show classification. In the late summer of 1981 moves were made to form the foundation of the proposed Tibetan Spaniel Association of Ireland, with thirty-five founder members. It is hoped that this move will encourage supporters of the breed in the North of Ireland also.

The points system in Eire for making up an Irish Champion, does seem very complex indeed. Whether this has any bearing upon the lack of support from English exhibitors the Author does not know, the system might be easier to understand if it was written in Tibetan! There are no Challenge Certificates, instead there are Green Stars and Reserve Green Stars, but to complicate matters not always is there a Green Star award for each sex at all the Irish Championship shows. This means that to make up an Irish Champion in a little known, numerically small breed can be a very slow and laborious process, which could account for the fact that by August 1981 there are still only six Irish owned Tibetan Spaniel Champions.

Officially, there were no Tibetan Spaniels registered on the Island of Guernsey in the Channel Isles, prior to Mrs S. Foley's first Tibetan Spaniel arriving there in 1976, but an old issue of the *Guernsey Evening Press* (March 22nd, 1963) shows that the first Tibetan Spaniel litter was born in Guernsey in that year, and was owned by Major and

Mrs D. Short. The Press cutting shows a photograph of a particolour bitch puppy and a black-and-tan male, with another puppy of uncertain colouring. The article states that the parents were uncle and niece and that the dam's litter-mates won most of the awards at Crufts Dog Show in February 1963. It goes on to say that there were only about a hundred of this breed in Europe, also that the parents of the sire were born in the Chumbi Valley of Tibet.

In 1955 Mrs J. Birchall of the Zepherine King Charles Spaniels purchased a Tibetan Spaniel male, Nakmingla, from Lady Wakefield. He was, in fact, the first post-war black-and-tan Tibetan Spaniel to be born, sired by Seng Ge La out of Shemo La. Mrs Birchall also purchased from Miss Braye and Miss Elam a bitch, Ranee of Padua, fawn with black points. When Mrs Birchall parted with her Tibetan Spaniels, only because they did not fit in with her other dogs, the male went to Guernsey and the bitch returned to her breeders. Mrs Birchall clearly recalls that the male resembled a miniature Tibetan Mastiff, and that both had good mouths with level bites.

Mrs Foley now has three Tibetan Spaniels as her nucleus, her male is Mingshang Benedict and her two bitches are Carrows Thari-Lo and Carrows Anna; she has also bred a litter of three puppies, from Anna, which she hopes will stay on the Island and help to found a Guernsey dynasty.

Also in the Channel Islands, in Jersey, Mrs J. Mourant has the first Tibetan Spaniels ever seen there; a male, Hormead Chi-Mu and a bitch, Hormead Maxe Mu. From this pair has come Mrs J. Garner's CC and Junior Warrant winning bitch Hormead Tsa Ku.

In an article entitled 'Trick of Forecasting the Top Breeds', in *The Times* (5th February, 1970), Wilson Stevens, at that time Editor of *The Field*, said: "Recently there was a market tip for Tibetan Spaniels, golden-coated lion-like dogs of pleasing temperament. Their stock met with a sudden demand".

Here lies a warning which applies even today. Yes, our breed is wanted for breeding, even for export to dubious countries where there are no cruelty laws, nor R.S.P.C.A. guardians, where the religion is anti-dog, and the climate and conditions are unsuitable for any breed.

In the Author's opinion, it is not a case of Caveat Emptor (let the buyer beware), but for all caring Tibetan Spaniel breeders to be very vigilant about where and to whom they sell their stock, especially bitches. If you do truly love the breed, you will know that this oriental breed of Asian origin does not suit everyone, and it should never be offered for sale in pet shops.

8 History of the Tibetan Spaniel in Sweden

It is perhaps difficult to imagine just how Champions are made up in other countries. All too often there is the ignorant criticism of 'cheap Champions', but every judge has the right to withhold a Challenge Certificate, Green Star or Challenge points, if the quality of the exhibit does not merit such an award.

The Kennel Clubs in Scandinavia come under the FCI or, to give this body its full name, the Federation Cynologique Internationale, which controls every aspect of shows and breeding in Europe, and South America, except for the United Kingdom. One major difference at shows is the classification which is regulated to only the following classes: for each sex, Junior, (which is nine to fifteen months of age, or occasionally twelve to eighteen months); Open (which is an age class, for dogs and bitches of either over fifteen months or eighteen months of age); Champion class; Veteran class (for dogs who are more than seven years old).

Again different from the United Kingdom, the classes are judged on a grading system, the first (and top) grade is 'Excellent', the second prize is given to a dog of good type and temperament and with minor faults which could not be considered 'Excellent' but can be given 'Very Good'. The third grade, 'Good', is given to a dog lacking condition and quality but who is not a really poor specimen of the breed. Finally 'Zero' is given to a dog of poor temperament which cannot be handled or one with a bad or disqualifying fault.

All dogs are given a written critique, which does slow down the number of dogs which can be judged; therefore the FCI countries usually limit a judge to seventy-five exhibits in a day, giving the surplus to another judge, which is very disappointing for the exhibitors.

There are two types of CCs; the first, the International Certificate is called the CACIB and this is awarded only at the International shows. It is not awarded until the best of each sex has been chosen and the exhibit must be over fifteen months of age and not yet an International Champion under the FCI rules. No dog can become an International Champion until it has won a CACIB not less than one year from the first. For an International title, CACIBs have to be won in all three Scandinavian countries of Sweden, Norway and Finland. Because of the risk of Rabies, Denmark is excluded from the Scandinavian 'block', as quarantine regulations will not permit the interchange of show dogs.

The second is the CAC which is for the National shows. Three CACs give the title of Champion, but these can be won under two different judges, whereas the four CACIBs must be won under three different judges. The title 'Scandinavian Champion' and 'Nordic Champion' are one and the same, the latter is merely an abbreviation. Once your dog has become a Champion, it may no longer compete for the CACs but must be entered only in the Champion class. So, if your dog is already a Swedish Champion, by winning another CC in Finland your dog would then become a Swedish and Finnish Champion. No dog may become a Champion in Sweden until he is fifteen months of age regardless of how many CCs he has won.

The Tibetan Spaniel is in the Toy group in Scandinavia, where there are about twenty-nine different breeds to compete with in the group judging, so it is difficult to get a group placing with a Tibetan Spaniel but, in spite of this, more Scandinavian Tibetan Spaniels have had group wins and placings than their English cousins. At the end of 1979, Tibetan Spaniels were running for the second consecutive year as the eighth most popular breed in Sweden.

The first English imports to Sweden and almost surely the first Tibetan Spaniels to go to Sweden, were sent by Miss J. Hervey-Cecil of the Furzyhurst kennel in the Isle of Wight and also by Colonel Hawkins. Six were registered with the Swedish Kennel Club in 1956, one of these was a bitch exported in whelp to Seng-Ge-La, sent to Margita Stroberg in 1955. Among the few descendants from these today is Mr G. Howard Smith's Spo Sihla, sired by his fourteen-year-old male Khoro-Yang, out of an English-bred imported bitch Chamdoh Shi-Sel Ayisha who is the litter-sister of Ch Chamdoh Shih-Sel Akbar. Mrs Rennerfeldt, who bred Khoro-Yang, has his litter-brother.

In 1964 Mrs Gunhild Vilén imported Sivas Khara and Sivas Khumbu; English Champion Rosaree Anak Agung followed in 1966, but unfortunately died young.

Mrs Marianne Baurne of the Krysants prefix, who has also bred Labradors, Tibetan Terriers and Lhasa Apsos, started in the breed in 1967 by importing Bragborough Bally Ho, a daughter of Ch Khan Dee of Curwenna out of Yakrose Sera, who became a Swedish Champion. Mrs Baurne also imported Bragborough Tammy who became a Nordic Champion, a daughter of Ch Braeduke Jhanki of

Wimaro out of Swedish Ch Bragborough Bally Ho. Other Tibetan Spaniels imported from England by Mrs Baurne have been Swedish Ch Rutherglen Tashi, a daughter of Huntglen Rosaree Bhabu and out of Braeduke Ti-Bo. International and Nordic Ch Daleviz Sivas Zebe who is a son of Ch Sivas Wimaro Ti-Mu out of Braeduke Cilla of Curwenna and the litter-brother of English Ch Sivas Zodi, who is now owned by Mr Einar Johannson; Swedish and Finnish Ch Braeduke Sinha, a son of Ch Windameres Braeduke Champa out of Braeduke Shan Hu of Northanger, is now owned by Lilian Lundquist; and more recently Mrs Baurne imported Braeduke Atisha Chu, a daughter of Ch Amcross Tarquin out of Braeduke Ama Chu, bred by Mrs Jenkins and Miss Hourihane. Like her two brothers English Ch Amcross Am-Ban and International and Nordic Ch Braeduke Amdo Chu, she has won her title of Champion. Mrs Baurne also imported a young male Skipsgreen Kung Fu, a son of Ch Clawson Braeduke Rampa out of Skipsgreen Do-Tso, bred by Mrs S. Nesbitt.

Mrs Baurne has bred Swedish and Finnish Ch Krysants Tarani, a daughter of Nordic Ch Rutherglen Shu-Sha out of Swedish Ch Bragborough Bally Ho, also Nordic Ch Krysants Tuna owned by Birgitta and Ulf Gustafsson who is a daughter of Swedish Ch Rutherglen Tashi. Mr and Mrs Gustafsson have imported Braeduke Rolwaling a daughter of Braeduke Dung-Ka out of Ch Braeduke Re-Ba.

Mrs Bibi Stäveby owns Swedish Ch Krysants Ama Rani, a daughter of International and Nordic Ch Braeduke Amdo Chu, and has bred two more CC winners, though Mrs Stäveby is well-known as a Lhasa Apso breeder as well.

There are many other Krysants CC winners and several kennels have purchased their foundation stock from Mrs Baurne, and Ch Bragborough Bally Ho is in the background of many successful lines.

In the late 1960s Gunhild Johannson and her husband Einar, who do not have a kennel name, started to breed Tibetan Spaniels with stock obtained from Mrs Vilén and Mrs Baurne. Since Mrs Johansson's death, her husband is carrying on breeding and showing. Mr and Mrs Johannson's first import was Whitewisp Chomolungma who became a Swedish Champion. Bred by Mr and Mrs G. W. Grounds, he is sired by Ch Braeduke Channa out of Braeduke Koko Nor, from a repeat mating which produced Ch Braeduke Whitewisp Hara Nor. They purchased from Mrs Baurne the dog International and Nordic Ch Daleviz Sivas Zebe and a bitch Krysants Zempa, who is a daughter of Ch Bragborough Bally Ho. Their other import was a bitch puppy bred by Mrs D. Ormsby, Braeduke Ka-Ma-Ru, a particolour daughter of T.S.C.A. Ch Braeduke Dung-Ka out of Kempton Keepa. From Ka-Ma-Ru has come Swedish Ch Fabiola, owned by Dagmar Larsson. Two other Champions have been bred here, Birgitta Carlsson's Swedish Ch Litte who is sired by Ch Zebe, and Mr Johansson's Swedish Ch Jenca, sired by Ch Whitewisp Chomolungma, both are daughters of Krysants Zempa.

In 1970 four more kennels commenced in Tibetan Spaniels: Mrs Aina Skarin who does not have a kennel name, Mrs Lisbeth Sigfridsson of Kennel Ulvus, Mr Börje and Mrs Monica Herjeskog of Kennel Strömkarlen, lastly Gunn and Sven-Erik Ödman of Kennel Lässebacken.

Mrs Skarin started with Swedish-bred stock, her Nordic Ch Florentina was sired by International and Nordic Ch Zodi of Zlazano out of Swedish Ch Huntglen Nova. This was from a half-brother and -sister mating, as both were sired by English Ch Braeduke Jhanki of Wimaro. In three litters, all sired by Nordic Ch Rutherglen Shu-Sha, this bitch Florentina produced International and Nordic Ch Baschi, Swedish and Finnish Ch Corinthia, CC winner Dhi-Lai-La as well as other CC winners. When Dhi-Lai-La was mated to Ch Lho-Cham of Windameres, she produced Mr Jonas Johansson's International and Nordic Ch Elko-Ti-Mo and, from the same litter, Solveig Berge's Swedish and Norwegian Ch Eicie-Kawanga. Florentina's other litter, sired by English, Swedish and Finnish Ch Amcross Kam-Dar, has produced R. Dufvenmark's Swedish and Norwegian Ch Floren-Thi-Noh and also Swedish and Norwegian Ch Fah-Ya-Noh. Sadly Florentina, Baschi and Dhi-Lai-la died in a fire and now Mrs Skarin only has Ch Fah-Ya-Noh left from her blood-lines. Mrs Skarin must be considered to be an influential breeder with all these Champions coming from only six litters.

Mrs Lisbeth Sigfridsson, who also breeds Japanese, Pekingese and German Shepherd dogs, purchased from Mrs Baurne her first bitch, a daughter of Ch Daleviz Sivas Zebe out of Ch Bragborough Bally Ho, named Krysants Zeba. Among the stock imported from England by Mrs Sigfridsson, four have had a great influence on her strain. Firstly, Nordic Ch Rutherglen Shu-Sha, a son of Mingshang Toto out of Rutherglen Lendzema, litter-brother of Mrs T. M. Smith's English Ch Rutherglen Jamba. Secondly, the bitch Braeduke Chu-Cel, imported in whelp to Ch Ramblersholt Ram-A-Din and from this litter came Ulvus Argon, which made history by becoming the first Swedish-born Tibetan Spaniel to become an International and Nordic Champion. Chu-Cel was the daughter of Ch Braeduke Jhanki of Wimaro out of Ch Braeduke Tam Cho, and litter-sister of Mrs Van

Den Boom's International Ch Braeduke Chura in Holland; like her litter-sister Chu-Cel became a Champion in Sweden. The third import was another bitch, Northanger Gur-Kum, sired by Huntglen Rosaree Bhabu out of Pan-Zi of Northanger. Willy Nilsson's International and Nordic Ch Ulvus Jollbart and the CC-winning Ulvus Gullmora are both out of Gur-Kum, who is also the grandmother of an interesting English import, Kalimpong Ming Dordja of Braeduke, born in St Louis, Missouri, U.S.A., whose dam is a Gur-Kum daughter.

Mrs Sigfridsson's Corinthia, purchased from Mrs Skarin, became a Swedish and Finnish Champion. The last import from England made by Mrs Sigfridsson was that of English Ch Amcross Kam-Dar, a son of Ch Rimpoche of Amcross out of Kosi of Amcross, who won Swedish and Norwegian Champion titles. Also from the Ulvus kennel has come Ulvus Dragon who has greatly influenced the kennel of Mrs Agneta Reis through her International and Nordic Ch Han-E-Ball; another is Marianne Nilsson's Swedish Ch Ulvus Kamphas, a son of Ch Ulvus Argon. Others bred here are Ingrid Carlsson's Swedish Ch Ulvus Sobel Sam who is sired by Ch Amcross Kam-Dar out of Ch Corinthia, and Swedish Ch Ulvus Yak Pansy who is sired by International and Nordic Ch Ulvus Argon out of Swedish Ch Ulvus Ludmilla. Ludmilla is the daughter of Swedish Ch Ba-Ba out of Krysants Zeba. Ch Ulvus Sobel Sam was the top winning Tibetan Spaniel for 1979. Perhaps Ch Shu-Sha has had the most influence on the Ulvus strain, he is the third top producing Tibetan Spaniel stud-dog with four Champions and many more CC winners.

Monica and Börje Herjeskog of the Strömkarlens kennel who earlier were breeders of Golden Retrievers and Kuvasz, started with the purchase of Nordic Ch Bragborough Tammy from Mrs Baurne, which proved to be a very good brood-bitch. The most important of the Herjeskog imports must be Ba-Ba from Honolulu, Hawaii. Bred by Mrs John Hacker and purchased as a puppy, Ba-Ba was sired by Braeduke Rimche Surkhang out of the Chinese-born Honeybun; this particolour dog is the litter-brother of English Ch Braeduke Ama Kuluh. Ba-Ba won his Swedish title and is the second top-producing stud-dog with six Champions and several CC winners.

Two other males imported from England have also influenced the Strömkarlens strain. Eulyn Impney a son of Ch Amcross Gu-Pa of Kethmora out of Geisha of Eulyn, became a Swedish and Norwegian Champion and is now owned by Mrs Gaardsmoen in Norway. The second male import is Braeduke Champa Namgyal, the first of the Indian blood-lines to be exported, to become a Nordic Champion. He is a son of Ch Windameres Braeduke Champa out of Braeduke

Northanger Cu-Li Dikki; his litter-brother and -sister in Holland are both International Champions. Solveig Smedstuen of Norway owns Swedish and Norwegian Ch Strömkarlens Dea Divina, a daughter of Ch Champa Namgyal.

Windameres Tar-Quin, a black-and-tan daughter of Ch Lho-Cham of Windameres out of Anke of Balgay, was imported from Mrs G. Vines, and was later joined by her sire who swiftly won his International and Nordic titles. Swedish Ch Strömkarlens Tsi-Rin was the top winning Tibetan Spaniel bitch for 1978, coming only one point behind the winning male; she is a daughter of Swedish Ch Ba-Ba out of Ch Tar-Quin. Another Ch Tar-Quin daughter is Swedish and Finnish Ch Strömkarlens Talika owned by Vera Ahs; this black-and-tan bitch is from a repeat mating of Ch Tsi-Rin.

Mr and Mrs Herjeskog purchased in Sweden a bitch Lässebackens Afrodite, sired by Swedish and Norwegian Ch Strömkarlens Bzanba, a son of Swedish Ch Ba-Ba out of Ch Bragborough Tammy. The dam of Afrodite is English-bred Swedish Ch Colphil Chu-Li, litter-sister of a South African Champion. Afrodite became an International and Nordic Champion between 1974 and 1976, when she was the top winning Tibetan Spaniel in Sweden with eight CACIBs, twelve times Best of Breed and four times placed in the Toy Group. Her highest placing in the Group was at the Stockholm International Show in 1974 when I made her Best of Breed and she went on to be placed Reserve (i.e. second) in the Group by Mrs Y. Bentinck. Stockholm is for the Swedish exhibitors their 'Crufts' dog show.

Ch Afrodite is the dam of Nordic Ch Strömkarlens Ang-Ela who was sired by English, International and Nordic Ch Lho-Cham of Windameres; Ch Ang-Ela was the top winning bitch for 1979. Another Champion offspring of Afrodite is Mia Lange's Strömkarlens Allegro, also sired by Ch Lho-Cham of Windameres. Nordic Ch Strömkarlens Angelina, also a Ch Afrodite daughter, was sired by Ch Eulyn Impney. From Ch Ba-Ba and out of Strömkarlens Näckros have come two more Champions, Marie Nilsson's Swedish and Finnish Ch Strömkarlens Doma, also Charlotte Nygren's Swedish Ch Strömkarlens Bang-A-Boomerang. The bitch Näckros carries three lines to Ch Braeduke Jhanki of Wimaro.

The Strömkarlens Kennel has been the top winning Tibetan Spaniel kennel in Sweden for many years; they hold the record of eleven home-bred champions. There is little doubt that English, International and Nordic Ch Lho-Cham of Windameres has had a very great influence both on the breed in Sweden and also on the Strömkarlens strain; he had up to early 1980, sired twelve Champions including two in England, and was the top winning Tibetan Spaniel in Sweden in 1977. He has also twice achieved Best of Breed at the Tibetan Breeds Show and is so far the only Tibetan Spaniel to have done so, last winning Best of Breed at the Stockholm International Show in 1980 when almost nine years old.

The last of the kennels founded in 1970 is that of Gunn and Sven-Erik Ödman of Lässebackens Kennels who started in the breed with two imported bitches. One is Braeduke Sarika, the daughter of Ch Windameres Braeduke Champa and out of Braeduke Shan Hu of Northanger; she is the litter-sister of Ch Braeduke Sinha and of International Ch Braeduke Spo-Sel in Holland, also the full sister from a repeat mating which produced Mrs M. Lundgren's Braeduke Su-Lin.

The other imported bitch was Colphil Chu-Li, the daughter of Ch Braeduke Channa out of Camleigh Shan Tsung, bred by Mrs H. Butler. Chu-Li's litter-sister South African Ch Colphil Chi-Lo produced English Ch Heyvan Jola and South African Ch Tong-Woo.

Colphil Chu-Li won her Swedish title and produced the beautiful Ch Afrodite. Another import was the male Heyvan Chu La, winner of a Reserve CC in England, purchased from his breeder Mrs C. Clapham. The Ödmans purchased from Mr and Mrs Herjeskog the male Strömkarlens Bzanba as a puppy; they also bred Ch Lässebackens Na-Nung sired by Ch Strömkarlens Bzanba out of Braeduke Sarika. This kennel was disbanded in 1980.

In 1972 Mrs Jorun Winberg started her breeding by importing three Tibetan Spaniels from Mrs Kangassalo's Zlazano kennel in Finland. They were International and Nordic Ch Zhade of Zlazano, also the English-bred male International and Nordic Ch Braeduke Phola, who was exported to Finland as a puppy. He was the son of Ch Braeduke Channa out of Clawson Che-Pa of Braeduke, who was at one time the top winning Tibetan Spaniel in Scandinavia. Mrs Winberg also owns the English-bred International and Nordic Ch Lha Buska of Copdene, a son of Huntglen Rosaree Bhabu out of Copdene Lha-Cam of Amcross. Ch Lha-Buska of Copdene is the sire of Finnish Ch Hårskas Clematis and of Nordic Ch Hårskas Golden Cream.

Mrs Maiden Lundgren has bred two litters of Cocker Spaniels. She purchased her first Tibetan Spaniel in 1972 and several of her foundation stock have come from Mrs Kangassalo's Zlazano kennel in Finland. One of these is International and Nordic Ch Zörryzöykky of Zlazano, sired by International and Nordic Ch Sivas Kirbah out of International and Nordic Ch Huntglen Braeduke Lhotse. When this bitch, Zörryzöykky, was mated to International and Nordic Ch

Northanger Tai Tsung she produced Mr Rune Lerudsmoen's Norwegian and Swedish Ch Zuzette. Mrs Lundgren does not have a kennel name.

Mrs Lundgren imported two males from Mrs Gidman's Clawson Kennel in England, Clawson Shha-Do became a Swedish Champion, sired by Da-Wa Dai-Sy of Clawson out of Clawson Shha Skup. The other was Clawson Ralpachen, a son of Ch Clawson Braeduke Rampa out of Zimbu Jewel. Mrs Lundgren imported an English CC winner, Braeduke Su-Lin, the younger full sister of Champions Sinha and Spo-Sel. When mated to International and Nordic Ch Han-E-Ball, among the winning progeny from Su-Lin came Mrs Inga Enstad's Nordic Ch Su-E-Ming. Mrs Lundgren now owns the CC winning male, Muskegon, bred by A. and K. Reis, and the Finnish and Swedish male particolour Ch Braeduke Oso Pando.

Mrs Agneta Reis and her daughter Kicki commenced breeding Tibetan Spaniels in 1973. Their first dog was Ulvus Dragon, a son of Ch Rutherglen Shu-Sha out of Ch Braeduke Chu-Cel, half brother of Ch Ulvus Argon. They purchased Strömkarlens Jasmin a daughter of Swedish Ch Ba-Ba out of Braeduke Kangri from Mr and Mrs Herjeskog, who has won a CC.

Mrs Reis and Kicki did not have a prefix for many years, but the home-bred winning litter brother and sister are well-known in Sweden – International and Nordic Ch Han-E-Ball, and International and Nordic Ch Hal-A-Li. I am told that it is considered that the most important influence on the Reis's Tibetan Spaniels has been the English import, Braeduke Nalina, the litter-sister of three other Champions, who herself won the title of International and Nordic Champion. Nalina was sired by Ch Ram Chandra of Amcross out of Ch Braeduke Whitewisp Hara Nor. 'The Terrible Twins', Han-E-Ball and Hal-A-Li, were sired by Ulvus Dragon out of Ch Nalina. Ch Han-E-Ball was the top winning Tibetan Spaniel in Sweden in 1978, and runner-up for this title in 1977 and fourth on the list in 1976. In a litter sired by Ch Karakorum, four out of five puppies from Ch Hal-A-Li were exhibited, producing Mrs Zollfranck's Nordic Ch Li-Tan, Nordic Ch Lo-Ma, Li-Si with two CCs and La-Po with one CC.

Strömkarlens Jasmin, when mated to Ch Lho-Cham of Windameres, produced Ann-Christin Söderholm's Swedish Ch Karakorum. From a repeat mating came Jonquil who now has two CCs. When mated to the English import Braeduke Dardo Tulku, litter brother of Mrs Kangassalo's Ch Braeduke Dolpo Dikki, Jasmin produced a CC winner, Nan Pai.

186

Mrs Reis and her daughter had the top winning kennel in 1978, and four out of five of their home-bred Champions won their titles during this year. In 1981 the prefix of Nalinas has been taken out by Mrs Reis and her daughter.

Mrs Inga Enstad's Ramblers prefix has been shared with Old English Sheepdogs and American Cocker Spaniels. She has imported two Tibetan Spaniel bitches; Woldscot Whitefoot, a black-and-tan bitch, sired by Shenlyn Zephyr out of Woldscot Braeduke Tunga, and Daleviz Snow White, a daughter of Ch Clawson Braeduke Rampa and Daleviz O-Se. Irene and Bengt Andersson's Swedish Ch Ramblers Ti Paljor was bred here. Mrs Enstad's home-bred Champion male Ch Ramblers Ti Wai Tangme, is a son of Nordic Ch Rutherglen Shu-Sha and Woldscot Whitefoot.

In 1974, Mrs Ingela Herrman, of John Blund's prefix, purchased from England a puppy, Braeduke Amdo Chu, bred by Mrs Jenkins and Miss Hourihane, which was sired by Ch Amcross Tarquin out of Ch Braeduke Ama Kuluh's daughter, Braeduke Ama Chu. Amdo Chu quickly became an International and Nordic Champion and, by winning twenty Best of Breed Awards and five Group placings, he must be the top winning Tibetan Spaniel of all time. Mrs Herrman was already an established breeder of Golden Retrievers.

Ch Amdo Chu was campaigned by Mrs Herrman until 1977 when she sold all her stock to Mrs Monica Zollfranck, who had a flying start in the breed. Together with Amdo Chu Mrs Zollfranck took over all Mrs Herrman's Tibetan Spaniels, including two other English imported bitches, Braeduke Likhi-Khola who won her Swedish title, and Braeduke Ranee who won two CCs; these were half-sisters sired by Ch Braeduke Nimmi, the dam of Likhi-Khola being Ch Braeduke Lhalu and the dam of Ranee being Ch Huntglen Braeduke Ta-Ra-Ni. Mrs Herrman had also purchased in Sweden, Kullabos Inzi, a daughter of Ch Braeduke Amdo Chu out of Braeduke Culi Cu-Cu, which carried the Anglo-Chinese blood-lines on both sides of her pedigree. Mrs Herrman only bred two litters before giving up the breed.

Mrs Zollfranck won two CCs with Ranee who, while still in Mrs Herrman's ownership, and, when mated to Ch Amdo Chu produced Swedish Ch John Blunds Bi-Ne, but Bi-Ne was campaigned to his title by Mrs Zollfranck. Mrs Zollfranck purchased, from Mrs and Miss Reis, Li-Tan which became a Nordic Champion. The first home-bred Champion for Mrs Zollfranck was Nordic Ch A-Bra-Ham, sired by Ch Amcross Kam-Dar out of Kullabos Inzi. Cocker Spaniels and Toy breeds are also bred by her, but she has no kennel name. Tragically,

International and Nordic Ch Braeduke Amdo Chu died in the autumn of 1978 at an early age, after he had passed from the ownership of Mrs Herrman, but he must be Sweden's top winning Tibetan Spaniel closely followed by Ch Lässebackens Afrodite.

Among other Tibetan Spaniel breeders and exhibitors in Sweden who deserve a mention is Siv Johansson, who bred Swedish Ch Rasmuss, sired by Ch Eulyn Impney out of Huntglen Raesheda. The Pallywoods kennel is that of Anna and Bjorn Strandbrink who are established Golden Retriever breeders. They imported the black-and-tan male Braeduke Chamdo Culi from England, a son of Huntglen Rosaree Bhabu out of Braeduke Northanger Cu-Li Dikki, who became a Swedish and Norwegian Champion. In 1972, after visiting Crufts Dog Show, Mr Strandbrink took back home with him Scotsmohr Sha-La and Whitewisp Shu-La, and in 1973 he purchased Mingshang Zinetta. Later he imported Mingshang Benjamin, a son of Ch Bu-Po of Amcross out of Mingshang Zuleika, who became a Swedish Champion. After this the only other import was that of a bitch puppy, Braeduke Su-Kya, a daughter of Ch Heyvan Jola out of Ch Braeduke Su-La. From Su-Kya has come Britt Lowenborg's Swedish Champion Pallywoods Fine-Mang, sired by Ch Chamdo Culi.

Kerstin Sjoberg, who also breeds Tibetan Terriers and Bernese dogs, imported the black-and-tan dog puppy Braeduke Pulak, which became a Swedish Champion. Pulak is the full brother of International and Nordic Ch Braeduke Phola. Also purchased, from Finland, was the black-and-tan bitch Nordic Ch Zuni of Zlazano, a daughter of Ch Braeduke Jhanki of Wimaro out of International and Nordic Ch Huntglen Braeduke Lhotse and litter-sister of International and Nordic Ch Zodi of Zlazano.

Soli Liden imported two bitches from Mrs Kangassalo's kennel in Finland; Zonata of Zlazano is a daughter of Ch Braeduke Lham and she won her International and Nordic Champion title, the other is Zyrinca of Zlazano, a daughter of Ch Braeduke Phola who became a Swedish and Norwegian Champion. Swedish Ch Yasmine was bred here, sired by Pajazzo out of Zorinta of Zlazano.

Gunilla Myrdal owns Swedish Ch Emma-Zeverina, bred by Soli Liden; also Amcross Kushi Tu, winner of two CCs, sired by Ch Amcross Vosta Kushi Kee out of Braeduke Ama Chu.

During 1980, Mrs Herjeskog handled to his title of Champion the dog Strömkarlens Straight Flush, a son of Strömkarlens Bzanba out of Swedish Ch Colphil Shan Hu; also the bitch Strömkarlens A-Dur Menuette, a daughter of Ch Lho-Cham of Windameres out of Ch

188

Lässebackens Afrodite. Both are now Swedish and Norwegian Champions for their owner Mrs Inger Svanberg, and Menuette was placed third in the Group at the Oslo International Championship Show under English judge, Mrs Pamela Cross Stern.

Menuette's full sister from an older litter, Strömkarlens Allegro Vivace, won her Champion title in 1979 for owner Mia Lange. Strömkarlens Talika is now a Swedish and Finnish Champion, a daughter of the Anglo-Chinese male Swedish Ch Ba-Ba, she is out of the English export Ch Windameres Tar-Quin.

The registration of Tibetan Spaniels in Sweden for the years 1956 to 1980 shows the progress of the breed and its popularity:

1956	1957	1958	1959	1960	1961	1962	1963	1964	1965	1966	1967	1968
19	4	20	1	–	3	–	4	2	4	3	11	3

1969	1970	1971	1972	1973	1974	1975	1976	1977	1978	1979	1980
25	36	39	67	157	237	241	349	380	415	405	359

The top winning Tibetan Spaniel for 1980 was Mrs Monica Zollfranck's male, Ch A-Bra-Ham, second to him was Mrs Agneta Reis' Ch Lan-Tan, a younger sister of Ch Lo-Ma.

There are some very dedicated breeders of Tibetan Spaniels in Scandinavia, especially in Sweden; having judged the breed in that country the Author can assure readers that some of the Swedish-bred Tibetan Spaniels (which of course, all stem from English blood-lines) could certainly become Champions in England.

9 History of the Tibetan Spaniel in Finland, Norway and Denmark

Finland

The history of the Tibetan Spaniel in Finland appears to have started in 1964, when Mrs Paula Kangassalo of the Zlazano kennel imported five Tibetan Spaniels from England, all bred by Miss Sara Selby of the Sivas prefix. The two males were Sivas Ang Arro a son of Ch Sivas Ten Sing of Myarlune out of Sivas Ang Ank; the black-and-tan dog, Sivas Kirbah, also a son of Ch Ten Sing out of Sema of Glenholme. The three bitches were the litter sister of Kirbah, Sivas Meta; Sivas Suzuki, sired by Kam Ga La out of Kyungu, and her daughter Sivas Suki sired by Sivas Kinzom. Both Kirbah and Meta won their International and Nordic Champion titles and Suzuki was the first ever Finnish Tibetan Spaniel Champion.

In 1967 Mrs Kangassalo imported Huntglen Braeduke Lhotse, a daughter of Ch Ramblersholt Ram-A-Din and Ch Braeduke Lotus Bud of Szufung, exported in whelp by Ch Braeduke Jhanki of Wimaro. This litter produced two puppies, a silver-sable male which became International and Nordic Ch Zodi of Zlazano and the black-and-tan female which became Nordic Ch Zuni of Zlazano, later to be owned by Mrs Baurne and then Mrs Sjoberg in Sweden.

Zodi was used a lot at stud and, among his progeny, were over ten Champions, including Zippe of Zlazano, an International and Nordic Champion and the winner of 1971 and 1972.

Lhotse, the dam of Zodi, became an International and Nordic Champion, and it is said that she has been the best brood bitch in Finland. The title 'The Winner of 19--' is given annually at the big International show in Helsinki. Among Lhotse's children to win this title are Zodi of Zlazano in 1969, Zorrizaykky of Zlazano in 1970; Zeva of Zlazano in 1973, and Zeelia of Zlazano in 1975; all of these became International and Nordic Champions. Other Tibetan Spaniels to have won this title are International and Nordic Ch Zippe of Zlazano in 1971 and 1972; International and Nordic Ch Zanzara in 1974; Ch Habanas Jabbache in 1976; International and Nordic Ch Zanzara of Zlazano in 1977; Ch Central Point Virginia, 1978. The

191

Zlazano Kennel also bred the top winning bitch of 1978 in International and Nordic Ch Zardiella of Zlazano.

Between 1964 and 1969 there were only three other breeders of Tibetan Spaniels in Finland, and all of them started with Zlazano stock. In 1968 Mrs Kangassalo imported Braeduke Tin-Ti-Lin which became a Finnish Champion; she was a daughter of Ch Sivas Ten Sing of Myarlune out of Braeduke Tamara of Szufung, which was exported in whelp by Huntglen Rosaree Bhabu and produced four puppies. Mrs Kangassalo also imported three more bitches; Bragborough Gyo-Po-Se-Mo, a daughter of Ch Khan Dee of Curwenna and Yakrose Sera; Sham of Copdene sired by Ch Sivas Wimaro Ti Mu out of Sivas Samantha; and Yum Yum of Copdene sired by Sivas Pin-Kin out of Yasmin of Copdene.

1969 brought a great flow of imports and, at the end of that year, there were one hundred and twenty-one Tibetan Spaniels registered at the Finnish Kennel Club. Mrs Rosendahl imported Witneylea Myurba, a son of Witneylea Choochy out of Geneau Millicentanna, which became a Finnish Champion. Mrs Kangassalo had eight imports of varied blood-lines. From Mrs Harper of Huntglen came English Ch Braeduke Sivas Padmini, a grand-daughter of Ch Kirbah, also Padmini's son Huntglen Rampa, sired by Ming-Y of Northanger; with them came Huntglen Northanger Tai T'sung, a son of Ch Braeduke Jhanki of Wimaro and Pan-Zi of Northanger. Both Rampa and Tai T'sung became Champions, and the top winner for the years 1974 and 1977 was International and Nordic Ch Zanzara of Zlazano, sired by Rampa; there was also Esteborne Akasha, the daughter of Huntglen Guoli Oli and Huntglen Braeduke Pema Choki. From Mrs Davies came Lu-Lu of Zlazano, the daughter of Ch Khan Dee of Curwenna and Furzyhurst Lal Ouina. From Mr Charlton came Cinders of Copdene the black-and-tan daughter of Ch Ti-Mu out of Cindela of Copdene, and Tilly of Copdene the black-and-tan daughter of Sivas Sreg-Gis out of Wimaro Tu Maraz of Copdene. From Mrs Young came the male Balgay Cho-Go of Amcross, a son of Ch Ramblersholt Ram-A-Din and Ch Seto of Rowcourt, and his two daughters, Balgay Tsan Ya and Balgay To-Go, both out of Braeduke Trangka of Balgay.

In 1970, Mrs Gronberg imported Witneylea Ka-Le, a daughter of Rama of Amcross and Kayla of Amcross, who became a Finnish and Swedish Champion; in 1971 Ka-Le was joined by her half-sister Witneylea Kati, sired by Witneylea Zil-Cam out of Amcross Kayla. Mrs M. Save imported Witneylea Zil-Cam, son of Witneylea Tuppence out of Zimbu Witch, who became a Finnish and Swedish

Champion. In 1972 Mrs Save imported the dog Witneylea Kul-La, a litter-brother of Finnish and Swedish Champion Witneylea Ka-Le. Kati became a Finnish Champion for Mrs Gronberg and Kul-La became a Finnish and Swedish Champion for Mrs Save. Mrs Rosendahl imported Witneylea Patchi Penny Piece in 1972, a particolour son of Witneylea Jack of Diamonds and Ramblersholt Zara, he made history by becoming the first ever particolour Champion in the breed by winning his Finnish and Swedish titles. This same year, Mrs Kangassalo imported a particolour male puppy, Braeduke Phola, son of Ch Braeduke Channa and Clawson Che-Pa of Braeduke, who won the title of International and Nordic Champion and was, at one time, the top winning Tibetan Spaniel in Scandinavia with more than ten CACIBs. He is now owned by Mrs Winberg in Sweden, as is Ch Le Buska of Copdene bred by Mr N. Charlton.

Five puppies from the half-sisters Ch Witneylea Ka-Le and Ch Witneylea Kati did a lot of winning and five of them won the Breeders class on four different occasions. One of the winning puppies is Nordic Ch Scedessan Talita, sired by Ch Witneylea Patchi Penny Piece. Ch Witneylea Myurba and five black-and-tans won the Breeders class at Rauman show in 1972.

In 1973, Mrs Kangassalo imported the dog puppy Braeduke Lham, a son of T.S.C.A. Ch Braeduke Dung-Ka out of Ch Braeduke Lhalu, also Wildhern Arabella in whelp to T.S.C.A. Ch Braeduke Dung-Ka. From Arabella's litter born in Finland came International and Nordic Ch Zalentino of Zlazano and Nordic Ch Zalamander of Zlazano. Among Zalentino's progeny is Mrs Salme Vestelin's Swedish and Finnish Ch Central Point Valentina and her litter sister Mrs Orvokki Keskinen's Nordic Ch and Winner 1978, Central Point Virginia; their dam is a daughter of International and Nordic Ch Huntglen Rampa and Finnish Ch Braeduke Tin-Ti-Lin. Ch Huntglen Rampa has sired more Champions than any other Tibetan Spaniel male in Scandinavia.

In 1975, Mrs Kangassalo again imported two dog puppies, Braeduke Sinji, the son of Ch Braeduke Nimmi out of Braeduke Shan-Hu of Northanger, and Braeduke Dolpo Dikki, the son of Ch Braeduke Am-Ra and Northanger Do-Lo Dikki, who took the first of the Anglo-Chinese blood-lines into Finland. Both Sinji and Dikki are now Champions.

In 1978 Mrs Kangassalo imported English Champion Bengagh Chensa, the daughter of Braeduke Rab-Shi and Ch Bengagh Chelsea, in whelp to Ch Amcross Vosta Kushi Kee. Ch Chensa has now won her Finnish Champion title. At the same time Mrs Kangassalo imported three male puppies, a particolour son of Ch Clawson Braeduke Rampa and Ch Braeduke Whitewisp Hara Nor named Braeduke Nan-Pai who has now won his Finnish Champion title; the second, Braeduke Oso Pando, also a particolour, and now a Swedish and Finnish Champion, the third was Braeduke Li-Tang.

Eero and Kirsti Karlstrom started their small Fieldlan prefix kennel in 1968, with a Cocker Spaniel bitch. They now have two home-bred Cocker Spaniel Champions and have bred another Champion Cocker. Their first Tibetan Spaniel which was purchased from Mrs Kangassalo, was Zeelia of Zlazano, the daughter of Ch Huntglen Northanger Tai T'sung out of Ch Huntglen Braeduke Lhotse; Zeelia became an International and Nordic Champion and was their foundation; she won the title of Winner 1975. Zeelia is in the pedigree of all their stock which consists of two Champion males, and two Champion bitches in International and Nordic Ch Fieldlan Fatima a daughter of Ch Huntglen Rampa, and Ch Zeelia of Zlazano. Their Nordic Ch Fieldlan Minya is a daughter of Ch Zalentino and Ch Fatima and is the Winner of 1979. Ch Minya's daughter Fieldlan Cosette has one CC.

Mr and Mrs Karlstrom's best known winner is the beautiful bitch Ch Fieldlan Fatima, which has been exhibited all over Scandinavia; she is a Group winner and has had many Group placings, and is possibly one of the very few Scandinavian Tibetan Spaniels to have won a Best in Show at an all breeds general Championship Show. The Author has judged her and considers that she is good enough to hold her own anywhere in the world.

Mrs Pirkko Linnus started in the breed in 1970 with a sable bitch which became International and Nordic Ch Zanzara of Zlazano, a daughter of International and Nordic Ch Huntglen Rampa. In the first-born litter, with the Saffron prefix from Zanzara, sired by Balgay Cho-Go of Amcross, came Nordic Ch Saffron Boojum and another with one CC. In Zanzara's second litter, sired by International and Nordic Ch Huntglen Northanger Tai T'sung came Finnish and Norwegian Ch Saffron Dolma.

In 1973, Mrs Linnus imported Braeduke Chung Culi, a son of Huntglen Rosaree Bhabu and Braeduke Northanger Cu-Li Dikki; he became a Nordic Champion and is the litter-brother of Swedish and Norwegian Ch Braeduke Chamdo Culi. The CC winner Saffron Gaissa, and show winners, Saffron Red Farda, and Saffron Lamleh, and Mrs Anna Liisa Passio's dual CC winner Millan Lam-De-Mo, are all sired by Chung Culi. Mrs Linnus is the breeder of the particolour Saffron Imandra with two CCs, of Finnish and Norwegian Ch Saffron Dolma, and of CC winner Saffron Jason.

Mrs Orvokki Keskinen of the Central Point prefix, owns Finnish Ch Zessica of Zlazano, the Winner of 1978, and from her bred Ch Central Point Virginia who is sired by Ch Zalentino of Zlazano. Zessica was sired by International Ch Huntglen Rampa out of Finnish Ch Braeduke Tin-Ti-Lin. Norwegian and Finnish Ch Central Point Neptunus, a son of Ch Huntglen Northanger Tai T'sung and Ch Zessica of Zlazano was also bred here.

Mrs Vestelin's Sajasan Kennel now has five Tibetan Spaniels, one of them is Swedish and Finnish Ch Central Point Valentina, who gained her title at eleven months old and is the litter sister of Ch Central Point Virginia. A young bitch, Central Point Frederika, has now won four CCs and is the litter-sister of Ch Central Point Valentina.

Mrs Sirkka Rautapuro of the Jadelia prefix, started in Tibetan Spaniels, when she was very young, with the purchase of Zumi of Zlazano which was never shown as Mrs Rautapuro was not interested in dog shows in those days. Zumi is the litter-sister of International and Nordic Ch Zeva of Zlazano and the full sister of International and Nordic Ch Zeelia of Zlazano. This is a very small kennel, and Mrs Rautapuro and her husband also have winning Cairn Terriers. Among the other Tibetan Spaniels here are the CC winner Zulma of Zlazano and the English born male, Finnish Ch Braeduke Narpo, which is the litter-brother of English Ch Braeduke Nimmi, Australian Ch Braeduke Numa and International and Nordic Ch Braeduke Nalina. The CC winner Jadelia Barbar was bred here. In early 1980, Mrs Rautapuro, in partnership with Mr Seppo Mattila of the Meriwia prefix, purchased a male puppy from England, Braeduke O-Pesa, a son of Ch Kensing O-So-Special sired by Rutherglen Lho-Ra-Ni, himself a son of English, International and Nordic Ch Lho-Cham of Windameres. Mr Mattila has three Tibetan Spaniel bitches and one English Bulldog.

Annaliisa Heikinnen, of the Mistyway American Cocker Spaniels, owns two Tibetan Spaniel bitches and bred her first litter in 1979. One of these bitches is Finnish, Swedish and Norwegian Ch Zhangri-La of Zlazano, who was the top winning Tibetan Spaniel for 1980 and the top winning Tibetan (of all the Finnish Tibetan breeds). She was exhibited at eight International shows and won CACIBs at all of them under different judges. She is a double grand-daughter of the late International and Nordic Ch Huntglen Braeduke Lhotse.

Mrs Riita Amperla, of the Habanas prefix, owns Finnish Ch Zarcina of Zlazano and in the first five years that she has owned Tibetan Spaniels, Mrs Amperla has bred seven Finnish Champions and two CC winners. The prefix is shared with a few Japanese Chins. Mrs Amperla's first Tibetan Spaniel bitch was Silences Habanera, a daughter of International and Nordic Ch Huntglen Rampa, Habanera is the dam of five Finnish Champions and her son Ch Jabbache was the Winner of 1976. Ch Jasperina a daughter of Int. Ch Braeduke Lham and Silences Habanera, is the dam of two Champions and her son, Finnish Ch Beedro now has two CACIBs. In 1979 Mrs Amperla imported Braeduke Mingbo, the only male in the first-born litter of American-born Kalimpong Ming Dordja of Braeduke, sired by Braeduke Lu Ting. Mingbo, now a Finnish Champion is the litter brother of New Zealand Ch Braeduke Mingmo and International and Danish Ch Braeduke Mingmar Choden. Mrs Amperla also owns Zinos of Zlazano which now has two CCs, and is a son of Finnish and Swedish Ch Braeduke Sinji.

Mrs Eila Mäenpää, of the Goldenrod Kennel, has a few Golden Retrievers and Tibetan Spaniels from the Habanas and Fieldlan Kennels. In 1979 Mrs Mäenpää imported Braeduke Norbu Linka a son of Windameres Ala Shan and Ch Braeduke Whitewisp Hara Nor.

Mr Erkki Annenberg of Arctica bred the top winning male for 1979, International and Nordic Ch Arctica Jöröjucca, sired by Finnish Ch Zombrero of Zlazano, a son of International and Nordic Ch Braeduke Lham, out of Arctica Ultra.

At the end of 1978 English Ch Amcross Pax was exported to the late Dr Brian Holcombe in Finland. Dr Holcombe already owned another English-born male, Finnish Ch Braeduke Lho-Tho-Ri, a son of Ch Braeduke Nimmi and Braeduke Lho-Ri-La, bred by Mr and Mrs Lindsay. From Mrs Gidman, in England, he imported Clawson Ku-Yin, a daughter of Ch Amcross Vosta Kushi Kee, and from Mrs Butler, Colphil Patiala, the litter-sister of the top English CC winner for 1979, Ch Braeduke Poo-Khyi. From Russia, Dr and Mrs Holcombe have a dog and bitch and both have now been bred from, with Mrs Gidman in England importing a bitch sired by the Russian dog Rin-Boj out of Clawson Ku-Yin originally bred by her.

The future of the breed lies in these hands and also in those of other kennels, a few more who breed and show being Asko Viljanen of the Junkertums prefix, Ritva Mattila of Bukefalos, Silva Gronberg of Scedessan, Riita Viitala of Silences, Tuula Kinnari of Polarsun, Anne Maki of Pounikon, Ulpu Lohikainen of Paarmuskan, A. Pikkarainen of El Prendo and Hilkka Laitamo of Lagoon prefix.

Registrations at the Finnish Kennel Club of Tibetan Spaniels have increased rapidly from 1964 until 1977 when there was a total of 2,137 Tibetan Spaniels registered, and they are still increasing. In 1977, four hundred and fifty-seven Tibetan Spaniels were registered, in 1978 the total was five hundred and fifteen with ninety-eight litters born. It is interesting to note that, in 1977, this breed was the top registration in the Toy and Companion Group, and the ninth most popular breed in Finland. As in other parts of Scandinavia, the Tibetan Spaniel is in the Toy Group in Finland. In 1979, five hundred and ninety-seven Tibetan Spaniels were registered in Finland, and the breed was then the eighth most popular breed. During 1979 there were thirty-five more Champions made up (i.e. Swedish, Norwegian, Finnish, Nordic and International) all Finnish owned; of these twenty were bitches and fifteen were males. From 1964–1977 there were seventy-four Champion Tibetan Spaniels made up in Finland, forty-six bitches and twenty-eight males, not all of them were Finnish bred, as these figures include the imported dogs and bitches which have become Champions.

Norway and Denmark

In 1974 Arvo and Solveig Smedstuen, of the Norwegian Dea Divina Kennel, started in Tibetan Spaniels with two Strömkarlens bitches; they imported Strömkarlens Dea Divina, now a Norwegian and Swedish Champion, and Strömkarlens Puccinella, sired by Ch Whitewisp Chomolungma out of Ch Bragborough Tammy, who now has two CCs.

The Rumens Kennel of Rune Lerudsmoen also started in Norway in 1974 with the importing of about ten bitches from Sweden and Finland. Among those to have influenced this kennel are Zuzette, now a Norwegian and Swedish Champion, bred by Mrs M. Lundgren in Sweden, and Zalamander of Zlazano, from Mrs Kangassalo in Finland which became a Nordic Champion. Zalamander is the litter-brother of International and Nordic Ch Zalentino of Zlazano. Mr Lerudsmoen purchased, from Mr and Mrs Strandbrink, Pallywoods Chanda and Pallywoods Jinga which have now won two CCs each, they are both sired by Ch Braeduke Chamdo Culi. From Mrs Lundgren also came Zonatha, who has now won two CCs; there is also Dilwel Doris, a daughter of Ch Amcross Tarquin which was imported from England, and the Finnish import International and Nordic Ch Zeva of Zlazano. From Zalamander have come three Norwegian Champions: Rumens Mailia, out of Dilwell Doris; Rumens Mette, out of Zuzette; and Rumens Martin, out of Pallywoods Chanda. Here also are Nordic Ch Rumens Movie Star, sired by Ch Eulyn Impney out of Ch Zeva and Rumens Mia his litter sister with two CCs, also Ch Sickow, a son of Ch Lho-Cham of Windameres.

Another Norwegian breeder and exhibitor is Mrs Margit Gaardsmoen, with the kennel name of Margibo. Ch Eulyn Impney purchased from Mr and Mrs Herjeskog now resides there, as does CC winning Strömkarlens Ramona, a black-and-tan daughter of Ch Strömkarlens Bzanba out of Braeduke Rak-Shi. Mrs Gaardsmoen's other bitch, Rumens Lady Zing, has produced Norwegian Ch Margibos Char-Man, a daughter of Ch Impney.

Solveig Berg, of Kennel Bergenova, started in dogs six years ago and has two Golden Retrievers and a Norwegian Champion Newfoundland bitch; she keeps only five or six dogs. She has won the Best Breeders award and the progeny class with her Newfoundland and her puppies. Her two Tibetan Spaniels, a dog and a bitch, came from Sweden in 1975. The dog died in an accident, but the bitch, Eicie-Ka-Gawa, is now a Norwegian and Swedish Champion bred by Aina Skarin, sired by Ch Lho-Cham of Windameres out of Dhi-Lai-La, a daughter of Rutherglen Shu-Sha out of Florentina.

Mrs Berit Mörk, who has the established Muskoko Golden Retrievers, owns Braeduke Pinuri, a daughter of Ch Braeduke Nimmi and out of Ch Braeduke Patlin, and has bred her first litter of Tibetan Spaniels. From this litter has come the 1981 Champion Muskokas Piro Piccolo, owned by Randi Eriksen of Billingstad, which was sired by Nordic Ch A-Bra-Ham out of Pinuri. He won the Toy Group under Mr J. H. Braddon at the Oslo International show in December 1980, after winning the CAC (being too young for the CACIB) under Mrs P. Cross Stern. He is the first Norwegian bred Tibetan Spaniel to win a Group.

While other puppies have been exported to Norway from Sweden and England they appear to be in pet homes and not used for breeding or exhibition.

Denmark

In about 1966 the Author sent to Mr Kurt Brendstrup in Denmark a sable male, Braeduke Ti Phu of Szufung and a particolour bitch, Sivas Lolita, to join his Pekingese. Ti Phu became a Swedish and Danish Champion and Mr J. H. Braddon, when judging in Denmark, had given them both the CACIBs. Lolita produced a litter of two puppies in 1968, and three puppies in June 1969. At the time the Author believed these to be the first Tibetan Spaniels in Denmark, and heard of another bitch, owned by someone else, being killed in a car accident just before she was due to whelp to Ti Phu in 1968. At the time of writing this book, both Lolita and Ti Phu are still alive, though they have been re-housed and no longer live with their original owner.

The Author is now only able to trace one active breeder and

exhibitor of Tibetan Spaniels and the latter had no idea that there had been any Tibetan Spaniels before hers in Denmark! Mrs Bente Rytter Jörgensen of Kennel Tenzing, started in Tibetan Terriers in 1975 and then had her first Tibetan Spaniels in 1976. By the end of 1979 Mrs Jörgensen had bred three Tibetan Spaniel litters.

Mrs Jörgensen purchased Fanfare for Skya Snar, a daughter of International Ch Braeduke Cham Kusho, from Mrs Van Den Boom in Holland. From Mrs Irmgard Wienekamp in West Germany she imported three bitches and one male. The dog is Uwong Jo-Gya-Kang, a son of Braeduke Chumna out of Gra-M of To Gya-Kang (a daughter of International and German Ch Beaver of Eulyn out of Clawson Pi-Ta), and he holds the record for being unbeaten; exhibited only twelve times, on each occasion he won Best of Breed, and he now holds the titles of International, Danish, Luxembourg and German Champion.

Mrs Jörgensen's foundation bitches are Hara of Jo-Gya-Kang, a daughter of Braeduke Chumna and Clawson Pi-Ta, which is now a Danish Champion. Another Chumna daughter, Dana of Jo-Gya-Kang, is a Danish and Luxembourg Champion. Baya of Jo-Gya-Kang is the daughter of International and German Ch Beaver of Eulyn, her dam is Clawson Chantin, Baya is now a Luxembourg Champion.

Since Denmark discontinued having any quarantine regulations at the frontier with Germany, Scandinavian dogs have not been able to be exhibited because of the quarantine regulations between Denmark and Sweden. Undoubtedly this has done a great deal to curb the popularity of the breed and to reduce the blood-lines in Denmark. The registration for Tibetan Spaniels at the Danish Kennel Club are not encouraging.

1973	1974	1975	1976	1977	1978	1979	1980
1	–	–	2	3	1	9	6

In the spring of 1979, Mrs Jörgensen visited England and took back home with her some fresh blood-lines, Braeduke Gon-Po, a sable son of Ch Amcross Am-Ban out of Tangwell Galaxy was a gift from the Author. A particolour bitch puppy Braeduke Mingmar Choden was purchased from the American imported bitch Kalimpong Ming Dordja of Braeduke's first-born litter, sired by Braeduke Lu-Ting. Gon-Po is now a Danish and International Champion, and Mingmar Choden won her first CAC while still a puppy at the Amsterdam International Show in November 1979, and has since become an International Champion and produced her first litter in 1981 sired by Ch Gon-Po.

10 History of the Tibetan Spaniel in Canada and the United States of America

The American Kennel Club signed a reciprocal agreement with the Canadian Kennel Club which is still in existence today, each agreeing to recognise the registrations of the other Club. Unfortunately this principle sadly does not apply to Tibetan Spaniels registered in Canada, as even the Tibetan Spaniel Club of America will not at the present time permit the exhibition of Canadian Kennel Club registered dogs at any of their Speciality shows.

Both these countries have a points system for their Champions and a judge can withhold a winner's points if he does not consider that the exhibit is of sufficient merit.

The points system is a little different in Canada from the United States, and slightly lower. A dog, and a bitch, requires ten points to become a Champion and must get these points under three different judges.

In America a dog must win fifteen championship points, but this total must include two majors. A major is a show with the rating of three, four or five points and these must be won under two different judges. The final points are based upon the number of dogs and bitches entered at each show for that breed, this is printed in each show catalogue. Five is the highest number of points given at any show, one is the lowest. There are five classes at the American Championship shows for each sex, Puppy, Novice, bred by Exhibitor, American bred, and Open. These points are only gained in the Winners class and it can vary for the sexes at the same show, with perhaps one sex gaining more points depending upon the entry.

Here again the American Kennel Club will only permit 175 dogs in a day to be judged by one judge, the surplus being given to another judge which is not always popular. No judges' critiques are given and of course the majority of dogs in the States go on a show circuit with a professional handler.

Some American exhibitors take their dogs to Mexico where the F.C.I. rules are in operation. I only know of Mr St. Clair in Missouri who has done this, in order to complete the title for one of his two Dutch imports.

Canada

Canadian Tibetan Spaniels have achieved something for which the American breeders are still striving, the full recognition and registration of the Tibetan Spaniel breed which came about on October 21st, 1978. Since January 1980, Tibetan Spaniels in Canada have been exhibited with Championship status and the first three Champions have been made up there. The proposed breed club is having difficulties because of the enormous distances between owners and, at the time of writing, there is, sad to relate, friction between the Canadian and American exhibitors who do not permit each other to exhibit outside their own countries. This matter will probably only be resolved by full American Kennel Club recognition and Championship status for American Tibetan Spaniels. This was anticipated as being imminent in mid 1981, and why the American Kennel Club have resisted this request for so long is a complete enigma to English Tibetan Spaniel breeders.

The first Tibetan Spaniel to arrive in Canada was probably Mr and Mrs W. R. Nesbitt's Braeduke Sa-Sky, which sadly died of poisoning at a comparatively early age and before she could be bred from. She was followed closely by two who emigrated to Kingston, Ontario, in May 1970 with their owner, Mrs Elaine Vaughan. When Mrs Vaughan applied to the Canadian Kennel Club to register her pair, she found that twenty-five individual dogs were needed in the country before the breed could be considered for Canadian registration.

In February 1957, Mrs Vaughan imported a male, Eulyn Lilac Domino, a son of Garrick of Eulyn out of Redgame Primrose. With him came a bitch, Cloudsmere Caraway, a daughter of Ch Amcross Gu-Pa of Kethmora out of Eulyn Cool Pepper. By early 1979 Mrs Vaughan had produced four litters and twelve puppies, one of which had been exported to America.

Mr and Mrs David Matear who now live in Calgary, Alberta, arrived from England in 1975 to live in Toronto, Ontario, bringing with them a dog Nomes Samso which unfortunately proved to be infertile, and a bitch Nomes Miss Zodi which died soon after her arrival. Their third, a bitch, was not bred from. Their fourth, a red-and-white particolour bitch, named Braeduke Rincen Bun-Ba, is the litter-sister of Australian and New Zealand Ch Braeduke Re-Gi-Na. Rincen Bun-Ba produced her first litter in late 1980, sired by Braeduke Gser-Phur, a bitch puppy has been exported to Mr W. St. Clair in St Louis, Missouri, U.S.A.

In 1976, Mrs C. C. Neville Thomas, a renowned all-breeds dog-show judge, both in Canada and America, imported a male, Tibskips

Khumbila, the son of Tibskips Kham Dong out of Tibskips Yam-Tsen. In 1977 Mrs Thomas imported a bitch puppy, Braeduke Patna, the daughter of Ch Braeduke Nimmi out of Ch Braeduke Patlin. From the first and, so far, only litter of these two only one dog puppy survived which was exported to America; subsequently Patna was spayed.

During 1977, Mrs J. Mason emigrated from England and took with her a black-and-tan dog and his sable half-sister; both were bred by Mrs Morgan and descendants of Mrs Mason's Tritou strain which had been recently established. Later, Mrs Mason became Mrs Chalmers and added to her Tibetan Spaniels by purchasing from Mr G. M. MacDonald of Ontario a sable bitch, Benagh Rue, which had been bred by Miss M. Moorhead in Southern Ireland and was the litter-sister of Irish Green Star winner Benagh Sage. Unfortunately, the dog puppy exported with Benagh Rue to Mr MacDonald had already been given to a pet home with Mrs W. Heafey of Cardinal, Ontario. Rue, a daughter of Ch Braeduke Nimmi out of Irish Green Star winner Clawson Me-Tsag was joined by two more English-bred bitches, as Mrs Chalmers imported a red-and-white particolour Braeduke Ru-Bi, a daughter of T.S.C.A. Ch Braeduke Dung-Ka out of Ch Braeduke Re-Ba and therefore, litter-sister of the Matear's Rincen Bun-Ba; also Braeduke Ne-To, a daughter of Ch Clawson Braeduke Rampa out of Ch Braeduke Whitewisp Hara Nor, litter-sister of Finnish Ch Braeduke Nan-Pai. In 1978, Mrs Chalmers imported a sable male, Braeduke Gser Phur, a son of Ch Amcross Am-Ban out of Tangwell Galaxy, carrying through his sire the Anglo-Chinese blood-lines from Ch Braeduke Ama Kuluh. Gser Phur is the litter brother of International Ch Braeduke Gon-Po and also of English Reserve CC winning Braeduke Gartok and of Ms Tamura's American winner Braeduke Garpon. Mrs Chalmer's Gser Phur was, for a time, exhibited in America with a professional handler. When Mrs Chalmers gave up her Tibetan Spaniels in 1979 most of them are believed to have gone to Mrs Diane Lilley of the Timothy Kennels in British Colombia.

While on holiday in England in 1977, Mrs Vaughan arranged for another male, Redgame Roc, and a bitch Redgame Jewel, to be sent to her in Ontario. Finally, with Mrs Vaughan's litters, there were twenty-five Tibetan Spaniels in Canada and it is hoped that there will soon be sufficient to form two divisions of the main breed club in the Western and Eastern provinces, each with its own administrative Secretary. Mrs Lois Tryon is doing noble work trying to establish a breed club from Kingston, Ontario; she, with her daughter Mrs Pat

Vaughan (daughter-in-law of Mrs Elaine Vaughan), and of course Mrs Elaine Vaughan herself, have been the main exhibitors in Ontario. Mrs Tina Kuroczka of Connecticut, U.S.A. imported Isabella of Rowfant which was bred by Mrs E. Vaughan and has done well with her. At the end of July 1980, Mrs Pat Vaughan's Seng Gay of Rowfant, bred by her Mother-in-law, won his Champion title – the first Canadian Tibetan Spaniel Champion. He was sired by Lilac Domino and is out of Elsie of Eulyn, Ch Seng Gay is now owned by Mr W. St. Clair in St Louis, U.S.A. On August 3rd, 1980, Mrs D. Lilley's Timothy's Bam-Bi, a daughter of Gser Phur out of Ne-To, finished her Championship. In April 1981, Timothy's Rajah became the third Canadian Tibetan Spaniel Champion. Ch Timothy's Bam-Bi has won a Group 4 at the end of April 1981; Tritou Jeremy has won a C.D. Obedience award and it is hoped will complete the third leg of his C.D.X.

In late summer 1981 Mrs E. Vaughan visited England and took home with her a sable male puppy Braeduke O Pingliang, son of Braeduke Lingbu out of Ch Kensing O So Special, thus taking fresh blood-lines into Canada.

In spite of the severe winters, the Canadian climate appears to suit Tibetan Spaniels and the breed is now only held back by the distances and lack of newcomers to the breed; so the fort is being held by just a few.

The United States of America

It is perhaps difficult for us in England to conceive of the enormous countries of Canada and America, and so, of course, of the enormous geographical areas which must automatically isolate some of the Tibetan Spaniel breeders and exhibitors.

In America, most Tibetan Spaniels are to be found on the East Coast where they have possibly been fostered and given more encouragement. With the formation of new area clubs other dedicated breeders do not feel quite so cut off and discouraged, it is to be hoped that the main parent club, the Tibetan Spaniel Club of America will take steps to keep alive the interest in the breed all over the United States, and not just the East Coast.

Although the Tibetan Spaniel Club of America was formed in 1971, the Author feels that the history of the breed started long before then and should not be ignored. It is sad but interesting to note that, in America, the breed has not made such great strides as in Canada with Kennel Club recognition and Championship status; but it is thankfully no longer in the hands of a very few people, so perhaps the possibility of full American Kennel Club recognition is now something which can be anticipated in the near future.

Mr Harrington of New York State claims to have bred the first American-born litter of Tibetan Spaniels in 1965, from two of his four Tibetan Spaniels which he says were obtained from a monastery at Saka Dzong. Evidence has also been found concerning a Tibetan Spaniel dog named Ching, which was purchased from a breeder in New York City in 1938; he is supposed to have lived until 1952 or 1953. Mrs Doris R. Culver of Lucver Kennels, Schodack Landing, New York, told me that one of the Harrington dogs was imported from Mrs Peach in England; another, Su-Su, was bred in England and exported by a Mrs Bennet; and a third, Kye Ho Jo Bo, was never used at stud.

Mrs Culver herself owned a black-and-white bitch, Polar Ryari, which was in whelp to Pontac Wei Simon in 1965 and later produced her second litter by him. Polar Ryari was bred by Lt.-Colonel Clery, and Mrs Gill bred Wei Simon; in addition to this pair, Mrs Culver owned a daughter from their first litter. All recent attempts to trace these dogs and their owners has failed.

Mr J. H. Braddon told me that, when he was judging in Los Angeles in 1968, someone brought a very nice Tibetan Spaniel along to the show for him to see.

Mr Leo Kearns, a Sexton of the Trinity Lutheran Church in New Haven, Connecticut, resurrected the breed in 1966 when he purchased Doghouse Dream Baby after seeing her in the window of the Dog House Grooming Salon in State Street. She had been bred in England and sold en bloc with her three litter-sisters, which have never been traced since. Two years later, Mr Kearns imported from the Amcross Kennels English Ch Yakrose Chiala of Amcross, Chiala and Dream Baby produced their first-born litter on Easter Sunday morning in 1968; Dream Baby is the daughter of Peterstown Drom of Szufung out of Moutai.

In 1967 Mr and Mrs Jack Isherwood imported three Tibetan Spaniels, which joined their established Sherwood Forest Kennel of Labradors. The male, Braeduke Po-Lo-Lin was the son of Ch Braeduke Jhanki of Wimaro out of Ch Braeduke Sivas Padmini. One bitch was the black-and-tan full sister of Ch Huntglen Braeduke Ta-Ra-Ni and the litter-sister of Finnish Ch Braeduke Tin-Ti-Lin. The second bitch, a sable, was the litter-sister of Ch Clawson Braeduke Rampa named Braeduke Ran-Si of Balgay. The first Isherwood litter was born in 1969, it is believed that Mr Isherwood changed the breed name to Khabacken Khyi dogs when selling his puppies and they have not been traced. After an accident and a head injury Mr Isherwood parted with all his Tibetan Spaniels which Mrs Jay Childs re-housed in 1975.

In 1967 Mrs St. Erme-Cardew exported a gold-and-white Tibetan Spaniel male to Colonel and Mrs Frank Harvan of Cadoga Park, California. Mrs Mae Zubeck of Ohio, at that time a well-known American Dog World columnist, purchased a Sherwood bitch from Mr Isherwood. A dog puppy was sold to Mr and Mrs Jacobsen of San Diego and Mr Isherwood tried to start a breed club. Mrs Zubeck undertook the task of organising the Mid West and Mr Kearns was approached to try and get something going in the East.

Mrs Boettiger's particolour Nepalese-imported dog, born in the city of Pokhara and bred by Tibetan refugees, Langtang Shimbu of Kyirong was used at stud once on a Sherwood bitch owned by Mrs Helen Fluckey, but unfortunately the resulting litter has not been traced

About 1970 Miss Mayhew exported Mingshang Zora to Mrs Jacobsen as a mate for her Isherwood male, but there is no record of any puppies being born from this pair.

Mr S. Dillon Ripley, former Curator of the Peabody Museum in New Haven and, at that time, the head of the Smithsonian Institute, had imported a dog and a bitch from Bhutan. The bitch was a very typical Tibetan Spaniel and he planned to breed from her; unfortunately, due to a car accident, this was not possible.

Also during 1970 Mr Bill Jobson, a well-known English judge, while judging in Italy, had three Tibetan Spaniels exhibited under him by an American Air Force Officer who was shortly returning to the States and taking his dogs with him. Unfortunately these and others purchased in England by American servicemen have never been traced, though we know that some, from the English kennels of Clawson, Kailas and the Irish Benagh kennel have definitely been exported to America in this way.

Going on to 1971, Mr Leo Kearns was doing a good job of obtaining Tibetan Spaniels through the Amcross kennels in England, to meet demand; Mr Kearns had been told, by the American Kennel Club, that three hundred would be required and he considered that this number could be reached if their popularity in the East continued. In 1970, he had imported and resold six sent out by the Amcross kennels, four going to local residents in his area, another three from Dream Baby's litter sold in the New Haven area, and he had orders for fifteen more.

The President of the Tibetan Spaniel Association was, at that time, The Lady Freda Valentine who, on a visit to America, went to see the

President of the American Kennel Club, then Mr Dick. He confirmed the information given to Mr Kearns, that three hundred would be required for American Kennel Club recognition. Unfortunately, later on this was denied and the supporters of the breed were told that the A.K.C. had now set a higher figure and while three hundred was the minimum required, it was more likely that eight hundred or nine hundred Tibetan Spaniels would be needed as one of the pre-requisites to the consideration of the opening of their stud book.

Mr Kearns managed to persuade the New Haven papers to give the breed some good copy with photographs, and the *New Haven Register* (February 10th, 1971), shows Mrs Peter Neckles and Mrs Patrick Child grooming a bevy of English-bred Tibetan Spaniels obtained through the Amcross kennel in England, in preparation for the training classes. At this time, the article stated, there were approximately forty Tibetan Spaniels in America. Mr Kearns was still doing a very noble job of importing Tibetan Spaniels and occasionally breeding a litter.

Mr and Mrs Joseph Shifman who lived in England while on an extended business trip, returned home to the States in October 1971 with Puckridge Za-Pa, a son of Ch Rimpoche of Amcross and Ciceter Cho Chu of Amcross. They also took home a bitch, bred by Mrs Greenland, a daughter of Rama of Amcross and Huntglen Akasha's Ming.

Ch Braeduke Tam Cho appeared on the Kasco Wall Chart and the Author wrote breed notes on Tibetan Spaniels from about 1970–1971 in the American magazine *Dog World* to try and boost the interest in the breed.

Miss Burnett, who was at the time Secretary of the Tibetan Spaniel Association in England, received a letter from a Mrs Joan Warner of Indiana, saying that she thought she owned a pure bred Tibetan Spaniel, but no further information was given.

1972 was quite a turning point for the breed, the T.S.C.A. held its first ever Fun Match sponsored by the St Hubert's Kennel Club. This was the year in which Mrs Jay Child started the Rare Breeds Club, there were twenty-nine Human members of the T.S.C.A. and thirty-four Tibetan Spaniels were registered.

Some more imports came from England; Mr and Mrs Kirk Schneider returned home from England taking with them some Cavalier King Charles Spaniels and some of the Tibetan Spaniels they had exhibited in England.

Mrs R. Kahan of Concord, Massachusetts, imported a male, Braeduke Lhamo Lam Tso, sired by Ch Amcross Tarka out of

Braeduke Lho-La and later imported a particolour bitch, Huntglen Zetta. Mrs Kahan said that her two would bring up to four the number of Tibetan Spaniels that she knew of in her State.

Mrs Bryant, of Ramsdell prefix in England, exported a puppy to Michigan to replace one killed in an accident, which had been purchased from an American pet shop.

In January 1971, with fourteen Charter members, the Tibetan Spaniel Club of America (T.S.C.A.) was formed. A news letter was started and has been published continuously since March 1971. The first Annual General Meeting was held in June of that year, at which time the Constitution and By-Laws were adopted, and the Club was incorporated as a non-profit corporation in 1973 under the laws of the State of Connecticut.

More important, the Stud Book was commenced in 1971, registering then a total of eighteen dogs. For the following three years only Tibetan Spaniels registered and imported from England, or the American-bred offspring of these T.S.C.A. registered dogs, were entered in the Stud Book.

There were then several requests for the registration of Tibetan Spaniels brought to the United states from Tibet, Nepal, India, etc. and, since the T.S.C.A. felt that these dogs with new blood-lines could be of great value, a Secondary Registration procedure was adopted in 1974. A Secondary Registered Tibetan Spaniel showing three generations of T.S.C.A. registered ancestors and/or three generations of reciprocal Kennel Club registered ancestors, may then apply for Primary Registration. Prior to 1978, only T.S.C.A. pedigrees or Import Pedigrees from England were acceptable, but in 1978 the Board of Directors passed a resolution to accept registration and import pedigrees from all other established Kennel Clubs, provided that those Kennel Clubs are recognised by the A.K.C. and E.K.C.

The first Annual Speciality Match was held in April 1972 and this has been held each ensuing year. In 1975 the T.S.C.A. instituted a Plan A type Match, thus following A.K.C. procedure for special shows. In 1973, the Board of Directors voted for guidelines for the establishment of local and regional Tibetan Spaniel Clubs. The first regional club was formed in New Haven in January 1974, followed by Hawaii in May 1974, and then the Mid-Atlantic chartered in May 1976.

Another big step forward was the T.S.C.A. Championship programme instituted by the Board in 1975; the awarding of T.S.C.A. Championship points is based on the same point system as that used by the American Kennel Club. The same point value is used as is assigned by the A.K.C. for 'All other breeds or varieties' where numbers exhibited do not warrant a higher scale of points.

Unfortunately once the A.K.C. recognises the Tibetan Spaniel breed and gives it Championship status, these titles will not be official, if the dogs are still young enough, they will have to be campaigned all over again at official A.K.C. shows under A.K.C. Rules. Nevertheless, it has been a healthy incentive to get good stock out into the ring whenever possible, into the Miscellaneous classes, where they can be seen by other breeders and exhibitors.

Mrs Jay Child of Wallingford, Connecticut, with the Amroth prefix could be considered the leading early breeder and exhibitor of Tibetan Spaniels in America; she has bred and finished the most Champions of any American breeder. Mrs Child became the initiating force in the exhibition of Tibetan Spaniels in the United States; she founded the T.S.C.A. and was instrumental in publicising the breed through her breed columns in nation-wide magazines. In America, the breed also owes a big debt to Mrs Child for establishing the Stud Book. She and her husband, Patrick, both acted as the liaison with the American Kennel Club, and gave all their energy and efforts for many years which finally resulted in that official body recognising the breed and granting exhibition status in the Miscellaneous classes, and also in Obedience Trials, as of February 1st, 1977.

To Mr Leo Kearns must be given the credit for being the 'Father of the Breed' in the United States; it was his imports and his breeding that began it all. His history of obtaining his first Tibetan Spaniel in England and his subsequent importing and breeding is legendary among the United States fanciers. T.S.C.A. Ch Rdo-Rje-Rig-Zin of Amroth, owned by Mrs Jay Child and bred by Mr Leo Kearns, will go down in American breed history as the top T.S.C.A. Champion producing stud dog to date, as well as the very first T.S.C.A. Champion, and it is indeed fitting that he should be bred and owned by these two people.

Ciceter Norbu was the first Tibetan Spaniel to be shown anywhere in the United States; though she had no competition, her first place Match ribbon so excited her owner Mrs Jay Child, that it inspired her to organise the Tibetan Spaniel Club of America. This little Tibetan Spaniel bitch, shown under judge Mr Gene Gasteiger at the January 25th, 1971, Match, sponsored by the Farmington Valley Kennel Club, should be the symbol of the T.S.C.A. as she was Mrs Child's inspiration which has led all these years later to the breed being recognised by the American Kennel Club and to the threshold of the breed being accepted for class competition. Wildhern Ambassador, who won his T.S.C.A. Champion title in 1976, was imported by Mrs Jay Child and Mrs Joan Child, who sadly died after an accident in 1979 and was a great loss to the breed.

Mrs Joan Child, has the Truk-Ku prefix and also lives in Connecticut. Mrs Child has been a successful breeder and exhibitor and has bred T.S.C.A. Champions.

Mrs Gwen Wexler of the Westerly prefix in Connecticut, owns one of the first ever Tibetan Spaniels to win its T.S.C.A. Championship, and she was the first person with a Champion to earn its C.D. title in an A.K.C. Obedience Trial.

Three Tibetan Spaniels have earned their A.K.C. Companion Dog Obedience titles, and one has won the title of Companion Dog Excellent. Ms Lily Hosticka, who resides on the West Coast in the State of Oregon, owns two of the Obedience title winners; her Khumbila Motha C.D. Ex is the highest scoring Tibetan Spaniel in Obedience as of July 1978. His dam, Khumbila Kahili of Trinity C.D., is the second highest scoring according to the Delaney Scoring System, and Mrs Phyllis Kohler's T.S.C.A. Ch Amcroth Su-Chan-La of Truk-Ku is the third highest.

Ms Hosticka who is now Ms Tamura has been the early leader in showing and breeding from imported blood-lines, her own imported stock coming from Nepal where she spent two years as a member of the Peace Corps. Ms Hosticka has integrated the imported blood-lines with American-bred primary registered stock. In 1978 she imported an English-bred dog puppy, Braeduke Garpon, a son of Ch Amcross Am-Bo out of the Reserve CC winning Tangwell Galaxy, who is one of only three Tibetan Spaniels in England to have won a Utility Group. Am-Ban carries outcross blood-lines through his grandmother Ch Braeduke Ama Kuluh.

Mr and Mrs Thomas Whiting of Fairfax, Virginia, have come to the fore with progeny from their Bim's Shri Brandywine. Brandy was bred by Mr and Mrs Whiting and is now the only producing progeny from their original imports from India. Their original dog, Bimbo, was born and registered at the Indian Kennel Club; he won a third placing at the Tibetan Dogs competition held annually by the Tibetan Embassy in New Delhi. They also own Ambrier's Tiger Lily, who won her T.S.C.A. Champion title at the end of 1979. During 1979, they bred a litter from Brandy's daughter Bim's Dusty Tara using the newly-imported dog, Braeduke Dung-Ka, and have retained two of their progeny, Bim's Tikka Dung and Bim's Bomber Sahb, which have made a successful start to their show careers.

210

Two imports who have not apparently been of much interest to the American Tibetan Spaniel breeders are Mrs Betsy Boettiger's Shimbu in California, found by her sister Ann Rohrer in Nepal; also Marguerite Cotsworth Perkins' Tashi Dorji in Washington D.C. Tashi Dorji was born in Darjeeling and some of his progeny are with Marguerite's parents Mr and Mrs Marlin Perkins in St Louis, Missouri, where Mr Marlin Perkins is the Director Emeritus of the Zoological Gardens.

Mr W. St. Clair has the Italia Cavalier King Charles Spaniels, founded in 1973 with stock imported from England, Holland and Sweden. From fifteen Cavalier imports have come five Canadian Champions and one Mexican Champion; from these imports, Mr St. Clair has made up two home-bred Canadian Champions and one Mexican Champion. As with Tibetan Spaniels, the Cavaliers are not yet given breed classes and can only be exhibited in Miscellaneous classes.

In 1977, Mr St. Clair, who lives in St Louis, Missouri, imported from Mrs C. Van Den Boom of the Fanfare kennel in Holland a black-and-tan Tibetan Spaniel male which became International and Mexican Ch Fanfare for Starlight. At under three years of age Starlight had won sixteen International Certificates, called CACIBs, throughout Europe and also in Mexico. His early death from an accident is a great loss to his owner and also to the breed. Mr St. Clair also imported a sable bitch from Mrs Van Den Boom which is now International and Mexican Ch Fanfare for Skya-Mar, and has fourteen CACIBs to her credit. As far as Mr St. Clair knows these are the first Tibetan Spaniels to be exhibited in Mexico which is governed by the FCI Rules and not by the A.K.C. Mr St. Clair also owns Bim's Laxmi Puff, bred by Mr and Mrs Whiting from their two Indian imports.

In mid 1979, Mr St. Clair in partnership with Mrs C. C. Neville Thomas of Ontario, Canada, imported a pair of puppies. From Miss Yvonne Border of the Sharbonne prefix in Scotland came Sharbonne Sa-Skya a son of Ch Braeduke Nimmi and the CC winner Friarland Bo-Peep of Sharbonne. The bitch, Braeduke Mandarava, is a descendant of both Yasodhara and Dikki Dolma, a black-and-tan daughter of Braeduke Lu-Ting and Mairmana of Priorswell. In mid 1981 Mr St. Clair purchased two more males. From Mrs V. Armstrong in Scotland he imported Friarland Trangka, a son of Irish Ch Balgay Artali out of Colphil Ku-Lu. From Mrs Pat Vaughan in Canada Mr St. Clair purchased the first Canadian Champion Seng Gay of Rowfant.

Ms Mallory Cosby (formerly Ms M. C. Haden) of Lynchburg, Virginia, has the Ambrier prefix and started in Tibetan Spaniels in 1974 with her purchase, from Mrs Joan Child of Truk-Ku She-Nay-Mo which became a T.S.C.A. Champion in 1977. In 1975, Ms Cosby in conjunction with Mrs Joan Child purchased from Mr Isherwood the male, Sherwood's Ku Omar, sired by Braeduke Po-Lo-Lin out of Braeduke Talika. In 1977, in partnership with Mrs Betty Rosen, she imported a particolour bitch from England, Braeduke Li-Tsi, a daughter of Ch Braeduke Channa out of Ch Kechanta Li-Sa, litter-sister of the English CC winner Braeduke Lu-Ting. In her first litter sired by T.S.C.A. Ch Braeduke Dung-Ka, Li-Tsi produced a parti-colour bitch Ambrier's Bet R Parti Girl, which has already eight points towards her T.S.C.A. Champion title; she is owned and exhibited with Mrs Betty Rosen. In December 1978, Ms Cosby in conjunction with Mrs Phyllis Kohler, imported Braeduke Dung-Ka, a red-and-white particolour adult son of Rama of Amcross out of Northanger Do-Lo Dikki, a daughter of the Indian-imported bitch Dikki Dolma. By 1981 Dung-Ka's progeny had made a lot of impact in the American show ring, and he won his T.S.C.A. Champion title in early 1980.

T.S.C.A. Ch Ambrier's Ti-Mu Ram-A-Din was bred by Ms Cosby, sired by her Sherwood's Ku Omar. From other litters there is Ambrier-bred stock with points towards their titles, in Diane Merritt's Ambrier's Funky Parfait, Susan Ross and Ms Cosby's jointly owned Ambrier's Rock N Roll Baby. Mr and Mrs Whiting's T.S.C.A. Ch Ambrier's Tiger Lily, a litter-sister of Ti-Mu Ram-A-Din, was bred by Ms Cosby. Before she had Tibetan Spaniels, Ms Cosby owned Norwegian Elkhounds and won Obedience awards with them, but was not a breeder.

Mrs Phyllis B. Kohler came into the breed in 1975, but has been active in breeding and showing Shetland Sheepdogs since 1969 having bred Champions in that breed. Her first Tibetan Spaniel, purchased in 1975, was a bitch puppy, jointly bred by Mrs Joan and Mrs Jay Child which became T.S.C.A. Ch Amroth Su-Chan-La of Truk-Ku in 1977. This bitch is also one of the two only T.S.C.A Champions to win an Obedience title, this she did in three shows in a record breaking three consecutive days. Sadly, she died in 1978 at three years of age, but has left behind winning progeny from her two litters. Mrs Kohler with Ms Cosby imported from England the English male Braeduke Dung-Ka which has now sired two T.S.C.A. Champions and ten other Champions all over the world.

Mr and Mrs Herbert Rosen of the Bet R's prefix, live in Lutherville,

Maryland. Before they commenced in Tibetan Spaniels, they owned and bred Lhasa Apsos and Miniature Pinschers with Champions in both breeds. All their foundation stock has been imported from England; the first was in 1974, a black-and-tan bitch Wildhern Winni Tu; as she was unable to be bred from, she was later joined by a bitch, Kempton Peony, then a male, Tsingay Tam Bo-Lin, which both won their T.S.C.A. Champion titles in 1977 and 1978 respectively. Another imported bitch Kharekhola Lasya, won her title in 1979; another bitch, Braeduke Gantsa, was also imported in 1979 and won her title in 1980, and has since produced her first litter. Another male, imported from England, was Fairstar Cho-Sun who is now a T.S.C.A Champion.

Mr and Mrs Herbert Rosen's expedition to Bermuda was very successful, with their dog, T.S.C.A. Ch Fairstar Cho-Sun, winning his Bermudian Champion title, as did their bitch, T.S.C.A. Ch Khareola Lasya – both imported from England as puppies. Further details of the blood-lines and Champions in America can be found at the end of this chapter.

Other Mid-Atlantic Club owners and breeders are Mr and Mrs Tom Whiting who bred Ms Cosby's T.S.C.A. Ch Bim's Twin Socks Kamla and her litter-brother Bim's Bomber Sahb which is on the way to an American Club title, descending from their Indian born original Pair. There is also Freeda Manley, Linda Foiles of Flolin prefix and Phyllis Kohler of Phylmarko who co-owns with Mallory Cosby the English-bred T.S.C.A. Ch Braeduke Dung-Ka. In the Lynchburg area are Mallory Cosby of Ambrier's prefix and Marianne Richardson.

In the south-west, perhaps due to the long distances, things are quieter, with Marie Rickett and Terri Solmson; there is Bette Merrill in Arizona, who appears to be about the only exhibitor at the time of publication. In Texas, there is Ms Dianna Smith of Houston and, in San Antonia, Miss Anna Armstrong the owner of the English-bred male, Braeduke Gompa.

In New England, there is Ellen and Brian Pickard in New York who are newcomers to this breed although they are exhibitors of a Bernese Mountain Dog. Joan Herrick and Beatrice Karstadt are others in this area. Mr Don Roy is another Tibetan Spaniel owner who does not breed or exhibit, but does sterling work for the main Club, including editing their newsletter and he collects oriental books as well.

Also on the East Coast, there is Mrs Joan Child, of Truk-Ku prefix, in Connecticut which is the Tri-Haven Club area, Patrick and Jay Child of Amroth, and Jean McNickle of Dynasty prefix. In late summer 1981 Mrs Valerie Robinson emigrated from Northern Ireland to Cape Cod, Massachusetts, with her three young sable bitches, Braeduke Lhotse Shar of Deetree, Braeduke Nima Dorji of Deetree and a particolour puppy; she hopes to breed her first Tibetan Spaniel litters in America. Lhotse Shar is a daughter of Ch Braeduke Nimmi out of Ch Kechanta Li-Sa, Nima Dorji is a daughter of Ch Kensing Ra out of Ch Braeduke Whitewisp Hara Nor, Braeduke Dhud Kosi is sired by Braeduke Lu Ting out of Whitewisp Duet.

Unfortunately, the pair owned by Mr Bryan Scott of California have not been integrated into the American blood-lines, the male was thought to be sterile and the bitch, imported from Mrs D. Norton when she lived in Toronto, Canada, has been rehoused and her whereabouts is now unknown.

Ann Rohrer lives in Pearblossom, outside Los Angeles, on the edge of the Californian desert, with two Tibetan Terriers, a family of Tibetan Mastiffs including a foundation stud dog for the West (an import from Nepal) and a few Tibetan Spaniels of English foundation. A bitch, Sketchley Chinki, was spayed after producing one litter; the male, Sketchley Yee Wong, is a son of Ch Clawson Braeduke Rampa out of a daughter of Ch Braeduke Jhanki of Wimaro out of Ch Yaso of Szufung. A very nice bitch, Lani's Kum-Chhe of Lantan which has been leased to Mrs M. Jennings, a double descendant of the late English Ch Huntglen Bràeduke Ta-Ra-Ni, with the Anglo-Chinese blood through a younger particolour sister of my English Ch Braeduke Ama-Kuluh.

Outside San Francisco, Mrs Marjorie Jennings of Los Altos, who has the Camas Japanese Chins, bred her first litter of Tibetan Spaniels in 1979. The sire was Braeduke Garpon owned by Ms Lily Tamura (formerly Ms Hosticka), the dam, Colphil Su-Li, was obtained from Mrs Hazel Eaton in Nassau. A dog puppy from Su-Li's first litter is owned and exhibited by Dixie McCulloch of the Chisai prefix who lives in Petaluma. Among the others on the West Coast who plan to show and breed Tibetan Spaniels is Mrs M. Gross of Santa Cruz who commenced with a stray male without a pedigree which looks to be a good particolour specimen. Late in 1979, Mrs Gross imported from England Braeduke Mutig Pren-Ba, a particolour daughter of Braeduke Lu-Ting out of Mairmana of Priorswell. There are also Dan Cooper and Jim McKinley; Bill and Rosanna Wells of the Tudorwells prefix, who have three Tibetan Spaniels and have been in dogs for over twenty-five years; and Virginia Newton of Los Altos who has been in Papillons for over thirty years and finished fourteen American Champions in that breed. Another breeder is Ms Cherie de Bonneville.

In the Mid-West area is Jeanne Holsapple who has the established Tashi kennel of Lhasa Apsos in New Castle, Indiana, importing her stock from England, Canada and Holland. In 1979 Mrs Holsapple purchased two bitch puppies, Whitewisp Pitti Sing and Ybroc Terribly Twee; both won their T.S.C.A. Champion titles in 1980. Tritou Charlotte, a daughter of Irish-bred Benagh Rue, came from Mrs Chalmers in Canada. Fanfare for Zepherine was obtained from Mrs C. Van Den Boom in Holland and she whelped one dog puppy in America sired by International and Dutch Ch Fanfare Dmar-Ba. In 1980, two more joined the Tashi Tibetans; a sable dog puppy, Braeduke Nam-Ra, a son of Ch Kensing Ra out of Ch Braeduke Whitewisp Hara Nor, and Braeduke Rincen Suna, a particolour daughter of Braeduke Lu-Ting out of Braeduke Rje-La. Later on, in 1980, two litter-sisters were imported from Miss Alison Leslie, sired by the CC winner Benagh Chang out of Weiden Su-Hi, the litter-sister of Ch Su-Li of Braeduke.

Others in this area are Sandi Lister, the Borkowskis, John and Evelyn Hanauer, the Don Crosses and Angela and Charles Wills. They all hope to plan two Rare Breed shows in this area, to be held annually in the spring and the fall.

In the Great Lakes district Gerald Turner and Jerome Clark of the Sundown prefix, already established in Norwich Terriers and Griffon Bruxellois with Champions in both these breeds, have bred their first Tibetan Spaniel litter in early 1981. Sired by Amroth Mot-Ta of Phylmarko, a male who was born in 1979, with two bitch puppies obtained from England in early 1980 – Braeduke Gur Kum, a daughter of Braeduke Su-Sun out of Tangwell Galaxy, and Braeduke O-Puskara, a daughter of Rutherglen Lho-Ra-Ni out of Ch Kensing O-So Special. Another Tibetan Spaniel owner in the Detroit area is Ilene Rowe, who has an American Champion Boxer.

The early breeders of Tibetan Spaniels in America who worked hard to form the Tibetan Spaniel Club of America (T.S.C.A.) and to get the breed going, should have an honourable mention; Ms Lucia H. Humphreys of the Lani's prefix who also has Tibetan Mastiffs, and Mr Charles Wills, both of Oklahoma; Mr and Mrs Robert Fecitt of the Belvedere prefix in Indiana; Mrs John Hacker in Honolulu, Hawaii, who bred the Author's English Ch Braeduke Ama Kuluh and Mr and Mrs Herjeskog's Swedish Ch Ba-Ba (from this litter-brother and -sister have come many Champions all over the world, a remarkable achievement); Mr and Mrs Pederstuen, who used to live in Hawaii; Mr and Mrs Don Langlois, Mrs Evelyn Lubenow, Mrs Tina Kuroczka of Ama-Kay prefix, all four come from Connecticut; Mr and Mrs W. L. Rickett of the Ric Ries prefix in Tenessee; Mrs Patty Auman in Philadelphia; Mr Leo Kearns of Trinity prefix who was the first importer of the foundation for the American dynasty; Mrs Joan Child of Truk-Ku and her sister-in-law Mrs Jay Child of Amroth – all of Connecticut.

The regional map at the end of this chapter clearly shows the progress of the breed, there being only seven States without any T.S.C.A. officially registered Tibetan Spaniels.

Undoubtedly there are many more Tibetan Spaniels in the States. Some have arrived with Service families who had returned home from England, and others could have mistakenly been thought not to be Tibetan Spaniels if they were purchased from Mr Jack Isherwood, at a time when he was selling them as Khabachen Khyi (watch dog of the snows!) when he lived in the Bellingham, Washington, area.

Miss Marguerite Cotsworth Perkins who became Mrs Peter Soman in July 1981, received from the Author, as a wedding present, a particolour Tibetan Spaniel puppy bitch, Braeduke Shen Ming, a daughter of Ch Kensing Ra out of Ch Su-Li of Braeduke. Ming is destined as a bride for the black-and-white Darjeeling-born male Tashi Dorji and Mrs Soman plans to show her in the future.

Let us hope that all those people who have dedicated themselves to the welfare and future of the breed in the United States of America, will see the long overdue reward of full Championship status for the breed in the not too distant future. It seems incredible to breeders and exhibitors of Tibetan Spaniels in England and Scandinavia, that the American Kennel Club has held back for so long. By the end of 1980 there was a total of three hundred and eighty-four Tibetan Spaniels registered with the T.S.C.A., there were one hundred and twenty-seven litters born during the period 1971 to 1980, the average size litter was three puppies, and of the total number of puppies born one hundred and nintey-six were males and one hundred and eighty-eight were females. The total number of imports to America at the end of 1980 was seventy-eight. It is high time they were removed from the Miscellaneous classification at the American Kennel Club.

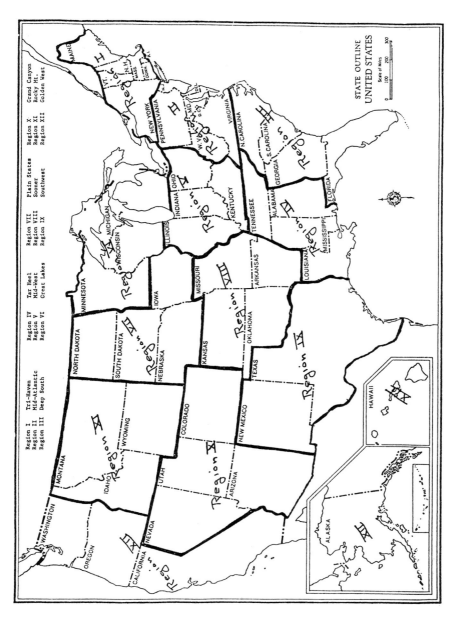

From the T.S.C.A. News Letter correct in April 1981.
Showing the Regional Tibetan Spaniel breed club areas.

217

Tibetan Spaniels in the United States being awarded their T.S.C.A. Championship titles

Finished in 1975

T.S.C.A. Ch Rdo-Rje Rig-Zin of Amroth (D) Born 8.7.71
Sire: English Ch Yakrose Chiala of Amcross
Dam: Doghouse Dream Baby
Breeder: Mr Leo Kearne
Owner: Mrs Jay Child

T.S.C.A. Ch Braeduke Sazi-La (B) Born 27.9.71
Sire: English Ch Braeduke Jhanki of Wimaro
Dam: Braeduke Si-Pu
Breeder: Mrs C. Clapham (U.K.)
Owners: Mrs Joan Child and Mrs Jay Child

T.S.C.A. Ch Witneylea Kulha (D) Born 31.8.69
Sire: Witneylea Melha
Dam: Kayla of Amcross
Breeder: Mrs A. L. Weller (U.K.)
Owner: Mrs Joan Child

Finished in 1976

T.S.C.A. Ch Wildhern Ambassador (D) Born 1.8.74
Sire: Ch Wildhern Genghiz Khan
Dam: Ch Northanger A-Su
Breeder: Mrs C. M. Micklethwait (U.K.)
Owner: Mrs Jay Child

T.S.C.A. Ch Chuni La of Amroth (B) Born 7.2.73
Sire: T.S.C.A. Ch Rdo-Rje Rig-Zin of Amroth
Dam: T.S.C.A. Ch Norbu's Tip Toes of Amroth
Breeder: Mr Wesley and the late Mrs Needham
Owners: Mrs P. Kohler and Mrs Jay Child

T.S.C.A. Ch Westerly Lotus of Amroth C.D. (B) Born 7.2.73
Sire: T.S.C.A. Ch Rdo-Rje Rig-Zin of Amroth
Dam: T.S.C.A. Ch Norbu's Tip Toes of Amroth
Breeder: Mr Wesley and the late Mrs Needham
Owner: Mrs Gwen Wexler

T.S.C.A. Ch Norbu's Tip Toes of Amroth (B) Born 16.11.70
Sire: T.S.C.A. Ch Witneylea Kulha
Dam: Ciceter Norbu
Breeder: Mrs Jay Child
Owner: Mr Wesley and the late Mrs Needham

T.S.C.A. Ch Amroth Hi Roller (D) Born 11.6.75
Sire: T.S.C.A. Ch Wildhern Ambassador
Dam: T.S.C.A. Ch Chuni La of Amroth
Breeder-Owner: Mrs Jay Child

T.S.C.A. Ch Kempton Peony (B) Born 27.5.76
Sire: Kempton Lombo-Moke
Dam: Kempton Keepa
Breeder: Mrs D. Ormsby (U.K.)
Owners: Mrs and Mrs H. Rosen

T.S.C.A. Ch Amroth Gandum So-Nam (D) Born 8.8.73
Sire: T.S.C.A. Ch Rdo-Rje Rig-Zin of Amroth
Dam: Camleigh Chirpi Chi
Breeder: Mrs Jay Child
Owner: Mrs Tina Kay Kuroczka

T.S.C.A. Ch Amroth Su-Chan-La of Truk-Ku C.D. (B) Born 4.1.75
Sire: English Ch Yakrose Chiala of Amcross
Dam: T.S.C.A. Ch Braeduke Sazi-La
Breeders: Mrs Joan Child and Mrs Jay Child
Owner: Mrs P. B. Kohler

T.S.C.A. Ch Ambrier's Ti-Mu Ram-A-Din (D) Born 11.1.75
Sire: Sherwood's Ku-Omar
Dam: T.S.C.A. Ch Truk-Ku She-Nay-Mo
Breeder: Ms Mallory C. Haden (now Ms M. Cosby)
Owners: Ms Anne C. Lewis and Mr William Cosby

T.S.C.A. Ch Truk-Ku She-Nay-Mo (B) Born 3.3.69
Sire: T.S.C.A. Ch Witneylea Kulha
Dam: Bu-Mo of Amcross
Breeder: Mrs Joan Child
Owner: Ms Mallory C. Haden

T.S.C.A. Ch Amroth Lotus of Belvedere (B) Born 12.8.76
Sire: T.S.C.A. Ch Rdo-Rje Rig-Zin of Amroth
Dam: Sherwood's Mu Tig
Breeders: Ann Fecitt and Mrs Jay Child
Owner: Mrs Jay Child

Finished in 1978

T.S.C.A. Ch Tsingay Tam Bo Lin (D) Born 24.6.76
Sire: English Ch Ram Chandra of Amcross
Dam: Wilhern Taranatha
Breeders: Mrs D. Ormsby (U.K.)
Owners: Mr and Mrs H. Rosen

T.S.C.A. Ch Wildhern Winni Tu (B) Born 1.8.74
Sire: Ch Wildhern Genghis Khan
Dam: Ch Northanger A-Su
Breeder: Mrs C. M. Micklethwait (U.K.)
Owner: Mr and Mrs H. Rosen

Finished in 1979

T.S.C.A. Ch Amroth Kung Dze Mo (B) Born date unknown
Sire: T.S.C.A. Ch Rdo-Rje Rig-Zin of Amroth
Dam: Amroth Kung T'say Mo
Breeder-Owner: Mrs Jay Child

T.S.C.A. Ch Phylmarko Tsam-Pa Ka-Mo (B) Born 11.1.77
Sire: T.S.C.A. Ch Rdo-Rje Rig-Zin of Amroth
Dam: T.S.C.A. Ch Amroth Su-Chan-La of Truk-Ku C.D.
Breeder-Owner: Mrs P. B. Kohler

T.S.C.A. Ch Ambrier's Tiger Lily (B) Born 11.1.75
Sire: Sherwood's Ku Omar
Dam: T.S.C.A. Ch Truk-Ku She-Nay-Mo
Breeder: Ms M. Haden (Now Ms M. Cosby)
Owners: Mr and Mrs T. Whiting

T.S.C.A. Ch Kharekhola Lasya (B) Born 15.9.78
Sire: Wildhern Warrior
Dam: Wildhern Dorje
Breeder: Mrs L. Dalgety
Owner: Mrs Betty Rosen

T.S.C.A. Ch Phylmarko Su-Chan Yin Erh-Tzu (D) Born 11.1.77
Sire: T.S.C.A. Ch Amroth Hi Roller
Dam: T.S.C.A. Ch Amroth Su-Chan-La of Truk-Ki, C.D.
Breeder: Mrs P. B. Kohler
Owner: Mrs Linda Foiles

Finished in 1980

T.S.C.A. Ch Braeduke Dung-Ka (D) Born 5.9.72
Sire: Rama of Amcross
Dam: Northanger Do-Lo Dikki
Breeders: Mrs Wynyard and Miss Forbes (U.K.)
Owners: Mrs P. B. Kohler and Ms Haden (now Ms M. Cosby)

T.S.C.A. Ch Bim's Twin Socks Kamla (B) Born 1979
Sire: T.S.C.A. Ch Braeduke Dung-Ka
Dam: Bim's Dusty Tara
Breeder: Mr and Mrs T. Whiting
Owner: Ms M. Cosby

T.S.C.A. Ch Italia's T. S. Artemus (D) Born 2.11.79
Sire: T.S.C.A. Ch Ambrier's Ti Mu Ram-A-Din
Dam: T.S.C.A. Ch Fanfare of Sky-a-Mar
Breeder: Mr W. St. Clair
Owner: Ms Mallory Cosby

T.S.C.A. Ch Whitewisp Pitti Sing (B) Born 14.9.78
Sire: Ch Braeduke Channa
Dam: Whitewisp Koko Nor
Breeders: Mr and Mrs G. W. Grounds (U.K.)
Owner: Mrs J. Holsapple

Bermuda Ch and T.S.C.A. Ch Fairstar Cho-Sun (D) Born 5.10.79
Sire: Wildhern Warrior
Dam: Windameres Indian Tigress
Breeder: Mrs F. M. McCartney (U.K.)
Owner: Mrs Betty Rosen

T.S.C.A. Ch Braeduke Gantsa (B) Born 5.2.79
Sire: Ch Windameres Lho-Zah-Mi
Dam: Tangwell Galaxy
Breeder: Mrs A. Wynyard (U.K.)
Owner: Mrs Betty Rosen

T.S.C.A. Ch Phylmarko Tonk-Ka (D) Born 20.5.79
Sire: T.S.C.A. Ch Braeduke Dung-Ka
Dam: T.S.C.A. Ch Phylmarko Tsam-Pa Ko-Mo
Breeder-Owner: Mrs P. B. Kohler

T.S.C.A. Ch Ybroc Terribly Twee (B) Born 25.11.78
Sire: Ch Heyvan Jola
Dam: Braeduke Ba-Byi of Ybroc

Breeders: Mrs and Miss Leslie (U.K.)
Owner: Mrs J. Holsapple

T.S.C.A. Ch Fanfare for Zepherine (B) Born date unknown
Sire: International and Dutch Ch Mingshang Zenith
Dam: International and Dutch Ch Fanfare for Jam-Po
Breeder: Mrs C. Van Den Boom (Holland)
Owner: Mrs J. Holsapple

Bermuda Ch and T.S.C.A. Ch Kharekhola Lasya (B) Born 15.9.78
Sire: Wildhern Warrior
Dam: Wildhern Djorja
Breeder: Miss R. Trethowan (U.K.)
Owner: Mrs Betty Rosen

Finished 1981 (incomplete list)

T.S.C.A. Ch Phylmarko Shan Hu (D) Born 3.9.80
Sire: T.S.C.A. Ch Braeduke Dung-Ka
Dam: Phylmarko Hua—Su
Breeder and Owner: Mrs Phyllis B. Kohler

T.S.C.A. Ch Ybroc Happy Go Lucky (B) Born 3.5.80
Sire: Benagh Chang
Dam: Weiden Su-Hi
Breeder: Miss A. Leslie
Owner: Mrs J. Holsapple

The Tibetan Spaniel Club of America
Summary of Registration Records
as of May 31st, 1981

	1971	1972	1973	1974	1975	1976	1977	1978	1979	1980	Through 5/31/81	Total
Puppies: American Bred												
Primary	3	16	26	58	40	22	27	30	45	47	34	348
Secondary	–	–	–	9	14	10	11	12	3	11	16	86
Total	3	16	26	67	54	32	38	42	48	58	50	434
Imports: Primary												
England	16	9	6	2	5	2	2	3	7	10	–	62
Holland	–	–	–	–	–	–	–	–	3	–	–	3
Canada	–	–	–	–	–	–	–	–	1	2	–	3
Total	16	9	6	2	5	2	2	3	11	12	–	68
Secondary	–	–	–	5	2	1	1	–	1	–	–	10
Total Imports	16	9	6	7	7	3	3	3	12	12	–	78
Total Registrations	19	25	32	73	61	35	41	45	60	70	50	512

This impressive tabulation showing Tibetan Spaniel registrations now over the 500 mark was presented to the T.S.C.A Board at their annual meeting, June 20th, 1981, by Thomas J. Whiting, T.S.C.A. Registrar.

223

11 Tibetan Spaniels around the rest of the world

Holland

Although I do not know the date, it was prior to 1970 when Mr Post imported into Holland a male Witneylea Dmar Pa, and a bitch Amcross Sophi. They produced Mr J. Kuif's Dutch International, Belgian and World Champion of 1976, Su Cheng van Tibets Stam, The litter-sister, Su-Ling van Tibets Stam, was campaigned by Mr Kuif to become a Dutch, International, Belgian and Luxembourg Champion and Bundessieger of 1975. There is no record of any progeny from either.

Mrs Constance Van Den Boom, who has the Fanfare prefix, was the pioneer of Cavalier King Charles Spaniels on the Continent, her stock coming from Mrs Amice Pitt's Ttiweh kennel. Braeduke Sivas Supi Yaw Lat, a black-and-tan daughter of Ch Sivas Zodi and Ch Sivas Mesa, was imported in whelp to Ch Braeduke Jhanki of Wimaro in 1970. Supi Yaw Lat had already won two Reserve CCs and her Junior Warrant in England, making history by being the first of her colour to win the latter. From this litter, born in Holland, came International Ch Fanfare for Jam-Po. This bitch and her litter-sister proved to be very good brood-bitches and have produced progeny which have become International Champions and Champions in Holland, Belgium, Austria, Italy and Luxembourg. Mrs Van Den Boom campaigned Supi Yaw Lat to the titles of International, Hungarian, French, Swiss and Dutch Champion, World Champion at Budapest and Bundessieger of 1971. Unfortunately, Supi Yaw Lat drowned under the ice on a pond. Mrs Van Den Boom still has several great-grandchildren and great-great-grandchildren of Supi's who are Champions or well on their way to becoming Champions in various countries. Mrs Van Den Boom exhibits her dogs all over Europe.

With Supi went a bitch puppy, Braeduke Chura, another daughter of Ch Jhanki out of Ch Braeduke Tam Cho. She was a great personality and her owner's little mascot. After starting a successful show career and winning her Champion title she died at an early age after an accident, and so was never bred from.

The next import was the male, Mingshang Zenith, a son of Ch Mingshang Jason and Ch Mingshang Yang Zom of Szufung, who became an International, Dutch, Belgian and Italian Champion and is still one of the keenest stud dogs in the Fanfare kennel; his blood-lines have blended well with the Braeduke and Fanfare blood-lines. In 1972 a litter-brother and -sister joined the Fanfare Tibetan Spaniels, only the second and third to be exported with the Indian imported blood-lines, the first being their brother who was exported to Sweden and became a Nordic Champion. This litter was sired by Ch Windameres Braeduke Champa out of Braeduke Northanger Cu Li Dikki. Mrs Van Den Boom says that this pair, the male Braeduke Chamba Sopa which became an International, Dutch and Luxembourg Champion, and the bitch Braeduke Cham Kusho who won her International title, have proved themselves to be a successful sire and brood-bitch. Cham Kusho has far too many Champion children to list, mostly sired by Mingshang Zenith or by her nephew, International, Dutch, German and Belgian Ch Fanfare for Sa-Skya, but among the most important of Ch Cham Kusho's progeny are International, Dutch and Austrian Ch Fanfare for Skya-Nar; and this bitch's litter-sister, International Ch Fanfare for Skya-Mar who has now been exported to Mr William St. Clair of St Louis, Missouri, U.S.A. Mrs J. Holsapple's Fanfare for Zepherine, a sable bitch, was exported by Mrs Van Den Boom to Indiana, U.S.A. when in whelp to International Ch Fanfare Dmar-Ba in 1979.

Three more Cham Kusho progeny that have almost completed their title of Champion are Fanfare for Starlet, Fanfare for Zembel and Fanfare for Zelamire. Another Champion is International, Dutch, Austrian and Luxembourg and German Ch Fanfare for Dmar-Ba; he, like Zembel and Zelamire, was sired by Mingshang Zenith. Mrs Van Den Boom has specialised in breeding black-and-tans.

Mrs Van Den Boom is an intrepid traveller and exhibitor as can be seen from all the different countries around Europe in which she has made up Champions; The Author considers that she has done more to pioneer and popularise the breed in Europe than anyone else. Apart from her twenty Tibetan Spaniels, all of which stem from the Ch Jhanki, Ch Supi Yaw Lat, Ch Zenith, Ch Braeduke Chamba Sopa and Ch Cham Kusho nucleus, she also shows and breeds Great Danes.

Mr H. R. J. Schipper of Amsterdam imported a bitch puppy, Braeduke Phu Phu in 1971. A daughter of Ch Braeduke Channa and out of Clawson Che Pa of Braeduke, Phu Phu became an International Champion in 1973; her litter-brother became an International and Nordic Champion and her litter-sister founded the

Benagh kennel in Eire.

In 1972, Mr Schipper imported Braeduke Spo-Sel, a daughter of Ch Windameres Braeduke Shan Hu of Northanger, which became Youth winner 1972 and Winner 1973 and later on an International Champion. From Mrs Clapham came Mr De Nooy's black-and-tan male, Braeduke Heyvan Minkar who at one time only wanted one more CC for his title of Champion. Mr Schipper also bred and exhibited Great Danes and, although he did breed one or two litters of Tibetan Spaniels with his Boeddah prefix, he has not exhibited them for some years.

Miss M. H. Iwes, of the van Markley affix from Breda, imported in 1971 a bitch puppy, Braeduke Rincen, litter-sister of English Ch Braeduke Re Ba and CC winner Braeduke Rab-Shi, sired by Rimsky Sun out of Ch Huntglen Braeduke Ta-Ra-Ni. Rincen became an International, Dutch and Luxembourg Champion and when mated to International Ch Braeduke Chamba Sopa produced Dutch Ch Kai-Lu van Markley who was Winner 1974. In another litter sired by International Ch Mingshang Zenith, Rincen produced Ch Reba van Markley who was Winner 1978. The latest star on the way to completing his title is Miss Iwes' home-bred Rab-Shi van Markley. They are all said to be so similar in type and colouring that it is difficult to identify them, which is a great compliment to pay this small selective kennel. The van Markley affix is also well-known in Cavalier King Charles Spaniels, bred by Miss Iwes' sister since 1958. They have the wonderful record of eighteen National Champions all owned and bred here in Cavaliers.

Mrs J. C. de Graaff-Guilloud owns Kechanta Lah-Di-Dah, bred by Mrs V. White, sired by Ch Kensing Oscar out of Redgame Luna.

Unfortunately there does not seem to be a great demand in parts of the European continent for Tibetan Spaniels, as either pets or for the show ring; this may seem very strange to the English and the Scandinavians in whose countries the breed enjoys great popularity and recognition. This must be very discouraging to the dedicated breeders, such as Mrs Van Den Boom and Miss Iwes, but surely the breed, in the hands of such experienced people, will some day reward all their efforts. Any influx of newcomers to carry on does not seem to be apparent, but perhaps other owners and breeders will soon take a second look at our breed and appreciate it!

West Germany

It is very difficult to know just when and by whom the first Tibetan Spaniel was brought into West Germany, or who bred the first litter, but among the first must be Mr Winfried and Mrs Hedy Nouc who imported a Szufung male and a bitch, Padme of Amcross.

In about 1970 Mrs Lotte Haas of Wuppertal-Cronenberg owned Chue of Szufung, and Pu-tse of Amcross, which was bred by Mrs A. L. Weller, was exported to Mrs Rose von Zitzewitz and became an International Champion. Frau von Zitzewitz still has a lot of Tibetan Spaniels, mainly from the Amcross kennels, her prefix is 'von Gre-Bin'. Mrs Laura Kleinsone near Hanover had a bitch, Ninah of Jo-Gya-Kang, bred by Mrs Wienekamp, but now owns Vosta Rum-Ba, a son of Ch Amcross Pax and out of Vosta Dhos-Sani. The Amritas kennel, owned by Mr Wilhelm Fleuchaus near Frankfurt has European Winner and World Champion Amritas Harmony. Mrs Marianne Luft of Hamburg has the kennel name of Djin-Ping-Meh, and Mr Gert Haenning of Wennigsen has the kennel name Alhambra.

Mrs Irmgard Wienekamp, of the Jo-Gya-Kang prefix, and who lives in Heidmühle, has bred German Shepherd dogs as well as Tibetan Spaniels and has, more recently, bred or exhibited Lhasa Apsos as well. Mrs Wienekamp has owned or bred six International Champions, six National Champions, seven Luxembourg Champions, three Champions of the World, four Bundessieger (German) Champions and many other dogs with different European Champion titles.

Mrs Wienekamp's first English imports were two daughters of Ch Clawson Braeduke Rampa. The dam of Clawson Chantin is Clawson Charming of Eulyn and the dam of Clawson Pi-Ta is Clawson Kham-Pu. The first male imported by this kennel was the English Reserve CC winner, Beaver of Eulyn, a son of Ch Braeduke Jhanki of Wimaro out of Deretta of Eulyn. Beaver became an International and German Champion. The next imports from England were a male, Daleviz Alpheus, then a bitch, Kitsown Khe-Sho, a daughter of Ming-Y of Northanger and Braeduke Lgo. Mrs Wienekamp then purchased, from Mr Jorg Haufschild, an English-bred bitch Camleigh Pema Tsu, a daughter of Rimsky Sun out of Braeduke Kan-Da. In 1973, Deanford Moon Daisy, a daughter of Ch Braeduke Channa out of Sivas Minette, was exported from England to Mrs Wienekamp with a male, Braeduke Chumna. Bred by Mrs C. Clapham, Chumna is the son of Braeduke Dung-Ka out of South African Ch Colphil Chi-Lo, and the litter-brother of English Ch Heyvan Jola. To date, Chumna has sired five Champions and has himself won CACs. Both Beaver and Chumna have been very influential stud dogs in this kennel.

In 1974 Mrs Wienekamp imported Braeduke Yasoda, a winning daughter of Ch Braeduke Jhanki of Wimaro and the Indian-born

Yasodhara. Yasoda was in whelp to Braeduke Dung-Ka and tragically died when her puppies were three days old, it is believed from eclampsia. The litter was hand reared and one of the survivors, Mara of Jo-Gya Kang has won CCs.

Other exhibitors in West Germany are Marianne Luft who owns Shymela Shakpa bred by Mrs J. Shearer, and her son Topas of Djin-Ping-Meh. Another English export here is Mr Wilhelm Fleuchaus' Clydum Kicking Horse, a son of Ch Shamau Ba-Ti-Ka out of Bruesown Tsampa of Clydum, bred by Miss H. Simper and Miss E. Scoates.

France

In 1971, Mrs A. L. Weller exported Witneylea Tarbu, a son of Witneylea Tupence out of Spro-Ba of Amcross, to a Miss M. Curto. In 1974, Mrs M. Prevost imported a male puppy, Braeduke Chugum; Mr Rene Trocque imported a pair in 1973, of which the male, Braeduke Sinji Chogyal, was later purchased by Mrs Berthier from a kennels outside Paris. The bitch, Braeduke Lhal-Pa La, has not been heard of again. In 1970, Mr and Mrs Le Hourry imported from Mrs Weller a son of Ch Amcross Vosta Kushi Kee, but there are no records of any Tibetan Spaniels being registered prior to 1973, apart from Miss Goulin's Ianke of unknown origins.

Miss Violette Dupont, who has the world-famous Annapurna Lhasa Apsos, now the President of the Club des Chiens du Thibet (which is affiliated to the Société Centrale Canine) is encouraging interest in Tibetan Spaniels. Mrs Brouilly of the De Rongbuk prefix now owns two bitches, one of which, Braeduke Gyara, a daughter of Braeduke Su-Sun out of Tangwell Galaxy, is the winner of two CACIBs, and is in fact the litter-sister of Mr and Mrs Mulford's Reserve CC winning male Braeduke Geruda. Early in 1981, Mrs Brouilly imported Braeduke Ma-Ni, a daughter of Kensing Ferdi out of Mairmana of Priorswell.

Mr Thomas Leathers Caldwell of the Malaku prefix, an American citizen, who is domiciled outside Paris, is already an established breeder and exhibitor of Tibetan Terriers and Lhasa Apsos. Late in 1980, Mr Caldwell purchased a male puppy, Braeduke Leh, a son of Ch Braeduke Nimmi out of Braeduke Lin-Ga-La. From this nucleus it is hoped to establish the first Tibetan Spaniel dynasty in France. During 1981 there has been stirring interest in the breed in France and both Leh and Gyara commenced their show careers at Luxembourg. As Leh was too young to win the CACIB or the CAC, he has the unofficial title of Luxembourg Youth Champion.

Madame Simonne Chauvin-Daroux of the De La Nerto Apsos, commenced with her first Tibetan Spaniel in mid 1981, Braeduke Pokhara, a daughter of Ch Kensing Ra out of England's top winning bitch Ch Braeduke Poo-Khyi.

In November 1981 Mrs Chauvin-Daroux imported from Mrs G. S. Vines in England, the Crufts Dog Show Tibetan Spaniel Dog Challenge Certificate winner in 1980, Tomarans Gwe-N-Daw. He was accompanied by two daughters of Ch Windameres Loo-Di-Pa, one of them was sired by Windameres Salvador. At the same time Mrs Brouilly imported a bitch, Langshi Zerena of Terra and Mr Caldwell purchased a male puppy, Wildhern Skyid.

Mrs Elizabeth Lecoq of Paris owns 'Ramdouk', a liver coloured bitch obtained from Nepal in 1979, pedigree and breeder unknown but she is already a CACIB winner in her own country.

There appears to be great opposition to the founding of a Tibetan Spaniel dynasty in France from many of the establihed Lhasa Apso breeders and exhibitors. Unfortunately the French system of registration is open to abuse, especially as it permits dogs and bitches of unknown origins and without pedigrees to be given a breed name and allows them to be used for show and breeding. There is no such safeguard as an import permit. It is to be hoped that the genuine devotees of the true Tibetan Spaniel breed will keep their English blood-lines 'pure'.

Switzerland

Mr F. Ruegg in Switzerland purchased a bitch Cho-Cho from her master who had walked from Tibet to a refugee camp in Kathmandu, Nepal. She was born in May 1960; she has since bred four litters in Switzerland, and is officially registered with the Swiss Kinologische Society. Her litters were sired by Beryll von Gre-Bin, a son of Pe-Sar of Amcross out of a daughter of Pe-Sar and Pu-Tse of Amcross, bred by Mrs Rose von Zitzewitz in West Germany.

From Cho-Cho's second litter, Mr Armin Ritz, of Kennel von Rakas, purchased a bitch, Bijou von Bodjul, which has been exhibited and won CACs and CACIBs. When Bijou was mated to Chuen of Szufung, she produced four males; in another litter sired by International and Swiss Ch Que-Sho-Wong of Jo-Gya-Kang who is a son of International and German Ch Beaver of Eulyn out of Clawson Pi-Ta, came litter-brother and -sister Bhutan von Rakas and Bhrikuti von Rakas, both of which are now Swiss and International

Champions. As far as is known, Cho-Cho's blood-lines have not been exported outside Switzerland and West Germany.

Mr Ritz exhibits his Tibetan Spaniels all over West Germany, France, Holland, Denmark and Austria as well as in his homeland of Switzerland. He also owns a Tibetan Mastiff.

Italy

In November 1975 Mrs David Alexander imported a male puppy, Braeduke Norbu Asma, sired by International Ch Braeduke Am-Ra and out of Ch Braeduke Whitewisp Hara Nor, litter-brother of the dual Reserve CC winner Braeduke Norbu Ambu owned by Mr and Mrs F. Ashton. He was followed in 1976 by Braeduke Pat-Me, daughter of Ch Braeduke Nimmi and Ch Braeduke Patlin, in fact the litter-sister of Mrs Butler's Braeduke Pye-Mi the dam of Ch Braeduke Poo-Khyi. Norbu Asma is now an International and Italian Champion, and Pat-Me is an International and World Champion.

In October 1976, friends of Mrs Alexander's imported a male, Braeduke Rgyul-Po, a son of Braeduke Dung-Ka out of Ch Braeduke Re-Ba. He has since become a Champion for Dr and Mrs Paolo Longoni. In August 1978, Mrs Alexander purchased another bitch puppy, Braeduke Rje Doma, a daughter of Braeduke Dung-Ka out of Braeduke Rje-La. Three litters have now been bred here and from the last, by Norbu Asma out of Rje Doma, has come a promising red-and-white particolour male, Yadruk-Pa Kang Tsup which is about to commence his show career.

Israel

In late 1975, Mrs L. Anderson exported a male puppy, Lindys Pembah, but he has not, to her knowledge, been exhibited in Israel. In early 1976, Mrs H. Dormont in Tel Aviv imported a brace of Tibetan Spaniels. The bitch, Balgay At-Sa-Ryá, was a black-and-tan daughter of International Ch Braeduke Am-Ra, bred by Mrs A. Young. The male, Bourton Tangu, was bred by the Hon. Mrs Field. Mrs Dormont gave the bitch to friends and there is no record of any litters born.

South Africa

Mr and Mrs G. Skeats, of the Sonnings prefix, imported a pair of puppies in mid 1975. The bitch, Braeduke O-Puku, quickly won her

Champion title, as did the male Braeduke Lhak-Pa-Lo. These were the first Tibetan Spaniels to be imported and exhibited in South Africa. In September 1975, Mrs Skeats imported two bitches in whelp; Colphil Chi-Lo, the litter-sister of a Swedish Champion, produced South African Ch Sonnings Tong Woo from this litter sired by Braeduke Dung-Ka. The other bitch, Braeduke Lhuntse, produced only one male puppy, a tricolour, a black-and-true-tan with a lot of white, to Tangwell Gu Cham Midas. Both Chi-Lo and Lhuntse became South African Champions. Puppies have been sold to Mrs E. M. H. Apfel of Johannesburg, also to Mr and Mrs A. Woods of Durban who are believed to have returned home to England with their Champion Tibetan Spaniel and Bearded Collies. There sadly appears little demand for the breed in South Africa and this has curtailed the breeding programme.

Australia

In Australia the Tibetan Spaniels come under the Non-Sporting Group which is slightly different from the English Utility Group with twenty-seven breeds. Classes are regulated to only Baby Puppy, Minor Puppy, Junior, Intermediate, Novice, Graduate, Limit, State Bred, Australian Bred and Open. Championship points can be awarded to dogs and bitches of six months and older. The Australian Challenge Certificates carry points allocated on a basic five points, plus one point for each exhibit of the same sex and breed being exhibited in all the above mentioned classes. Maximum number of points for a CC are twenty-five. A dog winning a minimum of one hundred points, consisting of at least four CCs won under four different judges, is eligible for the title of Champion. The owner has to apply and pay a fee.

Australia is another vast country, and each State has a different climate. It was apparent to the Author that judges still do not take the breed very seriously, and one can only hope that the desire to learn more about the breed points will encourage a higher standard of judging. It is fairly obvious that each breeder has to be fairly self-sufficient in blood-lines to avoid the pitfalls of inbreeding.

Toy group winning has not yet been achieved by a Tibetan Spaniel in Australia, though in other Asian breeds, notably the Lhasa Apso, there are exhibits winning Best in Show all breeds at Championship shows with an overall entry of two thousand dogs. Some Metropolitan shows are now having the foresight to separate the Asian Breeds under a Specialist judge from the Non-Sporting Group. There is no such thing as a 'Utility' Group in Australia.

Mrs Myra Leach of the Leagay prefix of Little Beach, New South Wales, brought in the first bitch in 1974. Skelbeck Cherry Bud which became an Australian Champion on October 13th, 1974, was sired by Daleviz High Hat out of Mingshang Tresa of Skelbeck. The second Tibetan Spaniel to be imported by Mrs Leach was Braeduke Numa, which won his Australian Champion title on November 30th, 1974. Numa is the litter-brother of English Ch Braeduke Nimmi, International and Nordic Ch Braeduke Nalina in Sweden and Finnish Ch Braeduke Narpo, sired by Ch Ram-Chandra of Amcross out of Ch Braeduke Whitewisp Hara Nor. Mrs Leach's first litter from these two was born on June 5th, 1975, and from this came two Champions, Mrs Olive Forbes' Ch Leagay Am-Mani and his litter-sister retained by Mrs Leach, Ch Leagay Am-Rita. From a second repeat mating came Mrs Forbes' Ch Leagay Bhabu and his CC winning litter-sister Bi-Di.

Mrs Leach then imported a black-and-tan male, Braeduke Lhak-Pa-Chedi which became a champion on December 3rd, 1977; through his sire Ch Braeduke Am-Ra he carries the Anglo-Chinese imported blood-line, his dam was Ch Braeduke Lhalu. Another import was Braeduke Sa-Di, a daughter of Braeduke Dung-Ka out of Braeduke Sipu and, through her dam, a granddaughter of Braeduke Sivas Supi Yaw Lat, won her title of champion posthumously in 1979. Unfortunately she lost her first litter in quarantine and only one survived in her second litter. Mrs Leach lost Cherry Bud in 1976 and Sa-Di in 1979.

Mrs Leach's last import was New Zealand Ch Braeduke Re-Gi-Na, sent originally to Mrs Joan Young in New Zealand, resold by Mr Young after his wife's death to Mrs Leach in Australia. This red-and-white particolour daughter of Braeduke Dung-Ka out of Ch Braeduke Re-Ba has had her Australian show career curtailed by a leg injury. In 1979 Re-Gi-Na produced her first litter sired by Ch Braeduke Lhak-Pa-Chedi. In 1980 New Zealand Ch Braeduke Re-Gi-Na won her Australian title and is the only Tibetan Spaniel so far to have become a Champion in both these countries.

Mrs Olive Forbes of Western Australia only has males, so she is not a breeder of Tibetan Spaniels, but she does fearlessly exhibit over very long distances.

Mrs Margaret Dogger and her daughter Lydia, of the Melm prefix, who live outside Sydney in New South Wales are now regular exhibitors and bred their first litter of Tibetan Spaniels in 1979, though they are established breeders and exhibitors in other breeds. Mrs and Miss Dogger have started with Leagay stock and hope to import some fresh blood-lines from England and New Zealand in the future.

Mr and Mrs Ken Talbot, of Pooraka in South Australia, already established breeders and exhibitors of Shetland Sheepdogs, imported their first pair of Tibetan Spaniels from England in early 1980. The dog puppy Braeduke O-Panka, is the son of Rutherglen Lho-Ra-Ni out of Ch Kensing O-So Special. The bitch puppy which accompanied him is Braeduke Rje-Ma, a daughter of Braeduke Lu-Ting out of Braeduke Rje-La, a granddaughter of Ch Huntglen Braeduke Ta-Ra-Ni. On June 29th, 1981, O-Panka became an Australian Champion and later on in that year he sired his first litter to Rje-Ma, containing some particolour puppies.

Mr and Mrs Talbot also own Leagay Khen Chung, another male, and plan to import a dog puppy Braeduke Solu Khumbu in early 1982, which is a son of Kensing Ferdi out of Ch Su-Li of Braeduke. They also purchased in late 1981 from Mrs Cassells, New Zealand Ch Kye-Mo, a particolour bitch who is now well on the way to her Australian title.

In the State of Queensland, Mrs D. Clatworthy imported her first Tibetan Spaniels in 1974 and can claim to have bred the first Australian-born litter and the first living particolour puppy born in Australia. Her original male was Mingshang Bino, a son of Ch Bu-Po of Amcross out of Ch Mingshang Zena. The two bitches which accompanied him were Jayne of Mingshang, a daughter of Mingshang Jason out of Carrow's Ampara, and Witneylea Zil-Pa, a daughter of Kensing Ano-rak of Amcross out of Ramblersholt Zara. Zil-Pa is the dam of Finnish Ch Witneylea Zachary.

The first litter to be born with Mrs Clatworthy's Koorabar prefix was sired by Bino out of Zil-Pa and was born on April 15th, 1975. Jayne's first litter to Bino was born a few days later, on April 17th, and from this came two Champions, both bitches, Koorabar Tashi-Nor which won her title in August 1976, and Koorabar Kar-Tse which was exported as a puppy to Mrs Jane Everson of New Zealand; another CC winner from this litter died before she could complete her title. In early 1980 Mrs Clatworthy imported from England Kingsbear Nam Khyi, a son of Wildhern Warrior and Lu-Lu of Kensing, bred by Mrs Mallinson, which is now an Australian Champion.

Mrs Leach was already an established breeder of Cavalier King Charles Spaniels and Mrs Clatworthy of Basenjis.

Mrs J. Stone, of Charters Towers, Queensland, imported in early 1980 a gold dog, Twinley Ra-Khee, sired by Ch Kensing Ra out of Nimana Khara of Twinley. In New South Wales, newcomers to the breed are Mr and Mrs Hammond, who have purchased their first two bitches from Mrs Mahony's Tygil kennels.

Mrs J. L. Mahony of Earlswood, New South Wales, has the Tygil kennels which started in 1974 with a Leagay Cavalier King Charles Spaniel bitch. In June 1978, Mrs Mahony purchased, from Mrs Clatworthy, Koorabar Ming Ma who has won Challenge Certificates.

Mrs Mahony has now bred four Champions out of her first litter of five Tibetan Spaniel puppies.

Mrs J. Gardiner of Cross Roads, New South Wales, has one Tibetan Spaniel male with her established Jogar Lhasa Apsos, Koorabar Druka won his Australian Champion title in early 1981.

Mrs Deidre Hunt, of Knoxfield, Victoria, is a Cavalier breeder and exhibitor, but her Tibetan Spaniel male, Leagay Gadon, gained his Australian Champion title in 1980; he is a son of Ch Braeduke Numa out of Leagay Chimurti, a daughter of Australian Ch Braeduke Lhakpa Chedi. Mrs Hunt also owns a Champion bitch Leagay Jahree.

Claire and Jenny Sims of Maroubra own the male Leagay Ghana Khri, a son of Ch Braeduke Numa and of Leagay Chumurti, who joined in 1981 with two of his litter brothers as an Australian Champion. They have now purchased two bitches also from Mrs M. Leach, sired by Ch Leagay Jhanki out of Ch Leagay Chiala.

In spite of driving long distances to exhibit at shows, there are in Sydney, for instance, at least two all breed Championship shows each weekend with entries of approximately two thousand dogs. In February 1979, for example, there were thirty-five Championship shows listed for New South Wales alone; of these twenty-nine were all breed shows, and the remainder were breed shows. This is actually the hottest month of the year in Australia with temperatures in New South Wales of around 38°–40° centigrade!

A fairly recent newcomer to the Australian Tibetan Spaniel scene in the South is Mrs Raelene Evans with a dog Wintersweet Wisp, a bitch Australian Ch Wintersweet Magnolia from Mrs Alexander of the North Island in New Zealand, and also from Queensland, Australia, another bitch Rintelma Po-Ni from Mrs Roy-Smith.

New Zealand

There is no points system in New Zealand, to become a champion a dog must win eight Challenge Certificates.

The first Tibetan Spaniel in New Zealand was Rosaree Cho-Ko-Gye, a son of Ch Kye Ho Za-Khyi who emigrated with his owner, Mrs W. Alexander's daughter and her husband, Mr Richard Williams, in 1972. Mr Williams has a son of Cho-Ko-Gye, Wintersweet Zac, which is doing very well in Obedience competitions. The New Zealand Obedience folk have christened him the 'Mouse Hound' and he has probably got more publicity for the breed than the show Tibetan Spaniels.

Mrs Alexander's prefix is Wintersweet which was well-known in England, and she also has Samoyeds. Mrs Alexander's two bitches are New Zealand Ch Wintersweet Zilla and Mintrode Lotus, a daughter of Kensing Ano-Rak of Amcross out of Mingshang Zsi-Zsi. There are also two English bred males here; New Zealand Ch Mobella Alexander, a black-and-tan son of Wildhern Sun King out of Wintersweet Ku-Cho; the other is New Zealand Ch Mobella Wizard, a son of Hatchibompato of Mobella out of Mobella Alexia.

Mrs Jane Everson, who now lives in California, U.S.A., imported a bitch, Koorabar Kat-Tse, from Mrs Clatworthy in Australia and later an English-born male, Braeduke O-Pam-Ra, a son of Ch Braeduke Am-Ra and Woldfoot Tsepame Opame. Both became New Zealand Champions. When Mrs Everson with her husband and family went to live in America, New Zealand Ch Koorabar Ka-Tse took up residence with Mr and Mrs Owen Roberts, also English emigrants, who are Pekingese breeders. Mr and Mrs Roberts have also bred Shetland Sheepdogs and Golden Retrievers; of the latter, the most notable was Ch Bart of Tygwyn. Trewilleath is their prefix for Tibetan Spaniels.

Among other Tibetan Spaniel owners, breeders and exhibitors in New Zealand is Mrs D. Ettrick, of the Chancery prefix, who has Ch Wintersweet Yin as well as Cavalier King Charles Spaniels. There is also Mrs K. Lockwood of Old Quarry prefix-affix, who has one Tibetan Spaniel, Sherpa Ranee, along with her Pekingese. Mr and Mrs J. Knipe also have winning Tibetan Spaniels based on the Everson blood-lines.

Mrs J. Cassells of Christchurch, who used to breed and exhibit Labrador Retrievers, purchased her first Tibetan Spaniel, a male, in 1978 from Mrs Leach in Australia. This was Leagay Ed Dzong, a son of Ch Braeduke Lhak-Pa-Chedi out of Leagay Bi-Di. He won his title in 1979. In that same year Mrs Cassells imported from England a particolour bitch, Braeduke Mingmo, bringing the new American line to New Zealand through her dam Kalimpong Ming-Dordja of Braeduke. Mingmo's sire, Braeduke Lu-Ting (a CC winner) also descends from the Indian-born Dikki Dolma. Mrs Cassells' Mingmo is now a New Zealand Champion, and had her first litter at the end of 1980.

Tragically, early in 1981, Mrs Cassells lost all but two of the litter from Parvo Virus at just under twelve weeks of age, with the only survivors being a particolour bitch, still with her breeder, and a previously sold male now on the North Island. This was the first particolour litter (with one sable bitch puppy) to be born in New Zealand.

From the two survivors came New Zealand Ch Tensing Kye-Mo who is now owned by Mr and Mrs K. Talbot in South Australia and is well on the way to winning her dual title. From a repeat mating Mrs Cassells has exported three puppies to Australia to Mrs and Miss Dogger, to Mrs M. Leach and to Mr and Mrs Talbot.

Mrs Sadie Reid of Rangiora purchased a dog puppy from Mrs Everson of Auckland in March 1978, sired by Ch Braeduke O-Pam-Ra out of Ch Koorabar Kar-Tse, he too won his Champion title to become Ch Pam-Jan of Tnan-Pso. Also in the South Island of New Zealand is Mrs Myra Dawson of Invercargill who imported Leagay Jindra from Mrs M. Leach of Australia. This bitch is a daughter of two English imports, Ch Braeduke Lhakpa Chedi out of Australia and New Zealand Ch Braeduke Regina. She too is now a Champion and her owner hopes to breed her first litter in 1982.

The breed appears slowly to be gaining ground and recognition in New Zealand, where the climate is not as hot as in Australia. In 1980 and 1981 there was a demand for New Zealand stock in Australia, which gave healthy encouragement. Greater interest is also now being taken in the breed by judges, prospective exhibitors and by breeders.

The biggest hazards for the exhibitor in Australia appear to be skin troubles, coat problems and the many varieties of worms.

At the present time, there does not appear to be any great demand for the breed as pets, nor has one of this breed yet hit the headlines at a general Championship show in Australia, but the Author feels that perhaps, with more people and a bigger pool of blood-lines, the Tibetan Spaniel could well go from strength to strength in the 1980s.

12 Tibetan Spaniel Imports and Discoveries

The Lady Freda Valentine, elder daughter of the Earl of Lanesborough and her sister, the Lady Vivian Younger, both had a tremendous interest in all Tibetan breeds, Lady Freda having Lhasa Apsos and Lady Vivian Tibetan Mastiffs. Lady Freda was, for many years, the President of the Tibetan Spaniel Association which profited from her immense knowledge and the Author feels tremendously honoured that she has written the Foreword to this book.

Historically, at the very first Tibetan Spaniel Association's Open show, Lady Freda issued a timely warning in her speech delivered before presenting the club trophies to the winners. She said that, out of the famous names and prefixes connected with Tibetan Spaniels, such as the Hon. Mrs McLaren Morrison who had started with what she called Afghan Spaniels, Mrs A. R. Greig of the Ladkok prefix who had revived the breed with imports in the 1920s and '30s, with the Rev. and Mrs Stutely Abbott of the Fanthorpe prefix and Mrs Brownlees, hers was now the only name still linked with the breed and she would like to stress how hard these people had worked to publicise and establish the breed.

The breed problems of the early 1950s were resolved by Lady Wakefield, assisted by Miss Braye and Miss Elam, with Miss J. Hervey-Cecil's strains, along with the dogs owned and bred by Colonel Hawkins. Their dogs and their blood-lines have gone to build up the excellent dogs which the modern breeders are now offering the world. In her speech, Lady Freda also mentioned that we should keep our ears and eyes open for any imported dogs, so that what has been so splendidly produced would not wilt from too much inbreeding, and that the main characteristics of this breed should be retained and bred for; the mane, shawl, the hare feet and last but not least, the inimical scowl, all of which are so typical of a good Tibetan Spaniel.

In 1966, the Author commenced searching for fresh blood-lines, and was hopeful when Mr and Mrs Hanstock's Bhalu, a male with a rich chestnut coat with sable shadings and white markings, came out of Mr Steele Bodger's quarantine kennels in late 1967. He was bred by Mr and Mrs Pratten, who lived in Kalimpong in West Bengal where they had a school for Tibetan orphans. He was approved by Mr A. O.

Grindey and registered at the English Kennel Club as Pride of Kalimpong and exhibited under Mr Fred Cross at the first Club show in 1967, winning a V.H.C. All hopes of breeding from him had to be abandoned. He resented the intrusion of a young female into his household, doubtless defending Mrs Hanstock's new baby. At this same show Sir Lionel Lamb brought along his eleven-year-old black-and-tan bitch which had been brought back from Tibet by his son; she was small, dainty and very typical, but unfortunately she was never bred from.

At one of the first shows held by the South Western Tibetan Spaniel Club, Mr and Mrs Southern brought along their Ci-Ci, purchased from a Chinese breeder in Hong Kong. She was thirteen years old when seen by the Author, a very pretty, dainty red-and-white parti-colour, nicely marked and with a good length of leg, but still well-balanced; she also had the 'old-fashioned' slight lift to her ears. Exhibited in Hong Kong, when her owners lived there, she had been given a prize by Mr Stanley Dangerfield. Once again, Ci-Ci was never bred from.

In West Germany Mrs Asta Blumel-Petersen owned two bitches, which had been brought home by her husband who was a Chief Engineer on a big motor vessel. Susi came from Mozambique and the other bitch from Ecuador in South America. From photographs, both are typical and very similar in head to Lady Wakefield's Dolma. I find this most interesting in view of the picture, which appeared in the *Sunday Times* (December 18th, 1960), of the Lion of Judah – Emperor Haile Selassie of Ethiopia – photographed in Brazil with what could only be a particolour Tibetan Spaniel. The Emperor was well-known as an animal-lover.

Miss Ann Rohrer, while working in Nepal for U.S. Aid, found a particolour male, Shimbu, which is now owned by her sister, Mrs Betsy Boettiger in California; he was used once at stud but the breeder of the litter and owner of the bitch were unable to be traced.

In 1967 the Author received from Mrs Furst in Assam a set of interesting photographs of Tibetan Spaniels owned and bred by H.H. the Maharani of Charkhari of Upper Shillong, India, who was prepared to sell her a male, but not a bitch, which is what she wanted. It was through contact with Nawab Nazeer Yar Jung that the Author received a copy of the *Indian Kennel Gazette* (May 1967), showing the registration of two Tibetan Spaniels: a dog named Jigme Khampa, born 26.2.66, which was dark red, and a bitch named Yang Chelna with no date of birth, coloured red-gold. The owner was Mrs D. N. K. Banerjee of Poona, but it took a long time to make contact with Mrs

Banerjee and, eventually, a pair of litter-sisters from these parents arrived in England on February 24th, 1968. Mrs G. Howard Joyce purchased and owned Dikki Dolma, Miss H. F. J. Forbes and the Author jointly own Yasodhara.

Mrs Maryse Choisy in France purchased a black-and-tan male Braeduke Chentze of Szufung, as a future mate for her black-and-white bitch, Shakti, which had been given to her when she visited H.H. The Dalai Lama in India. Shakti was very devoted to her owner and even accompanied her to church; she was exhibited in Deauville in 1967 where she won the CACIB. She had no intention of permitting Chentze to take any liberties so, sadly, no family resulted.

Through an illustrated advertisement showing Ch Braeduke Tam Cho, which appeared in *Country Life*, Crufts edition, the Author received a letter from Mrs John Hacker who at the time lived in Nassau. The Author corresponded with Mrs Hacker for a number of years and learned about her gold-and-white particolour bitch named Honeybun which was raised by a wealthy Chinese family who lived in Shatin, in the New Territories, and which was given to Mrs Hacker as she was leaving Hong Kong. The Author later sent her a sable male, which sadly died soon after arrival as a result of an accident, to be replaced by a black-and-tan dog, Braeduke Rimche Surkhang, the litter-brother of Ch Clawson Braeduke Rampa. Honeybun's first litter to Rimche was born August 11th, 1970; from this litter came Ama Kuluh, who arrived in England on December 11th, 1970, to spend her six-month quarantine period in Lt.-Col. R. H. Cuming's Hill Farm Kennels. Ama was registered, having been approved by Mr L. C. James, just before the Kennel Club changed their registration requirements for dogs of part unknown, or unknown ancestry, or from unregistered parents. She won her first CC under Miss P. M. Mayhew in 1972, maternal duties for her first litter prevented her winning her second and third Challenge Certificates until 1974, when she became Champion Braeduke Ama Kuluh.

The Author was invited to take Ama Kuluh to the Friends Meeting House, Euston Road, London, where, on October 25th, 1973, His Holiness the Fourteenth Dalai Lama spoke to her and patted her on the head, after asking the Author in perfect English if she would bite him. From Ama Kuluh and her litter-brother owned by Mr and Mrs Herjeskog in Sweden, have descended many Champions all around the world; Ama Kuluh's descendants include her son International English and Irish Ch Braeduke Am-Ra and her daughter Ch Braeduke Ama Dablam.

Miss Marguerite Cotsworth Perkins, now Mrs P. Sorum, met Tashi

Dorji on a cold, damp morning in Darjeeling, Northern India, at the Tibetan Refugee Self Help Centre; he was residing in a makeshift chicken wire kennel which was attached to the Tibetan refugee village. A very old, bearded Tibetan man, the caretaker of the 'kennel' was cutting clumps of fur from the belly of an Apso. The kennel was perched on a ledge, overlooking the tea estate and the majestic Himalayas in the background. So, in 1973, this little black-and-white particolour dog puppy attached himself to Miss Perkins, who was on her way to Sikkim for an audience with the King and Queen. Having had his first ever bath, and then been violently car-sick, he eventually arrived with Miss Perkins at Kalimpong, where they were greeted, at the Himalaya View Hotel, by Mrs Perry, the proprietress, who was half Scottish and half Tibetan, her father having been the British Emissary to Tibet. Mrs Perry kept dogs, Apsos and Bhutanese Spaniels, and took an immediate interest in Tashi; as he was full of fleas, she even made him a flea collar from the ends of three old ones. Miss Perkins says that she does not know when she has been more moved, as this gift of a flea collar was a real sacrifice and, ever since, a parcel of them has been annually despatched at Christmas time from St Louis, Missouri, America, to Mrs Perry.

Tashi and Marguerite journeyed home through Sikkim and the lowlands of India. En route Tashi stayed in the Imperial Hotel in Vienna, the darling of the room boy and the Hotel staff, his dinner was delivered on a silver salver at the ring of a bell – just five days after being taken from a Tibetan village! Just over a year later, Mr and Mrs Marlin Perkins purchased from the Author Braeduke Gon-Zu, taking her home as a future bride for Tashi. Two litters were produced and, included in the second was the Author's Kalimpong Ming Dordja of Braeduke. Ming arrived in England on March 12th, 1977, going into quarantine at Hill Farm Kennels. With support from the Tibetan Spaniel Association and the Tibetan Terrier Association, the Author had a long fight with the English Kennel Club to obtain Ming's official Kennel Club Registration. As early as January 1973 she had written to the English Kennel Club about the possibility of importing another Tibetan Spaniel. So, Miss Elam's prophecy, made in *Dog World* (September 6th, 1973), almost, but thankfully did not, come true. She had written "It would be serious for us if the proposal not to register dogs of unknown pedigrees ever became a Kennel Club rule . . . The proposal was made, I gather, but it seems to have been withdrawn, but one never knows if it will be suggested again."

Miss F. Hamilton the Editor of *Dog World* was unstinting in her publicity; Mr Richard Marples and Mr Rasbridge wrote offering some excellent suggestions which the Author implemented. Eventually Lt.-Cdr. J. S. Williams, then Secretary of The Kennel Club, wrote on June 23rd, 1977, to say that it had been resolved that a decision should be deferred until the bitch (Ming) had been inspected by two independent Championship show judges of the breed and a report received from them.

Major L. H. H. Glover, who was at that time the Chairman of the Stud Book and Registrations Sub-Committee of the Kennel Club, and Miss M. C. Hourihane of the Famous Amcross Tibetan Spaniels, visited Ming in quarantine and reported back favourably. Just eighteen days after leaving quarantine Ming was exhibited at the Richmond Championship show, under Mrs Y. Bentinck, where she won a Reserve Challenge Certificate and qualified for an English Kennel Club Stud Book entry. It was a wonderful climax which justified the Author's faith and persistence. From Ming's first litter, born on January 21st, 1979, has come a New Zealand Champion, a Champion daughter in Denmark, and the only male, which is in Finland, is now a Champion.

Mr and Mrs Thomas J. Whiting in Virginia, U.S.A., were among the first Americans to acquire a Tibetan Spaniel in Asia when they purchased Bimbo and his litter-sister, Dido, born on April 18th, 1967. Their sire, Johnie, and dam, Brownie, were registered by the Kennel Club of India, as were Bimbo and Dido. Bimbo was placed third at the Tibetan Dogs Competition held annually by the Tibetan Embassy in New Delhi. Two litters resulted from Bimbo and Didi, but from the second litter, born on March 25th, 1974, came their son Bim's Shri Brandywine, although being an inbred offspring, he is a fine example of the strength and soundness of his hereditary make-up. Later he was mated to an American-bred bitch of Braeduke and Amcross bloodlines, and a bitch was retained by the Whitings. She was subsequently mated in 1979 to T.S.C.A Ch Braeduke Dung-Ka, an English import; puppies from this mating have done extremely well in Miscellaneous classes in America.

Early in 1979, Mrs Gidman of the English Clawson prefix-affix imported a dog and bitch from Finland from the late Dr B. Holcombe's Russian-bred male Rin Boj, which was brought back from Russia with a bitch, in payment for a debt. These two were known in Russia as Chinese Polonko, or 'Dwarf Chinese Dogs'. The grandsire of the male had won three gold medals at Russian shows making him their equivalent of a Champion. There are more of these dogs in Russia, but they are only owned by the diplomats and other important people such as ballerinas, as they are still considered 'special'. In Russia, Dr Holcombe said that they were also called 'Pekin Spaniels' as they originally came from Peking. This, in relation to the reference in the chapter on Chinese dogs gives food for thought. Mrs Gidman's bitch, named Clawson Raibrai Yin, produced her first litter in January 1981, sired by Ch Clawson Braeduke Rampa.

The outstanding unsolved mystery is the race of dogs so closely resembling the Tibetan Spaniel, which appears to abound on Teneriffe in the Canary Islands.

Some of us have caught a brief glimpse of a Tibetan Spaniel in Television documentary programmes on Asia or Tibet; in a 1970 ATV programme on Cambodia, the Prince was shown with his constant companion, a cream-and-white particolour Tibetan Spaniel. Another dog was featured in the Asia Magazine of August 11th, 1968, His Majesty the King of Bhutan, Jigme Dorji Wangchuk, was seen with Khomto (said to mean 'my little baby') also a particolour Tibetan Spaniel.

America has probably more fresh and imported blood-lines than any other country, yet sadly, these are not being requested as the American Kennel Club, in its wisdom, still has not granted the Tibetan Spaniels Championship status nor admitted them into the Stud Book. Professor Alvin Novick of Yale University, who breeds and exhibits Shih Tzus, sent his Chinese houseboy on holiday to Hong Kong and asked him to bring home a good specimen Shih Tzu. What was brought home was Lucky, which looked very like a Tibetan Spaniel. Lucky eventually went to Mrs Baurne and Mrs Ekelof in Sweden where he mated an English imported bitch and produced one litter, but none of them have been heard of since; perhaps this is because there was some doubt about Lucky's soundness, although Professor Novick said that he had been involved in a car accident while in America.

Mr S. Dillon Ripley brought a pair of dogs back from Bhutan, a golden-sable bitch and a black-and-white rough coated dog. The bitch was unable to be bred from due to a car accident which broke her pelvis, but she was a very typical Tibetan Spaniel.

Mrs Lily Hosticka, now Ms Tamura, while working with the U.S.A. Peace Corps, found and brought back to America a pair of Tibetan Spaniels, which she purchased from Tibetan families in Kathmandu. Their descendants, Khumbila Jampa and Khumbila Trindzin, have done well at shows and two from these imported blood-lines have won their Obedience Companion Dog titles at A.K.C. shows.

The Bhutanese Dumci looks to be very similar to a Tibetan Spaniel, both in colouring and head type, but it is said to be bigger. Those on the postage stamps do not look in the least bit like the one owned by Mrs M. Furst from Assam, India.

Lastly, mention must be made of Tigger, given to an American diplomat by his breeder, a high-class lady in Kathmandu, Nepal, who only very occasionally bred from her Tibetan Spaniels, giving them to the Royal Family or to important diplomats. The diplomats who had been given her 'nod of approval' would only receive one of her dogs if they would take them out of Nepal, and if they would promise not to breed them to the 'hoi poloi' there in Kathmandu! Tigger was born on August 15th, 1971; his new owner left Kathmandu during the Indian-Pakistan war and Tigger somehow survived the direct trip from Bombay to Boston, U.S.A. via Tel Aviv, Rome and Paris. Living with his owner, for a while first in Boston and then in Dallas, Texas, he spent seven years with the diplomatic family. When the family were posted to Japan, Tigger was sent to old friends of theirs in New Hampshire. Eventually, through ill health, as they could not care for him any longer, they decided to have him put to sleep.

Tigger's story has a happy ending, for Mrs Jay Child (known in America as 'Mrs Tibetan Spaniel') heard of Tigger's plight fourth hand, and immediately contacted his last owners and offered to rescue him. So Tigger then went to live with Jay and Patrick Child and their family, and joined the Amroth Tibetan Spaniels and Smooth Standard Dachshunds on May 3rd, 1979. So far, he has only sired one litter, born in October 1979, but two more are planned; one of his daughters, Chagsum Morgan L'fe of Amroth, jointly owned by Mrs Child and her daughter Victoria in conjunction with Susan Banner, has won at the T.S.C.A.'s speciality show in July 1980. To give him his full official name 'Amroth's Own Tigger', he is gold in colour with lovely dark pigment and should be a valuable asset to the breed in America with his fresh blood-lines. Let us hope that some of them will find their way over to England in the near future.

The Author hopes that more effort will be made to obtain more outcross blood-lines, through stock known to have come directly from Tibet. It may well be found that it is going to be increasingly difficult, or well nigh impossible, to obtain more later on when they may be wanted. Even now, in Tibetan refugee camps in India and Nepal, the Tibetan people do not mate like to like. They are, more often than not, just breeding for the tourist trade, aiming to produce pretty eye-catching puppies. No longer are the Tibetan people in isolated communities where strains and breeds were kept 'pure' from necessity.

13 The Three Tibetan Spaniel English Kennel Club Breed Standards, Illustrations and Character of the Breed

The Original English Kennel Club Standard for the Tibetan Spaniel 1934
Usually found in the Chumbi Valley of Tibet.

In judging these dogs, breed characteristics are of paramount importance.

1. General appearance: a dainty active Toy.
2. Character: gay and assertive but chary of strangers.
3. Size and weight: variable, 5–14 lbs.
4. Colour: golden, fawn, black, black and tan, particolour, cream, white or brown.
5. Body shape: length from point of shoulder to point of buttocks longer than the height at withers. Chest of medium width.
6. Coat: double coated, lies rather flat, a decided mane on neck and shoulders.
7. Head and neck: medium size, skull slightly domed. Neck symmetrical, well covered with hair.
8. Mouth and muzzle: level: otherwise slightly undershot preferable. Strong cushioned muzzle of medium length. Nose black with all colours.
9. Ears: pendant and feathered at base.
10. Eyes: brown of medium size.
11. Legs: fore-legs smooth but feathered at back, appear straight but there is a slight bend in the bone. Hind legs smooth, feathering on buttocks.
12. Feet: smooth, of medium size.
13. Tail and carriage: tail plumed, carried in a gay curl over back, set on high.
14. General remarks: large prominent eyes, domed forehead, accentuated stop and broad flat face are all objectionable.

The 1959 English Kennel Club Breed Standard

CHARACTERISTICS: gay and assertive, highly intelligent, and aloof with strangers.

GENERAL APPEARANCE: should be small, well balanced, active, alert.

HEAD: should be of medium or small size in proportion to the size of body.

SKULL: slightly domed, muzzle fairly short and blunt.

NOSE: black, but brown or liver permissible.

EYES: should be dark brown in colour, bright expressive, set fairly wide apart, not full or prominent.

EARS: pendant, well feathered, they can have a 'slight' lift away from the side of the head.

MOUTH: slightly undershot preferable, teeth should not show when the mouth is closed.

NECK: short, well covered with a mane, is more pronounced in dogs than in bitches.

FOREQUARTERS: the bones of the forelegs are slightly bowed but firm at the shoulder. Well feathered at back.

BODY: longer from the point of the shoulder to the root of the tail, than at the height at the shoulder.

HINDQUARTERS: hindlegs smooth, feathered at back, with heavy feathering on buttocks.

FEET: hare footed, small and neat with feathering between the toes often extending beyond the feet. White markings allowed.

TAIL: set high, richly plumed and carried in a gay curl over the back.

COAT: double coated, silky in texture, lies rather flat with a mane on neck and shoulders.

COLOURS: golden, cream, white, biscuit, fawn, brown, shaded-sable, red-sable, black, particolour or tricolour.

WEIGHT: dogs from 10–16 lbs. Bitches from 9–15 lbs.

HEIGHT: dogs up to 11 inches. Bitches up to 9½ inches.

FAULTS: large full eye. Broad flat face. Very domed head. Accentuated stop. Pointed muzzle.

The 1975 English Kennel Club Breed Standard

CHARACTERISTICS: gay and assertive, highly intelligent, aloof with strangers.

GENERAL APPEARANCE: should be small, active and alert. The outline should give a well-balanced appearance, slightly longer in body than height at withers.

HEAD AND SKULL: small in proportion to body and proudly

carried giving an impression of quality. Masculine in dogs but free from coarseness. Skull slightly domed, moderate width and length. Stop slight, but defined. Medium length of muzzle, blunt with cushioning, free from wrinkle. The chin should show some depth and width. Nose black preferred.

EYES: dark brown in colour, oval in shape, bright and expressive, of medium size set fairly well apart but forward looking, giving an ape-like expression. Eyerims black.

EARS: medium size, pendant, well feathered in the adult and set fairly high. They may have a slight lift from the skull, but should not fly. Large, heavy, low-set ears are not typical.

MOUTH: ideally slightly undershot, the upper incisors fitting neatly inside and touching the lower incisors. Teeth should be evenly placed and the lower jaw wide between the canine tusks. Full dentition desired. A level mouth is permissible provided there is sufficient width and depth of chin to preserve the blunt appearance of Muzzle. Teeth must not show when mouth is closed.

NECK: moderately short, strong and well set on. Covered with a mane or 'shawl' of longer hair, which is more pronounced in dogs than bitches.

FOREQUARTERS: the bones of the forelegs slightly bowed but firm at shoulder. Moderate bone. Shoulder well-placed.

BODY: slightly longer from point of shoulder to root of tail than the height at withers, well-ribbed with good depth, level back.

HINDQUARTERS: well made and strong, hocks well let down and straight when viewed from behind. Stifle well developed, showing moderate angulation.

FEET: harefooted, small and neat with feathering between toes often extending beyond the feet. White markings allowed.

GAIT: quick-moving, straight, free, positive.

TAIL: set high, richly plumed and carried in a gay curl over the back when moving. Should not be penalised for dropping the tail when standing.

COAT: double coat, silky in texture, smooth on face and front of legs, of moderate length on body, but lying rather flat. Ears and back of forelegs nicely feathered, tail and buttocks well-furnished with longer hair. Should not be overcoated and bitches tend to carry less coat and mane than dogs.

COLOUR: all colours and mixture of colours allowed.

WEIGHT AND SIZE: weight 9–15 lbs. being ideal. Height about 10 inches.

FAULTS: large full eyes, broad flat muzzle, very domed or flat wide skull, accentuated stop, pointed weak or wrinkled muzzle, overshot mouth, long plain down face without stop, very bowed or loose front, straight stifle, cow hocks, nervousness, cat feet, coarseness of type, mean expression, liver or putty-coloured pigmentation, light eyes, protruding tongue.

NOTE: male animals should have two apparently normal testicles fully descended into the scrotum.

The Hon. Mrs Bailey wrote in the Dog Fanciers column of *Our Dogs* (1934):

> During the past few years we have got standards for our Tibetan Terriers and Tibetan Spaniels. These standards have not yet been printed, but that is only because the Tibetan ideals were not secured without difficulty, in fact it was only through influential friends she made in her medical work in India, that Dr Greig was able to get these two Standards. Apart from that, we must not forget that both these Tibetan breeds are known in the Indian show rings.

Both the English Tibetan Terrier and Tibetan Spaniel Breed Standards of 1934 were practically identical with those previously adopted by the Indian Kennel Club for these two breeds, in fact they were identical, save that the British versions have been clarified and made more explicit.

Comments on the Breed Standards

Hutchinson's *Dog Encyclopedia* makes its comments on the standard of points in the 1930s from the Indian Kennel Club:

> In appearance they are rather like a Pekingese with straight legs, narrow-pointed muzzles which must not give the dog's face a triangular appearance, and skulls that are not flat. The plume is not so busy as that of the Pekingese, nor is it carried quite so tightly curled. It should, however, be carried over the back. The coat lies flat and the mane is not prominent, though there is a good frill around the throat when the dog is in full coat. Head and muzzle are of natural shape. Eyes full and expressive but not so large as a Peke's. The feet are well padded with hair. Legs short, back of moderate length. The most prized specimens weigh 5–6 lbs., the usual weight being 10–12 lbs., though some have been known to weigh as much as 15 lbs. In colour they may be black, black and tan, biscuit or fawn with dark shadings, sandy red or parti-colour. In fact nearly all recognised colours are seen in the breed. For show purposes the same colours are allowed as in the Pekes – liver or chocolate colour is a disqualification and so is a liver or chocolate nose.

250

The nose must be black in every specimen that hopes to compete in the show ring whatever the colour of its coat . . . the little dogs are reputed to be hardy and to have a high degree of intelligence.

At this time, in India, a club had been formed to look after the interests of the small breeds of Tibet. As the Hon. Secretary of the Kennel Club of India had, at that time, over thirty years experience of judging Tibetan Spaniels, he was asked to give the Club a rough description of the breed to act as a basis for the standard. His reply was quoted verbatim in Hutchinson's *Dog Encyclopedia*, so that breeders in Britain might also have the benefit of his experience. It is also interesting to learn that judges in India, who have specialised in this breed, considered that Doma, belonging to Mrs Greig of Royden, was about the best Tibetan Spaniel ever obtained from Tibet. Then, as up to about ten years ago, the Tibetan Spaniel was very little known outside Tibet; hence the natural mistake most people make when seeing one for the first time and saying, "Surely that is a Pekingese gone wrong"! This is illustrated by the opening sentences of the Indian Kennel Club Secretary's letter. He wrote:

The Standard might be put into a few words, viz: 'A Peke gone wrong', the face is not flat, and the muzzle is as prominent as in any ordinary breed; the skull, instead of being flat is more rounded. The body is long for the dog's height, the coat like a Pekingese, the plume not so full as the Peke but the tail lighter feathered and curled over the back; legs short, but the forelegs quite straight; chest not wide like the Peke, the body much the same from the chest to the loin, which of course is quite different from the Peke.

Our Dogs (April 21st, 1911) under 'Foreign Dog Fancies', states:

An army officer and a well known Tibetan traveller, who is deeply interested in the Tibetan Spaniel and anxious for its progress in the British fancy, kindly sends us the following standard, which is the one in its native land. The diversity of opinion as to what constitutes an ideal Tibetan Spaniel has certainly retarded the Breed's progress as a fancy animal, and this gentleman hopes that with the native standard known this drawback will pass away.

The true Tibetan resembles the Pekingese more than any other breed, but with this difference – that although the noses of the former should not be pointed, they should not be the regular snub of the Pekingese. The Tibetan Spaniel shows none of the instincts of the lapdog, and in fact, has a good deal of the wild animal in it, being very hardy and most independent. It is remarkably intelligent, and has a

251

highly developed sense of smell. In colour, Tibetans vary considerably, from pure black to black and white, and brown. The coat should be long and rather silky, with a distinct ruff, or mane, on the neck, and very long feathering on the hind legs. The ideal tail is thick and bushy, and carried curled over the back. The forelegs should be turned out from the knees down, but should not be bent above the knee. Tibetan Spaniels have a wonderful ability for travelling, considering their size; and our correspondent has one which has no difficulty in keeping pace with a fast pony over rough roads and long journeys. They inherit this characteristic, as the Tibetan Merchants usually take one or two dogs with them on their travels through the snow clad passes of their native land, and the dogs never seem to tire. The breed has been known in Tibet for many hundreds of years, and it is thought so much of there that it is extremely difficult to procure a really good specimen, even at a fancy price.

In the 1970s and early 1980s judges, especially Specialist Breeder-Judges, have commented on the different types and the variation that there is still in the breed. With the advent of the freshly imported blood-lines in the late 1960s and early 1970s into England, as well as in other countries lucky enough to have found or imported genuine Tibetan Spaniels, this should not be too surprising.

Looking at the three English Kennel Club breed standards there are some significant differences between them. The Author questions whether in fact the final one is an improvement on the first!

One would expect dogs to become heavier with better balanced diets, scientific improvements and vitamins. It may well have been a retrograde step to delete the permission of the level bite. Certainly the Author would not go along with allowing a brown or liver nose as in the 1959 standard. Whether the oval eye wanted in the 1975 standard will produce more weeping eyes and possible entropion, remains to be seen.

A great deal of what is written in a breed standard is common sense, intended to assist a breeder to produce a sound, well made dog but it should be stressed that always when judging dogs, breed characteristics are of paramount importance.

The timely words of wisdom of our Patron, the Lady Freda Valentine, should most certainly be kept in mind – the ape-like look (or the marmoset face), the scowl which is not always seen in the late 1970s and early '80s, the splendid shawl (or mane) in the male, with the flowing bib on the chest, the definite hare-shaped foot – the only Tibetan breed to have this, must not be forgotten or bred out.

The Author feels that the late Mr Leo Wilson's show report on his winners at Crufts Dog Show in 1960, where Challenge Certificates were offered for the first time in our breed, is something that every Tibetan Spaniel breeder should ponder upon:

> Tibetan Spaniels were a good muster competing for their first CCs. As a rule I am meticulous in following Breed Standards, but if I had followed the revised (i.e. 1959) Standard, several of the best here would have had to go cardless, as the new Standard makes the level mouth a fault. This I consider a retrograde step. The original 1934 Breed Standard still allowed for a slightly undershot mouth such as is often seen in the bred and I cannot see any advantage in making a level mouth subject to penalty. It is said that this move is made to prevent the breeding of undesirable snub noses. I would respectfully point out that all the snub nosed breeds are undershot and so the undershot mouth accentuates snub noses. Type was reasonably level but there is still a lot of room for judges to differ in their awards. Personally I was glad to find a young dog to win this first CC, but nothing could beat the Veteran bitch for Best of Breed.

For the record, the dog CC winner was Mrs E. Peach's Kye Ho Tumi, and Reserve to him was Lady Wakefield's Senge La. The bitch CC winner and also Best of Breed, was Miss J. Hervey-Cecil's Chuni La, bred by Lady Wakefield, with Miss Braye's and Elam's Rowena of Padua as the Reserve CC winning bitch. At that time Chuni La was ten years old and had whelped five litters, one of them by caesarian.

From old newsletters and Year Books from the Tibetan Spaniel Association, the Author would like to pass on observations made by Miss Hilda Elam of the Padua Tibetan Spaniels which gives us an insight into the Tibetan Spaniel breed and its problems in the 1950s. Miss Elam said that a lot of people do not nowadays realise that the correction of faults in Tibetan Spaniels had to be done slowly, because of the limited stud dog situation. More often than not, it was impossible to get a stud dog of your choice to mate your bitch; bitches then only came into season once a year. Temperaments were good, and often in the show ring many of the exhibits were swapped around with strange handlers, as many of the owners entered a lot of dogs in one class as shows had a very limited classification and mixed sex classes. Miss Elam recalls that these dogs usually showed well for their stranger handlers.

The breed faults at that time, Miss Elam remembers, were liver and badly off-coloured noses, uneven teeth which were often crossed or with gaps of bare gum. There was also a great variation in coats, too bowed front legs, many were far too undershot, others had a level bite with sufficient depth and width of chin, but none with a scissor bite. There was also a great variation in size, both in the overall height and in the length of leg. Some were more 'aloof' than others and these could be difficult to exhibit, as they usually dropped their tails – even when walking in the ring – and this became a fairly common trait.

One of the worst faults at this time was the late closure of the skull in puppies, known as an open fontanelle. In 1971, Miss Elam told the Author that she felt judges were passing mouths which were, in her opinion, far too undershot. In order to define what is too undershot, she suggested that you should not be able to place the tip of your little finger (i.e. fifth finger) between the top and bottom jaws when the mouth was closed (but obviously when the lips were lifted).

Looking at the close breeding done by the early breeders in this country, as illustrated in the pedigrees in the appendix section, we must today be reaping the benefit of the skill and care taken by these breeders, who, like Miss Elam, only kept and bred from their best and soundest stock.

All who own a Tibetan Spaniel know how versatile this breed can be, equally at home within the walls of the smallest and most humble cottage, or in one of the stately homes of England, their popularity extends widely over the social scale. Many are natural clowns with a wicked sense of humour and others will seize any chance to play to the gallery. Yasodhara, born in Poona, was probably the first Tibetan Spaniel to appear on television; on August 28th, 1968, she was invited to appear on the ATV 'Today' programme shortly after leaving quarantine kennels. In 1969, Annabelle of Eulyn, a black-and-tan show-winning daughter of Ch Kye Ho Za-Khyi appeared with the comedian Harry Worth, co-starring with a cross-bred Newfoundland x Pyrenean Mountain Dog. On December 7th, 1970, Ch Braeduke Tam Cho and Ch Braeduke Jhanki of Wimaro appeared with their four puppies, joined by four more sired by Huntglen Rosaree Bhabu out of Mingshang Tansy of Braeduke. Another 1970 TV star was Witneylea Chamba, then owned by Mr John Holmes, who appeared in a series called 'So you think you know how to train a puppy?'. More recently, in 1980, Major and Mrs Tye's Dockenfield Beech showed off in Mrs Barbara Woodhouse's series on Dog Training. Two television stars themselves own Tibetan Spaniels, Mr and Mrs Shaw Taylor have two, and Anthony Booth of 'Till Death do us Part' had another.

It could only have been a Tibetan Spaniel which managed to slip the 'net' and get into Crufts Dog Show in February 1970, without ever having qualified. This same dog, Ogre, owned by Earl Peel, was bred by Mrs G. Bowring, and was the subject of an amusing article written by Mrs Mary Roslin Williams in her Northern Topics column in *Dog World Weekly*, (October 1972).

Describing a shoot on the grouse moors of Bleasdale as "very tough going and can be equated with walking up two thousand stairs", she said Ogre clearly illustrated the hardiness and the good scenting powers of his ancestors dating back to neolithic times, from the Kitchen Midden Dog and its immediate descendant the Small Soft-Coated Drop-Eared Hunting Dog (mentioned in the Evolution chapter), used for hunting small game and eventually being denigrated to a simple mouse catcher!

Ogre skipped lightly up and down over the roughest heather all day. There were several assorted gundogs working alongside Mrs Roslin Williams' own famous Mansergh black Labradors, but Ogre provided the light relief. He was well-named! He was the most interested in all the four-legged females at the shoot, and challenged every leg lift from the other males present; he then went into his master's butt just like a custom bred gundog. He hunted the game with verve and obvious enjoyment, and when he did find a shot grouse he did not bother to retrieve it himself, but sat on it until his minion and master, Lord Peel, came to retrieve it.

Mrs Roslin Williams concluded by saying that, while the Tibetan Spaniel may look like a sleeve and cushion breed, you only have to put them on a grouse moor to know that this is really their true environment.

The Wildhern Tibetan Spaniels are not steady to shot, but their owners Mr and Mrs Micklethwait often take them 'beating' at some of their local shoots, and they have proved themselves to be worthy of the misnomer 'Spaniel'.

Oriental disobedience does not apply to them all; Mrs V. Rickett of the Knockindu German Shepherd Dogs started in 1969 with a bitch, Tad-Bu of Amcross, and now also has her son and grandson. Tad-Bu is Obedience trained and works alongside the German Shepherds which include Obedience Champion Vicki of Knockindu.

Miss Betty Deane owns Sophie of Cleish, a daughter of Redgame Gnome out of Tamas of Cleish, a granddaughter of Ch Kye Ho Za-Khyi. Sophie has passed her elementary Obedience tests and attends a local dog club, competing against the much bigger and more conventional Obedience breeds.

So, the Tibetan Spaniel is a truly versatile breed, but it is indeed what the breeder and then the owner makes of it.

Good overall balance with correct amount of daylight underneath.

A good illustration of a male head, showing required scowl which commences in the stop, between the eyes.

Set 1 Hindquarters

a) Cow Hocked.

b) Weak behind.

c) Correct.

Set 2 Heads.

d) Correctly balanced.

e) Too round in skull and too
   short in muzzle.

f) Incorrect skull shape, too
   long in muzzle, the whole head
   is unbalanced and the muzzle
   lacks the desired cushioning.

257

Set 3 Heads

g) Correctly balanced head and muzzle showing required amount of chin.

h) Too round in skull (apple-headed), wrinkle on muzzle with deep stop, too round in eye, unbalanced and with too much turn up of bottom jaw.

i) Lacking in stop, overshot jaw, mean exression and incorrectly balanced head comparing length of skull and muzzle.

Figures (h) and (i) have bad breed faults.

Set 4 Fronts

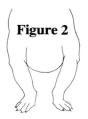

Figure 2

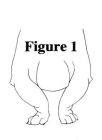

Figure 1

Figure 3

Fig. 2. Weak pasterns. Front feet turn out.

Fig. 1. Knuckling over of pasterns. Too bowed in front. Out at elbow, which can be minimised by a heavy mane, but the pasterns cannot be hidden.
Would expect very poor front action.
Feet incorrect shape.

Fig. 3. Pin toed, would expect poor front action.
Shoulder angulation is not correct.

258

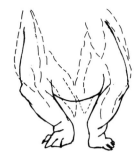

A very bad front which can be partially concealed by a heavy mane and bib, out at elbow, too bowed in front. The hare foot is held in ball position to maintain action, which will probably create poor front movement.

Set 6 Overall Balance

Fig. 1. Too long, straight in stifle, pasterns knuckle over.
Too short on leg for overall correct balance.
Round cat feet which are incorrect.

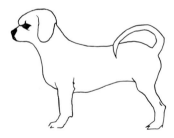

Fig. 2. Too high on leg, unbalanced overall. Weak hind muscles and thin in loin.

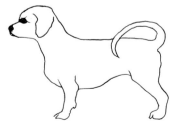

Fig. 3. Correct overall balance.
Good stifle and hind muscle.

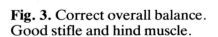

259

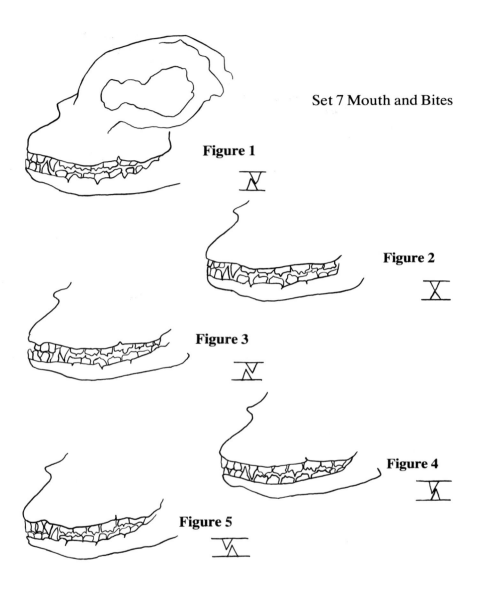

Set 7 Mouth and Bites

Figure 1

Figure 2

Figure 3

Figure 4

Figure 5

Fig. 1. Very good, slightly undershot.
Fig. 2. Level bite, with good depth of chin. Good.
Fig. 3. Very undershot, may show bottom teeth when mouth is closed, a bad fault.
Fig. 4. Scissor bite, insufficient depth of chin, undesirable.
Fig. 5. Overshot, receding chin, a bad fault.

Set 8 Gaits

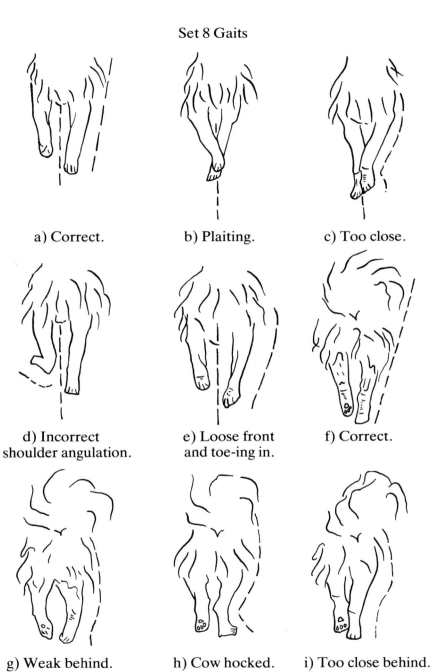

a) Correct.

b) Plaiting.

c) Too close.

d) Incorrect
shoulder angulation.

e) Loose front
and toe-ing in.

f) Correct.

g) Weak behind.

h) Cow hocked.

i) Too close behind.

14 Appendix 1
Key Pedigrees of Early English Tibetan Spaniels

Researching pedigrees with Mrs A. Keen and Miss E. Cherry, we came across various discrepancies, whether through poor handwriting on past pedigrees, or spelling errors or misprints in the *Kennel Gazette*, perhaps even unwittingly perpetuated by breeders over generations – we cannot tell.

It is impossible to write all the alternatives into the manuscript, the alternatives which have been in use generally throughout the breed all over the world, but the spellings in the following pedigrees are those which the three of us believe to be accurate.

Seng Ge La, Senge La or Seng La.
Ran-Ba (not Ranba).
Chumurti La (and not Chimurti La, Chirmurti La, or Churmurti La).
Fanthorpes Nanki Poo, although other Fanthorpe registrations do not have an 's'.
Ama Dablam of Furzyhurst (and not Furzyhurst Ama Dablam).
Furzyhurst Tamar (and not Furzyhurst Tamara).
Glenholme Skuid (and not Glenholm Skyid, or Glenholme Skjid).
Mondo La (and not Monda La).
Mrs Peach's prefix of Kye Ho has also been written as one word.

Key Pedigrees which will assist readers to trace back their own pedigrees to the Greig Imports.
TINA OF LADKOK born 14.11.32.
SKYID born 25.5.43.
RAMBA OF ARMADALE born 20.5.53.
RANEE OF PADUA born 12.8.55.
RAJAH OF GLENHOLME born 24.5.58.
Ch KYE HO ZA KHYI born 1.7.58.
Ch ROSAREE MAI LEI (and also of ROSAREE PERI LUSTRE) born 26.6.59.
Ch SIVAS TEN SING OF MYARLUNE born 1.11.60.
Ch RAMBLERSHOLT RAM-A-DIN born 7.8.62.
BRAEDUKE TAMARA OF SZUFUNG (and also of AMCROSS SETO OF SZUFUNG) born 25.11.63.

BREED Tibetan Spaniel
SEX Female
COLOUR & MARKINGS Red
DATE OF BIRTH 14.11.32
BREEDER Mrs A. R. Greig

THE PEDIGREE OF:
TINA OF LADKOK.
(Also of Pitti Sing of Ladkok.)

PARENTS	GRANDPARENTS	GREAT GRANDPARENTS	GT. GT: GRANDPARENTS
SIRE TUTTOO OF LADKOK (imported)	*Sire* Unknown, Bred by Buddiman Lama	*Sire*	*Sire*
			Dam
		Dam	*Sire*
			Dam
	Dam of Thibet. Unknown	*Sire*	*Sire*
			Dam
		Dam	*Sire*
			Dam
DAM DODO OF LADKOK	*Sire* Tuttoo of Ladkok	*Sire* unknown	*Sire* Bred by Buddiman
		{ Bred by Buddiman / Lama of Thibet	*Dam* Lama of Thibet
		Dam unknown	*Sire*
			Dam
	Dam Dizaree of Ladkok	*Sire* Tuttoo of Ladkok (imported)	*Sire* unknown Bred by Buddiman
			Dam unknown Lama of Thibet
		Dam Ru Ru of Ladkok	*Sire* George of Ladkok (imported)
			Dam Bits of Ladkok (imported)

264

BREED Tibetan Spaniel
SEX Male
COLOUR & MARKINGS —
DATE OF BIRTH 26.5.43
BREEDER Mr J. H. Sabin

PEDIGREE OF: SKYID.

PARENTS	GRAND - PARENTS	G. G. - PARENTS	G. G. G. - PARENTS	G. G. G. G. - PARENTS
SIRE FANTHORPES NANKI POO	**SIRE** Zemu of Lamleh 10/32	**SIRE** Namdgyal (unregistered)	**SIRE** unknown	
			DAM unknown	
		DAM Dullee Doma of Lamleh 10/32 Bred by Tikbir Dhojay Lama	**SIRE** Lhamoo (unregistered)	
			DAM Yongdoo (unregistered)	
	DAM Pitti Sing of Ladkok 10/33	**SIRE** Tuttoo of Ladkok (imported) 2/29	**SIRE** unknown } Bred by Buddiman Lama of Thibet	
			DAM unknown }	
		DAM Dodo of Ladkok	**SIRE** Tuttoo of Ladkok	unknown
				unknown
			DAM Dizaree of Ladkok	Tuttoo of Ladkok
				Ru Ru of Ladkok
DAM KA RA	**SIRE** Rajah 11/34	**SIRE** Ju Ju of Ladkok 3/31	**SIRE** Tuttoo of Ladkok	unknown
				unknown
			DAM Ru Ru of Ladkok	George of Ladkok (imported)
				Bits of Ladkok (imported)
		DAM Buckie of Winchmore 2/34	**SIRE** Ju Ju of Ladkok	Tuttoo of Ladkok
				Ru Ru of Ladkok
			DAM Buddhi of Ladkok (born 11.6.31)	Tuttoo of Ladkok
				Dizaree of Ladkok
	DAM Fanthorpe Golden Ranee 11/38 (Best Bitch W.E.L.K.S. show 1939)	**SIRE** Rajah	**SIRE** Ju Ju of Ladkok	Tuttoo of Ladkok
				Ru Ru of Ladkok
			DAM Buckie of Winchmore	Ju Ju of Ladkok
				Buddhi of Ladkok
		DAM Fanthorpe Rubie 7/37	**SIRE** Zemu of Lamleh	Namdgyal
				Dullee Doma of Lamleh
			DAM Pitti Sing of Ladkok	Tuttoo of Ladkok
				Dodo of Ladkok

PEDIGREE OF:
RAMBA OF ARMADALE

BREED Tibetan Spaniel
SEX Male
COLOUR & MARKINGS Sable
DATE OF BIRTH 20.5.53
BREEDER Mrs O. Sabin

Also the pedigree of Ta-Le (female) born 10.10.50 owned by Lt Colonel and Mrs A. W. Hawkins.

PARENTS	GRANDPARENTS	GREAT GRANDPARENTS	GT. GT. GRANDPARENTS
SIRE SKYID	**Sire** Fanthorpes Nanki Poo, Best of Breed Crufts 1938 (red and white particolour)	**Sire** Zemu of Lamleh	**Sire** Namdgyal
			Dam Dullee Doma of Lamleh
		Dam Pitti Sing of Ladkok	**Sire** Tuttoo of Ladkok
			Dam Dodo of Ladkok
	Dam Ka Ra	**Sire** Rajah (sable)	**Sire** Ju Ju of Ladkok
			Dam Buckie of Winchmore
		Dam Fanthorpe Golden Ranee	**Sire** Rajah
			Dam Fanthorpe Rubie
DAM SUSAN OF DEDDINGTON	**Sire** Garpon (deep, bright red)	**Sire** Tashi	**Sire** unknown, bred in Tashi Gong Monastery in Tibet
			Dam unknown, bred in Tashi Gong Monastery in Tibet
		Dam Mughiwuli	**Sire** Nashpu bred in Takla Kot Monastery in Tibet
			Dam Duma
	Dam Potala (black-and-tan)	**Sire** Tashi	**Sire** unknown
			Dam unknown
		Dam Mughiwuli	**Sire** Nashpu
			Dam Duma

BREED Tibetan Spaniel
SEX Female
COLOUR & MARKINGS Golden Sable
DATE OF BIRTH 12.8.55
BREEDERS The Misses Braye and Elam

THE PEDIGREE OF:
CHAMPION ROWENA OF PADUA
and also of Ranee of Padua (female)

PARENTS	GRAND - PARENTS	G. G. - PARENTS	G. G. G. - PARENTS	G. G. G. G. - PARENTS
SIRE SHIM RDE LA OF PADUA	**SIRE** Seng Ge La (Best of Breed Crufts show 1959)	**SIRE** Lama	**SIRE** Tashi	unknown — bred at the Tashi Gong unknown — Monastery in Tibet
			DAM Mughiwuli	Nashpu / Duma
		DAM Dolma	**SIRE** unknown — bred in the **DAM** unknown — Phari Dzong Monastery in Tibet	
	DAM Shemo La	**SIRE** Lama	**SIRE** Tashi	unknown
			DAM Mughiwuli	unknown
		DAM Dolma	**SIRE** unknown	unknown
			DAM unknown	unknown
DAM FURZYHURST SERMO OF PADUA	**SIRE** Ramba of Armadale	**SIRE** Skyid	**SIRE** Fanthorpes Nanki Poo	Zemu of Ladkok / Pitti Sing of Ladkok
			DAM Ka Ra	Rajah / Fanthorpe Golden Ranee
		DAM Susan of Deddington	**SIRE** Garpon	Tashi / Mughiwuli
			DAM Potala	Tashi / Mughiwuli
	DAM Chuni La (Bitch CC and Best of Breed at Crufts show 1960)	**SIRE** Lama	**SIRE** Tashi	unknown / unknown
			DAM Mughiwuli	Nashpu / Duma
		DAM Dolma	**SIRE** unknown	unknown
			DAM unknown	unknown

BREED Tibetan Spaniel

SEX Male

COLOUR & MARKINGS Red sable

DATE OF BIRTH 24.5.58

BREEDER Mrs L. W. Westbrook

Also the pedigree of Glenholme Skuid (male) born 4.4.59.

PEDIGREE OF:

RAJAH OF GLENHOLME

PARENTS	GRANDPARENTS	GREAT GRANDPARENTS	GT. GT. GRANDPARENTS
SIRE FURZYHURST VIRTUOUS DRAGON	*Sire* Ramba of Armadale	*Sire* Skyid	*Sire* Fanthorpes Nanki Poo
			Dam Ka Ra
		Dam Susan of Deddington	*Sire* Garpon
			Dam Potala
	Dam Ama Dablam of Furzyhurst	*Sire* Kyipup (winner of two CCs)	*Sire* Garpon
			Dam Potala
		Dam Ta Le	*Sire* Skyid
			Dam Susan of Deddington
DAM RANEE OF GLENHOLME	*Sire* Ramba of Armadale	*Sire* Skyid	*Sire* Fanthorpes Nanki Poo
			Dam Ka Ra
		Dam Susan of Deddington	*Sire* Garpon
			Dam Potala
	Dam Toya of Furzyhurst	*Sire* Mondo La	*Sire* Lama
			Dam Dolma
		Dam Chuni La	*Sire* Lama
			Dam Dolma

PEDIGREE OF:

BREED Tibetan Spaniel
SEX Male CHAMPION KYE HO ZA-KHYI
COLOUR & MARKINGS Red with black fringes
DATE OF BIRTH 1.7.58
BREEDER Mrs L. Jones

Also of his litter-sister Ske-Tse and younger full sister Yan.

PARENTS	GRAND - PARENTS	G. G. - PARENTS	G. G. G. - PARENTS	G. G. G. G. - PARENTS
SIRE TOOMAI OF FURZYHURST	**SIRE** Ramba of Armadale	**SIRE** Skyid	**SIRE** Fanthorpes Nanki Poo	Zemu of Lamleh
				Pitti Sing of Ladkok
			DAM Ka Ra	Rajah
				Fanthorpe Golden Ranee
		DAM Susan of Deddington	**SIRE** Garpon	Tashi
				Mughiwuli
			DAM Potala	Tashi
				Mughiwuli
	DAM Chuni La	**SIRE** Lama	**SIRE** Tashi	unknown
				unknown
			DAM Mughiwuli	Nashpu
				Duma
		DAM Dolma	**SIRE** unknown	
			DAM unknown	
DAM KU-SBURPA	**SIRE** Nyi Khyi	**SIRE** Shipki La	**SIRE** Lama	Tashi
				Mughiwuli
			DAM Dolma	unknown
				unknown
		DAM Chumurti La	**SIRE** Lama	Tashi
				Mughiwuli
			DAM Dolma	unknown
				unknown
	DAM Yang Ga-U La	**SIRE** Seng Ge La	**SIRE** Lama	Tashi
				Mughiwuli
			DAM Dolma	unknown
				unknown
		DAM Shemo La	**SIRE** Lama	Tashi
				Mughiwuli
			DAM Dolma	unknown
				unknown

BREED Tibetan Spaniel
SEX Female
COLOUR & MARKINGS Black with tan markings
DATE OF BIRTH 26.6.59
BREEDER Miss Mason

PEDIGREE OF:
CHAMPION ROSAREE MAI LEI
also of Rosaree Peri Lustre (male) brindled fawn with black mask.

PARENTS	GRANDPARENTS	GREAT GRANDPARENTS	GT. GT. GRANDPARENTS
SIRE			
KYE HO TUMI (winner of two CCs)	*Sire* Nak Lok La (black-and-tan)	*Sire* Seng Ge La	*Sire* Lama
			Dam Dolma
		Dam Shemo La	*Sire* Lama
			Dam Dolma
	Dam Ran-Ba	*Sire* Toomai of Furzyhurst	*Sire* Ramba of Armadale
			Dam Chuni La
		Dam Yang Ga-U La	*Sire* Seng Ge La
			Dam Shemo La
DAM			
MILADY ZETTA	*Sire* The Prince of Dzun	*Sire* Garpon	*Sire* Tashi
			Dam Mughiwuli
		Dam Potala	*Sire* Tashi
			Dam Mughiwuli
	Dam Ta-Le	*Sire* Skyid	*Sire* Fanthorpes Nanki Poo
			Dam Ka Ra
		Dam Susan of Deddington	*Sire* Garpon
			Dam Potala

270

BREED Tibetan Spaniel
SEX Male
COLOUR & MARKINGS Sable and white
DATE OF BIRTH 1.11.61
BREEDER Mrs M. H. Bailey

PEDIGREE OF:
CHAMPION SIVAS TEN SING OF MYARLUNE
also of Ming-lin of Myarlune (female).

PARENTS	GRANDPARENTS	GREAT GRANDPARENTS	GT: GT: GRANDPARENTS
Sire SIVAS SHERPA (white with black patches)	*Sire* Pubu Levens	*Sire* Shipki La	*Sire* Lama
			Dam Dolma
		Dam Chumurti La	*Sire* Lama
			Dam Dolma
	Dam Gser-Pho La	*Sire* Nyi Khyi	*Sire* Shipki La
			Dam Chumurti La
		Dam Shemo La	*Sire* Lama
			Dam Dolma
Dam KYUNGU (sable)	*Sire* Seng Ge La	*Sire* Lama	*Sire* Tashi
			Dam Mughiwuli
		Dam Dolma	*Sire* unknown
			Dam unknown
	Dam Pingu La	*Sire* Mondo La	*Sire* Lama
			Dam Dolma
		Dam Dolma	*Sire* unknown
			Dam unknown

BREED Tibetan Spaniel
SEX Male
COLOUR & MARKINGS Fawn and white
DATE OF BIRTH 7.8.62
BREEDER Mrs F. Dudman

CHAMPION RAMBLERSHOLT RAM-A-DIN

PARENTS	GRAND - PARENTS	G. G. - PARENTS	G. G. G. - PARENTS	G. G. G. G. - PARENTS
SIRE RORY OF PADUA (winner of one CC)	**SIRE** Nak Lok La	**SIRE** Seng Ge La	**SIRE** Lama	Tashi
				Mughiwuli
			DAM Dolma	unknown
				unknown
		DAM Shemo La	**SIRE** Lama	Tashi
				Mughiwuli
			DAM Dolma	unknown
				unknown
	DAM Ch Rowena of Padua	**SIRE** Shim Rde La of Padua	**SIRE** Seng Ge La	Lama
				Dolma
			DAM Shemo La	Lama
				Dolma
		DAM Furzyhurst Sermo of Padua	**SIRE** Ramba of Armadale	Skyid
				Susan of Deddington
			DAM Chuni La	Lama
				Dolma
DAM RAMBLERSHOLT LA TRU	**SIRE** Glenholme Skuid (unshown)	**SIRE** Furzyhurst Virtuous Dragon	**SIRE** Ramba of Armadale	Skyid
				Susan of Deddington
			DAM Ama Dablam of Furzyhurst	Kyipup
				Ta-Le
		DAM Ranee of Glenholme	**SIRE** Ramba of Armadale	Skyid
				Susan of Deddington
			DAM Toya of Furzyhurst	Mondo La
				Chuni La
	DAM Furzyhurst Tamar	**SIRE** Furzyhurst Virtuous Dragon	**SIRE** Ramba of Armadale	Skyid
				Susan of Deddington
			DAM Ama Dablam of Furzyhurst	Kyipup
				Ta-Le
		DAM Furzuhurst Tiger Lily	**SIRE** Ramba of Armadale	Skyid
				Susan of Deddington
			DAM Ama Dablam of Furzyhurst	Kyipup
				Ta-Le

BREED Tibetan Spaniel

SEX Female(s)

COLOUR & MARKINGS Red sable

DATE OF BIRTH 19.10.62 (Tamara) and 25.11.63 (Seto)

BREEDER Mrs D. M. Battson

THE PEDIGREE OF:

BRAEDUKE TAMARA OF SZUFUNG and of

AMCROSS SETO OF SZUFUNG

This is also the pedigree of:
Ch Peterstown Drom of Szufung born 22.5.63.
Ch Mingshang Yang Zom of Szufung born 7.5.65.
Yangpel of Szufung born 23.11.63.

PARENTS	GRAND - PARENTS	G. G. - PARENTS	G. G. G. - PARENTS	G. G. G. G. - PARENTS
SIRE CHAMPION TOMU OF SZUFUNG	SIRE Champion Kye Ho Za-Khyi	SIRE Toomai of Furzyhurst	SIRE Ramba of Armadale	Skyid
				Susan of Deddington
			DAM Chuni La	Lama
				Dolma
		DAM Ku Sburpa	SIRE Nyi Khyi	Shipki La
				Chumurti La
			DAM Yang Ga-U La	Seng Ge La
				Shemo La
	DAM Szufung Traza Truly Fair	SIRE Rajah of Glenholme	SIRE Furzyhurst Virtuous Dragon	Ramba of Armadale
				Ama Dablam of Furzyhurst
			DAM Ranee of Glenholme	Ramba of Armadale
				Toya of Furzyhurst
		DAM Traza Truly Gold	SIRE Seng Ge La	Lama
				Dolma
			DAM Rosella of Padua	Shim Rde La of Padua
				Furzyhurst Pyari Larki of Padua
DAM SZUFUNG LOTUS OF FURZYHURST	SIRE Furzyhurst Virtuous Dragon	SIRE Ramba of Armadale	SIRE Skyid	Fanthorpes Nanki Poo
				Ka Ra
			DAM Susan of Deddington	Garpon
				Potala
		DAM Ama Dablam of Furzyhurst	SIRE Kyipup	Garpon
				Potala
			DAM Ta-Le	Skyid
				Susan of Deddington
	DAM Furzyhurst Tiger Lily	SIRE Ramba of Armadale	SIRE Skyid	Fanthorpes Nanki Poo
				Ka Ra
			DAM Susan of Deddington	Garpon
				Potala
		DAM Ama Dablam of Furzyhurst	SIRE Kyipup	Garpon
				Potala
			DAM Ta-Le	Skyid
				Susan of Deddington

273

BREED Tibetan Spaniel
SEX Male
COLOUR & MARKINGS Red sable
DATE OF BIRTH 16.11.66
BREEDERS Mrs D. Jenkins and
                    Miss M. C. Hourihane

PEDIGREE OF:

CHAMPION RIMPOCHE OF AMCROSS

PARENTS	GRAND - PARENTS	G. G. - PARENTS	G. G. G. - PARENTS	G. G. G. G. - PARENTS
SIRE ENGLISH Champion YAKROSE CHIALA OF AMCROSS (red) (exported U.S.A.)	**SIRE** Yangpel of Szufung (red)	**SIRE** Ch Tomu of Szufung (red, black fringes)	**SIRE** Ch Kye Ho Za-Khyi (red sable, black fringes)	Toomai of Furzyhurst
				Ku Sburpa
			DAM Szufung Traza Truly Fair (red)	Rajah of Glenholme
				Traza Truly Gold
		DAM Szufung Lotus of Furzyhurst (golden red)	**SIRE** Furzyhurst Virtuous Dragon (brown)	Ramba of Armadale
				Ama Dablam of Furzyhurst
			DAM Furzyhurst Tiger Lily (sable)	Ramba of Armadale
				Ama Dablam of Furzyhurst
	DAM Traza Truly's Tribute (fawn)	**SIRE** Rajah of Glenholme (red sable)	**SIRE** Furzyhurst Virtuous Dragon	Ramba of Armadale
				Ama Dablam of Furzyhurst
			DAM Ranee of Glenholme (fawn)	Ramba of Armadale
				Toya of Furzyhurst
		DAM Traza Truly Gold (golden sable)	**SIRE** Seng Ge La (fawn)	Lama
				Dolma
			DAM Rosella of Padua (sable)	Shim Rde La of Padua
				Furzyhurst Pyari Larki of Padua
DAM Nyi Shu of Rowcourt (fawn)	**SIRE** Chimpet of Rowcourt (red)	**SIRE** Toomai of Furzyhurst (red sable)	**SIRE** Ramba of Armadale (sable)	Skyid
				Susan of Deddington
			DAM Chuni La (red)	Lama
				Dolma
		DAM Traza True Gold (golden sable)	**SIRE** Rajah of Glenhome	Furzyhurst Virtuous Dragon
				Ranee of Glenholme
			DAM Traza Truly Gold	Seng Ge La
				Rosella of Padua
	DAM Kora (fawn)	**SIRE** Kye Ho S'Go-Kyi (fawn)	**SIRE** Nak Lok La (black and tan)	Seng Ge La
				Shemo La
			DAM Ran-Ba (fawn, black mask)	Toomai of Furzyhurst
				Yang Ga-U La
		DAM Ske-Tse (black-and-tan)	**SIRE** Toomai of Furzyhurst	Ramba of Armadale
				Chuni La
			DAM Ku Sburpa	Nyi Khyi
				Yang Ga-U La

Bibliography

Anon. (1911), 'Foreign Dog Fancies', *Our Dogs*, April 21st, 1911.

Anon. (1925), 'Two valuable dogs from Tibet', 'Chat of the Week', *Dog World*, Vol. 39, No. 1211, April 23rd, 1925.

Anon. (1934), 'The Tibetan Breeds Standards', *Our Dogs*, November 9th, 1934.

Bailey, The Hon. Mrs F. M., (1934), *Kennel Gazette*, Vol. 44, No. 649, April 1934.

——, (1934), *Kennel Gazette*, Vol. 55, No. 650, May 1934.

——, (1934), 'Notes on Tibetan Dogs', *Kennel Gazette*, Vol. 55, No. 653, August 1934.

Bell, Sir Charles Alfred, (1934), *Notebooks on Tibet, Bhutan, Sikkim and Chumb Valley*, 4 Vols. typewritten mss., British Library.

The People of Tibet, (1928), Clarendon Press, Oxford, 1928.

Portrait of the Dalai Lama, (1946), London, Collins, 1946.

Bode, S. H., (1949), 'The Sacred Shih Tzu', *Dog World*, Vol. 32, No. 1076, May 27th, 1949.

Bower, Captain Hamilton, (1893), *Diary of a Journey across Tibet*, Calcutta, Office of the Superintendent of Government Printing, India, 1893.

Buffon, Le Clerc, Count of, *Table de l'ordre des Chiens*.

Burckhardt, Col. V. L., *Chinese Creeds and Customs*, Hong Kong South China Morning Post, 3 vols., 1953–58.

Bush, The Rev. H. W., *Dogs of Tibet*, Kennel Encyclopedia, 4 vols., 1908.

Bylandt, Count Henri de, (1897), *Le race des chiens, leurs origines, points descriptions, etc*, Bruxelles, 1897.

——, *Dogs of all Nations: their varieties, characteristics, points, etc.*, (1905), London, Kegan Paul & Co., 1905.

Carl, K. A., (1905), *With the Empress Dowager of China*, London, Eveleigh Nash, 1905.

Chandra, Sarat, (1885), *Narrative of a Journey to Lhasa*, publisher unknown, 1895.

Collier, V. W. F., (1921), *Dogs of China and Japan in Nature and Art*, London, William Heinemann, 1921*.

Compton, Herbert, (1904), *The Twentieth Century Dog. Compiled from the contributions of over five hundred experts*, 2 vols., London, Grant Richards, 1904.

Cottesloe, Lady, (1970), 'Spaniels from Tibet', *Field Magazine*, October 22nd, 1970.

Croxton Smith, A., (1931), *About Our dogs*, London, Ward Lock, 1931.

Cutting, Suydam, (1947), *The Fire Ox and Other Years. An account of travel in the Far East*, London, Collins, 1947.

Desideri, Ippolito, (1932), *An Account of Tibet. The travels of Ippolito Desideri of Pistoia S. J. 1712–1727*, translated and prepared by Janet Riss. Edited by Filippo de Filippi. With an introduction by C. Wessels, George Routledge & Sons, London, 1937.

Drury, W. D., (1903), *British Dogs – their points, selection and show preparation*, London, L. Upcott Gill, 1903.

Duncan, M. H., (1964), *Customs and Superstitions of Tibetans*, London, Mitre Press, 1964.

Duncan, Ronald Cardew, (1950), *Tomu from Tibet and other Dog Stories*, London, Methuen & Co., 1950.

Ekvall, R. B., (1968), *Fields on the hoof. Nexus of Tibetan nomadic pastoralism*, New York etc., Holt Rinehart & Winston, 1968.

Epstein, H. (1969), *Domestic Animals of China*, Commonwealth Agricultural Bureau, Slough, 1969.

Este (Mrs J. Murray Aynsley), (1880), 'Thibetan Method of the Use of Dogs in their Funeral Rites', *Kennel Gazette*, No. 11, September 1980.

Ferris, A., (1952), 'Tibetan Breeds', *Dog World*, February 8th, 1952.

Fitzgerald, Brian Vesey, Ed., (1948), *The Book of the Dog*, London, Brussels, Nicholson & Watson, 1948.

Fraser, James Baillie, (1820), *Journal of a Tour through Part of the Snowy Range of the Himala mountains, and to the sources of the Rivers Jumna and Ganges*, London, Rodwell & Martin, 1820.

*In Clifford L. B. Hubbard's catalogue of rare and interesting dog books of the world from the Hubbard collection. Bakewell 1968 the author of this book is given as:

Collier-Collins. Dogs of China and Japan in Nature and Art, London 1921.
First Issue with the title page crediting the author as V. W. F. Collier.

Also as:

Collins/Collier Dogs of China and Japan in Nature and Art. London 1921.
Second Issue with the title page crediting the author as W. F. Collins.
Front cover reading V. W. F. Collier, the spine titled similarly; and the dust jacket similarly, but the original title page removed and reset cancel title page mounted on the original stub, giving the author as W. (William) F. (Frederick) Collins. The contents the same as the first issue.

The Collier (plain and simple) version is itself a rare book but the Collins version is unrecorded, even in America where Collins wrote earlier on the history of Ford Omalia. The Publishers in Britain (Heinemann Ltd.) have no copy of the Collins version and know nothing of it.

British Museum catalogue – COLLIER V. W. F.
Library of Congress Catalogue – COLLIER V. W. F. London edition 1921.
New York edition 1921.
English Catalogue of books – COLLIER V. W. F.
U.S.A. Catalogue Supplement – COLLIER V. W. F.

Gelder, S. & R., (1964), *The Timely Rain. Travels in new Tibet*, London, Hutchinson, 1964.

Gill, W., (1880), *The River of the Golden Sand*, Vol. 1, John Murray, 1880.

Goldsmith, Oliver, (1876), *An history of the earth and animated nature. Preceded by a memoir of the author by John Francis Waller.* 2 vols., London, Blackie & Son, 1876.

Gray, T., (1940), 'Journal', *Dog World*, Vol. 23, No. 600, March 22nd, 1940.

Gregory, J. W., (1923), *To the Alps of Chinese Tibet, An account of a journey of exploration*, London, Seeley, Service & Co., 1923.

Hally, Will, (1930), 'Foreign Dog Fancies', *Our Dogs*, October 3rd, 1930.

——, (1931), 'Foreign Dog Fancies', *Our Dogs*, January 23rd, 1931.

——, (1932), 'Foreign Dog Fancies', *Our Dogs*, June 24th, 1932.

Hamilton, Ferelith, (1971), *The World Encyclopedia of Dogs*, London, New English Library, 1971.

Hayden, Sir Henry and Cosson, Cesar, (1927), *Sport and Travel in the Highlands of Tibet*, London, Richard Cobden-Sanderson, 1927.

Hayes, Mrs Geoffrey, (1932), 'The Many Breeds of Mysterious Tibet', *Our Dogs*, June 3rd, 1932.

Hedin, Sven, (1922), *Southern Tibet*, Stockholm, Lithographic Institute of the General Staff of the Swedish Army, 1922.

Hedley, J., (1910), *Tramps in Dark Mongolia*, London, T. Fisher Unwin, 1910.

Herbel, Norman and Carolyn, (1979), *The complete Lhasa Apso*, New York, Howell Book House Inc., 1979.

Hermanns, M., (1949), *Die Nomaden von Tibet*, Wien, Verlag Herold, 1949.

Hodgson, B. H., (1842), 'Notice on the Mammals of Tibet', *Journal of the Asiatic Society of Bengal*, Vol. 1, 1842.

Hubbard, Clifford, (1945), *The Observer's Book of Dogs*, London and New York, F. Warne & Co., 1945.

Huc, E. R. and Gabet (trs William Hazlitt), (1851), *Travels in Tartary, Thibet and China 1844–1846*, London, 1851.

Hutchinson, W., Ed., *Hutchinson's Popular Illustrated Dog Encyclopedia*, 3 vols., London, Hutchinson, 1934–5.

Jacobs, Lionel, (1901), *Indian Breeds*, Dog Owner's Annual, 1901.

Johnston, R. F., (1908), 'From Peking to Mandalay', *Dogs*, 1908.

Kaulback, R., (1934), *Tibetan Trek*, Hodder & Stoughton, London, 1834.

Kipling, J. L., (1891), *Beast and Man in India. A popular sketch of Indian animals in their relations with the people*, London, Macmillan & Co., 1891.

Kircher, Athanasius, (1667), *China monumentis, qua sacris, qua profanis, nec non variis naturae et artis spectaculis aliarumque rerum memorabilium argumentis illustrata*, Amsterdam, 1667.

Lampson, S. M., *The Observer's Book of Dogs*, Warne.

Landon, Perceval, (1905), *Lhasa: an account of the country and people of*

Central Tibet and the progress of the mission sent there by the English Government in the year 1903–4, etc., 2 vols., Hurst & Blackett, London, 1905.

Landor, A. H. S., 'In the forbidden land', *Dogs*, Vol.1, 1898.

Lane, C. H., (1902), *Dog Shows and Doggy People*, London, Hutchinson & Co., 1902.

Laufer, Berthold, (1909), *Chinese Pottery of the Han Dynasty*, New York, American Museum of Natural History, East Asiatic Committee, 1909.

Legl-Jacobsson, Elisabeth, (1978), *East Asiatic Breeds*, Tryck Produktion, Sweden, 1978.

Leighton, Robert, Ed., (1907), *New Book of the Dog. By Eminent Authors*, London, New York, Toronto and Melbourne, Cassell & Co., 1907.

Lhalungpa, Mr Lobsang, (1970), *A Brief Account of Tibetan Dogs by the Apso Committee, Tibet House*, New Delhi, India, 1970.

Lu, Madame Zee Yuen Nee (trs by M. Chow Sze King), *The Lhasa Lion Dog*, publisher and year of publication unknown.

Lytton, The Hon. Mrs Neville, (1911), *Toy Dogs and their Ancestors, including the history and management of toy spaniels, pekingese, Japanese and pomeranians*, London, Duckworth & Co., 1911.

McGovern, W. M., (1924), *To Lhasa in Disguise*, London, Thornton Butterworth, 1924.

Markham, C. R., (1876), *Narratives of the Mission of George Bogle to Tibet and of the Journey of Thomas Manning to Lhasa*, Dogs, Vol. 1, 1876.

Marples, Theophilus, (1926), *Show Dogs: their points and characteristics. How to breed for prizes and profit*, Our Dogs Publishing Co., Manchester, 3rd Edition, 1926.

Matthiessen, Peter, (1979), *The Snow Leopard*, London, Chatto & Windus, 1979.

Mayhew, Miss P. M., *The Tibetan Spaniel*, published privately 1972, and revised in 1974.

Morrison, The Hon. Mrs McLaren, (1895), 'Asiatic Dogs', *Our Dogs*, July 13th, 1895.

——, (1908), 'The Dogs of Tibet', *Kennel Encyclopedia*, 4 vols., 1908.

——, (1911), 'The Coloured Tibetan Spaniel', *The Kennel*, Vol. 2, No. 16, July 1911.

Moulton, H. L., (1939), *Shi Tzu Shavings*, H. L. Hawkins, 1939.

Mulliner, Mrs Angela, (1977), *The Tibetan Terrier*, Holywell Press, Oxford, 1977.

Our Kennel Correspondent, (1930), 'Strange Dogs from Tibet. Some new importations', *The Times*, Monday, December 11th, 1930.

Rawling, C. G., 'The Great Plateau: being an account of exploration in Central Tibet 1903 and of the Gartok expedition 1904–5, *Dogs*, London, E. Arnold, 1905.

Rees, Abraham, (1784), *The Cyclopaedia; or Universal Dictionary of Arts, Sciences and Literature*, 39 vols., London, 1819. (First published 1784.)

Rennie, Dr David Field, (1866), *Bhotan and the Story of the Dooar War*, *including sketches of a three months' residence in the Himalayas*, London, 1866.

Riencourt, Amaury de, (1950), *Lost World, Tibet, key to Asia*, Victor Gollancz, London, 1950.

Rohrer, Ann and Larsen, Linda, *The Tibetan Mastiff Book*, California, CG Publishers, 1981.

Ruttledge, Hugh, *Everest 1933*, 5th Edition, Hodder & Stoughton, 1936

Sellar, A. J., (1980), *The Tibetan Terrier Association Year Book 1980*, The Tibetan Terrier Association, 1980.

Shaw, Vero Kemball, (1879–81), *The Illustrated Book of the Dog. With an appendix on Canine Medicine and Surgery by W. G. Stables*, London, Paris and New York, 1879–81.

Siber, Max, (1897), *Der Tibethund*, Wintherthur, 1897.

Simsova, Mrs Sylva, (1979), *Tibetan and Related Dog Breeds. A Guide to their History*, Tibetan Terrier Association, 1979.

Smith, Dr R. N., (1972), *An Anatomy of the Dog*, London, Quartilles International Ltd., 1972.

Soman, W. V., (1963), *The Indian Dog*, Bombay, Popular Prakashan, 1963.

Suyin, Miss Han, (1977), *Lhasa, the Open City: Journey to Tibet*, London, Jonathan Cape, 1977.

Tafel, Dr Albert, (1914), *Meine Tibetreise, Eine Studienfahrt durch das nordwestliche China und durch die innere Mongolei in das östliche Tibet*, Stuttgart, Berlin, Leipzig, Union Deutsche Verlagsgesellschaft, 2 vols., 1914.

Temple, W. R. H., (1899), 'Foreign Dogs', *Kennel Gazette*, Vol. 20, No. 226, January 1899.

Trendells Ltd., *Year Book of British Tibetan Spaniel Champions 1971–1975*, Trendells, date of publication unknown.

Tucci, Professor Giuseppe, (1967), *Tibet, Land of the Snows*, London, Paul Elek Ltd., 1967.

Turner, J. Sidney, General Editor, (1908), *The Kennel Encyclopedia*, 4 vols., *The Kennel*, 1908.

Turner, Captain Samuel, (1800), *An Account of an Embassy to the Court of the Teshoo Lama, in Tibet*, London, G. & W. Nichol, 1800.

Vaton, A., (1854), *Relations d'un voyage au Thibet en 1852 et d'un voyage chez les abors en 1835*, publisher unknown, 1854.

Waddell, L. A., (1905), *Lhasa and its Mysteries. With a record of the expedition of 1903–1904*, London, John Murray, 1905.

Watson, James, (1905), *The Dog Book*, London, New York, Doubleday Page & Co., 1905.

Widrington, Mrs Gay, *Shih Tzu Handbook*, publisher and date of publication unknown.

Wynyard, Mrs Ann L., (1980), *The Dog Directory Guide to Owning a Tibetan Spaniel*, The Dog Directory, 1980.

——, (1974), The Dog Directory Guide to the Tibetan Spaniel, The Dog Directory, 1974.

Young, Dr C. Walter, (1933), *Some Canine Breeds of Asia*, publisher unknown, 1933.

Yule, H., 'The Book of Marco Polo', *Dogs*, Vol. 2, London, J. Murray, 1903.